CAPTAIN ED BAXTER

& HIS TENNESSEE ARTILLERYMEN, C.S.A.

BY

DENNIS J. LAMPLEY

WESTVIEW BOOK PUBLISHING, INC. NASHVILLE, TENNESSEE

ISBN 1-933912-83-9

First Edition, June 2007

Printed in the United States of America on Acid-Free paper.

Front and back cover artwork by John G. White, La Mesa, California

Cover design by Landon Earps

Interior Layout by Tracy Lucas

Author Representative: Bob Allen, Author's Corner, LLC

WESTVIEW BOOK PUBLISHING, INC.
P.O. Box 210183
Nashville, Tennessee 37221
www.westviewpublishing.com

FOREWORD

My interest in Civil War history began in 1964 as a junior high student in Fairview, Tennessee. It was the 100th Anniversary of the Battle of Franklin. Many activities took place in Williamson County to commemorate the battle and we studied it in school under an inspirational history teacher, Mrs. Mildred Overby Bethshears. I asked at home if we had any ancestors who fought in the Civil War. My mother had no knowledge of it. My dad said: " Sure grandpa Arter Lankford was a Sergeant in the Rebel Army." Dad didn't know what unit grandpa served in or what battles he fought in, but did have some oral history about him which was passed down from his mother.

It took me over 25 years, but I finally had time to do some research on grandpa and he indeed was a Sergeant in the Rebel Army, serving in Baxter's Company Tennessee Light Artillery. I continued to research and collect information on the unit and soon realized that I was related to about 20 of the men in the unit. I was fortunate to receive personal information on several of the soldiers from their descendents and was encouraged by many of the descendents to put my research into book form so other descendents and future generations could learn more about their Confederate ancestors. Most of the information in this book comes from the soldier's service records and pension applications and *OFFICIAL RECORDS OF THE WAR OF REBELLION.* I was also able to obtain much oral history of the men, which had been handed down in their families over the years. Much of the oral history matched service records, some could not be verified, but is included and is noted as oral history.

The goals of this book are to: record the wartime experiences of the men in Baxter's Company Tennessee Light Artillery, 2nd Organization, highlight the life of Edmund Baxter, and to reflect on the effects of the war on the soldiers' families at home in Middle Tennessee.

I would like to express sincere appreciation to those individuals and institutions that provided records, photos, letters, oral history and other information for this publication:

Alabama Department of History and Archives, Montgomery, Alabama.
Captain Ed Baxter Camp 2034, Sons of Confederate Veterans, Fairview, Tennessee.
COLUMBIA HERALD, Columbia, Tennessee.

Dickson County Archives, Charlotte, Tennessee.
Dickson County Public Library Dickson, Tennessee.
DICKSON HERALD Dickson, Tennessee.
FAIRVIEW OBSERVER Fairview, Tennessee.
Fayette County Historical Society Fayetteville, Georgia.
Georgia State Archives Morrow, Georgia.
Heritage Foundation of Franklin & Williamson County, Franklin, Tennessee.
Hickman County Public Library Centerville, Tennessee.
Kentucky State Library & Archives Frankfort, Kentucky.
Missouri State Archives Jefferson City, Missouri.
Nashville Public Library Nashville, Tennessee.
National Archives Washington, D.C.
Oklahoma Department of Library & Archives Oklahoma City, Oklahoma.
Old Hickory Chapter 747, United Daughters of the Confederacy Dickson, Tennessee.
Paulding County Historical Society Dallas, Georgia.
Tennessee State Library & Archives Nashville, Tennessee.
THE TENNESSEAN Nashville, Tennessee.
Vanderbilt University Archives & Special Collections Nashville, Tennessee.
Williamson County Archives Franklin, Tennessee.
Williamson County Historical Society Franklin, Tennessee.
Williamson County Public Library Franklin, Tennessee.

Mr. Joseph R. Bailey Dickson, Tennessee.
Mrs. Betty Hall Beard Fairview, Tennessee.
Mr. Mitchell Beard Fairview, Tennessee. (Deceased)
Mrs. Alice Blake Dickson, Tennessee.
Mr. William "Jack" Bowker Charlotte, Tennessee.
Mrs. Sharon Diane Breyfogle Huntsville, Alabama.
Mr. M. Todd Cathey Burns, Tennessee.
Mr. Jerry W. Cook Wartrace, Tennessee.
Col. Robert J. Dennison Franklin, Tennessee.
Mrs. Margarite Duke Burns, Tennessee.
Mr. Thomas A. Forehand, Jr. Clarksville, Tennessee.
Mrs. Verna Halcomb Forney, Texas.
Mr. Rick Hollis Charlotte, Tennessee.
Mr. Billy A. Jones Crestwood, Kentucky.
Mr. Larry C. Lampley Nashville, Tennessee.
Mrs. Imogene Green Lewis Bon Aqua, Tennessee.
Mrs. Louise Lynch College Grove, Tennessee.

Mr. David Mangrum   Smyrna, Tennessee.
Mr. Ronny Mangrum   Franklin, Tennessee.
Mr. Charlton Queen   Winchester, Kentucky.
Mr. Bryan A. Sharp   Burns, Tennessee.
Mrs. Linda Smith   Dickson, Tennessee.
Mr. James R. Spicer   Franklin, Tennessee.
Mr. Carlos Tidwell, Sr.   McEwen, Tennessee.
Mr. Lance Varden   Springfield, Tennessee.
Mr. Joe Walker   Waco, Texas.

Special appreciation goes to: Mr. John G. White of La Mesa, California for cover artwork, photos and letters; Mr. Rick Warwick of Franklin, Tennessee for photos, proofing and guidance, Mr. Bob Bowser of Fairview, Tennessee for photo preparation and to my wife, Irene, for her assistance, encouragement and patience with this project.

Dennis Lampley
7346 Sack Lampley Road
Bon Aqua, Tennessee. 37025
615-799-0916
lampleydj@aol.com

TABLE OF CONTENTS

CHAPTER 1

RECRUITMENT

April 1861, the clouds of war loomed over the state of Tennessee. Twenty-three year old Ed Baxter discussed the upcoming war with Baxter Smith; his cousin, close friend and future law partner. Both were young attorneys with young families. Both were building their law practices, Baxter in Nashville and Smith in Gallatin, Tennessee. Both agreed it was their duty to defend the Southland. Smith enlisted in the Confederate Cavalry and later became Colonel of the 8th Tennessee Cavalry Regiment, which was referred to as Baxter Smith's Cavalry. Baxter enlisted in the Harding Artillery and later commanded a battery of artillery which bore his name. [23]

Edmund Dillehunty Baxter was born August 22, 1838 in Columbia, Tennessee to a prominent Maury County family. He was the eldest son of Judge Nathaniel Baxter, Sr. and Martha Hamilton Baxter. He was named for his father's friend, the noted Jurist and District Attorney, Edmund Dillehunty. [13]

Judge Nathaniel Baxter later became Davidson County Circuit Court Judge and moved his family to Nashville. In Nashville, young Edmund completed an academic course at the University of Nashville. He worked in the office of the Circuit Court Clerk and served as a Deputy Sheriff under Sheriff Edmundson. Baxter decided to follow his father's footsteps in the practice of law and began a systematic study of law on his own. He also read law in the office of Attorney Andrew Ewing in Nashville. He passed the state bar exam at age twenty with high scores. Nashville was a city full of prominent lawyers and Baxter was destined to earn his place among them, only to have his career interrupted by war. [13]

Ed Baxter married Miss Eliza T. Perkins on August 6, 1859 in Davidson County. At the time of their marriage, he was twenty years old and she was fifteen. Their first child, Catharine, whom Ed affectionately called Katie, was an infant when her father left for the war. His grandmother, Nancy Hamilton, and the family slaves were living with his wife and daughter when he departed for the war.

Captain Edmund D. Baxter

In May 1861, a month before Tennessee seceded from the Union, Baxter enlisted in Captain George H. Monsarrat's Battery of Artillery of the Provisional Army of Tennessee. The battery was better known as the Harding Artillery. The unit was organized May 15, 1861 at Camp Harris in Nashville. Baxter was elected First Lieutenant and was placed in charge of Company B of the battery. [1]

With the election of Abraham Lincoln as President of the United States, South Carolina became the first state to secede from the union in

December 1860. Six other southern states soon followed suit. Tennessee Governor Isham G. Harris was pro-secession and had called for a referendum on secession. A slate of union and secession delegates were quickly put together. The vote in the February 1861 referendum the citizens of Tennessee voted 68,282 to 59,449 against calling for a convention. Union delegates captured 91,803 votes to the secession delegates 24,749 votes. [5]

On April 12, 1861 Confederates forces fired on Fort Sumpter, South Carolina, the start of four long, bloody years of war. President Lincoln called for 75,000 troops to suppress the rebellion. This action incited the people of Tennessee and other southern states. Governor Harris telegraphed President Lincoln:

> " Tennessee will not furnish a single man for purposes of coercion, but 50,000 if necessary for the defense of our rights and those of our Southern brothers." Harris called a special session of the legislature on April 25. On May 6 a Declaration of Independence from the United States was drawn up and a referendum was set for June 8, 1861. [5]

The attitude of Tennesseans toward secession had greatly changed since the February referendum when the people strongly favored staying in the Union. The June 8 vote was 108,399 to 47,233 for leaving the union, with the majority of the pro-union votes coming from East Tennessee. The vote in Dickson County was 1,141 to 71 for secession. Williamson County voted 1945 to 28 for secession, Davidson County voted 5,686 to 492 for secession, Humphreys County voted 1,012 to 0 for secession and Hickman County voted 1,400 to 3 for secession. [5]

In May and June 1861 companies were being raised in communities across the state to enter Confederate service. Emotions were running high among the citizens of the state and the glory of war and quick southern victory were being preached by the secessionist politicians. Circulars such as the one prepared by Centerville Lawyer Thomas Bateman were widely distributed.

TO ARMS !

We are now in a state of revolution, and Southern soil must be defended, and we should not stop to ask, Who brought about the war ? Or Who is at fault ? but let us go and do battle for our native, or adopted soil, and then settle the question of who is to blame.

I have the acceptance of a company to go to the South and fight for Tennessee and the South, provided it can be mustered into service between the 1st and 10th of May next. Come forward and enroll yourselves immediately at my office in the town of Centerville.
April 23d, 1861   T. P. BATEMAN [21]

The company Bateman recruited became Company H of the 11th Tennessee Volunteer Infantry Regiment. Bateman served as the first captain of the company and later as Lieutenant Colonel of the regiment. [23]

The following appeared in the May 18, 1861 issue of the *NASHVILLE DAILY GAZETTE:*

THE FLAG OF TENNESSEE
Unfurl our Banner to the breeze,
And let all traitors see.
'Midst those that float for Southern rights,
The Flag of Tennessee !
Fry paints them-cheap at the Bridge and,
But dear to a foe will be;
The foremost in the battle's van,
The flag of Tennessee
W.J.F.
Nashville, April 21, 1861—tf

On May 20, 1861, before Tennessee had seceded from the Union, the Williamson County Quarterly Court levied a four and one half cent tax per one hundred dollars of property value for the relief and support for families of volunteers while in active service. The Court also established a County Home Guard of Minute Men consisting of fifteen men from the 9th Civil District and ten men from the other civil districts of the county. John M. Winstead was appointed commander of the home guard and was directed by the commission to elect a captain and sergeant. [26]

On June 10, 1861 the Dickson County Quarterly Court also appointed a Home Guard of Minute Men to help defend the county in the event of an invasion by Federal Troops. Ten men from each of the county's twelve civil districts were appointed to serve for three months in their respective limits. Colonel Allen Nesbit was appointed General Commander of the Dickson County Home Guard of Minute Men. Eight of the Home Guards later enlisted in Baxter's Company: B. F. Brown, Hiram

Spencer, John H. Tidwell, Arter Lankford, Richard P. Jackson, David C. Beck, John Jefferson Johnson, Jr. and William Herrin. [8]

At its August 5, 1861 session, the Dickson County Quarterly Court made provisions to care for indigent families of men from the county who had volunteered for Confederate service: "This ordered by the Court that the Tax Collector of Dickson County in year 1861, receive and pay accounts of persons for provisions furnished to families of volunteers, upon the following conditions to wit; provided that said accounts are sworn to before one Justice of the Peace of the county; and provided that said accounts are hoped before the two magistrates of the district where the families live, and are certified by them to be correct; then said collector shall receive and pay them. And it shall be the duty of the Justices of the Peace in each district to ascertain the numbers of families of volunteers who are indigent and needy circumstances, and who from poverty or affliction are unable to support themselves, the number of children in each family, in their district and make a minute of awe and also report the same to the County Clerk; and that each woman and child that may be entitled to the provisions of law and this order, receive provisions not to exceed the following rated list: 3 ½ pounds of bacon per week or 8 ¾ pounds of beef each week, one half bushel of meal of corn or wheat each month.   And it shall be the duty of each of said Justices to keep an account of the amounts furnished to each one and see that they do not exceed the foregoing rates, and not certify account of any one where they are going over the foregoing rate." [8]

The Hickman County Quarterly Court minutes were destroyed when the Courthouse war burned by Confederate guerrillas in 1864. [21]

THE NASHVILLE REPUBLICAN BANNER
Sunday June 16, 1861
REPRESENTATION—ELECTION OF MEMBERS OF CONGRESS
The people of Tennessee having declared themselves independent of the despotic Government at Washington, and with almost equal unanimity their recorded desire that the "Volunteer State" should become a member of the Confederate States of America, the next step will be election of Representatives to Congress.

The formal admission of Tennessee into the Confederacy will take place immediately upon the reassembling of Congress at Richmond, on the 20th proximo. The permanent Constitution provides that new States shall be admitted by "a vote of two-thirds of the whole house of Representatives, and two-thirds of the Senate—the Senate voting by

States". Until this vote is taken, Tennessee is in form an independent State, except so far as she is bound by the Military League.

The act of the Legislature entitled "An Act to submit to a vote of the people a Declaration of Independence, and for other purposes," provides:

SECTION 7. That in the event the people shall adopt the Constitution of the Provisional Government of the Confederate States at the election herein ordered, it shall be the duty of the governor forthwith to issue writs of election for delegates to represent the State of Tennessee in the Provisional Government. That the State shall be represented by as many delegates as it was entitled to members of the United States of America, who shall be elected from the several Congressional Districts, as now established by law, in the mode and manner now prescribed for the election of members of the Congress of the United States.

Unless this act should be amended by the Legislature, to reassemble on Monday, (which we presume is not likely, as it has received the sanction of the people) it will be the duty of the Governor "forthwith to issue writs of election," & c; and in order that our State may be represented at Richmond at the earliest possible moment, it will be necessary to fix the election at an early date.

THE NASHVILLE REPUBLICAN BANNER
Tuesday Morning June 18, 1861
THE FLAG OF THE SOUTH.

The flag of the Southern Confederacy was yesterday raised over our magnificent State Capitol, destined, perhaps, in the future to be the Capitol of the Southern Confederacy, amid the cheering of the people, the military, and the booming of guns. Short and stirring speeches were made by Hon. WM. Ewing of Williamson, and Hon. R. G. Payne of Shelby.

Tennessee had become the eleventh and last state to leave the union and join the Southern Confederacy.

THE NASHVILLE REPUBLICAN BANNER
July 5, 1861
DICKSON COUNTY

At a meeting of a portion of the people of Dickson county at Charlotte on the first Monday in July, 1861, irrespective of former political parties, John C. Collier, Esq, was chosen President, and E. H. Wiley Secretary of the meeting. The President explained the objective of the meeting in a brief, patriotic and feeling manner, whereupon a committee of five was appointed to draft resolutions expressive of the sense of the meeting, who reported as follows:

RESOLVED, that we highly approve of the patriotic course of our present executive, Isham G. Harris, and we heartily recommend him for re-election as Governor of Tennessee

RESOLVED, That the patriotic stand taken by Hon. James M. Quarles, our late member of Congress in favor of the South against the usurpations and tyranny of the Lincoln government, meets our entire approbation, and we cordially recommend him as a candidate for a seat in the Confederate Congress from this district.

RESOLVED, That we fully and cordially approve the course of our Senator, Tho. McNeilly in our State Legislature, and we present him as our candidate for re-election to that position and respectfully ask the counties of Hickman, Lewis and Maury irrespective of former politics to co-operate with us in his election.

RESOLVED, That we have full confidence in all these men; that they are true and tried friends of Southern interests, and we can indorse them as men in whom implicit confidence can be placed.

RESOLVED, These proceedings be published in the Nashville papers.

There was but one dissenting voice to the passage of the foregoing resolutions.

JOHN C. COLLIER, PRESIDENT
R. E. WILEY, SEC.

The Harding Artillery and other units of the Provisional Army of Tennessee soon became part of the Confederate Army. A supply requisition by Lieutenant Ed Baxter on October 24, 1861 in Nashville showed his unit was manned by sixty non-commissioned officers and privates. The battery was stationed at Camp Lookout near Chattanooga, Tennessee in November 1861 and in Knoxville, Tennessee and Mill Springs, Kentucky in December, 1861.[22]

In a December 9, 1861 report from Brigadier General William H. Carroll to Major General G. B. Crittenden, Carroll reported on the number and condition of troops in his command: " Artillery-Captain, George H. Monsarrat; first senior lieutenant, E. Baxter; first junior lieutenant, Brian; second senior lieutenant, Freeman; 140 men, 4 guns, 3 caissons, 103 horses. This company is now stationed near this city; is under command of one of the most active and efficient officers in the service. It is thoroughly drilled and disciplined. Six more guns will be obtained in a few days and the command will increase to 250 men."

Later in December 1861, Captain Monsarrat was appointed commander of the post of Knoxville and the Harding Artillery was divided into two separate batteries while stationed at Mill Springs. Captain H. Baker was assigned command of Company A, which became Baker's Battery. Baxter was promoted to Captain and given command of Company B, which became Baxter's Battery (First Organization)[22]. Other officers in Baxter's Company were; 1st Lieutenant Samuel Freeman, 2nd Lieutenant A. L. Huggins, 3rd Lieutenant Tulley Brown, and 4th Lieutenant E. H. Douglas.[23] Baxter's Battery continued to be known as Monsarrat's Battery for several months. Lieutenant Tulley Brown, who in later life became Adjutant General of the state of Tennessee, recalled accompanying Lieutenant Ed Baxter on a recruiting trip while organizing this company: " I gave my little speech to the men at a barbeque, then I had the pleasure of hearing a man talk." Baxter said to those men on that occasion: "The conflict is already begun, why stand ye idle ?"

HEADQUARTERS WESTERN DEPARTMENT
Bowling Green, January 24, 1862
Captain M. H. Wright
Ordinance, C. S. Army, Nashville:

Sir:

You will send to General Crittenden, by the Cumberland River, for Monsarrat's battery, composed of three 6-pounders smooth bore and one 8-pounder rifled cannon, a supply of spherical case for the 6s and shell for the rifled gun. I understand there is no deficiency except in these particulars.

There will be also needed a full supply of ammunition for 4,000 muskets-about 2,500 Harper's Ferry percussion and 1,500 flint-lock, old pattern, and perhaps some small supply for shot-guns.

With great respect, your obedient servant,
A.S. JOHNSTON,
General, C. S. Army [1]

Captain Baxter nicknamed the first cannon fired by his command "Katie", in honor of his daughter.

On February 16, 1862, Confederate forces under Major General Simon Bolivar Buckner surrendered to Union forces at Dover, Tennessee after the Battle of Fort Donelson on the Cumberland River. Fort Henry on the Tennessee River had already been captured by the Federals. The occupation of Middle Tennessee by Union troops had begun. Clarksville was occupied by Federal forces a few days after the surrender of Fort Donelson. Federal occupation stopped the printing of southern sympathizing newspapers.   The last edition of the *CLARKSVILLE JEFFERSONIAN* was printed February 12, 1862, four days before the fall of Fort Donelson.

CLARKSVILLE JEFFERSONIAN
CLARKSVILLE, TENN. FEBRUARY 12, 1862

The defeat of our forces at Fort Henry and the fall of that fortification seems to have taken a great majority of our people by surprise. They had imagined that a work upon which six or eight months of labor had been expended and about which so much had been said must be impregnable and their disappointment was proportionally great. Our readers can attest that we have time after time expressed our opinion in regard to the weaknesses of the defenses on the Cumberland and Tennessee rivers and have protested against the neglect of this section of the country between this and the Ohio river, which has been so long and persistently exhibited by our authorities. We continued to raise our voice in favor of better and more reliable defenses for the two rivers until we were rebuked by the military leaders and it was plainly hinted to us that we were meddling with matters that did not concern us, and which were in abler hands than ours. The result has proved the wisdom of our warnings and in the abandoned Fort and ruined bridge and an endless catalogue of other evils, the world may read the results of trifling, with the public safety. Now that the evil is done and the terrible consequences are before our eyes, every nerve is strained to mitigate and arrest the consequences of a disaster which might have been averted by the display of one half the energy and expense now brought in to exercise to redeem the fault. If the present disaster shall teach wisdom and lead to the adoption of more vigorous means and a more complete defense, such as can readily be made, our experience will have been cheaply purchased and we candidly confess that from what we see going on around us, we are induced to hope that this disaster will insure our more perfect security and the glory of our cause. We believe that the scales will now fall from eyes which have not heretofore looked in this direction.

During the past week our city has been overrun with soldiers. Where they came from or where they are going to the Federalist will scarcely find out by reading this paragraph. But they have been here, and given our usually quiet city, an unusually lively and bristling appearance. Our hills have been covered, and our streets crowded with them all daring enthusiastic souls eager for a chance to measure arms with our invading foe.

PROCLAMATION

To the Inhabitants of Clarksville, Tenn.:

At the suggestion of the Hon. Cave Johnson, Judge Wisdom, and the mayor of the city, who called upon me yesterday, after our hoisting the Union flag and taking possession of the forts, to ascertain my views and intentions towards the citizens and private property, I hereby announce to all peaceably-disposed persons that neither in their persons nor in their property shall they suffer molestation by me or the naval force under my command, and that they may in safety resume their business avocations with the assurance of my protection.

At the same time I require that all military stores and army equipment shall be surrendered, no part of them being withheld or destroyed; and further, that no secession flag or manifestation of secession feeling shall be exhibited; and for the faithful observance of these conditions I shall hold the authorities of the city responsible.

A.H. FOOT,
Flag-Officer, Commanding Naval Forces Western Waters,
U.S. FLAG-STEAMER CONESTOGA,
Clarksville, Tenn., February 20, 1862 [1]

The conquest and occupation of Middle Tennessee by Union troops continued. The Confederate army evacuated Nashville on February 23, 1862 and retreated to Murfreesboro, taking as many provisions as possible with them. The citizens of Nashville had turned into a mob, breaking into warehouses and taking meat and other provisions. Colonel Forrest and his cavalry broke up the mob before leaving the city. [1]

Union Brigadier General Don Carlos Buell's troops entered the city of Nashville on February 25. The flag of the Confederacy was lowered from the Tennessee State Capital and the Stars and Stripes were raised. [1]

HEADQUARTERS DISTRICT OF WEST TENNESSEE,
Nashville, February 27, 1862

General D. C. Buell,
Commanding Department of the Ohio:

I have been in the city since an early hour this morning, anxious and expecting to see you. When I first arrived I understood that you were to be over to-day, but it is now growing too late for me to remain longer.

If I could see the necessity of more troops here I would be most happy to supply them. My own impression is, however, that the enemy are not far north of the Tennessee line. I was anxious to know what information you might have on the subject.

General Smith will be here this evening, with probably 2,000 men, as requested by you, and should still more be required, address me at Clarksville. To-night I shall return to Fort Donelson, but will take up my headquarters at Clarksville the next day.

Should you deem the command under General Smith unnecessary to your security, I request that they be ordered back.

I am in daily expectation of orders that will require all my available force.

U. S. GRANT
Major-General, Commanding [1]

In February 1862 both Baxter's and Baker's batteries were assigned to the Central Command at Murfreesboro, Tennessee in Brigadier General William Henry Carroll's First Brigade of Major General George B. Crittenden's Second Division.   The batteries were in route from Murfreesboro to Corinth, Mississippi during the Battle of Shiloh. [1]

A report dated April 26, 1862 at Corinth listed Baxter's Battery in the First Brigade of Lt. General William Hardee's Corp under the command of Colonel R. G. Shaver with a total of 73 effective troops. [1]

The army was reorganized in May 1862 while in camp at Corinth. Under orders of General Hardee, Captain Baxter was assigned to post duty in Knoxville, Tennessee and the battery was turned over to Lieutenant Samuel L. Freeman. [22] Freeman was promoted to Captain and the battery became known as Freeman's Battery. Baxter's younger half-brother, Sgt. Nathaniel Baxter, Jr. remained with the battery and was cited for valor in the December 31, 1862 Battle of Parker's Cross Roads, Tennessee by General Nathan Bedford Forrest. The Battery was captured April 19, 1863 in battle at Franklin, Tennessee. Captain Freeman was killed by the Federal captors and the men of the battery were sent to Union Prison. Upon release from Union prison at Fort Delaware, the battery was reorganized under Captain Amariah L. Huggins as Huggin's Battery and served with distinction the remainder of the war. [22] Nat Baxter, Jr. served as a Lieutenant in the reorganized battery. [23]

General Hardee was a West Point graduate and had written *HARDEE'S TACTICS,* an infantry tactical manual used widely by both sides during the war. He was strictly an infantryman. Many of his officers complained that he did not know how to utilize artillery and cared little for it. [23]

In May 1862, Captain Baker resigned as commander of his battery. General Braxton Bragg appointed Captain W. R. Browne as commander of the battery on June 16, 1862 and it became known as Browne's Battery. [22]

October 1862, after four months of post duty at Knoxville, Captain Baxter was given a new assignment by the Department of East Tennessee; return to Middle Tennessee and recruit a second organization of artillery. [22]   After the fall of Fort Donelson and the occupation of Nashville in February 1862, much of Middle Tennessee was under Federal occupation.   After the Battle of Shiloh in April 1862, most of West Tennessee was also in Union hands. The Army of Tennessee, after having been defeated at the Battle of Perryville, Kentucky on October 8,1862 was also headed back to Middle Tennessee to lay groundwork for the upcoming Battle of Murfreesboro. [1, 22]

The twenty-four old Baxter came first to Williamson County. Skirmishes between Union and Confederate Cavalry in the northern part of the county between Brentwood and Franklin were frequent.   Around Franklin, Baxter recruited several men who had previously served in the Confederate Army.   John Marshall, Jr. had served as Commissary Captain in the 20th Tennessee Infantry Regiment and had resigned his commission. John Gault had served in Company C of the 1st Tennessee Infantry Regiment.   Robert Scales from Nolensville and John Demonbruen from College Grove had served in Co. D of the 20th Tennessee Infantry Regiment, both had been discharged for medical disability. George Hogan, Jr. had served as a Sergeant in Company I of the 55th Tennessee Infantry Regiment (The Nashville Confederates) and had also received a medical discharge. Edwin Paschall had served in Company C of the 1st Cavalry Regiment and the Belmont Artillery. Aaron Beard from the First District of Williamson County, a Mexican War Veteran, had served in Co. B 24th Tennessee Infantry Regiment and had been discharged after the Battle of Shiloh under the Conscription Act for being over 35 years of age.   Vachel Barnhill, also from the First District, had served in Company C 9th Tennessee Calvary Battalion (Gantt's).   He escaped capture at the Battle of Fort Donelson, returned home and enlisted in Baxter's Battery November 5, 1862.[23]

One section of Middle Tennessee not under Federal occupation in the fall of 1862 was the hill country thirty miles west of Nashville. Western Williamson, southern Dickson, east Hickman, and southern Cheatham Counties were still in Confederate hands. This was a sparsely populated area of small farms and few slaves. No railroad, major river or turnpike ran through the area. The area was pioneered in the early 1800's by settlers from Virginia, Kentucky, Georgia and the Carolinas who settled along Big Turnbull Creek and its tributaries: Little Turnbull Creek, Parker's Creek, Barren Fork Creek, Beaver Dam Creek and numerous spring branches.

Colonel Nathan Bedford Forrest had escaped capture with his command at the fall of Fort Donelson in February 1862.   He came through Cumberland Furnace and Charlotte in Northern Dickson County on his way to Nashville. Federals soon came to the area and Dickson County began to experience guerrilla warfare. [5] By the summer of 1862, guerrilla warfare had broken out in several areas of Middle Tennessee and Federal troops were entering the remote areas of the region.

August 11, 1862
Affair near Kinderhook, Tenn.
Reports of Brig. Gen. James S. Negley, U.S. Army
Columbia, Tenn., August 11, 1862—3 p.m.

My movement against the guerrillas who have committed the great outrage has been completely successful. Megowan's command of Third Kentucky Cavalry and First Tennessee Cavalry, 108 men, engaged 175 of the enemy near Kinderhook at 5 a.m., continuing the contest fiercely for four hours. Seven were found killed, numbers wounded, 27 prisoners among a number of whom are officers. Our loss was 3 killed. The woody and broken character of the country and the combatants scattered prevents an accurate estimate of the enemy's loss. I have received news from Maj. F.H. Kennedy, of my staff, commanding another portion of the expedition. He is driving the enemy in every direction.

Jas. S. Negley
Hon. E. M. Stanton
Brigadier-General, Commanding [1]

Columbia, August 13, 1862—11p.m.

Col. J.B. Fry:

Fourth Ohio Cavalry left Franklin at 11 a.m. toward Centreville, to disperse a considerable force near that point. After accomplishing this object will pass through Hickman via Centreville to Lawrence to break up the band there. The Third Kentucky are en route east, north side of Duck River, to Wallace Ford, where they will cross and engage if possible several parties in that vicinity, one of which is the one you refer to.

There is undoubtedly a force of 300 to 500 in that neighborhood, but poorly armed. Their location is favorable for safety and escape unless surprised.

The two companies First Kentucky are en route via Bigbyville and Mount Pleasant to surprise if possible a party of 55 near Potts' Mills, southwest of Mount Pleasant.

The troops along the line to Franklin are expecting an attack tonight, particularly at Carter Creek Bridges. Two hundred guerrillas are reported near that place. I am at a loss to know where they all come from, unless composed of citizens of the vicinity.

Jas. S. Negley [1]

Columbia, August 16, 1862

Maj. Rogers, Kennett's Cavalry, has just returned from Centreville, having driven the guerrillas from that place.

The Third Kentucky are just in from a scout. Part of the battalion is in Nashville getting horses. The two companies First Kentucky are in readiness to surprise a small party of guerrillas at Cedar Springs.

The defeat of the guerrillas at Kinderhook was of greater importance than first reported, both in killed, wounded and dispersion of the band.

Jas. S. Negley
Brigadier-General [1]
Col. J.B. Fry

Columbia, August 17, 1862

You will be pleased to hear that the defeat of Napier's and Anderson's guerrillas near Kinderhook was more complete than reported. Upwards of 20 are reported killed, the band stricken with terror, and scattered in every direction. A prisoner captured yesterday gives the following, I believe, reliable information: Headquarters Cooper's band removed to Persimmon Branch, 6 miles west of Ashland; Tom Williams' Buffalo Creek, 8 miles southwest of Henryville.

When the Third Kentucky get their horses if they could be used against these nests it would be good policy. These sudden surprises frighten many of the scoundrels back to their homes. Six hundred citizens of this county have taken the oath this week. I hope to have every prominent citizen in this county under oath or out of the lines by the end of next week.

Jas. S. Negley, Brigadier-General [1]
Col. J. B. Fry, Chief of Staff.

On September 22, 1862 President Lincoln signed the emancipation proclamation which would free slaves in all states still in rebellion on January 1, 1863.

Captain Baxter, by this time a seasoned commander with experience in training green recruits, came to Dickson County in late October and established a camp on Charlie Jones' farm near the Turnbull Creek Bridge on the Franklin to Charlotte Road . He spent about six weeks crisscrossing the area of western Williamson, southern Dickson and the bordering areas of Hickman, Cheatham, Davidson and Maury Counties enlisting recruits. Several men heard of the company being organized and came to the camp to enlist. Over eighty percent of the original recruits for Baxter's 2nd Organization of Artillery came from the Turnbull Creek area. [23]

Most of the men who enlisted in Baxter's Battery were first or second generation native born Tennesseans, a few were born in Virginia and North Carolina. Harvey Clark was born in Indiana. Most of the men were of English and Scotch-Irish descent, some with Cherokee ancestry. These were men of hardy pioneer stock who were used to the hardships of frontier life and the hard work of farming. Like all country boys, these men grew up hunting and many were superior marksmen when they entered the Confederate Army.   Most of the recruits listed their occupation as farmer. Other occupations listed in the service records included: blacksmith, carpenter, cooper, shoemaker, harness maker, school teacher, preacher, physician, woodworker, miller, boilermaker, wheelwright, and brick mason [23] Abe, Hiram and Samuel Spencer worked in the family grist mill on Parker's Creek in Dickson County. The Confederate government generally allowed one man from each community to be exempted for military service to operate a grist mill. Samuel Spencer, eldest son in the family stayed behind to operate the mill. He had been appointed to the Home Guards of Minute Men of Dickson County in June 1861.   Many of the recruits had little or no education. Many were illiterate. Some of those who could read and write were later appointed as non-commissioned officers. [23]

SAMUEL SPENCER, DICKSON COUNTY HOME GUARD, STAYED BEHIND
DURING THE WAR TO OPERATE SPENCER'S MILL.

As with most companies recruited in rural areas, there were numerous kinships in the unit. Twenty-two sets of brothers, as well as cousins, uncles, and brothers-in-law were in the company. John and Nancy Lankford of Dickson County furnished four sons to the battery, the largest number of any family. All four brothers survived the war. The Lankfords had three nephews who served in Company K 11th Tennessee Infantry Regiment, all three died in the war: Robert and Lawrence Lankford died of disease in Camp Douglas Prison in Chicago, Illinois in 1864 and John Lankford died of disease in camp at Cumberland Gap, Tennessee in 1862.[18]

There were two William Buttreys and two James Buttreys in the unit. The older William and James were the uncles of the younger Buttreys. There were also two Andrew Jackson Lampleys in the unit, an uncle and nephew. Nicknames were common among Baxter's men. The older James Buttrey was know as "Big Jim" and the younger known as "Little Jim". The older Andrew Lampley was known as "Bud" and the younger was known as "Jack". Thomas Jefferson Carr and Thomas Jefferson Parker were both known as "Jeff", George Washington Carr was known as "Wash". Dillard Lankford went by "Dee". Tillman Lankford was known as "Till" Andrew Parker and Anderson King went by "Andy". Most of the Williams in the unit were known as "Billy". William Sullivan, being older than most of the troops was known as "Uncle Billy". [10, 17]

At the outbreak of the war, many men of the Turnbull Creek area enlisted in the Confederate Army. Several of the early recruits had brothers and other relatives who would later join Baxter's Company. Over fifty men from west Williamson County joined Company H 20th Tennessee

Infantry Regiment in Franklin in May 1861, accounting for about one third of the men who enlisted in that company. A few men from the First District of Williamson County ventured to Nolensville to enlist in Company B of the 24th Tennessee Infantry Regiment in June 1861. Many of the men from southern Dickson County enlisted in Company K 11th Tennessee Infantry Regiment in May 1861. Other units with area men were: Co. D of Feild's 1st Tennessee Infantry Regiment (The Williamson Grays), Company G 48th Tennessee Infantry Regiment (Voorhies'), Company B 42nd Tennessee Infantry Regiment, Company H 11th Tennessee Infantry Regiment, Company B 49th Tennessee Infantry Regiment, Company C 9th Tennessee Cavalry Battalion (Gantt's), and Companies H & I 24th Tennessee Infantry Regiment. Company G of the 50th Tennessee Infantry Regiment received several recruits from southern Cheatham and western Davidson Counties. In August 1862, a few of months before Baxter's Company was recruited, several area men traveled to Franklin and enlisted in Captain Thomas Fern Perkins' Company of Douglass' Battalion of Tennessee Partisan Rangers. This unit later became Company I of the 11th Tennessee Calvary Regiment.[23]

The war had been raging for a year and a half when Captain Baxter came to the Turnbull Creek area to recruit his second company of artillerymen. The war had already taken its toll on several of the area men who entered the army early in the war. In the January 19, 1862 Battle of Fishing Creek, Kentucky (Mill Springs), several local members of the 20th Tennessee Infantry Regiment were casualties. Private William Rials of Company G, Private David Anglin of Company A and Privates Asa Ivy and Nelson Newcomb of Company H were killed in the battle. Ivy was the first soldier of Company H killed in the war.   Privates Daniel Harrison and Ben Givens of Company H were badly wounded, captured and escaped. Private Thomas Pewitt of Company H died of disease in camp at Mill Springs on January 5, 1862. Several other local men had died of disease early in the war in various camps and hospitals. Private Drury Overby of Company G 48th Tennessee Infantry Regiment died of measles in camp at Danville, Tennessee, Privates Thomas Turman, and Henry Groves of Company I 24th Tennessee Infantry Regiment died in camp at Bowling Green, Kentucky. Private James Pinkerton of Company H 24th Tennessee Infantry Regiment died in 1861 at Camp Trousdale, Tennessee. Private Wash Pritchard of Company H 20th Infantry died in camp at Knoxville. Sergeant Thomas Garton Newton McCord of Company A 48th Tennessee Infantry Regiment had died of measles in a hospital in Columbus, Mississippi on June 21, 1862. [18, 19]

The Confederate loss at the fall of Fort Donelson, Tennessee in February 1862 had meant more heartache for area families. The 42nd and 48th Tennessee Infantry Regiments with numerous soldiers from east Hickman County and the 49th Tennessee Infantry Regiment with several men from southern Dickson County were heavily engaged in the Battle of Fort Donelson. Fort Donelson was surrendered February 16, 1862, with a majority of the Confederate troops being captured.   Most of the captured Confederate enlisted men were sent to prison at Camp Douglas in Chicago, Illinois. The death toll at Camp Douglas was high, including several men of the area: Private J. W. Ham of Company B 49th Tennessee Infantry Regiment; Privates Samuel Forrester and James Forrester of Company G 48th Tennessee Infantry Regiment and Private Joel Chandler of Company F 42nd Tennessee Infantry Regiment. [23]

The Battle of Shiloh fought April 6 & 7 1862 took another heavy toll on the Confederate soldiers from Williamson and Hickman Counties. The 49th and 50th Tennessee Infantry Regiments had been captured at Fort Donelson and most of the soldiers were in prison during the Battle of Shiloh.   The 11th Tennessee Infantry Regiment was stationed in East Tennessee during the battle. No Dickson County Infantry units were engaged at Shiloh.   Killed at Shiloh: Private Granville Pritchard of Company H 24th Tennessee Infantry Regiment, Privates William King and Thomas York of Company H 20th Tennessee Infantry Regiment, Private James H. Pewitt of Company I 44th Tennessee Infantry Regiment, and Privates W. G. Griffin and Thomas Curl of Company I 24th Tennessee Infantry Regiment.   Several other area men were wounded, maimed and lost limbs at Shiloh. [23]

Private Mason Foley Buttrey of Company C 55th Tennessee Infantry Regiment had been captured at Island Number Ten at Columbus, Kentucky and died May 9, 1862 in Union Prison at Camp Randall in Madison, Wisconsin. He was the brother of James F. E. Buttrey and William G. D. Buttrey who served in Baxter's Company. The other Buttrey brother, John, served as a drummer in Company B 20th Tennessee Infantry Regiment and was discharged as a non-conscript for being over 35 years of age. [23]

Though an area of no large plantations and few slaves, the sentiment of the citizens of the Turnbull Creek area was strongly pro-confederate. The citizens were like most Tennesseans, reluctant to leave the Union when the question of secession first appeared and then reluctant to stay after President Lincoln's call for troops. Aaron Beard, a Mexican War Veteran, was said to have been the only man in the 1st District of

Williamson County to vote against secession in the June 8, 1861 vote, but when Tennessee seceded, he soon joined the 24th Tennessee Confederate Infantry Regiment.

Few, if any men from the area joined the Union Army early in the war. As the war progressed, a few area men joined Federal units as they came through the area. Leroy Bradford enlisted in Company D 56th Illinois Infantry Regiment. Descendents of John A. Greer, who moved to the Turnbull Creek area after the war, reported he enlisted in Company E of the 2nd Tennessee U. S. Mounted Infantry Regiment after being given the choice of joining the unit or going to prison as a Confederate sympathizer. At least one area man changed sides from Confederate to Union. William Burr Stinson had enlisted in Company B 24th Tennessee Infantry Regiment in June 1861 at Nolensville. He was reported as having deserted after the Battle of Murfreesboro and later went to Nashville and enlisted in Company A of the 9th Tennessee U. S. Calvary Regiment. Knowing the lay of the land and locations of farms, he is said to have led Union foraging parties through western Williamson County. He eventually deserted from the Union Army, taking the horse and rifle which had been issued to him. Said to have been the most hated man in western Williamson County for his role in the foraging parties, after the war he relocated to New Orleans for several years before returning to the county. A few local Confederate joined the Union Army to get out of Union Prisons. These soldiers were referred to as "galvanized Yankees". The "galvanized" Yankees were typically sent to outposts in the western states as Indian fighters to prevent them from rejoining the Confederate Army or from deserting.[23, 17]

Many of the men who enlisted in Baxter's Company were married with children and were reluctant to leave their families when the war broke out in 1861. Others were too young for service in the spring of 1861, by the fall of 1862 a year and a half had passed, making them old enough for service. With the passage of the Conscription Act by the Confederate States Congress on April 16, 1862, all men between the ages of 18 and 35 were required to serve in the army unless exempted by owning twenty or more slaves. This law caused much discontentment within the ranks of the Confederate army and led to the creation of the saying: "It's a rich man's war and a poor man's fight." [25]

Several of the recruits in Baxter's Company were over thirty-five years of age and did not have to serve under the law, but did. Those men were: A. P. Beard, William Sullivan, Ira Castleman, William Herrin, Benjamin Gilliam, John J. Johnson, Jr., Andy King, Reuben Lane, James Martin,

John Sayers, Joseph Terrell, Harvey Clark and Hiram Sears.   The
company also had it's share of young recruits. Wesley Welch was said
by family members to have lied about his age and was only fifteen years
old at the time of his enlistment. Other teenagers in the company were:
Malachia Beggs, William Bethshears, John Black, James M. Buttrey,
William G.W. Buttrey, John Cunningham, Samuel Davis, Jesse Edwards,
James Garland, Jack Lampley, Dillard Lankford, James Lewis, Robert
Loveall, Alfred McCaslin, Freeling McKay, Andy Parker, Robert Scales,
James B. Thompson, Sol Tidwell, Elisha Varden, and James P. White.[23, 17]

With Federal troops moving nearer the area, the men knew it was time to
choose to either fight to defend the homeland or be forced to take the
oath of allegiance to the United States and support the invading Federal
Troops. Most of the eligible area men volunteered for service for a
period of three years or the duration of the war and were paid a $50
bounty for enlisting.   Several area men who did not volunteer for
Confederate service were later conscripted into service by Conscription
Corp Officers based in Columbia.[23]

With the men of the community marching off to war, the chores of
farming, cutting fire wood and making a living for the families were left
up to the women, children and the elderly.

On November 27, 1862 Baxter and the new recruits marched from the
Turnbull Creek camp in Dickson County to Smith Springs in Williamson
County. In later years, some of the old soldiers recalled talking, singing,
and laughing on their first march. This was the first of many miles the
men would march in the next two and one half years. For eight of the
new recruits, this was to be their last look at Dickson County. Cheatham
County recruit James B. Thompson's mother had knitted him socks and a
helmet to cover his neck, head, and chest and spun yarn and wove him a
blanket to take to war. Upon his departure from home he had been given
the best horse "on the place" by his father to take to war. Thompson
reported the men were having so much fun on the march, that he gave the
horse to a farmer near Franklin so he could walk with the other men. He
reported they went to Bethesda through the woods because the yanks
were in Franklin. The new soldiers remained at Smith Springs for three
days and added more recruits. On November 30, the company marched
seven miles from Smith Springs to West Harpeth. December 9 the
company marched from West Harpeth nineteen miles to Bethesda. On
December 10, 1862, the first death in the company occurred. Private
John D. Groves of Dickson County died of hypertrophy of the heart in

camp at Bethesda, the day before the unit was inducted into Confederate service.[18, 24]

While Baxter's men were on the march in southern Williamson County, a sharp skirmish was fought in the northern part of Williamson County at Brentwood on December 9. The Federals then made a reconnaissance toward Franklin and skirmished again on December 12.[1] Federal troops in Middle Tennessee were foraging on the area farms and guerrilla activity continued to heat up.

No. 2
Report of Lieut. Sylvanus H. Stevens,
Stoke's (Chicago Board of Trade) Illinois Battery
IN CAMP ON FRANKLIN PIKE
Near Nashville, Tenn., December 14, 1862
(Received headquarters Eight Division, Dec. 15, 1862)

Sir:

I have the honor to report that, in obedience to your orders, I proceeded with 3 wagons and a detail of 6 men to obtain forage on the Franklin pike; that before leaving the lines I had the pass from General McCook approved by General Negley, authorizing such commands. While on the road I was informed by Lieutenant Wood, of General Negley's command, commanding a party of forage wagons, that he had just obtained a quantity of forage at a place about 2 ½ miles outside of the pickets, and that other teams, under an escort commanded by Colonel Scott, had gone beyond this place. Before commencing the loading of the wagons, I made a thorough reconnaissance of the position and placed my sergeant on an eminence to observe the country around. While proceeding to load, about 20 or 30 guerrillas, mounted and well armed, surrounded my men. They fought as long as there was a chance of a defense, and then surrendered. Rather than be taken a prisoner, I fought my way through, escaping on foot. In consequence of the gateway being blocked up by one of my wagons, the sergeant and myself held the party at the gate with our pistols while the teams were escaping. Five privates and 1 corporal were taken prisoners; 1 private wounded in the back. This man we brought away. Five horses were captured and 2 killed. The guard under Colonel Scott with train had passed without my knowledge, leaving my party about a half mile in the rear.

I am captain, very respectfully, your obedient servant,

S. H. Stevens, Jr.
First Lieutenant [1]

On December 11, 1862, in camp at Bethesda, Baxter's Company was organized into Confederate service and officers were elected. Ed Baxter of Davidson County was elected Captain. Elected First Lieutenant was John Marshall, Jr. of Franklin. Second Lieutenants elected were John Gault of Williamson County and William Herrin of Dickson County. Matthew F. Maury of Williamson County was elected Orderly Sergeant.

Other Sergeants elected were: Aaron P. Beard of Williamson County, William M. Gault of Williamson County, George W. Hogan, Jr. of Davidson County, James A. Martin of Dickson County and Hiram Sears of Dickson County. Elected Corporals were: James F. E. Buttrey of Williamson County, John Cunningham of Williamson County, Alfred McCaslin of Dickson County, James McCrory of Davidson County, Albert Green of Williamson County, Arter Lankford of Dickson County, Edwin Paschall of Williamson County and Joseph Sweeney of Williamson County. Dr. Robert B. Sayers of Williamson County was appointed company physician.[23]

Confederate artillery units were typically named for the Captain commanding the unit. Baxter's unit was named Baxter's Company Tennessee Light Artillery. It was also referred to as Baxter's Battery and Baxter's Tennessee Battery. The unit was referred to in some records as Baxter's Battery second organization to differentiate it from his first command.

MUSTER ROLL OF PRIVATES OF ORIGINAL MIDDLE TENNESSEE RECRUITS
BAXTER'S COMPANY TENNESSEE LIGHT ARTILLERY
2ND ORGANIZATION

Pvt. James W. Allen Williamson Co., TN.
Pvt. James G. Barnhill Williamson Co., TN.
Pvt. Vachel Isiah Barnhill Williamson Co.TN.
Pvt. David C. Beck Dickson Co., TN.
Pvt. John T. Beck Dickson Co., TN.
Pvt. Malichi Beggs Cheatham Co., TN.
Pvt. James E. Bentley Williamson Co., TN.
Pvt. William H. Bethshears Williamson Co.,TN.
Pvt. Harding Bilbrey Overton Co., TN.
Pvt. John S. Black Williamson Co., TN.
Pvt. Benjamin F. Brown Dickson Co., TN.
Pvt. Carter T. Brown Hickman Co., TN.
Pvt. Charles L. Brown Dickson Co., TN
Pvt. George M. D. Brown Dickson Co., TN.

Pvt. James Monroe Buttrey Williamson Co.,TN.
Pvt. William G. D.Buttrey Dickson Co., TN.
Pvt. William G. W. Buttrey Williamson Co.,TN.
Pvt. George W. Carr Dickson Co., TN.
Pvt. Thomas J. Carr   Dickson Co., TN.
Pvt. Ira Castleman Hickman Co., TN.
Pvt. Harvey Clark Williamson Co., TN.
Pvt. Samuel Davis Williamson Co., TN.
Pvt. Thompson Davis Williamson Co., TN.
Pvt. John F. Demonbruen Williamson Co., TN.
Pvt. John B. Dillard   Cheatham Co., TN.
Pvt. Jesse B. Edwards Dickson Co., TN.
Pvt. William M. Ellison Dickson Co., TN.
Pvt. John L. Forehand Hickman Co., TN.
Pvt. William P. A. Frashier Dickson Co., TN.
Pvt. James Garland Dickson Co., TN.
Pvt. John Gatlin Williamson Co., TN.
Pvt. Benjamin F. Gilliam   Cheatham Co., TN.
Pvt. William Goodgene Williamson Co., TN.
Pvt. John D. Groves Dickson Co., TN.
Pvt. John T. Groves Dickson Co., TN.
Pvt. Napoleon Groves Dickson Co., TN.
Pvt. James H. Hall Williamson Co., TN.
Pvt. Robert G. Hall Williamson Co., TN.
Pvt. William B. Hill Williamson Co., TN.
Pvt. John N. Hood Dickson Co., TN.
Pvt. William J. Hood Dickson Co., TN.
Pvt. Thomas J. Hooper Dickson Co., TN.
Pvt. William Hooper Dickson Co., TN.
Pvt. Richard P. Jackson Dickson Co., TN.
Pvt. John J. Johnson, Jr. Dickson Co., TN.
Pvt. Felix M. Jones Calloway Co., KY.
Pvt. Wilson B. Jones Williamson Co., TN.
Pvt. Anderson King Williamson Co., TN.
Pvt. John O. Ladd Dickson Co., TN.
Pvt. William H. Ladd Dickson Co., TN.
Pvt. Andrew Lampley Dickson Co., TN.
Pvt. Andrew J. Lampley Dickson Co., TN.
Pvt. Radford T. Lampley Dickson Co., TN.
Pvt. Reuben Lane Williamson Co., TN.
Pvt. Dillard H. Lankford Dickson Co., TN.
Pvt. Tillman P. Lankford Dickson Co.,TN.
Pvt. William J. Lankford Dickson Co., TN.

Pvt. Thomas R. Laughlin Williamson Co., TN.
Pvt. James T. Lewis   Cheatham Co., TN.
Pvt. Robert B. Loveall Dickson Co., TN.
Pvt. John C. Mangrum Williamson Co., TN.
Pvt. Freeling H. McKay Williamson Co., TN.
Pvt. William McCrory Davidson Co., TN.
Pvt. Pvt. John W. McLaughlin   Dickson Co.,TN.
Pvt. William McPherson Williamson Co.,TN.
Pvt. Joseph A. Nall Williamson Co., TN.
Pvt. Linden A. Nall Dickson Co., TN.
Pvt. George W. Neely Williamson Co., TN.
Pvt. Andrew J. Parker   Dickson Co., TN.
Pvt. Thomas J. Parker Dickson Co., TN.
Pvt. George Peach Williamson Co., TN.
Pvt. George A. Petty   Williamson Co., TN.
Pvt. James Richardson Williamson Co., TN.
Pvt. Isham Roberts Williamson Co., TN.
Pvt. Samuel Saunders Williamson Co., TN.
Pvt. John G. Sayers   Williamson Co., TN.
Pvt. Robert S. Scales   Williamson Co., TN.
Pvt. Joseph M. Sears   Dickson Co., TN.
Pvt. Eli G. Sherman   Williamson Co., TN.
Pvt. William T. Smith Hickman Co., TN.
Pvt. Abraham Spencer   Dickson Co., TN.
Pvt. Hiram Spencer Dickson Co., TN.
Pvt. Amos Spicer   Dickson Co., TN.
Pvt. William M. Sullivan   Williamson Co.,TN.
Pvt. David Basil Talley Cheatham Co., TN.
Pvt. Benjamin H. Terrell Williamson Co., TN.
Pvt. Joseph R. Terrell Williamson Co., TN.
Pvt. James B. Thompson Cheatham Co., TN.
Pvt. Lewis E. Thompson Cheatham Co., TN.
Pvt. Aquilla Tidwell   Dickson Co., TN.
Pvt. John H. Tidwell   Dickson Co., TN.
Pvt. Soloman Tidwell Dickson Co., TN.
Pvt. Felix G. Truett   Williamson Co., TN.
Pvt. Elisha Varden   Cheatham Co., TN.
Pvt. Wesley B. Welch   Dickson Co., TN.
Pvt. Daniel White Dickson Co., TN.
Pvt. James P. White Dickson Co., TN.
Pvt. Jesse White Dickson Co., TN.
Pvt. John Williams   Williamson Co., TN.

Recruits continued to trickle into camp until the company moved out from Bethesda on December 22, 1862 with 107 men. The company marched five miles to Peytonsville and remained there until December 28, spending their first wartime Christmas away from home. Skirmishing between the opposing armies continued to increase, on December 26 & 27 skirmishes were fought at Franklin and in the vicinity of LaVergne in Rutherford and Davidson Counties.[1]

As the men marched off to war, most had no idea of what they were getting into. Several of the men who had previously served in the army had already experienced the horrors of war. Aaron Beard and George Hogan had been heavily engaged at Shiloh. Vachel Barnhill had escaped capture at Fort Donelson after a heated battle. John Gault, Edwin Paschall and several of the other men had been under enemy fire in various other battles and skirmishes. [23]

December 27 Private Freeling McKay was captured by Union Troops while on duty at Franklin. He was transported to a Federal Prison at Louisville, Kentucky and remained there until transported to Baltimore, Maryland May 2, 1863. He was exchanged at City Point, Virginia July 7, 1863 and later reunited with Baxter's Battery.[23] December 28, the men marched to Caney Springs in Marshall County. December 31 the company marched 9 miles to Farmington in Marshall County. The company was first mustered for pay on December 31, 1862. Pay vouchers were later issued by Captain E. L. Hord. Baxter was paid $140 per month as Captain, 1st Lieutenant Marshall was paid $100 per month, 2nd Lieutenants Gault and Herron were paid $90 per month.

Orderly Sergeant Matt Maury was paid $20 per month, other Sergeants were paid $17 per month, Corporals were paid $15 per month and Privates were paid $12 per month. Artificers (blacksmiths, harness makers & other skilled positions) and teamsters were paid twenty-five cents per day more than other soldiers of the same rank. Dr. Sayers was paid twenty-five cents per day bonus for serving as Company Physician. Captain Baxter, the three Lieutenants and others who furnished their own horses were paid forty cents per day for furnishing horses.[23]

December 31, 1862, the Battle of Murfreesboro started at dawn and lasted for three days. While being in the Confederate Army less than three weeks and being unequipped, Baxter's Battery was listed as reserve artillery in Brig. General John A. Wharton's Brigade, McCowan's Division of Hardee's Corp in the order of battle for the Battle of Murfreesboro.[1] Being green recruits, un-equipped and un-drilled, the battery was never ordered to Murfreesboro and proceeded on to its assignment in East Tennessee. The Battle of Murfreesboro brought more death and suffering to the families and neighbors of Baxter's men. Private John Chandler of Company H 11th Tennessee Infantry Regiment and Private Claiborne Chester of Company C 11th Tennessee Infantry Regiment were killed in the battle. Private James Butts of Company H 20th Tennessee Infantry Regiment was killed in Breckenridge's Charge. Privates William H. Pewitt, Adam Pewitt, John W. Mangrum, Wes Mangrum, and John Ivy of   Company H 20th Tennessee Infantry Regiment were wounded, as was Private Jack Stinson of Company B 24th Tennessee Infantry Regiment and Captain Franklin Fulton Tidwell of Company K 11th Tennessee Infantry Regiment. [23]

Rail cars at Chattanooga of the type Baxter's men were transported in.
(Note Union Cavalry in rear)

January 1, 1863 the men marched thirteen miles toward Shelbyville. January 4th the battery marched fifteen miles toward Fayetteville. The company marched on to Cowan Station in Franklin County where they boarded a train for Knoxville on January 9, 1863. The train traveled from Cowan Station to Chattanooga, then northward to Knoxville.

Knoxville and East Tennessee furnished men to both armies, with a majority joining the Union Army. The sentiment of the citizens of the region was heavily pro-union. Only five of the twenty-nine counties in East Tennessee voted in favor of secession, all five were in the southeastern section of the state: Monroe, Sequatchie, Rhea, Meigs, and Polk Counties. Representatives of the East Tennessee counties held conventions in May and June 1861 and requested that they, along with any bordering counties of Middle Tennessee who wished to join them, to be allowed to secede from the state of Tennessee and form a separate state. The Confederate occupation of East Tennessee was resented by the citizens of the area, just as Union occupation of Middle and West

Tennessee was resented by the pro-southern citizens of those parts of the state.

Confederate President Jefferson Davis had imposed martial law in East Tennessee on April 8, 1862. Brigadier General William H. Carroll, commander of the post of Knoxville, had imposed martial law in the city of Knoxville on December 11, 1861: " I have been greatly annoyed by the interference of the civil authorities with what I conceive the proper and faithful discharge of the duties incumbent upon me in my capacity of military commander of this portion of East Tennessee. Several attempts have been made to take offenders out of my hands by judicial process to be tried by the civil tribunals, which trials I am satisfied would in many instances have resulted in the release of those who are guilty and should be punished. In order to avoid these embarrassments, I felt myself justified in placing the city under martial law until such time as all the prisoners charged with military offenses now in my custody can be tried by military tribunal. If after this is done any should remain whose offenses come legitimately under the jurisdiction of the civil courts. I will turn them over to the proper officers to be disposed of in that way. I have only been prompted to venture upon this stringent course by strong conviction that the public good imperatively demanded it. The traitorous conspiracy recently so extensive and formidable in East Tennessee is, I think, well-nigh broken up, as there is at present but little or no indication of another outbreak. I have small detachments of my force out in every direction, suppressing any rebellious spirit that may be manifested and arresting those who are known to have been in arms against the Government. I am daily receiving the most encouraging evidences that the people are beginning to return to a sense of duty and patriotism, as many of those who were heretofore unfriendly towards us are coming forward and giving every assurance of future fealty. [1]

PROCLAIMATION
HEADQUARTERS RIFLE BRIGADE
Knoxville, Tenn., December 11, 1861

The exigencies of the time requiring, as is believed, the adoption of the sternest measures of military policy, the commanding general feels called upon to suspend for a time the functions of the civil tribunals.

Now, therefore, be it known that I, William H. Carroll, brigadier general in the Confederate Army, and commander of the post at Knoxville, do hereby proclaim martial law to exist in the city of Knoxville and the surrounding country to the distance of 1 mile from the corporate limits of said city.

By order of Brig. Gen. William H. Carroll:
H. C. Young
Assistant Adjutant-General [1]

GENERAL ORDERS
WAR DEPARTMENT, A. AND I.G.O.
NO. 21
Richmond, April 8, 1862

I.   The following proclamation is published for the information of all concerned:

PROCLAMATION

By virtue of the power vested in me by law to declare the suspension of the privilege of the writ of habeas corpus, I, Jefferson Davis, President of the Confederate States of America, do proclaim that martial law is hereby extended over the Department of East Tennessee, under the command of Maj. Gen. E. K. Smith; and I do proclaim the suspension of all civil jurisdiction (with the exception of that enabling the courts to take cognizance of the probate of wills, the administration of the estates of deceased persons, the qualification of guardians to enter decrees and orders for the partition and sale of property, to make orders concerning roads and bridges, to assess county levies, and to order the payment of county dues), and the suspension of the writ of habeas corpus in the department aforesaid.

In faith whereof I have hereunto signed my name and set my seal this eight day of April, in the year one thousand eight hundred and sixty-two.

JEFFERSON DAVIS.

II.   Maj. Gen. E. K. Smith, commanding the Department of East Tennessee, is charged with the due execution of the foregoing proclamation. He will forthwith establish an efficient military police, and will enforce the following orders:

All distillation of spirituous liquors is positively prohibited, and the distilleries will forthwith be closed. The sale of spirituous liquors of any kind is also prohibited, and establishments for the sale thereof will be closed

III.   All persons infringing the above prohibition will suffer such punishment as shall be ordered by the sentence of a court-martial; provided that no sentence to hard labor for more than one month shall be inflicted by the sentence of a regimental court-martial, as directed by the sixty-seventh Article of War.

By command of the Secretary of War:
S. COOPER
Adjutant and Inspector General [1]

HEADQ'RS DEPARTMENT OF EAST TENN.
Office Provost Marshall
April the 21st, 1862

Mrs. Maynard, Knoxville
MADAM:

By order of Major General E. Kirby Smith, I am directed respectfully to require that yourself and family pass beyond the Confederate States lines in thirty six hours from this date.

Passports will be granted you at this office.

Yours respectfully,
W. M. Churchwell,
Colonel and Provost Marshall [1]

HEADQ'RS DEPARTMENT OF EAST TENN.
Office Provost Marshall April 23, 1862

To the Disaffected People of East Tennessee:

The undersigned, in executing martial law in this Department, assures those interested, who have fled to the enemy's lines, and who are actually in the army, that he will welcome their return to homes and families; they are offered amnesty and protection if they come to lay down their arms and set as loyal citizens within thirty days, given them by Gen. E. Kirby Smith to do so. At the end of that time those failing to return to their homes and accept the amnesty thus offered, and provide for and protect their wives and children in East Tennessee, will have them sent to their care in Kentucky, or beyond the Confederate States lines, at their own expense. All that leave after this date, with a knowledge of the above facts, their families will be sent immediately after them. The women and children must be taken care of by husbands and fathers, either in East Tennessee or in the Lincoln Government.

W.M. CHURCHWELL
Colonel and Provost Marshall [1]

Baxter's Company arrived in the hostile confines of Knoxville January 11, 1863. Captain Baxter had been commissioned to recruit the company by the Department of East Tennessee, so the men were sent to Knoxville rather than remain in Middle Tennessee with the Army of Tennessee.

Recruiting Officers, Major James Nicholson and B. T. Gillam of the Conscription Corp, along with Major John L. House of the 1st Tennessee Infantry Regiment continued to roundup recruits on into March 1863. The men were inducted into the army at Columbia, Headquarters of the

Volunteer and Conscript Bureau. The bureau was commanded by Brig. General Gideon J. Pillow. The volunteers and conscripts were forwarded on to meet the battery in East Tennessee. Several of the conscripts deserted and returned home without ever being inducted into the army.[23]

Desertion was common in both the Union and Confederate Armies and Baxter's Company was no exception. A report dated January 1, 1863 listed five members of the company: Privates John Black, William Goodgene, Reuben Lane, George Peach, and John Demonbruen as AWOL. Demonbruen rejoined the company April 13, 1863 at Cumberland Gap. Lane was later reported to be dead. Private George A. Petty was reported as having deserted on January 4, 1863. Privates James Bentley, Wilson Jones and Samuel Saunders were detached from the company to serve as government coopers under Special Order # 19 issued by General Braxton Bragg December 9, 1862 in Murfreesboro. Both Jones and Saunders were reported as deserters later in the war.[23]

Upon arrival in Knoxville the company was assigned to the 3rd Brigade of the Army of East Tennessee commanded by Brigadier General Archibald Gracie, Jr. Gracie was a thirty year- old native of New York City and West Point graduate. He had moved to Mobile, Alabama before the war to enter business with his father and had served in the Alabama Militia. The elder Gracie returned to New York upon the outbreak of the war. His son remained in Alabama to defend his adopted Southland and entered the Confederate army as a Captain of his militia unit, Washington Light Infantry, which was incorporated into the 3rd Alabama Infantry Regiment and was sent to Virginia. Gracie was promoted to Major and in early 1862 returned to Mobile to raise his own regiment, the 43rd Alabama Infantry Regiment. Gracie was promoted to Brigadier General November 4, 1862.

Gracie's Brigade, in January 1863 was headquartered at Cumberland Gap, the strategic passage thorough the Appalachian Mountains at the point where the Tennessee, Kentucky and Virginia state lines meet. The Cumberland Gap had been used as a passage through the mountains for centuries by wildlife and Indians. It was the route used by Daniel Boone and other pioneers in the settlement of Kentucky. It was a prime route for Union troops to enter East Tennessee and for Confederate troops to enter Kentucky. Forts had been constructed by the Confederates early in the war. Trees had been felled to create an abattis to slow the movement of large bodies of troops. Gracie's Brigade was assigned the task of defending the Gap and tracking the movement of Union troops in the area. The Gap eventually changed hands four times during the war.[1]

The other units in Gracie's Brigade were: 43rd Alabama Infantry Regiment commanded by Col. Y. M. Moody, 2nd Battalion Hillard's Alabama Legion commanded by Lt. Col. B. Hall, Jr., 16th Georgia Calvary Battalion (one company) commanded by Capt. J. D. Simms, 55th Georgia Infantry Regiment commanded by Col. C. B. Harkie, 63rd Tennessee Infantry Regiment commanded by Col. R. G. Fain, Mabry Tennessee Artillery commanded by Capt. W. C. Kain, and Rhett Tennessee Artillery commanded by Capt. William Burroughs. Gracie's Brigade formed part of the Department of East Tennessee headquartered in Knoxville and commanded by Brig. General Daniel Smith Donelson. Donelson assumed command of the department only a few days after Baxter's Battery arrived in Knoxville. Donelson took over command from Brigadier General Henry Heth who was transferred to the Army of Northern Virginia. Heth had assumed the command from Major General E. Kerby Smith who was transferred to command the Army of the Trans-Mississippi. Major General Dabney H. Maury assumed command of the department upon the death of General Donelson in April 1863. Maury was later assigned to the Department of the Gulf and Major General Simon Bolivar Buckner was assigned to command the department.   Buckner had been forced to surrender the Confederate troops at the capture of Fort Donelson and had been imprisoned at Fort Warren, Massachusetts.[1]

In addition to troops stationed in Knoxville and Cumberland Gap, Col. John Palmer's Brigade was stationed at Big Creek Gap, Brig. General A. E. Jackson's Brigade was stationed at Strawberry Plains, and Brig. General John Pegram's Brigade was in Kentucky. Other troops were stationed in Loudon, Kingston, Greeneville, Haynesville, Clinton, Bristol and Watauga Bridge. Brig. General Sam Jones' Brigade moved back and forth in East Tennessee and Southwestern Virginia. [1]

On January 13, 1863, after being issued uniforms, canteens, knapsacks, haversacks and other equipment, the company departed Knoxville for Cumberland Gap, marching eight miles from town. January 14, the company marched fourteen miles. On January 15 the company marched 13 miles to the Clinch River and camped on its bank. January 16 the company camped two miles North of Tazewell after marching thirteen miles. On January 17 the company reached Cumberland Gap.[1]

SPECIAL ORDERS   ADJT. AND INSPECTOR GENERAL'S OFFICE
NO. 14
Richmond, Va., January 17, 1863

XII.   Brig. Gen. D. S. Donelson is assigned to the command of the
Department of East Tennessee, which will hereafter include
within its limits the counties of Washington, Russell,
Buchanan, Wise, Scott, and Lee, in Virginia. The command of
Brig. Gen. Humphrey Marshall will be considered as embraced
within this department.

XIII.   Brig. Gen Henry Heth, now in command of the Department of
East Tennessee, on being relieved by Brigadier-General
Donelson, will repair to Fredericksburg, Va.; and report for
duty to General R. E. Lee, commanding, &c.

By command of the Secretary of War:
JNO. WITHERS
Assistant Adjutant-General [1]

Chattanooga, January 21, 1863
General Joseph E. Johnston,
Commanding, & c.:

Sir:

The following is the aggregate and distribution of the force in the
Department of East Tennessee present for duty: Aggregate, 8,520, of
which 6,136 are infantry, 348 artillery, and 2,036 cavalry; distributed
thus-Cumberland Gap: Infantry, 1,643; Artillery, 207; cavalry, 263; total
2,113. Big Creek Gap: Infantry, 1,037; artillery 84; cavalry, 353; total
1,474. Scattered: Infantry 3,456; artillery, 57; cavalry, 1,420; total
4,933. This is sent to enable you to decide more readily on General
Heth's proposition. In the artillery at Cumberland Gap are included a
company of sappers and miners, 55 strong. The numbers are accurate,
Pegram's brigade is excepted, which is suppose to contain 1,200
effectives at least.

Respectfully, your obedient servant,
Benj. S. Ewell
Assistant Adjutant-General [1]

Brig. Gen. Gracie

Brigadier General Archibald Gracie, Jr., first General to command Baxter's Battery 2nd Organization. Gracie was killed by Union Artillery fire December 2, 1864 during the siege of Petersburg, VA.

CHAPTER 2

CUMBERLAND GAP

Skirmishing between Union and Confederate troops around Cumberland Gap began in February 1862 and continued until the forts and fortifications built by Confederates early in the war were occupied by Union troops June 18, 1862. Skirmishing resumed and Cumberland Gap was evacuated by Union troops on September 17, 1862 and reclaimed by the Confederates. The 11th Tennessee Infantry Regiment served much of its time on garrison duty defending Cumberland Gap from July 1861 until the summer of 1862. Numerous soldiers in that regiment had relatives and neighbors who served in Baxter's Battery. Most of the men in Company K were from southern Dickson County. Company H was comprised mainly of men from Hickman County. [23, 22]

Gracie's Brigade had the multiple responsibilities of defending the Gap and other strategic locations north of Knoxville, guarding railroad bridges, and of scouting for enemy troop movements. In his correspondence with Headquarters, Gracie expressed fear of an invasion of Union troops trough the gap. Other Confederate Generals in the Department of East Tennessee speculated that Federal troops would try to enter Tennessee trough passages farther west. [1]

At Cumberland Gap, Baxter's Battery was organized into a four-gun battery with two sections designated as left and right. Captain Ed Baxter commanded the company, 1st Lt. John Marshall served as second in command, 2nd Lt. William Herrin commanded the left section and 2nd Lt. John Gault commanded the right section. Each section was armed with two three-inch rifled cannon. [1]

On the march, each cannon was hooked up behind a limber, which carried an ammunition chest, and was drawn by a team of six horses. Each cannon had a caisson, carrying three ammunition chests, also drawn by a six-horse team. These two units made a platoon, commanded by a sergeant and two corporals. The battery was accompanied by a traveling forge and a battery wagon carrying tents and supplies. Other wagons, some pulled by mules, carried forage and other supplies. Each six-horse team had three drivers, who rode the horses on the left side. The typical gun crew consisted of nine men. The cannoneers typically rode on the ammunition chests or walked behind the guns. In the company were several men designated as artificers, these men were skilled as blacksmiths, harness makers, etc. and were paid a twenty-five cents a day bonus for their skills. Those who served as artificers in Baxter's Battery were: William P. A. Fraisher, Benjamin Gilliam, Albert Green and Joseph R. Terrell. [23]

With his previous experience in artillery tactics, Captain Baxter drilled and quickly trained his new company in the procedures of firing cannon.

On January 20, 1863 Corporal Arter Lankford and Private Benjamin Gilliam, by order of Brig. General Archibald Gracie, Jr. were furloughed to return to their homes to dispose of their private horses. Lankford was later reported to be sick at home in Dickson County and rejoined the company at Cumberland Gap in February. Family members recalled after the war that he brought lice home from camp and infested the family. Gilliam had not returned to camp from his home in Cheatham County at the end of his furlough and was feared to have been captured by the Federals. He returned to Cumberland Gap in March 1863.[23, 17]

Privates Amos Spicer, Aquilla Tidwell and David C. Beck of Dickson County who had been conscripted by Major John L. House on December 22, 1862 in Maury County, reported to the company at Cumberland Gap on January 26, 1863. [23]

Headquarters Department of East Tennessee
Knoxville, February 10, 1863
Colonel Ewell, Assistant Adjutant-General:

I inclose you a document from Brigadier General Marshall which has arrived since I assumed command of this department. I respectfully ask that it be forwarded to General Joseph E. Johnston, for his consideration and instructions in the matter. Having just entered on my duties, having no knowledge of the causes inducing the order, I have not thought proper to take action until properly advised.

I would further state respectfully, for the information of the general commanding, that, as far as my investigations have gone, I find the army here in the worst possible condition, on the score of discipline and efficient military government; no returns made, no reports of brigades, not giving data upon which reliable returns can be made and forwarded to headquarters; great complaint in getting the necessary forage. The disloyal spirit of East Tennessee seems not to have improved by the lenient course hitherto pursued. I am of the opinion more stringent measures should be adopted. I would advise that a reliable force be at once placed in the field, and conscript all persons of the proper age, and the disaffected disloyal portion be sent to our army in the extreme south, and their places supplied by troops from the south. In this way you rid East Tennessee of a population that always has and will give aid and comfort to our enemies,   I would advise, further, that some of the prominent leaders be arrested, put in prison, and held as hostages to such men as Judge Marchbanks of Middle Tennessee. The suggestions are furnished for the consideration of General Johnston, and such action taken as his better judgment may suggest.

Respectfully yours,
D. S. Donelson, Brigadier-General, Commanding Department

Brigadier General Daniel Donelson

Desertion was a major problem in the Department of East Tennessee. The 63rd Tennessee Infantry Regiment was the only Tennessee Infantry Regiment in the Department. The other East Tennessee Infantry Units were assigned to the Army of Tennessee and the Army of the Trans-Mississippi.   Desertion was rampant among the North Carolina Regiments in the Department of East Tennessee. Several of their officers professed to be unionists. Many of the Florida troops stationed in East Tennessee had returned home and requested their regiments be reassigned to defend their home state.[1]

Of the 18,761 troops listed as aggregate present and absent in the Department of East Tennessee, only 9,005 were listed as effective and present. Gracie's Brigade listed an aggregate present and absent of 3,400 men, of these, only 1,732 were effective and present.[1]
The Army of Tennessee had settled into winter camps in Middle Tennessee at Shelbyville, Tullahoma, Wartrace, Fairfield, Fosterville,

and Spring Hill. The soldiers in the Department of East Tennessee continued to maneuver during the winter of 1863. [1]

One of the first missions assigned to Baxter's Battery after arriving at Cumberland Gap was to forage for horses. Under orders of General Gracie on February 15, Sgt. William Gault along with Privates; James Barnhill, Vachel Barnhill, Thomas Parker, William Bethshears, James Lewis, Sol Tidwell, Jesse White, Thomas Carr and James Hall were detached near Knoxville and ordered into the East Tennessee country side to take horses from the pro-union citizens. No record of the number of horses procured was given.[23]   In less than a year, Union troops would be foraging their farms and homes back in Middle Tennessee. [17]

Early spring in 1863 saw an increase in troop movements and skirmishing in the mountains of eastern Kentucky. On March 2, 1863 the battery marched out of the Gap on a scout into Kentucky. They crossed Yellow Creek twice, swimming the horses once and toting the ammunition across the water on horseback. They later crossed the Cumberland River on a pontoon bridge and marched thirteen miles. March 3 the company marched fifteen miles, set up camp and remained two nights before returning to Cumberland Gap March 6.[1]

Private John Dillard, serving in the right section of the battery under the command of Lt. John Gault, reported he first came under enemy fire during March 1863 while on patrol in Kentucky with the command of Colonel John Hart of the 6th Georgia Cavalry. During this time, Radford Lampley was nicknamed "Duck", when the battery came under fire and the other soldiers yelled: "duck, Lampley, duck!"[17] Members of the left section serving under Lt. William Herrin reported they first came under enemy fire at the Battle of Chickamauga. [10]

No. 3
Report of Maj. Augustus Norton, Seventh Ohio Cavalry
Hdqrts. 2D Battalion, 7th Ohio Volunteer Cavalry
Lexington, Ky., March 16, 1863
   General: In obedience to your request, I submit the following statement of the manner in which Colonel Runkle's command was marched from Winchester to Mount Sterling, on the 2nd day of March, 1863; also the condition of the commanders:
   About 7 a.m. the command was on the road, a detachment of the mounted infantry and one piece of Captain Marsh's battery as an advance guard; the Seventh Ohio Volunteer Cavalry in advance of the column; Tenth Kentucky next, followed by the mounted infantry and artillery. After we had proceeded about 3 miles, Colonel Runkle ordered

me to take my command (giving me a guide) and move off to the right through fields and come into the road again about 6 miles ahead, stating that the rebel pickets were reported stationed at a bridge some 5 miles (distant), and he wanted to capture them. I immediately proceeded with my command in the direction ordered, moving as rapidly as circumstances would permit, making the route of 8 or more miles in about one and one-fourth hours, striking the road at the point designated, and on my arrival I found the advance guard and Tenth Kentucky Cavalry in advance of the point named.

The movement of the column to this point before it was possible for me to reach it, defeated the whole object of the circuitous march I was ordered to make, at which I was very much surprised. I took my place behind the Tenth Kentucky, as ordered, and moved on with the column about 1 mile, when Lieutenant (H.E.) Ware, one of Colonel Runkle's aides rode up beside me, and I suggested the propriety of sending a detachment to within 1 mile of Mount Sterling, and there turn to the right and intercept Tick Town road, so as to cut off their retreat in that direction, with which suggestion the lieutenant coincided, and went back to consult with the colonel in regard to the movements. In a few moments he came back with an order for me to take my command and move forward "like hell" to the point where he fired shells at the pickets on our first visit to Mount Sterling, which is about 1 mile from town. I moved forward with my command lively, but before reaching the point designated I ran into their pickets, and took after them at full speed (knowing that they would be able to get around on the pike before I could cut across the fields and intercept them on the Tick Town road, should they choose to retreat in that direction). We pursued them very closely, and captured 1 prisoner before reaching town. On their arrival at the center of the town, they wheeled into line and fired one volley at us, wounding 1 man, but our chase being to hot for them, they left in a hurry, holding up their hands and arms, showing wounds they received to the citizens as they left. Just before entering town I sent back a courier to Colonel Runkle for re-enforcements. We pursued them hotly, capturing 12 prisoners, 2 of whom were wounded, and killed several horses for them. After we had pursued them some 3 miles from town, a majority of our horses had given out, and no re-enforcements had come up, I dispatched another messenger for re-enforcements, and he found Colonel Runkle with part of this troops in line of battle about 1 ½ miles from town. We kept up the pursuit until we ran them into their camp across Slate Creek, which was about 6 miles from Mount Sterling, after which I took a commanding position in full view of their camp, and was watching their movements until the column should come up. I had been in that position but a few moments when I received an order from

Colonel Runkle to take my command and move across the Owingsville pike and join the column. I debated for a moment the propriety of obeying such an order under the circumstances, but concluded to obey it, and proceeded in that direction, leaving the enemy to dispose of their forces as they pleased.[1]

March 7, 1863 Corporal Edwin Paschall and Private Robert Scales were given medical discharges at Cumberland Gap. Paschall was suffering from secondary syphilis and Scales of hypotrophy of the heart. Both returned to Williamson County. Paschall joined Company F of the 4th Tennessee Confederate Cavalry. Scales died at home October 14, 1863. Private William McCrory was promoted to corporal to replace Paschall.[23]

On March 7, Joseph H. Cox of Fayette County, Kentucky enlisted in Baxter's Company. Cox had joined the Confederate Army while the Army of Tennessee was in Kentucky during the Perryville Campaign. He was serving in the Orderly Department at Cumberland Gap at the time of his transfer to Baxter's Battery. He served as company bugler and remained with the company to the end of the war. In later years, he drew a Confederate pension from the state of Kentucky for his service in Baxter's Battery.[16] While stationed in East Tennessee, five other men enlisted in Baxter's Company: Andrew J. May, Robert Earl, Joseph F. Foard, George Isler, and William Reed. Earl and Reed both deserted. Foard transferred to the 8th Tennessee Calvary and was captured and sent to Union Prison at Fort Delaware, Delaware. He was later exchanged at Bermuda Hundred, Virginia. Isler transferred to the Quartermaster Department and was paroled at the end of the war at Clarksburg, West Virginia. Privates Benjamin Brown and Linden Nall of Dickson County, Basil Talley of Cheatham County and Joseph Nall of Williamson County had been recruited by Recruiting Officer B. T. Gilliam of the Conscription Bureau in Columbia and forwarded to Cumberland Gap in March.[23]

Captain Baxter had paid for food and subsistence for his men while recruiting the company and while on the march from Bethesda on to Knoxville.

The Confederate States
To Captain Ed Baxter on March 12, 1863
    To expenses actually incurred and paid by him in subsisting his company from December 28, 1862 to January 1, 1863 and from January 4, 1863 to January 8, 1863 $211.70.

I certify upon honor, that the above amount is correct, that the expenses were actually incurred and paid by me in subsisting my company consisting of ninety enlisted men during the times stated, and while on a march under orders from H$^{dg.}$ The Dept. of E. Tenn., from Williamson County, Tennessee to Knoxville, Tennessee. That it was impossible to procure said subsistence from the Government, there being no commissaries at the time and place, and that I have not received pay for any part of the above amount.

Cumberland Gap, March 12, 1863
Ed Baxter, Capt. Lt. Arty.
Approved
A. Gracie, Jr.
Brig. Gen. [23]

During the Civil War, more soldiers died of disease than were killed in battle. Baxter's Company was no exception. An outbreak of typhoid fever struck the camp at Cumberland Gap. Dr. W. J. Abraham, Chief Surgeon at Cumberland Gap, ordered some of the sickest men sent to Fairgrounds Hospital in Knoxville.   William G.D. Buttrey, Robert Loveall, Jesse Edwards, James Garland, Albert Green, James Richardson, George Neely and William McPherson were admitted to the hospital on March 29. Loveall died in Fairgrounds Hospital April 13, 1863. Edwards, Garland, Green, Richardson and Neely recuperated and returned to the battery. Buttrey and McPherson were given 30-day furloughs to return home by Surgeon W. C. Hillard. Neither returned to the company and were listed as presumed deserted. At this point in time, the Federal presence in Middle Tennessee had greatly increased and getting trough the Union lines was difficult. Being unable to return to his command, Buttrey enlisted in Captain A. Duval McNairy's Company of Scouts. This was an irregular Confederate unit attached to Captain Albert Henon Cross' Battalion of Harvey's Scouts. Known as a guerrilla band by the Federals, McNairy's Scouts raided Union camps on the Northwestern Railroad line in Cheatham, Dickson and Humphreys Counties and had numerous skirmishes with Federal Cavalry. Buttrey was paroled with McNairy at the end of the war on May 16, 1865 at the Dean House on Lick Creek in Hickman County.[23] No official muster rolls were kept on McNairy's or the other irregular Confederate units in the area. It was possible that some other men of Baxter's Battery who returned to Middle Tennessee before the end of the war also served in these irregular units.

While the Federal Troops were trying to eliminate the guerrillas and bushwhackers in Middle Tennessee, the Confederates were faced with similar problems in East Tennessee and North Carolina.

WAR DEPARTMENT, C.S.A.
Richmond, March 27, 1863
General D. S. Donelson, Knoxville, Tenn.:

Grave complaints are made by Governor Vance and others of the presence and depredations of marauding deserters and refugees lurking in the mountains of North Carolina, near Asheville, and in the neighboring mountain districts. Send, if you can, an efficient detachment to sweep the country of such bands, conscripting all of proper age. I will write to Governor Vance, asking him to co-operate.

J. A. Seddon, Secretary of War [1]

March 29, the battery was again on the march, traveling thirteen miles and spending the night one mile south of Tazewell, Tennessee. March 30, the soldiers marched twelve miles and camped one mile south of the Clinch River. March 31 the company walked fourteen miles. April 1, 1863 the right section marched five miles to Louis Springs, the left section was assigned to camp at Strawberry Plains in Knox County with the duty of guarding the railroad bridge over the Holston River. Lt. Herrin procured a ration of corn for the twenty-six horses and four mules assigned to his left section of the battery on April 1 at Strawberry Plains. [23]

Pvt. Abraham Spencer

Railroad bridge over the Holston River at Strawberry Plains, TN. (Note fort in background.)

General Orders,
HDQRTS. DEPT. OF EAST TENNESSEE
No. 64
Knoxville, March 30, 1863

I.   To non-combatants and persons exempt from military duty residing within the Department of East Tennessee, desirous of removing beyond Confederate lines, permits will be granted upon application to the department commander.

II.   Applications for passports will be made through the deputy provost marshal, within whose district the applicant resides, to Col. John E. Toole, provost marshal for the department, and by him referred to the department commander, who will indicate the route to be traveled.

By command of Brig. Gen. D. S. Donelson:

J. G. Marti, Assistant Adjutant-General [1]

April 5, 1863 Captain S. H. Reynolds, Ordinance Officer at Knoxville issued a supply requisition which showed the battery with ninety-six non-commissioned officers, musicians and privates under Captain Baxter's command. Including the three Lieutenants, the company then listed one hundred men on its roll.[23]

April 16 the left section of Baxter's Battery stationed at Strawberry Plains was sent on a scout, marching thirty miles. The right section based at Louis Springs headed back to Cumberland Gap, marching fourteen miles. April 17, the right section marched fourteen more miles and arrived at the gap. The left section also arrived at Cumberland Gap on April 17 and went on patrol in Virginia, where they remained until April 23, when they departed for Bean Station, Tennessee. The company received a supply of ammunition on April 19 at Cumberland Gap. It consisted of: sixty-nine 6-pounder fixed solid shots, forty-two 6-pounder unfixed solid shot, ten 6- pound fixed canisters, thirty-one 6-pounder spherical based fixed, thirty-three 1 ¼ blank cartridges and nine 12-pounder Mountain howitzer sphericals. On April 22 Captain Baxter received a supply requisition which consisted of: fifteen artillery horses, sixty pairs of men's shoes, ten gallons of wagon grease, one side collar, three four horse wagons, two sets of lead harnesses, seven mules, five gallons of tar, and fifty pounds of salt. On April 23, Lt. Herrin received a supply of five hundred pistol caps for the company.[23] Most men in artillery companies were armed with pistols to defend the battery at close range. Some men in each battery were armed with rifles. Several of Baxter's men reported bringing their own arms to war with them. [17]

The right section departed Cumberland Gap for Bean Station on April 24 and marched seventeen miles. The right section marched eleven miles on April 25 and arrived at Bean Station. The left section also arrived in Bean Station on April 25.[1]

Typhoid fever continued to take its toll on Baxter's Company and the other Confederate units stationed in East Tennessee. While on the march and patrol more men had fallen ill and were left behind at Lea Springs, Louis Springs and Strawberry Plains. Corporal James F.E. Buttrey had been order by Brig. General Gracie to remain at Louis Springs in March and April in charge of the sick and baggage. On April 16, Private James Lewis was ordered to Lea Springs in charge of non-commissioned officers by Brig. General Gracie. On May 9, Lewis was reported sick in S. A. Smith Hospital in Mossy Creek, Tennessee. June 21, 1863 he was captured by Union troops near New Market, Tennessee. He later returned to the company. On April 23, Private William Sullivan, a teamster, was ordered to Strawberry Plains to assist Sgt. A. P. Beard in caring for the sick and baggage. On April 23 Private Felix Grundy Truett, who had been permanently detailed as a teamster, was ordered by Captain Baxter to Lea Springs to assist Corporal Buttrey in caring for the sick and baggage.[23]

April 29, 1863 Company Physician, Dr. Robert Sayers, was ordered by Captain Baxter to go to Lea Springs to get medicine for the sick.[23]

GENERAL ORDERS
HEADQUARTERS ARMY OF TENNESSEE
NO. 85
Tullahoma, April 24, 1863

The general commanding announces to the army the death of Brig. Gen. D. S. Donelson. He died in the Department of East Tennessee, which he had commanded. The regret with which his death is announced will be felt by the army and his country. He was an educated soldier, of great purity of character, singleness of purpose, and goodness of heart. Conspicuous for gallantry on the field, after the excitement had passed he was foremost in providing for the wants of his command, and devoted to the sick and wounded. His comrades in this army, and those who served under his orders, will long remember his deeds and virtues.

BRAXTON BRAGG, General.[1]

General Donelson was replaced as commander of the Department of East Tennessee by Major General Dabney H. Maury. Maury was a Virginia native with family ties to Williamson County. Matthew F. Maury of Baxter's Battery was his cousin.[1]

Major General Dabney Maury

Reports continued to indicate Union Troop movement in Kentucky and an impending invasion of East Tennessee. The forces in East Tennessee were also alerted to the possibility of being sent to Middle Tennessee to reinforce the Army of Tennessee.[1]

Back home in Middle Tennessee, the war also continued to escalate. The Federals had constructed Fort Grainger on the Harpeth River in Franklin. Large camps had been established at Franklin and Triune. A cavalry garrison had been established at Leiper's Fork.[1]

The Confederate cavalry under Major General Earl Van Dorn had defeated Union troops in the Battle of Thompson Station on March 5. In the battle, Private Anderson Lampley of Dickson County, serving in Company I 11th Tennessee Cavalry Regiment, was wounded by a minie ball in the right arm. The arm was amputated and he remained in a hospital in Columbia, Tennessee until the Confederates withdrew from Middle Tennessee. He was sent to an invalid corps camp in Georgia and remained in Georgia after the war and drew a Georgia Confederate pension. He was a brother of Andrew "Bud" and Radford Lampley who served in Baxter's Battery.[12, 23]

General Forrest conducted a successful raid on the Federal fort and camp at Brentwood on March 25. Forrest led an attack on Franklin on April 19. Captain Freeman, Baxter's successor in command of his first battery of artillery was captured and killed by his captors in the fight. Baxter's younger half-brother, Nathaniel Baxter, Jr. was captured with the rest of the command and sent to the Union Prison at Ft. Delaware, Delaware.[22]

Headquarters Department of East Tennessee
Knoxville, April 30, 1863
Brig. Gen. Arch. Gracie, Jr.
Commanding & c, :

General:

It is important to hold all of the forces of the department available as reserves in such position near the railroad as will enable the general commanding to concentrate them on short notice. He therefore desires that, after assigning to the bridge defenses the very smallest force sufficient to hold them, you will be ready to move the remaining available infantry and a battery of artillery, if you have one near you, with the greatest possible promptness to any point which may be indicated to you from this office.

Let your brigade quartermaster at once inform himself as to the amount of railroad transportation which may be held available for the movement without interfering with the necessary transportation of supplies.

These instructions are given in consequence of a telegram from General Johnston last night, requiring that all the available reserves be held ready for a prompt movement if called for.

Very respectfully, & c.
D. W. Flowerree, Assistance Adjutant-General [1]

RICHMOND, May 1, 1863
General Samuel Jones, Dublin Depot, Va.:
The following dispatch just received:
TULLAHOMA, May 1

Reports of our scouts in Kentucky indicate the invasion of East Tennessee by a strong force under Burnside. Cannot our troops there be re-enforced from Western Virginia?

J. E. JOHNSTON, General.

The Secretary of War directs that if it is in your power to render this aid, you will do so; but you must exercise your judgment in view of the circumstances and your own forces.

S. COOPER, Adjutant and Inspector General. [1]

GENERAL ORDERS
HDQRS. DEPT. OF EAST TENNESSEE
NO. 8
Knoxville, May 1, 1863

The following general order from headquarters Department of East Tennessee is republished for the information of all concerned. It will be strictly enforced:

I.   The transportation of flour, bacon, corn, and oats from the Department of East Tennessee it strictly prohibits.

II.   When Government supplies are purchased for shipment from the department, authority must be obtained at department headquarters for their transportation.

III. Railroad and steamboat companies will in every case require this authority to be presented before shipping such supplies.

By command of Maj. Gen. D. H. Maury:
D. W. FLOWERREE, Assistant Adjutant-General. [1]

Brig. General Donelson had complained of lax discipline in the Department of East Tennessee. That was not the case in Baxter's Company. Though not a military man by training, Captain Baxter's legal training led him to follow rules and regulations to the letter of the law and he expected as much of his men. Baxter did not hesitate to demote a soldier for neglect of duty or incompetence. On May 1, 1863 Sgt. James Martin, Sgt. Hiram Sears and Cpl. Albert Green were demoted in rank to privates for incompetence.

Sears was replaced by Private Eli Sherman, Green was replaced by Private William Hill and Martin was replaced by Cpl. Arter Lankford. Lankford served as "horse sergeant" of the company. He was assigned the responsibility for the company's horses and mules because of his experience with livestock. Lankford could not read or write. His close friend, Sgt. John Cunningham did his paper work for him. [17, 23]

May 3, 1863 under Special Order # 7 by Maj. General Dabney Maury, Lt. William Herrin was ordered to Dickson County for the purpose of bringing men to the company. He was allotted ten days for the assignment. On May 24, Privates Carter T. Brown, Charles L. Brown, George M. D. Brown and John T. Groves were left sick in Dickson County by Lt. Herrin. None were ever heard from, never reported to the command and were never paid. They were listed as: believed deserted, time and place unknown. Lt. Herrin was paid a $60 travel allowance for the six-hundred mile round trip from Morristown to Dickson County. [23]

HEADQUARTERS DEPARTMENT OF EAST TENNESSEE
Knoxville, May 5, 1863
Brig. Gen. Arch. Gracie, Jr.
Commanding, &c.:

My Dear General: So far as I can see, the indications of the enemy's purposes do not point to Cumberland Gap, as strongly as to a route into Tennessee much farther west. They have a considerable force at Williamsburg and Somerset, and have driven our forces out of Monticello and Albany, and occupied these places in a force represented to be quite formidable. Therefore it was that I desired you to send Hart's regiment to General Pegram. But, in consideration of your information and your orders to Colonel Hart's regiment to move forward in another direction, Pegram will have to do without him for the present.

I do not think it necessary to move your battery to Morristown yet. I told Colonel Trigg to send you his infantry, if he can spare it.

I have applied to General Jones to put some of his troops on the railroad, near Zollicoffer. I am compelled to make all dispositions of troops with reference to my ability to concentrate my infantry rapidly.

Very truly, yours,
DABNEY H. MAURY, Major-General, Commanding

P. S.—My cousin, M. F. Maury, came to see me this morning, and I have transferred him on direct application to the engineer department. This is wrong, of course, but I hope will not be of any serious injury to the service. [1]

On May 6, 1863 Privates Thompson Davis, John C. Mangrum, James Garland, Isham Roberts and William T. Smith were captured by Union troops near Richmond, Kentucky, located about one hundred miles north of Cumberland Gap. Company reports of June 1, 1863 list the men as having deserted at Cumberland Gap. The men were taken to prison in Lexington, Kentucky. They were sent from Lexington to the Union Prison at Camp Chase, Ohio where they arrived June 6, 1863. The prisoners departed Camp Chase for Johnson's Island Prison at Sandusky, Ohio on June 20, 1863. They remained imprisoned at Johnson's Island until October 30, 1863, when they were transported to the Federal Prison at Point Lookout, Maryland. Smith was released upon taking the oath of allegiance to the United States at Point Lookout on April 11, 1864. Point Lookout Prison gave Baxter's Company its first "galvanized Yankees". Mangrum took the oath of allegiance and enlisted in the 1st United States Volunteer Infantry to gain release from Point Lookout on April 7, 1864. Davis joined the Union army to gain release from prison on April 8.

Mangrum deserted from the Union Army in September 1864 and returned to the First District of Williamson County and was reunited with his wife and three children.   Roberts was released on oath April 12, 1864. Garland was exchanged at City Point, Virginia on October 30, 1864 and sent to Chiambrazo Hospital in Richmond, Virginia.[23]

May 6, 1863 Orderly Sergeant Matthew Maury was transferred to the Engineering Department under orders of his cousin, Maj. General Dabney Maury. Cpl. John F. Cunningham was promoted to Orderly Sergeant to replace Maury. Private Daniel White was promoted to Corporal to replace Cunningham. General Maury admitted in a letter that transferring his relative was not the right thing to do, but that he had the authority to do it. He felt his relative would be safer in the Engineering Corp than serving in a field battery.[1, 23]

HEADQUARTERS DEPARTMENT OF EAST TENNESSEE
Knoxville, May 7, 1863
Brig. Gen. Arch. Gracie, Jr., Commanding & c., Bean Station :
General:
Written orders were sent on yesterday for Hart's cavalry to report to General Pegram. You were telegraphed last night to move your infantry to Morristown, and hurry up Hart's cavalry to Clinton. The later orders were given in consequence of Chenault's and Pegram's cavalry being forced back by Yankee cavalry from Monticello and Albany. Please hurry forward Hart to Clinton, where he will receive instructions from General Pegram. The major-general commanding directs that you will order a regiment of infantry to Knoxville at once.
Very respectfully, your obedient servant.
D.W. FLOWERREE, Assistant Adjutant General [1]

HEADQUARTERS DEPARTMENT OF EAST TENNESSEE
Knoxville, May 8, 1863
Brig. Gen. Arch. Gracie, Jr., Commanding, &c:
General :
Your battalion will probably be returned to you in a few days. I have already authorized you to move at once toward Cumberland Gap, without waiting for orders from me, if you find that your command is required there. Meanwhile your infantry, from the indications now before me, had better remain on or near the railroad.
I ordered Colonel Trigg to communicate with you. Can you tell me anything about him or where his troops are, for I do not know, and I have received no report from him since he left here? Push forward the works

at Strawberry Plains as rapidly as possible. Do not let the troops stop laboring on them. I understand they have done so. You can then concentrate all of your infantry, which is desirable on the score of discipline and efficiency.

Very respectfully, your obedient servant,
DABNEY H. MAURY, Major-General. [1]

On May 11, 1863 Major General Simon Bolivar Buckner arrived in Knoxville from Mobile and assumed command of the Department of East Tennessee on May 12. General Maury assumed command of the Department of the Gulf headquartered at Mobile. [1]

Major General Simon Bolivar Buckner

WAR DEPARTMENT, C.S.A.
Richmond, May 12, 1863
General Samuel Jones, Dublin Depot, Va.:
    General Maury telegraphs East Tennessee to be in imminent danger of invasion by superior forces. Do your plans allow you to so arrange your forces as to send re-enforcements or go to the rescue ?
J.A. SEDDON, Secretary of War. [1]

May 19, 1863 the company moved out from Bean Station marching fourteen miles and camped for the night on the bank of the Clinch River. The sick were left behind at Bean Station, including Dr. Sayers, who was ordered behind by Chief Surgeon Abraham. Dr. Sayers was later detached to hospital duty under orders of Maj. General Buckner. He was later captured and took the oath of allegiance. May 20 the battery marched 16 miles to the Powell River. May 21, marched 4 miles back to Cumberland Gap. May 23 the left section marched ten miles into Kentucky on a scout and returned the same day. The battery remained camped about one mile southwest of Cumberland Gap until June 18.[23]

June 1, 1863 a thirty-day ration of forage for the company livestock was received at Morristown, Tennessee. The requisition showed the company had sixty-five horses and eighteen mules. Each animal was issued a daily allowance of twelve pounds of corn and fourteen pounds of hay.[23]

HEADQUARTERS DEPARTMENT OF EAST TENNESSEE
Knoxville, June 2, 1863
General Gracie, Cumberland Gap:
    Enemy reported advancing on Burkesville from Columbia. One regiment only at Williamsburg.
                    J. N. GALLEHER, Assistant Adjutant-General [1]

June 5, 1863 Gen. Gracie was advised by dispatch from Headquarters that there were indications of a general advance by the Federals. Ten regiments of infantry, three of cavalry and four batteries were reported at Somerset, Kentucky with two additional brigades expected shortly. The Federals reportedly had cooked eight days rations. Gracie was advised two Parrott guns would be sent to his command the next day. [1]

Members of the company suffering from typhoid remained at Bean Station under the care of private physicians.[23] Private James Thompson of Cheatham County recalled being among 18 soldiers suffering from typhoid at Bean Station. He recalled the sick men weren't allowed to have water. Catching the guard asleep, Thompson drank his fill from the water tub and encouraged others to do likewise. He reported those who drank water survived and those who didn't died within a few days. Thompson thought he was dying and brushed his hair back and crossed his hands on his chest because he "wanted to make a nice looking corpse." [24]

Private Lewis Thompson was the first to die of typhoid at Bean Station on May 27, 1863. Private Joseph Terrell died May 28. Private William Hooper died May 29. Cpl. James McCrory died June 7. Private George Carr died June 8. Private Richard Jackson died June 10. The men were buried in unmarked graves near the Bean Station Baptist Church. Lt. William Herrin attended to the legal matters concerning personal processions of the deceased soldiers and was granted letters of administration by the Knox County Court because there were no military personnel at Bean Station at the time of the men's deaths. Private Thompson's belongings were given to his nephew, Private James. B. Thompson. Cpl. McCrory's belongings went to his brother Private William McCrory. Private Hooper's items were given to his brother Private Thomas Hooper. Private Carr's belongings were taken by his brother Private Thomas Carr. Private Terrell's belongings were given to his brother Private Benjamin Terrell. All six of Baxter's men who died at Bean Station were married, adding six more widows to the growing number of Confederate widows in Middle Tennessee. Corporal McCrory was survived by two sons. Private Terrell left behind four children with his widow in the 1st District of Williamson County.[23]

MOUNT VERNON, June 7, 1863
Brig. Gen. S. P. Carter

General:

The communication which called forth the following was a notice to citizens of Knox County, who might become the victims of rebel malignity, setting forth that I would, on their application to me here, locate such as were driven from their homes there on account of their loyalty to the United States and to the State of Kentucky on farms of disloyal persons in this vicinity. It was not sent to or intended especially for the commanding officer of the rebel forces at Cumberland Gap: Nor was there anything in its contents to call forth or justify the ungentlemanly language used in the following. Being at a distance of about 80 miles, and in a strongly fortified mountain pass, this valiant general no doubt considered himself perfectly safe in indulging in abusive epithets and ridiculous blustering. This communication would indicate this individual as the true prototype in mind, as he is in person, of Shakespeare's famous knight, Sir John Falstaff. Deserters from his command represent his men in fully as sad a plight as the tatterdemalions led out to battle by Sir John. God speed the day when those poor fellows shall be relieved from the oppressive rule of such bogus chivalry.

SAMUEL A. GILBERT, Colonel

(Inclosure)

(CIRCULAR)   HEADQUARTERS GRACIE'S BRIGADE
June 4, 1863

There has been brought to my notice a communication issued from the headquarters Second Brigade, Fourth Division, Army of the Cumberland, Kentucky, May 26, 1863, signed by S. A. Gilbert, colonel commanding, notifying the commandant of the rebel forces at Cumberland Gap, in the State of Tennessee, that said colonel will cause the families of rebel sympathizers to be removed from their homes on account of the alleged removal of the families of certain (unarmed) citizens of Knox County, Kentucky.

Without condescending to further notice the abusive character of the article or its author, I deem it due to the truth of history to remark that no families have been removed from their homes by my command until the order recently issued for the removal of the notorious Green Turner, his brothers, Ben and Jim Turner, and John Howard, with their families, living in close proximity to my lines.

Green Turner was guide to the Yankees in their late raid on this place; shot one of my men, and would have murdered him had he not been prevented by those with him. He was known to harbor spies, to steal horses, and was capable of any service or atrocity required by the enemy. His brothers and Howard were united with him in treasonable purposes, and only differed from him in the fact of being lesser villains. From that respect and sympathy due to the helplessness of women and children which has so distinguished the Confederate army they were permitted to leave unmolested, with their families and all their moveable property, to the place of their choice, whereas the mean spirit which has actuated the Northern Army and Government would have consigned them to the halter or the dungeon. Detachments sent to Barboursville, which could at any time destroyed it, have been particularly instructed to commit no violence against its citizens or touch any of their property, and it stands now, an evidence of my clemency.

The infamous threat against helpless families contained in the notice issued under the false pretense of retaliation is the braggadocio of a cowardly braggart, who, with the valor of the ass in the lion's skin would attack the weak and helpless, and flee like a spurned cur from the strong, and adds, if possible, to the already merited infamy and disgrace of the Government he serves. The depraved Lincolnites on either side of the mountains have hitherto been the objects of my forbearance rather than justice, but if the homes or lives of "rebel sympathizers," as they are called, are put into peril or destroyed, the retaliation that shall instantly follow will teach those warriors on women a lesson not soon to be forgotten.

The civilized world stands shocked at the falsehood and despotic tyranny of that hated Government, which has deprived its best citizens of their political and civil rights, condemned them, without trial, to the dungeon of the felon, for the mere expression of their political opinions; shed the blood of the innocent, depopulated New Orleans of its most virtuous citizens, after robbing them of all their property. The threat of the minion of such a Government will not be regarded and my orders will be carried into effect.

A. GRACIE, JR.
Brigadier-General, Provisional Army of the Confederate States
(Indorsements)
This was brought from the Gap by John G. Newley, at the request of General Gracie. We are expecting them down upon us every hour. I will not be here.

Very respectfully, yours,
H. K. WILSON

LONDON, June 6, 1863
Colonel:
This circular was brought in by a courier at 11 o'clock to-day. I will get out a reconnoitering force in that direction this p. m.

W. D. HAMILTON [1]

SPECIAL ORDERS   ADJT. AND INSPECTOR GENERAL'S OFFICE
NO. 136
Richmond, June 8, 1863

XXI.   The following will hereafter be the western limits of the Department of East Tennessee, viz: Following the Little Tennessee and Tennessee Rivers to Kingston, thence up Clinch river to mouth of Emery Creek, up Emery Creek to the Cumberland Mountains, and following said mountains to Cumberland gap. All the country in Tennessee west of this line will be added to the command of General Bragg.

By command of the Secretary of War.
JNO. WITH, Assistant Adjutant-General. [1]

Knoxville, June 8, 1863
Brig. Gen. Arch. Gracie, Jr.
Cumberland Gap:
All quiet on the 6th in Pegram's front. It is possible that enemy is making only a feint near Monticello, and intends advancing from Somerset on Williamsburg. Watch approaches from that point. An engineer has been sent you. What rations do you need to supply you for thirty days?

V. SHELIHA, Chief of Staff [1]

HEADQUARTERS DEPARTMENT OF EAST TENNESSEE
Knoxville, June 18, 1863
General S. Cooper,
Adjutant and Inspector General, Richmond, Va.:

GENERAL: I returned yesterday from an inspection of the troops of the department and of the Mountain Gaps, from Clinton to Cumberland Gap. The troops I inspected were in a bad condition, with the exception of Gracie's brigade at Cumberland Gap. The defenses of the gaps are very imperfect; scarcely any work has been bestowed on them during the past twelve months. I set the troops at work to strengthen the defenses at Cumberland Gap at once. In connection with the chief engineer and my chief of staff, I have devised a system of small, strong defenses at the gaps, which will be commenced at once if the enemy's movements justify it, and which, when completed, will enable a small force to check for a considerable time a very large one. With the present resources at my control, it is very difficult to prevent a surprise of some of the more important gaps.

I am, sir, very respectfully, your obedient servant.
S. B. BUCKNER, Major-General, Commanding [1]

Knoxville, June 18, 1863
Col. R. G. Fain, Cumberland Gap:

Send courier to General Gracie, with orders to move the bulk of his command to Jacksborough Gap, leaving sufficient garrison at Big Creek Gap, keeping open communication with General Frazer, who will concentrate his brigade at or near Clinton. Send tents to General Gracie's command.

V. SHELIHA, Chief of Staff. [1]
Knoxville, June 18, 1863

Col. R.G. Fain, Cumberland Gap:

Inform General Gracie that his command will remain at big Creek Gap until further orders.

V. SHELIHA, Chief of Staff [1]

HEADQUARTERS DEPARTMENT OF EAST TENNESSEE
Knoxville, June 18, 1863
Brigadier-General Frazer,
Commanding Brigade:

General:

The major-general commanding directs you first, to collect your brigade as rapidly as possible at or near Clinton, according to circumstances; secondly, to avoid an engagement with the enemy should he occupy Kingston with a large force; but thirdly, to try and cut him off should he cross the river in inferior strength; fourthly, to keep in constant communication with Brigadier-General Gracie, who will leave a sufficient garrison at Big Creek Gap and move the main body of his command to Jacksborough Gap, and fifthly, to keep these headquarters fully advised of the movements of the enemy. A private dispatch was received eight hours before your official dispatch arrived.

The Fifty-fourth Virginia Regiment has been ordered to support McCant's battery, at Kingston, against the attack of an inferior enemy, but to serve as escort to the battery and fall back on Loudon, keeping between Clinch and Tennessee Rivers, should the enemy approach in too strong a force.

I have the honor to be, general, very respectfully, your obedient servant,

V. Shelia, Chief of Staff. [1]

HEADQUARTERS DEPARTMENT OF EAST TENNESEE
Knoxville, June 18, 1863
Brig. Gen. Arch. Gracie, Jr.,
Commanding Brigade:

General:

The major-general commanding directs that you leave at Big Creek Gap a garrison sufficiently strong to guard against all surprise, and to take position with the main body of your command at Jacksborough Gap. You will please keep in constant communication with Brigadier-General Frazer, and support him in case he should attack or be attacked by an enemy approaching from the direction of Kingston.

I have the honor to be, general, your obedient servant.

V. SHELIHA, Chief of Staff [1]

Knoxville, June 19, 1863
General S. Cooper
Adjutant and Inspector General, Richmond, Va:

The enemy made a demonstration in force against Big Creek Gap night before last, but retired after heavy skirmishing. He now threatens Cumberland Gap and Loudon, telegraphic communication to which point is already interrupted. This morning at 5 o'clock 2,000 cavalry were near Loudon. The bridges along the railroad and the mountain gap are guarded by garrisons deemed strong enough to prevent surprise, while General Buckner, who left here this morning, is concentrating his forces near Clinton.

A raid on Knoxville is not improbable. Proper measures for the protection of the place are being taken.

V. SHELIHA, Chief of Staff [1]

Knoxville, June 20, 1863

General S. Cooper:

Major-General Buckner is at Clinton, concentrating his forces. Enemy, 2,000 strong, attempted to burn the railroad bridge yesterday, but failed. Attempted to burn depots here last night, but failed again, and retired this morning, after severe cannonading, in the direction of Rogersville.

V. SHELIA, Chief of Staff [1]

Morristown, June 21, 1863

Major-General Jones, Dublin:

The enemy burned the bridge over the Holston, 16 miles east of Knoxville, last evening. They advanced to within 14 miles of this place this morning and burned a bridge and depot. No troops here except my regiment, Brigadier-General Jackson in command.

G. C. WHARRTON, Colonel. [1]

Knoxville, June 22, 1863

General Braxton Bragg, Shelbyville:

The enemy appeared near Knoxville on the 19th and attacked on 20th. Were repulsed. They burned the railroad bridges at Flat Creek and Strawberry Plains. Please grant permission to Maxwell, bridge-builder, to rebuild them at once.

S. B. BUCKNER, Major-General, Commanding. [1]

On June 15 Private William Ellison was promoted to Corporal to replace James McCrory who had died at Bean Station. [23]

Following orders handed down by General Gracie, on the night of June 18, Baxter's Company departed from its camp near Cumberland Gap for the last time and marched seventeen miles in the direction of Big Creek Gap. June 19 the company marched eighteen miles and arrived at Big Creek Gap. June 20 was spent marching twenty-six miles to Clinton. On June 21, the battery marched eighteen miles toward Strawberry Plains. On June 22 the company returned to Clinton and remained there until June 26 when the men marched eighteen miles to Knoxville and set up camp near the depot. [1]

VIEW OF KNOXVILLE FROM SOUTH SIDE OF THE TENNESSEE RIVER.
THE BUILDING ACROSS THE RIVER IS EAST TENNESSEE UNIVERSITY,
PREDECESSOR OF THE UNIVERSITY OF TENNESSEE.
BAXTER'S COMPANY CAMPED IN THE VICINITY.

On June 26, 1863, Lieutenant John Marshall, Jr. had drawn rations of whiskey for the men in the company and kept five quarts for himself. Men in the company reported on June 27 that Lt. Marshall got drunk and the "flies blowed him". On June 28 and 29, Marshall was seen taking whiskey which had been procured for the sick and used it himself. On July 18, Lt. Marshall gave a soldier a pass to kill a pig in exchange for whiskey. [17]

On July 1, 1863, Sgt. A. P. Beard and Sgt. George Hogan, Jr. both resigned as Sergeants and took demotions to the rank of Private. Beard was replaced by Corporal Alfred McCaslin. Hogan was replaced by Corporal James F. E. Buttrey. McCaslin's Corporal slot was filled by Private Robert Hall. Buttrey's Corporal position was assumed by Private William Lankford. [23]

Lt. John Marshall, Jr.

By special order #3 of General Gracie, on July 8, Lt. John Marshall was ordered to Chattanooga to arrest all stragglers belonging to the brigade. He was allotted nine days to accomplish the task and was paid $14.80 in travel expenses for the 148 mile round-trip from Knoxville. No report as to the number of men arrested was given. [23]

HEADQUARTERS DEPARTMENT OF EAST TENNESSEE
Knoxville, July 9, 1863
Hon J. A. Seddon
Secretary of War, Richmond, Va.:

SIR:
I replied two days since your telegram relative to a forward movement. With a view to a more complete understanding, and also to procure arms long since promised by the Ordinance Department, but which have not yet been sent to me, I send Maj. J. Stoddard Johnston, of my staff to confer with you. A large portion of my cavalry are most indifferently armed. They cannot render efficient service in their present condition. I have to request that you will give such orders as will secure the immediate forwarding of the necessary arms. Major Johnston will give you more detail than I can furnish in a letter the general plans which I propose- plans which of course may be modified by the development of facts in relation to the enemy. I will remark that if a forward movement is designated from East Tennessee the column should be as strong and as well organized as the Government can make it. The troops of this department are raw. They are the residuum left after taking the best troops under General Kirby Smith to the Army of Tennessee. They have not yet passed the ordeal of fire and consequently should be mingled

with veteran troops to give them stability under fire. If therefore, it be designed for me to advance, I would respectfully suggest that Wharton's small brigade from General Jones' force be added temporarily to Preston's command, and that as many brigades as General Bragg can spare be added to my division. With the small force likely to be placed at my disposal I do not expect to hold Kentucky, but if I can start with 10,000 infantry, Morgan's cavalry, now in Kentucky, be ordered to report to me, I can certainly occupy until the autumn as many as 20,000 or 30,000 of the enemy in Kentucky. The effect would be a powerful diversion in favor of the other armies. It is for the War Department to judge of its expediency.

I am, very respectfully, your obedient servant,
S. B. BUCKNER, Major-General, Commanding. [1]

On July 10, Privates John and William Hood were reported as having deserted. Both eventually returned to Middle Tennessee to rejoin their wives and children. [23]

July 13, Captain Baxter's legal training was put to use. By General Order # 75 of Maj. General Buckner, he was ordered to Court Judge Advocate duty. [23]

The company remained in Knoxville until July 16. Before departing, the company turned in to Major E. L. Hord of the Quartermaster's Department: one four horse wagon listed as unfit for service, four poor mules, two single sets worn wheel harnesses and one wagon saddle. It then marched six miles out of town on the Knoxville and Clinton Railroad, where it remained until August 10, 1863.

HEADQUARTERS DEPARTMENT OF EAST TENNESSEE
August 3, 1863
Brig. Gen. Arch. Gracie, Jr.,
Commanding Brigade:

General:

The major-general commanding directs the speedy concentration of your brigade at Strawberry Plains. You will please give the necessary directions for the execution of this order, and instruct the three battalions of the Alabama Legion now stationed at Cumberland Gap and Big Creek Gap to join you as soon as relieved by Brigadier-General Frazer's command. The Forty-third Alabama will remain at Knoxville until relieved by the Sixth Florida Regiment. Colonel J. J. Finley.

I have the honor to be general, very respectfully, your obedient servant,

V. SHELIHA, Chief of Staff

P.S.-Report to these headquarters the line of march ordered for your different regiments and battalions.   The North Carolina regiment at Cumberland Gap will not be ordered to move until further instructions are received.

S. B. BUCKNER, Major-General, Commanding [1]

On August 6, 1863, Cpl. William Lankford and Privates: James W. Allen, John Gatlin, Bud Lampley, Duck Lampley, Jack Lampley, John Tidwell, Amos Spicer, Napoleon Groves, and   George Neely were reported as having deserted near Knoxville.   Most of these men had wives and some had children at home in Middle Tennessee.   In 1910, Jack Lampley's application for a Confederate Pension was rejected because the military records showed he had deserted. He stated that he and the other men did not desert, that they became detached from the company while on patrol and were captured by Union troops near Lebanon, Tennessee and taken to the State Prison in Nashville. He stated they were paroled from the prison at the end of August or first of September 1863 and sent home without parole papers. He stated the took the oath of allegiance at the end of the war at Clarksville, Tennessee.   Records of the Assistant Provost Marshall at Clarksville show he was given authority to parole area guerrillas at the end of the war.[23]   It is possible some men in this group joined the irregular Confederate bands after returning to Middle Tennessee. Tales passed down through the generations in the Lampley family tell of the days when: "the men went off on the horses with their rifles on killing sprees." Included in this group were Joseph "Doad" Lampley, Jr. and his eldest son, John.[17]

August 8 a supply of hats for the men was procured through a requisition by Lt. John Marshall. Hats were not issued when the company was equipped in January.[23]

August 10 the battery moved back toward Knoxville and camped on the hill about one mile north of town.

While the men in Baxter's Battery maneuvered around East Tennessee. The war was close to home back in Middle Tennessee and guerrilla activity was rampant. On August 19, 1863 on the way to Bon Aqua in pursuit of Major Dick McCann, Federal cavalry attacked pickets from McCann's Confederate cavalry near Turnbull Creek in western Williamson County near the Hickman County line. Records were not kept on much of the guerrilla fighting. Four unknown Confederate soldiers were buried in the Walker Family Cemetery on the Williamson-

Hickman County line.   Whether they were killed in action or died of disease was not documented. [17]

August 19, 1863---Skirmish at Weem's Springs, Tenn.
Report of Capt. James Clifford, First Missouri Cavalry
Nashville, TN. August 23, 1863

Captain:

I have the honor to submit the following report of the expedition to Weem's Springs, Tenn.:

In compliance with your instructions from headquarters District of the Cumberland, I left camp at Nashville, Tenn., with my company (F), First Missouri Cavalry, Maj. Gen. G. Grainger's escort, at daybreak on the morning of the 18th instant and proceeded to Hillsborough, Tenn., where I arrived at 1 p.m.   Here in accordance with your instructions, I was joined by Company C, Fourteenth Michigan Infantry (mounted), under command of Captain Mackey.   I left there at 9 p.m. traveling all night, and arriving within half a mile of Weems' Springs at 8 o'clock on the morning of the 19th instant.

Here I halted and gave directions to Captain Mackey how he should maneuver his company, dividing both companies into four platoons, each under command of a commissioned officer.   Every man being in readiness, I ordered the charge, which resulted in the capture of Maj. Dick McCann and 14 others, together with 27 horses, their arms and equipments.   The notorious guerrilla chief was captured by Private Martin W. Culp, of my company, and first recognized as the same by Liet. William Davis, who immediately introduced the gentleman to me.   I of course had him well cared for, with the others of his command who fell into my hands.   I fed my horses and rested at Weems' Springs until noon, when I started for Franklin, Tenn., where I arrived with my command soon after dark on the 19th instant.   Here I turned Maj. Dick McCann and prisoners over to the provost-marshal, and rested my men and horses until the afternoon of the 22nd instant, when I departed with my company for Nashville, arriving there about 8 p.m. without the loss of a single man or horse.

Too much praise cannot be bestowed on Captain Mackey and the officers and men of his company, also to First Lieut. William Davis and men of my company, for their gallant behavior throughout the entire expedition, having traveled 105 miles in less than twenty-four hours.

I have the honor to be, captain, very respectfully, your obedient servant,

James Clifford
Captain Co. F, First Missouri Cav.
Maj. Gen. G. Granger's Escort, Comdg. Expedition [1]

Capt. William C. Russell
Assistant Adjutant-General
Headquarters District of the Cumberland
Nashville, August 27, 1863
Respectfully referred to department headquarters. Dick McCann and his associates are confined in Nashville penitentiary.

G. Grainger, Major-General, Commanding. [1]

Headquarters Buckner's Corps
Knoxville, August 20, 1863
Brigadier-General Gracie
Strawberry Plains:
General:
the major-general commanding directs you to march with your brigade at once to this point. Make an early start so that the brigade can be here at latest by to-morrow night. There are sure indications of an immediate attack by the enemy in force.

I have the honor, general, to remain your obedient servant.

V. Sheliha, Chief of Staff [1]

Baxter's Company remained in camp in Knoxville until August 22, departed from the fairgrounds camp in Knoxville and marched six miles down the Kingston Road where the men camped for the night. August 23, an eleven mile march to Campbell's Station on the Kingston Road. The company departed Campbell's Station about 7 o'clock the night of August 24 and marched all night covering fourteen miles, arriving at Loudon at sunup. The battery crossed the Holston River on the railroad bridge and camped about half a mile out of Loudon. Brig. General Gracie was ordered to move his entire brigade to Loudon.[1]

Headquarters Buckner's Corps
Knoxville, August 24, 1863
Brigadier-General Gracie,
In the Field
General:
You will move at once with the whole command concentrated at Turkey Creek (Colonel Palmer's Regiment and Colonel Moore's Georgia regiment) to Loudon, where you will confer with Brigadier-General Johnson, who, by the time of your arrival at Loudon, will have received orders from General Bragg to move his command to some other point.

It will be well to leave one battery, with sufficient infantry support, in the works constructed this side of the river. You are expected to reach the point of your destination to-night.

I have the honor, general, to be your obedient servant.

V. Sheliha, Chief of Staff [1]

The company remained in Loudon with Gracie's Brigade until moving out August 30, marching four miles. March 31 the unit marched trough Philadelphia Station covering sixteen miles. September 1 seventeen miles were marched. September 2 the brigade marched trough Charleston covering sixteen miles. On that day, General Buckner reported the enemy had shelled Loudon and Federal cavalry had entered Knoxville. September 3 the brigade camped on Candy Creek eight miles west of Charleston in Bradley County.[1]

Headquarters Preston's Division. Buckner's Corps
In the Field, September 3, 1863
Colonel Sheliha:

Colonel:

My command is bivouacked with its right (Gracie) at Carmichael's Ford: center near McCracken's 6 miles on the road from Charleston, and its left toward Ross' Ford of Candy Creek, on the south and east bank of Candy Creek, and at the base of Candy Hills. I have just received your dispatch in reference to the steamboats, and have given the requisite orders in regard to them. Will you inform me if there are any cavalry between the Hiwassee and the Tennessee covering my right, and direct their officers to inform me of any movements of the enemy on the east of the Hiawassee?

I am colonel, very respectfully,
W. Preston, Brigadier-General Commanding [1]

Headquarters Buckner's Corp
Charleston, September 3, 1863

(General Preston:)

You will proceed with Brigadier-General Gracie's and Colonel Kelly's Brigades and three batteries of artillery, via Georgetown, on the Blythes Ferry road, to a point about 1 mile beyond Georgetown, select a suitable camping-ground, and support the cavalry in your front and flank.

The cavalry force of this corps will be under command of Brigadier-General Forrest. Colonel Trigg' brigade, with one battery of artillery, will remain at Candy Creek until relieved by Major-General Stewart's command, and then return to this point.

I remain, general, very respectfully, your obedient servant.

V.Sheliha, Chief of Staff. [1]

For the first time during the war, Baxter's Company served in the same command with General Nathan Bedford Forrest "The Wizard of the Saddle" during the march from Loudon to Georgia.

September 4 the brigade marched through Georgetown and camped in Hamilton County, Tennessee. September 5 marched twelve miles and camped near Blythe's Ferry on the Tennessee River.   September 6 marched eight miles during the night. The marching continued with the destination of joining the Army of Tennessee in the state of Georgia, south of Chattanooga. The Federals were approaching Chattanooga from the west, requiring Buckner's Corp to bi-pass Chattanooga and take an indirect route into Georgia from the east.

The main body of the Army of Tennessee had left its winter camps in Shelbyville, Wartrace and Tullahoma in June and marched toward Chattanooga.   A sharp engagement was fought June 24, 1863 at Hoover's Gap, Tennessee.   The 20th Tennessee Infantry regiment was heavily engaged in the fight, bringing more casualties among the soldiers of Company H from west Williamson County. Private Thomas Knight was killed in the battle. Private Ben Givens was wounded for the second time in the war and later died from the wound in a hospital in Dalton, Georgia. Private James Castleman lost an arm from a wound received at Hoover's Gap.   Privates John McIntosh and Wiley P. Mangrum were also wounded in the engagement.[19]

In 1863 Chattanooga was a relatively small city, but was a strategic point due to its railroad connections to Knoxville, Atlanta, Nashville and Memphis.

General Braxton Bragg withdrew the Army of Tennessee from Chattanooga on September 8 without a fight and moved to the west bank of Chickamauga Creek in north Georgia.   The Federals moved into Chattanooga on September 9 and soon began their pursuit of the Confederates. [1]

Of the one hundred original Middle Tennessee recruits of Baxter's Company who reached Knoxville in January 1863, almost one-third were gone when the company left Tennessee and entered Georgia in September 1863, after ten months service. Seven had died, thirteen had deserted, one transferred to another command, two had been unable to return from furloughs home, and six had been captured and were in union prisons.[23]

Pay voucher of Private William Bethshears.

CHAPTER 3

CHATTANOOGA

On September 7, 1863, Baxter's Battery entered the state of Georgia with Gracie's Brigade after marching twelve miles. The next day, the company marched six more miles and camped one mile west of Ringgold, Georgia. The marching continued with the brigade covering ten miles on September 9. [1]

Private Felix Jones was born in Dickson County and had moved with his family to Calloway County, Kentucky before the war. He returned to his native county and enlisted in Baxter's Battery December 19, 1862. Jones had been left behind sick at Cumberland Gap in May, but later rejoined the company. He again became separated from the company and was reported as deserted on September 9 at Rock Springs, Georgia. He was captured at Chattanooga on September 12 and sent to military prison at Louisville, Kentucky. He was paroled and released on oath to return to his home in Calloway County on October 30, 1863 by order of Brig. General Boyles. [23]

On September 10 the battery traveled eight miles. September 11, the men had marched about two miles and were ordered into line of battle in McLemore's Cove at the foot of Pigeon Mountain. Heavy skirmishing with the enemy broke out and lasted about two hours. Buckner's Corp and Hindman's Division had been ordered to attack Union Major General James Negley's isolated Division. Negley's Division escaped with only minor casualties. No casualties were reported on Baxter's men in the fight. [1]

On September 12 the company crossed Pigeon Mountain and marched seven miles to Lafayette, Georgia. September 13 the company was ordered to march four miles in the direction of Snow Hill, where a skirmish was being fought. The company headed back to Lafayette and were followed by the enemy. More skirmishing was reported both to the right and left of Lafayette. The company remained at Lafayette until September 17 and marched ten miles on the Chattanooga-Georgia Road. September 18 at noon, the company was ordered to form in line of battle. Skirmishing erupted at about 3 p.m. and lasted about two hours. Baxter's Battery had no report of casualties in the skirmish. [1]

The Union Army of the Cumberland under command of Major General William S. Rosecrans numbering 55,000 troops had marched out of Chattanooga soon after its occupation in pursuit of the Confederate Army of Tennessee under command of General Braxton Bragg.   General Robert E. Lee had ordered Lt. General James Longstreet and his Corp from the Army of Northern Virginia to Georgia to re-enforce Bragg. With the arrival of Longstreet's Corp on the evening of September 19, Bragg's force numbered about 70,000 men. [1]

September 19, 1863 the Battle of Chickamauga began at daybreak with a Confederate attack on Union positions.   Baxter's Battery, armed with two 3-inch rifle cannon, was assigned to Major Samuel Williams Reserve Artillery Battalion of Major General Simon Bolivar Buckner's Corp.   Williams Battalion was held in reserve the first day of battle. Other batteries in Williams Battalion were: Captain R. F. Kolb's Alabama Battery (Barbour Artillery) armed with two 12-pound howitzers and two 6-pound bronze cannon; Captain Robert P. McCant's Flordia Battery equipped with one 10-pound Parrott cannon and three 6-pound bronze cannon and Darden's Mississippi Battery, commanded by Lt. H. W. Bullen. Major Thomas Porter, an Annapolis graduate who had been severely wounded at Fort Donelson, served as Buckner's Chief of Artillery.   Including William's Battalion, Porter commanded seven batteries armed with twenty-nine field pieces. [1, 22]

Baxter's Battery was detached from William's Battalion on September 19 and returned to Brigadier General Gracie's Brigade. Gracie's Brigade had taken position at Dalton's Ford on the Chickamauga Creek on the evening of September 18. On the morning of the nineteenth, the brigade formed in line of battle facing the enemy's works near Lee and Gordon's Mill, where it was exposed to the fire of enemy artillery.   Several members of the 63rd Tennessee Infantry Regiment were injured by the artillery fire. Gracie placed Baxter's Battery on a ridge on the far left of the battle line near Lee and Gordon's Mill, with Jeffress' Virginia Battery (Nottoway Artillery).   The 43rd Alabama Infantry Regiment reported on the 19th that about 2 p.m. it moved to the right several hundred yards to the top of a slight elevation and was left with the 3rd Battalion of Hilliard's Alabama Legion to support Baxter's and Jeffress' Batteries.   The position was shelled by the enemy throughout the afternoon and evening, but received no casualties. [1, 22]

The first day of the Battle of Chickamauga closed without either side claiming victory. Confederates in their camps reported hearing the work of axes in felling trees on the Union lines, while they also were busy fortifying their positions. The Federals were preparing breastworks for the next days fight. Longstreet's Corp arrived in the evening. [1]

The morning of September 20 was cold with the temperature in the low thirties and a heavy frost on the ground. A dense fog rose from Chickamauga Creek and mixed with the smoke from the fires in the woods. The area had received little rain in the six weeks before the battle and exploding shells ignited fires in the dry woods. General Braxton Bragg had ordered his troops to attack at daybreak on September 20. Due to failure in following orders, the battle did not resume until later in the morning. General Bragg blamed Lieutenant General Leonidas Polk for failure to attack as ordered and later tried to have him relieved of his command. [1]

Baxter's and Jeffress's Batteries remained in the same position on September 20. The 43rd Alabama Infantry Regiment and 3rd Battalion of Hillard's Alabama Legion rejoined the main body of Gracie's Brigade. The 65th Georgia Infantry Regiment of Kelly's Brigade was left to support the batteries. On the morning of the 20th, Gracie's Brigade was ordered to near Dyer's house on the Chattanooga Road where it formed line of battle and was exposed to enemy shelling. [1]

Between 4 and 5 p.m., the brigade was ordered to support Kershaw's Brigade posted to the left of the Chattanooga Road. Gracie's Brigade advanced, passing through Kershaw's command and suddenly found itself in the presence of the enemy, strongly posted behind breastworks of logs and rails on the crest of an opposite hill. The fury of musketry, grape and canister immediately commenced, but undaunted, the brigade scaled the precipitous heights, driving the enemy before it and took possession of the hill. General Gracie's horse was shot out from under him during the charge. Gracie's Brigade held the hill about an hour, until it's supply of ammunition was almost exhausted. The brigade withdrew to replenish its empty cartridge boxes upon the arrival of Kelly's and Trigg's Brigades. [1]

On September 20, Baxter's Company expended thirteen rounds of ammunition. The long-range 3-inch guns proved ineffective in the heavily wooded terrain of the Chickamauga Battlefield. Jeffress' Battery, commanded by Captain William C. Jeffress, was armed with one 12-pound Blakely cannon and four 10-pound Parrott cannon. Jeffress' Battery fired sixty-seven rounds of ammunition in the battle. The batteries had been supplied with poor quality ordinance. Reports stated that not more than one fourth of the projectiles fired by William's

Artillery Battalion exploded. The reports of William's Battalion also showed no guns were exchanged, lost or abandoned on the battlefield. No casualties were reported in either Baxter's or Jeffress' batteries. Kolb's battery fired sixty-six rounds of ammunition and lost two men killed and one wounded. Kolb also had one horse killed and two horses wounded. McCant's battery fired eighty-five rounds of ammunition and its lone casualty was one soldier wounded. [1, 22]

The men of Baxter's Battery were fortunate to survive the Battle of Chickamauga with no killed or wounded. The Battle of Chickamauga had become the bloodiest two -day battle of the war. The South had won a costly victory at Chickamauga. Estimated casualties in killed and wounded were 18,454 for the Confederates and 16,170 for the Union.

Lee and Gordon's Mill near Baxter's position at Battle of Chickamauga.

In Gracie's Brigade of about 1,870 carried into action, 90 were killed, 615 wounded and 27 missing in action. Among the casualties were some of the neighbors and kin of Baxter's men from Middle Tennessee who weren't so fortunate. Private Granville Johnson, Jr. of Company H and Private Berry Jordan of Company K, 11th Tennessee Infantry Regiment were killed in the battle. Captain F. F. Tidwell received his second wound of the war at Chickamauga. Private Alfred Hutchinson of Company H 20th Tennessee Infantry Regiment lost an arm due to a Chickamauga wound.   Others   from   Company   H   wounded   at Chickamauga were: Privates Fred Beech, Jesse Ham and James Vowel. They were among the eighty-eight casualties suffered by the 20th Tennessee Infantry Regiment in the battle. [19]

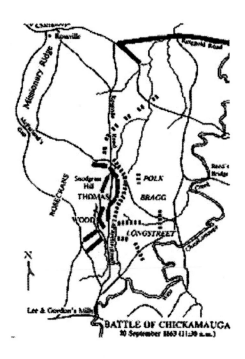

Baxter's position during the Battle of Chickamauga, far left of the line near Lee & Gordon's Mill

September 21, Baxter's Battery was assigned the gruesome task of burial detail and traveled about two miles to the main section of the battlefield to remove bodies. The battery wagons were used to haul corpses from the battlefield to the burial trenches. Private Sol Tidwell recalled to family members after the war that he was on duty as a teamster after the Battle of Chickamauga, loading corpses onto his wagon and hauling them from the battlefield to the burial trenches at Bird's Mill near Chickamauga Station.   He recalled that the stench of the decaying corpses made him sick to his stomach and he would have to stop working to vomit and then resume loading the bodies. Many of the corpses were charred and burned from the fires started by exploding shells. Many of the wounded had been burned to death. Other burial details buried the dead on the spots where they fell, both blue and gray. Visitors searching the battlefield several weeks after the battle reported seeing unburied corpses, some reported seeing decapitated heads of Union soldiers on fence posts in some sections of the battlefield. Dr. Urban G. Owen of Williamson County, a Surgeon with the 34th Tennessee Infantry Regiment was still on the battlefield on November 1 caring for soldiers in a field hospital. The soldiers were too badly wounded to be moved to a hospital. He recalled dead men and horses were strewn for miles in every direction on the main road, in cornfields and in the woods. He reported the smell was bad everywhere. [11, 17]

Tuesday September 22, Baxter's Company marched about six miles in the direction of Ringgold and spent the night on the bank of Chickamauga Creek. September 23, the battery was placed in line of battle in Hamilton County, Tennessee about two miles south of Chattanooga. The battery was engaged in heavy cannonading which began about 2 o'clock in the afternoon and lasted about four hours. On September 24, the men of the company were awakened at daylight by Yankees shelling the woods near where they were camped. The fighting resumed with heavy skirmishing and cannonading at 10 p.m. The fight lasted about an hour and a half, until the Union Troops fell back to their fortifications. Friday September 25 skirmishing and cannonading commenced at 2 p.m. Sporadic cannonading continued frequently through out the night. At day break on the 26th, the company moved to fortifications. Skirmishing broke out at 5 a.m. Captain Baxter ordered open fire and the company started shelling the enemy at 6 a.m. and continued firing for two hours. Sunday September 27 was reported as all quiet, except about fifteen minutes of skirmishing at 10 p.m. September 28 was reported as all quiet. [1]

Lookout Mountain, September 28, 1863
Captain Manning:
 The enemy are crossing five regiments of infantry and four pieces of artillery by the lower bridge.

DUVALL, Lieutenant. [1]

Lookout Mountain, September 29, 1863.
Captain Manning:
 The enemy are busily engaged this a.m. in strengthening Fort Cheatham and enlarging a heavy earth-work on their left flank. Last night their fires were fewer than usual on this and more numerous on the other side of the river from the toe of the Moccasin to the lower bridge.

They also planted a battery of field pieces opposite the tan-yard last night.

DUVALL, Lieutenant. [1]

The Federals had retreated back into Chattanooga, fortifying the defenses built by the Confederates earlier in the war.   The strategy of the Confederates was to lay siege to the City of Chattanooga and starve the Yankees out.   Colonel E. Porter Alexander was assigned the duty of commanding the artillery in bombarding the city.   Alexander had commanded the artillery bombardment of Cemetery Ridge on the third day of the Battle of Gettysburg before Pickett's Charge.   Alexander and his artillery battalion had come to Chattanooga from the Army of Northern Virginia following Longstreet's Corp on September 25. Alexander made no secret that he was not impressed with the Army of Tennessee or its artillery.   He found the organization of the artillery imperfect, the fixed ammunition of poor quality, and the guns of inferior caliber.   Alexander's artillery battalion consisted of: Captain Piqhegru Wolfolk, Jr.'s Virginia Battery, Captain George V. Moody's Louisiana Battery, Captain Osmond B. Taylor's Virginia Battery, Captain William W. Fickling's South Carolina Battery, Captain Tyler C. Jordan's Virginia Battery, and Captain William W. Parker's Virginia Battery with a total of twenty-three guns. [1]

Alexander placed his batteries around the heights above Chattanooga and on September 29 commenced daily shelling of the Federals. Firing from heights as high as 1,500 feet, the Yankees were too far out of range for the Confederates to inflict great damage. One of the best rifled guns of the Army of Tennessee, a 20-pound Parrott in Massenburg's Georgia Battery burst at the muzzle on September 30, injuring two of the artillerymen. Baxter's Company and other Army of Tennessee batteries were also engaged in almost daily shelling of enemy positions and receiving counter fire from the Union batteries, as well as rifle fire from the Yankee pickets. Alexander's attack on Chattanooga lasted about a month. His artillery left Chattanooga with General James Longstreet for the siege of Knoxville on November 4 and remained under his command until eventually returned to Virginia.[1]

Food and other supplies for the Federal Troops were scarce. The Union could move large quantities of supplies from Louisville and Nashville by rail on the Nashville and Chattanooga railroad to Stephenson, Alabama. where the line connected with the Memphis and Charleston Railroad. From Stephenson, the Memphis and Charleston ran through Bridgeport,

Alabama, thirty miles away, on into Chattanooga. The Federals could move supplies no further than Bridgeport. From Bridgeport to Chattanooga, the Confederates had all routes: rail, river, and road blocked by artillery, sharpshooters and pickets. The Rebels occupied Lookout Mountain, Lookout Valley and Raccoon Mountain. The only supply route for the Federals was a sixty mile route from Bridgeport up the Sequatchie Valley and crossing Waldon's Ridge and entering Chattanooga from the north. This was a rough, narrow route that provided only a trickle of the supplies needed by the troops. On October 3, Major General Joseph Wheeler's Cavalry raided the Sequatchie Valley supply line, capturing a supply train estimated from 800 to 1,500 wagons of supplies. The supply train was said to have been five miles long. Wheeler's men took what supplies and wagons they could and burned the rest. What mules were not needed by Wheeler were shot or sabered to death. Shells and ammunition exploding in the fires were said to have sounded like a battle in progress and could be heard by the Federal Troops in Chattanooga. [1]

September 30, two of Baxter's four guns were moved in the direction of Lookout Mountain, with heavy picket firing to the left. The guns returned to post the same day. October 1 through 3 reported as all quiet with rain. Sunday October 4 reported quiet with preaching conducted.[1]

Near Chattanooga, October 1, 1863
(Via Chickamauga)
Jefferson Davis,President, Richmond, Va.:

There was probably no mistake in the cipher. Heavy loses resulting from a desperate and prolonged fight and heavy straggling from the re-enforcements have depleted us. The later are coming up so that our force is increasing. It would be murderous to assault the enemy's superior forces in his intrenchments. Our efforts will be devoted to drawing him out.

BRAXTON BRAGG [1]

Near Chattanooga, October 1, 1863
(Received 3d)
Jefferson Davis, Richmond, Va.:

My action in the case of Lieutenant-General Polk was only after the receipt of an unsatisfactory written explanation. The case is flagrant and but a repetition of the past. If restored by you to his command the amnesty should extend to all. In the crisis now upon us might he not be exchanged for Hardee ? Our cause is at stake. Without vigorous action and prompt obedience cannot be saved. My personal feelings have been yielded to what I know to be the public good, and I suffer self-reproach for not having acted earlier.

BRAXTON BRAGG [1]

Raccoon Mountain, October 2, 1863

Captain Manning:

The enemy still cross the river. They are cutting cornstalks for forage. No apparent change otherwise.

Watson [1]

No. 393
Report of Brig. Gen. Archibald Gracie, jr.,
C.S. Army, commanding brigade
Headquarters Gracie's Brigade
In front of Chattanooga, October 2, 1863

Captain:

I have the honor of herewith forwarding the report of the operations of my brigade-composed of the Sixty-third Regiment Tennessee Volunteers, Lieut. Col. A. Fulkerson commanding, Forty-third Regiment Alabama Volunteers, Col. Y. M. Moody commanding, First Battalion Alabama Legion, Lieut. Col. J. H. Holt commanding, Second Battalion Alabama Legion, Lieut. Col. B. Hall commanding; Third Battalion Alabama Legion, Lieut. Col. J. W. A. Sanford commanding- on the days of September 19 and 20:

Taking position on the evening of the 18th instant at Dalton's Ford, on Chickamauga River, early on the morning of the 19th the brigade formed its first line of battle, facing the enemy's works near Lee and Gordon's Mills. It was exposed to the fire of the enemy's shell, wounding Lieutenant Lane and others of the Sixty-third Tennessee Regiment. Further than this, the brigade was not engaged on this day's fight.

On the morning of the 20th, the brigade was ordered to near Dyer's house, on the Chattanooga road, where again forming line of battle, it again received the fire of the enemy's shell.

Between 4 and 5 p.m. orders were received to support Kershaw's brigade, posted to the left of the Chattanooga road. Word was sent to General Kershaw that the brigade was ready, and he ordered it to advance. Passing through Kershaw's command, the brigade found itself suddenly in the presence of the enemy, strongly posted behind breastworks of logs and rails on the crest of an opposite hill. The fury of musketry, grape and canister immediately commenced, but, undaunted, the brigade scaled the precipitous heights, driving the enemy before it, and took possession of the hill. Holding these heights for nearly an hour, and ammunition becoming scarce, I informed Brigadier-General Preston, commanding the division, that unless supported the brigade could not much longer hold out. Trigg's and Kelly's brigades were ordered to my relief. Though with ammunition nearly exhausted, the brigade held its own till the scattering fire of its musketry betrayed its condition to the enemy. Trigg's and Kelly's brigades arriving, the command withdrew to replenish its empty cartridge boxes.

Early the next morning the brigade resumed the position it had so nobly won. The number of killed and wounded shows the desperate nature of the contest. Of about 1,870 carried into action, 90 were killed and 615 wounded.

Where so many distinguished themselves, it would be difficult to particularize. All nobly did their duty. I would, however, call attention to the following named officers:

Lieut. Col. A. Fulkerson, Sixty-third Regiment Tennessee Volunteers, who, in the absence of the colonel, commanded the regiment and led it into action. To him it owes its discipline and efficiency. Colonel Fulkerson was severely wounded in the arm, making, with the one received at Shiloh, the second during the war. He is deserving of a much higher position.

Col. Y. M. Moody, of the forty-third Alabama Regiment, always at the head of his regiment on the march, maintained the same position on the field, rallying and encouraging his men.

Lieut. Col. J. J. Jolly, of the same regiment, though seriously wounded in the thigh, remained on the field until no longer able to walk, and then had to be carried off.

Lieut. Col. J. H. Holt, of the First Battalion, Alabama Legion, This battalion sustained the heaviest loss. Of 239 carried into action, 169 were killed and wounded. Among the latter was Lieutenant Colonel Holt, seriously in the knee.

Lieut. Col. Boling Hall, commanding the Second Battalion, Alabama Legion. It was this battalion that first gained the hill and placed its colors on the enemy's works. Its colors bear marks of over eighty bullets. Its bearer, Robert Y. Hiett, though thrice wounded and the flag-staff thrice shot away, carried his charge throughout the entire fight. He deserves not only mention, but promotion. Lieutenant-Colonel Hall behaved most gallantly, receiving a severe wound in the thigh.

Lieut. Col. John W. A. Sanford, commanding the Third battalion, Alabama Legion and Major McLennan, commanding the Fourth battalion, Alabama Legion, nobly did their duty, sustaining heavy loss in officers and men.

Capt. W. D. Walden, Company B, Second Battalion, Alabama Legion, was wounded in the breast, arm and shoulder, inside the enemy's works. His case deserves special mention.

Asst. Surg. James B. Luckie, of the Third Battalion, Alabama Legion, both in the field and at the hospital, was most attentive to the wounded, as, indeed, were all the medical officers of the command.

Capt. H. E. Jones, my assistant adjutant-general was most conspicuous for coolness and gallantry. Carrying orders into the thickest of the fight, he was more exposed than any one in the field: also my aide-de-camp, Lieut. E. B. Cherry. I am happy to state that, though both these officers had their horses shot from under them, both escaped unhurt.

To Lieut. J. N. Gilmer, adjutant of the Alabama Legion, who, during the absence of its commander, has acted as my assistant inspector-general, and Messrs. George C. Jones and J. S. Harwell, both wounded, my thanks are due for services rendered.

Maj. E. L. Hord, my quartermaster, who so completely equipped my brigade, was constantly at his post performing his onerous duties.

Maj. C. D. Brown, my commissary, who by untiring energy, kept the brigade constantly supplied with cooked rations. My thanks are also due to Lieut. A. M. MacMurphy, my efficient ordnance officer.

Among the noble dead I have to record the names of Capt. James T. Gillespie and Lieut. S. M. Deadrick, Company I Sixty-third Tennessee Regiment; Capts. O. H. Prince, Company A, and J. A. P. Gordon, Company C; Lieut. William H. Watkins, Company B, Forty-third Alabama Regiment, and Lieut. R. H. Bibb, of the First Battalion, Alabama Legion.

I am, captain, very respectfully, your obedient servant.

A. Gracie, Jr., Brigadier-General

Capt. J. L. Sandford
Assistant Adjutant General [1]

Richmond, Va., October 3, 1862
General Braxton Bragg,
Near Chattanooga, Tenn.:

GENERAL:

Your letter of the 25th and telegram of the 1st instant have been received. I can well appreciate the disappointment resulting from the delays and disobedience of orders which you refer, and I sincerely regret the consequences which resulted there from. When I sent you a dispatch recommending that Lieutenant-General Polk should not be placed in arrest, it was with a view of avoiding a controversy which could not heal the injury sustained, which I feared would entail further evil. Believing that he possessed the confidence and affection of his corps, it seemed better that his influence in your favor should be preserved by a lenient course. Your letter furnished the only information I possessed. In that it did not appear that there was any intention to disobey your orders, and it might be well that no repetition of the objectionable conduct would occur.   To change the commander involves the necessity of an investigation, with all the crimination and recrimination to be thus produced. The opposition to you both in the army and out of it has been a public calamity in so far that it impairs your capacity for usefulness, and I had hoped the great victory which you have recently achieved would tend to harmonize the army and bring to you more just appreciation of the country. It must be a rare occurrence if a battle is fought without many errors and failures, but for which more important results would have been obtained, and the exposure of these diminishes the credit due, impairs the public confidence, undermines the morale of the army, and works evil in the cause for which brave men have died, and for which others have the same sacrifice to make. I can but regret that the explanation you have received has been found insufficient to enable you to overlook the offense, and you will not be surprised that I am at a loss to see how the delay of one general should be regarded as a higher offense than the disobedience of orders by another officer of the same grade, especially when to the latter is added the other offenses you specify, each giving point to the disobedience charged. You will not fail to perceive how readily others predisposed to censure you will connect the present action with former estrangement said to have followed an expression of opinion by your generals in answer to interrogatories propounded by you. I may be mistaken as to what is the wisest course, and do not intend either to decide the question of necessity or suggest that any policy so adopted which does not promise success to our cause. It not infrequently happens that in a state of excitement one believes himself impelled to do that which a calm observer will regard as easily pretermitted. You have a much better knowledge of the facts than myself, and I frequently pray that you may judge correctly, as I am well assured you will act purely for the public welfare.

Very respectfully yours,
JEFFERSON DAVIS [1]

HEADQUARTERS OF GENERAL BRAGG'S ARMY
Tennessee   October 5, 1863
President Davis
Richmond, Va.:

Your immediate presence in this army is urgently demanded. Come if possible. Reply to me in duplicate - one here, to care of General Bragg; the other to me at Atlanta, where I go today.

JAMES CHESNUT
Colonel and Aide-de-camp to the President. [1]

Raccoon Mountain, October 5, 1863

Captain Manning:

A large number of wagons encamped near the head of Moccasin disappeared during the night.

WATSON. [1]

Lookout Mountain, October 5, 1863

Captain Manning:

The little steamer Paint Rock is running from bridge to bridge, apparently picking up the bridge material afloat.

DUVALL, Lieutenant. [1]

October 5, 1863

Lieutenant Duvall:

You try and ascertain the number of guns from your post, and let the general know by courier.

Manning, Captain [1]

Lookout Mountain, October 5, 1863

Captain Manning:

There are but few guns visible in fixed position, their pieces being well masked in order to prevent observation from this point. For several days they have kept field pieces harnessed up in readiness to move. On the toe of Moccasin there are visible one casemated gun and two exposed. On their extreme right we can see three pieces between the river and railroad, and four midway from the railroad to star fort. By the firing this a.m. four pieces have been revealed in the star fort. Immediately beyond star fort six pieces can be seen. Farther we can discover none until reaching the large earth-work on the extreme left. On their interior lines earth-works mounting guns begin at the base of Cameron Hill, crossing the railroad about 300 yards south of the depot, continuing through woods to rear of star fort. The number of guns in those works cannot be ascertained by aid of best glasses.

DUVAL, Lieutenant. [1]

Monday October 5, cannonading began at 10 a.m. and lasted until after 5 p.m. October 6 and 7 reported all quiet, with rain on the 7th. Thursday October 8 was reported all quiet until 4 p.m. when the yanks started shelling Baxter's position from their camps. Friday October 9 again reported as all quiet until 4 p.m. when the yanks began shelling the battery's position again. Saturday October 10, more shelling of the position by the yanks and more skirmishing. Sunday October 11, President Jefferson Davis visited the camps. Baxter's Company along with the other commands were ordered into line of battle to be reviewed by the President and his staff. Preaching was also held. The following week October 12 through 16 was reported as all quiet with rain. [1]

On October 3, 1863, with a lull in the action, Private John Bryant Dillard wrote to his parents in Cheatham County:

Dear honored parent
Tis once more the much mercies of God that I take the few lapsed moments that is serene to me to write to you to let you know that I am yet in the land of the living and in good health truly hoping if these lines should reach you they find you in good health and doing well. I've been on this line of late for about a month...commenced firing...regular engagement commenced on the 19th and lasted until the twentieth at Chickamauga. The Federals was driven to Chattanooga...has remained there ever since strongly fortified. Dear parent it has fell to my lot to participate in one of the bloodiest fights that has ever been fought on the Southern sand ever. I hope I shall never be in such another. The loss on our side was estimated 18 thousand, while that on their side was at thirty thousand. Dear mother I have seen death in so many forms since I saw you last, it has taught me. I have saw them mangled in every shape that human mention could invent on man. I have saw them butchered, shot, laid out and in every other way that is to be named that man might suffer.

The regular engagement commenced a melee was the 19th. There was no abatement in the roar of the fire arms until nine o'clock that night. Strange to say that both armies slept...that same ground by one massing many young savages...bustles...high with ambition. That night was to dream of home and slept his last sleep. There was no advantage going there first day...except the loss of so many man on battalions lately we upon them again and by sun up, their canon and shouts of our boys told too well that they was gradually hurting them inch by inch. At nine o'clock the roar of their canon, report of small arms rising forth flames of fire and death. The cries of the dying and wounded men. The day painful to be told. Chickamauga the battlefield...extended southwest a few miles, beyond that rises toward here too. They seem already before our eyes the wind being savage, high and dry. The sierras taken fire and spread rapidly and arise the battlefield, burning up the dead and wounded. Poor fellahs my heart bleeds especially when I call to mind their timely end, but those are gone and left us to mourn those departed. I hope they have gone to rest, it was not my purpose to give you a minute detail of this fight, it would take more time and space than is allowed me here.   So I will drop the subject before I wear your patients.   Dear Mother, Just be assured that your Christian admonition is daily appreciated and often thought of...give my respect to all inquiring friends.   Varden is well and sends his compliments to you all.   James Thompson and James Lewis also send their respects, his compliments too and says that he is under allegations you to for her from his family. So I must close my scrawling note to la farewell.   Find gardens of my influence.   If I never more see you on earth, I hope to meet you in heaven.

John Bryant Dillard. [9]

No. 411
Report of Maj. Samuel C. Williams, Reserve Corps Artillery Battalion
Headquarters Williams' Battalion
October 7, 1863

Sir:

In compliance with instructions, I have the honor to submit the following report of the part taken by my command in the late battle of Chickamauga:

I crossed the Chickamauga at Alexander's Bridge early on the morning of September 19 with my battalion, composed of Kolb's, Darden's, Baxter's, and McCant's batteries, and arrived on the field just before the infantry became engaged. I was held as the reserve artillery of Buckner's Corps, and was posted accordingly in rear of his line, where I remained for several hours. While at that place Baxter's battery was detached and ordered to report to Brigadier General Gracie, and remained under his orders until the close of the battle. McCant's battery was detached and ordered to report to Colonel Trigg

About 2 p.m. I was ordered to take a position with my two remaining batteries to check the enemy in case our infantry, which was then hotly engaging him in my front, should be driven in. I remained in this position about two hours, subjected to a very heavy fire of artillery from the enemy, without returning it, losing several men and horses killed and wounded. I was then removed to a position near the one I occupied in the morning. McCant's battery returned to me.

I remained here until 11 or 12 o'clock on the morning of the 20th, when I was moved forward and placed in several positions without engaging the enemy until about 4 or 5 p.m., when I was ordered to move up and open fire on the enemy, who was crossing from his right to his left. I opened fire first with eight and then with eleven pieces, one piece having been disabled. The fire was kept up in intervals from half to three-quarters of an hour, with considerable effect on the enemy, his line being broken, and Major General Stewart having crossed in my front, I ceased firing. While in this position, I was subjected to a fire from the enemy's artillery at about 900 yards until he was driven away by our fire.

The officers and men of my command behaved with great coolness, notwithstanding most of them had never been in an engagement before.

Accompanying this please find reports of the several captains of my command, also a report of the casualties and losses sustained.

Respectfully submitted.

S.C. Williams

Major, Commanding Battalion Artillery[1]

SPECIAL ORDERS   HEADQUARTERS ARMY OF TENNESSEE
No. 268
Missionary Ridge, October 17, 1863

The following changes in the organization of the army are announced:
1.   Major-General Buckner's division is assigned to Polk's Corps. Brigadier-General Preston will be assigned to one of the brigades in Buckner's Division. Major-General Walker's division will remain in Longstreet's corps.

By command of General Bragg:

George WM. Brent, Assistant Adjutant-General.[1]

Meridian, Miss, October 23, 1863

General Braxton Bragg,

Near Chattanooga, TN.:

General Polk is relieved from duty with your command. General Hardee will join you with such expedition as your circumstances require. If needed for immediate service, two brigades of his command here will accompany him. Telegraph me at Mobile and to General Hardee at Demopolis.

JEFFERSON DAVIS.[1]

No. 368

Report of Maj. Thomas K. Porter, Chef of Artillery

Headquarters Buckner's Division

Near Chattanooga, November 10, 1863

Major:

I have the honor to submit the following report of the operations of the artillery of General Buckner's corps at the battle of Chickamauga.

It consisted of Williams' battalion of four batteries, Leyden's battalion of three batteries, and three batteries of Major General Stewart's division acting with their brigades. Leyden's battalion was attached to Brigadier General Preston's Division, and by his order one battery was attached to each of his brigades. As most of the ground over which the battle was fought was very thickly wooded, we could not see more than 300 yards to the front, and consequently could very seldom use artillery. For this reason the batteries of Major General Stewart's Division fired but a few shots, though they were left in exposed positions, and lost between 20 and 30 horses.

Two of the batteries of Leyden's battalion were engaged Saturday and Sunday, but, owing to the thickness on the timber and undergrowth, continued but a short time. They were unable to ascertain the damage they inflicted. They suffered but a slight loss themselves. One of his batteries (Jeffress') was kept on the extreme left of the original line till the battle ceased.

Williams' battalion was kept as a reserve, and on Saturday morning was placed in position on the ridge which Preston's division occupied. When Stewart's division was carried to the right of the line, Brigadier General Mackall, General Bragg's chief of staff, ordered that all the artillery that could be spared from the corps should be placed in the position just vacated by General Stewart. In obedience to this order, Major Williams was directed to post two of his batteries there and remain to repel any assault that the enemy's infantry might make. He remained there several hours, part of the time under heavy artillery fire, which he could not return, as our fuses are so uncertain he would have run the risk of killing our own men by firing over their heads. He remained there until about sundown, when he was moved back to his former position, where he remained till the left made its move to the front and right on Sunday. He was then ordered to leave Baxter's battery to assist Jeffress in holding the bluff on the extreme left of the line, and move with his other three batteries in rear of Preston's division. After getting to the Chattanooga Road he was placed in several positions to check the expected moves of the enemy, but did not get into action till about 5 p.m. This was when Preston's division was in the hottest of the fight, and the enemy were crossing the Chattanooga road in large numbers to re-enforce that part of their army holding the hill to the left. Major Williams was then ordered to take position about 1,000 yards from where they were crossing and open fire with his three batteries. This he did with great execution, silencing the enemy's artillery, cutting off the re-enforcements, and enabling the infantry to capture between 500 and 600 prisoners.

All the officers and men acted, whenever they had an opportunity of doing so, with courage and coolness.

Enclosed are reports of the battalion commanders.

Very respectfully, your obedient servant,
Thomas K. Porter, Major and Chief of Artillery [1]

Many soldiers of the Army of Tennessee recalled their duty at Chattanooga and Missionary Ridge as being some of the most miserable of their service in the Confederate Army. Sam Watkins of Columbia, Tennessee, a Private in Company H 1st Tennessee Infantry Regiment recalled: "In all the history of the war, I cannot remember of more privations and hardships than we went through at Missionary Ridge. And when in the very acme of our privations and hunger, when the army was most dissatisfied and unhappy, we were ordered into line of battle to be reviewed by Honorable Jefferson Davis. When he passed us by, with his great retinue of staff officers and play-outs at full gallop, cheers greeted with the words, 'Send us something to eat, Massa Jeff. Give us something to eat, Massa Jeff. I'm hungry! I'm hungry!' [25]

The men in Baxter's Company shared Watkins' sentiments. Sgt. Arter Lankford recalled going three days with nothing to eat but a piece of moldy bread. Private John Dillard stated he had gone up to three days without eating. Private Wesley Welch blamed his health problems while in the army as due to "lack of eatibles". Private Sol Tidwell relayed to family members that his army ration once consisted of "seven grains of corn for seven days." The Confederate strategy was to starve the Yankees out, but they also suffered from lack of food and supplies due to poor transportation. The Rebel troops had been on half rations most of their tour of duty at Chattanooga. Union troops started on half rations and were later reduced to one-quarter rations. [1, 10, 17, 25]

On October 19, General William Rosecrans was relieved of duty as commander of the Army of the Cumberland and was replaced by General George H. Thomas, "The Rock of Chickamauga". Lt. General Ulysses S. Grant arrived in Chattanooga on October 23 and took command of all Federal forces. Grant ordered Maj. General William T. Sherman to bring his command from Mississippi to Chattanooga. [1]

On October 25 Private Thomas Kent, who had been transferred to Baxter's Battery from Company F 34th Alabama Infantry Regiment, deserted from a field hospital on Missionary Ridge. He was later reported to have joined another unit. [23]

RICHMOND, October 25, 1863
President Davis,
Atlanta, Ga.:

Northern papers just received inform that Rosecrans has been superseded by General Thomas, and Grant placed in command of all forces in the West and Southwest. The iron-clad in England has been actually seized by the Government. The question relative to them is to be submitted to the courts. General Lee has withdrawn with his army this side the Rappahannock. Meade's purposes uncertain. Some indications that he may advance. No movements on the Peninsula or in North Carolina, and no late intelligence from East Tennessee. All well in the city.

Jas. A. Seddon, Secretary of War. [1]

Chickamauga, October 25, 1863 (Received Mobile 26th)
The President:

Shall call for General Hardee and his troops immediately. Hope to drive Burnside. Rosecrans holds on, and we cannot operate on our left for constant rains and bad roads. General Buckner continues to give me great trouble about his right command in Southwestern Virginia. He gives orders and sends officers from here to there without consulting me, whilst I have requested General Jones to assume command there and move on the enemy, now that Mead has fallen back. Might not a division be sent to Jones ? It would insure Burnside' discomfiture.

BRAXTON BRAGG. [1]

Chickamauga, October 25, 1863 (Received Mobile 26th)
His Excellency Jefferson Davis
Mobile, Ala.:

Colonel Clift, Federal Army, an East Tennessee tory, now on recruiting service in Tennessee, was captured yesterday carrying dispatches from Chattanooga to Burnside. Rosecrans is relieved from duty and Thomas succeeds him. Grant assigned to command; both departments united. I shall try colonel Clift as Burnside does our officers for recruiting in Kentucky.

BRAXTON BRAGG [1]

HEADQUARTERS NINTH KENTUCKY CAVALRY
October 25, 1863

General Longstreet:

The enemy reported yesterday in Nickajack Cove, suppose to be a pioneer corps, are engaged in removing the engine and works from

Gordon's Mills. They evidently intend it for a mill at the bridge or a boat to forage on the river. With a regiment of infantry from General Law's brigade and my cavalry I will capture them or stop their work on the mill. Will an order for the regiment be sent?

AUSTIN, Major.[1]

GENERAL LONGSTREET'S HEADQUARTERS
October 25, 1863
Major Austin
Ninth Kentucky Cavalry:

Your dispatch received. General Jenkins will send a brigade to capture the party at Nickajack Cove, with which you will co-operate.

LONGSTREET, General [1]

HEADQUARTERS NINTH KENTUCKY
October 25, 1863

Captain Manning:

The enemy have moved the engine from Gordon's Mill to Shellmound Depot and are now engaged in building a bridge over Nickajack Creek. They are 500 strong, as reported by a scout.

AUSTIN, Major, Ninth Kentucky Cavalry. [1]

The soldiers were not the only ones suffering the shortage of supplies at Chattanooga. Feed and forage for horses were in short supply. Many horses in the Army of Tennessee were reported as too weak to pull wagons. Disease among livestock was rampant. It was estimated the life expectancy of an artillery horse in the Confederate Army was about seven and one- half months. Baxter's October 31, 1863 requisition for forage for sixty-eight horses and nineteen mules was given a ration of corn only, no hay or fodder was available. Soldiers on both sides were guilty of stealing corn from the horses to eat themselves. Some of the Union units only fed their horses with armed guards present. Baxter's livestock fared much better with the November forage requisition; corn, barley, oats, hay and fodder were provided. This was short- lived relief as sources of forage dried up and railroad lines were destroyed. [23]

In a surprise attack on October 27, the Federals had captured Brown's Ferry. This allowed General Grant to establish a shorter supply route from Bridgeport and the flow of supplies to the Union troops greatly increased with the opening of Grant's "cracker line". [1]

The Chattanooga Campaign was a time of great spiritual revival for the Army of Tennessee. Regular worship and revival services were held.

Private Aaron Beard of Baxter's Battery was a Primitive Baptist Preacher. He reported of his days stationed at Chattanooga as being "cannonading by day, praying by night". While stationed at Missionary Ridge, Private Beard was given a pass to visit his brothers, Alex and George Tall Pine Beard in the camp of the First Tennessee Infantry Regiment. The Beards and their cousin, Jacob Beard, were serving as Privates in Company D "The Williamson Grays". Both Alex and George T. P. were captured after the Battle of Missionary Ridge and sent to the Union Prison at Rock Island, IL. where they "galvanized" to get out of prison. Alex Beard returned to Williamson County after the war. George Tall Pine returned briefly and relocated to Arkansas. Aaron and George Tall Pine had served in the Mexican War together in Company K of the 3rd Tennessee Volunteer Infantry Regiment. [17, 23]

Private Wesley Welch was also allowed to visit his brother, John Shadrack Welch, in the camp of the 11th Tennessee Infantry Regiment. Descendents recall family members were told Wesley was mad at John because he sent him home in May 1861 when he tried to enlist in the 11th. It was said he walked into the camp and found John sitting by a campfire drinking coffee and shot a hole in his coffee mug. [17]

November 1, Private William A. Moore was transferred from Company I 44th Consolidated Infantry Regiment to Baxter's Battery under order of General Braxton Bragg. Moore was a resident of Williamson County who had enlisted at Tullahoma April 1, 1863. Private John B. "Bailey" Moore. a Dickson County native, had joined the 44th in December 1861. He had been ordered transferred to Baxter's Battery by General Bragg in March 1863, but became ill and died in a Tullahoma hospital before joining the battery. [23]

Chattanooga, Tenn., November 3, 1863
11:30 p.m. (Received 3:30 a. m.)

Major:

General R. S. Granger reports from Nashville that he sent a detachment of cavalry from that place, under Lieutenant Colonel Shelley, to pursue Hawkins and other guerrilla chiefs. Overtook Hawkins near Piney Factory. Routed and pursued him to Centreville, where he made a stand. Routed him again and pursued him until his forces dispersed. Rebel loss, 15 or 20 killed and 66 prisoners. Our loss, 1 severely and several slightly wounded.

Rebels have fired 40 or 50 shells from top of Lookout today without doing any damage. We are getting supplies by steam-boat up the river as fast as they arrive by railroad at Bridgeport. We shall need more rolling stock on the railroad immediately to keep this army supplied. One of my scouts today reports that 20,000 or 30,000 rebels, under Buckner, have moved in direction of Knoxville to attack Burnside. The movement of troops in that direction is corroborated by other scouts, but they do not agree as to numbers.

My river guards, stationed as high up as Piney Creek, report all quiet in their front.

GEO. H. THOMAS, Major-General. [1]

November 4, Longstreet's Corp was detached for an assault on General Burnside's Union troops in Knoxville.   Buckner's Corp, including Gracie's Brigade was ordered to join Longstreet's command.

Baxter's men had been in the Confederate Army for almost a year in November 1863. Most of their service had been with the Department of East Tennessee, a department known for slack discipline. The men were now serving under General Braxton Bragg, a strong disciplinarian. Since assuming command of the Army of Tennessee shortly after the Battle of Shiloh, Bragg had gained a reputation for discipline. He did not hesitate to send men before a firing squad for execution. Bragg constantly issued orders to the troops.

General Orders
HDQRS. Army of Tennessee
No. 205
Missionary Ridge, November 14, 1863

1. Hereafter, there will be a daily parade inspection under arms of each regiment, battalion, and battery in this army by their respective commanding officers.   Each brigade shall be inspected weekly by its commander. Each division will in like manner be inspected.

2. Written inspection reports will be forwarded weekly to the inspector-general of the army through the proper channel. The report of each regiment will show the number of effective men present, non-effective present and cause thereof;   names of officers on leave, by whose authority, from and what time; number and names of officers and men absent without leave or overstaying their time;   the number and condition of arms and accouterments;   amount of ammunition to each man and condition of same;   amount in reserve;   condition of clothes; quality and condition of provisions received (whether full rations or not);   quality of forage received;   number of horses, whether

public or private, in possession of the regiment; how many stragglers or citizens with command and whether liable for conscription; condition of camps; whether a proper police is observed; health of the command.

3. Brigade commanders in their weekly inspections will verify the reports of the commanders of regiments, giving their attention particularly to the points specified for guidance of regimental commanders, and see to the prompt correction of all abuses and to supply all deficiencies. They are especially enjoined to see that their commands are always prepared and ready for action in every particular.

4. Artillery battalion commanders will inspect thoroughly the batteries in their commands, and report upon their condition, number of men for duty, & c., amount of ammunition on hand, number and condition of horses.

5. Brigade commanders will see that the necessary roads are made and kept in good repair within the limits of his brigade and leading to and from it.

6. Division commanders will verify reports of the brigade commanders and give their personal attention to the points specified above for guidance of regimental and brigade commanders. They will inspect carefully, monthly, the papers of the quartermasters and commissaries of the divisions, brigades, and regiments and report accurately any irregularity existing, and report upon the manner in which each officer of these departments discharges his duties. Each division commander will have the pickets in his front inspected by a staff officer every night, and will report in writing anything unusual or important, and will promptly correct all errors and neglects.

By command of General Bragg:

George WM. Brent, Assistant Adjutant General. [1]

General Orders
Headquarters Hardee's Corps.
No. 4
Near Kirkpatrick's, November 14, 1863

Pursuant to instructions from headquarters of the army, Lieutenant-General Hardee assumes command of all the troops west of Chattanooga Creek.

Major-General Stevenson is assigned to the command of the troops and defenses on the top of Lookout Mountain.

The ranking officer of Cheatham's division will assume command of the troops and defenses at and near the Craven house.

The ranking officer of Walker's division will have charge of the line from the base of Lookout Mountain east to Chattanooga Creek, and all the troops not at the points above named.

Official papers will continue to be forwarded according to organization.

By command of Lieutenant-General Hardee:

T. B. Roy, Assistant Adjutant General [1]

Headquarters Hardee's Corp
November 15, 1863
Major-General Stevenson
Commanding Mountain:

General:

The lieutenant-general commanding directs me to say, in answer to your note of last night, that it will be impossible to furnish you with three brigades for the mountain as you desire. The length of the line to be defended below is such that an extra brigade in addition to the two you have cannot be spared. The general hopes you will be able to hold your line with the force you have, and when it becomes necessary, you can be re-enforced before endangered.

He wishes you to thoroughly block up all the roads leading up the mountain, and this will enable you to get timely notice of any advance of the enemy. In regard to the matter of the cavalry, he says he has no control of it, but will refer the matter to General Bragg, but the difficulty of foraging on the mountain is so great that it is almost impossible to maintain any considerable cavalry force up there.

I am general, respectfully, your obedient servant.

T. B. Roy, Assistant Adjutant-General [1]

Headquarters Department of Tennessee
Mission Ridge, November 15, 1863
General S. Cooper
Adjutant and Inspector General, Richmond:

General:

By a rigid inspection a great reduction has been made in the number of horses to be foraged in this army. The inspection and close inquiry have convinced me, and I am fully sustained by other general officers, that forage is allowed to many more animals than are necessary to junior staff officers.

Medical officers, quartermasters, and commissaries, except those engaged in purchasing, adjutants, aides-de-camp, assistant adjutants-general, ordinance officers, signal officers, field officers of regiments, except the commander, and subalterns of artillery, can all do just as well with forage for 1 horse each. Many of these have but 1 horse, but take another of some friend to forage, and thus impose that burden on the army. When supplies are so costly and so difficult to obtain, I beg the attention of department to the policy, if not necessity, of limiting the officers above indicated.

I am general, very respectfully, your obedient servant,

Braxton Bragg, General , Commanding [1]

General Orders
Headquarters Army of Tennessee
No. 206
Missionary Ridge, November 15, 1863

Publications in violations of orders have recently appeared in the public journals giving information of the organization of this army and changes made therein. All such publications are highly improper and positively prohibited. Commanding officers furnishing or allowing copies of orders to be furnished from their headquarters to persons not entitled to receive them, will be held responsible for their publication.

By command of General Braxton Bragg:
George WM. Brent, Assistant Adjutant-General [1]

General Orders
Headquarters Army of Tennessee
No.207
Missionary Ridge, November 15, 1863

To enable the commissary department to meet the heavy demands upon it, for the present three-quarters of a pound of fresh meat will be the daily ration, and in lieu of the deficiency, the ration of rice will be increased to 10 pounds to 100 rations, and an issue of sugar will be made at the rate of 18 pounds in lieu of 100 pounds of meat. These issues will be regularly and promptly made. Nothing but an impossibility will be accepted as an excuse, and that must be promptly reported by the commissaries to their respective commanders at the time of the failure.

By command of General Bragg:
George WM. Brent , Assistant Adjutant-General. [1]

On November 15, Private DeWitt Houston of Marshall County, Tennessee was transferred to Baxter's Battery from Company I of the 4th Georgia Cavalry under orders of General Braxton Bragg. [23]

General Orders
Headquarters Army of Tennessee
No. 208
Missionary Ridge, November 16, 1863

That the enemy does not intend to carry out in good faith the cartel agreed on between his Government and the Confederate States for the exchange of prisoners of war has long been demonstrated by his acts and is now officially recognized.

Such a cruel proceeding so opposed to the laws of humanity and an enlightened civilization is a virtual acknowledgement by the enemy of his inferiority, and it shows a craft and cunning worthy of the Yankee in imposing upon us the maintenance of thousands of his prisoners, that they may consume the subsistence which should go to the support of our gallant men and their families.

This should be known to our officers and men. They should know that if taken prisoner those who survive their cruel treatment will be forced to languish in Northern dungeons until the close of the war, subjected to the taunts and barbarity of a merciless foe. If their liberty and lives must be lost, the alternate of honorable death on the field of battle, nobly fighting for the cause of freedom, will be accepted by brave and patriotic Southern soldiers.

The general deems it his duty to announce these facts to the troops of his command. The designs of the enemy are transparent, and our officers and soldiers are forced to accept the policy imposed by him.

By command of General Bragg:
George WM. Brent, Assistant Adjutant-General [1]

General Orders
Headquarters Army of Tennessee
No. 212
Missionary Ridge, November 18, 1863

The general commanding has regretted to discover that officers and men of this army, under color of the law of impressments, have been engaged in seizing upon the property of citizens in an irregular and illegal manner.

Defenseless women, peaceable and loyal citizens, and the families of soldiers who are fighting with their colors, have been deprived of their subsistence. Such outrages are unworthy of the Confederate soldier, alienate the affection and confidence of the people, and embarrass the provisioning of the army. Such proceedings are no less than marauding and robbery, and, unless promptly checked, will create just discontent and destroy the morale of the army.

All officers are enjoined to take necessary precautions to suppress such lawless and wanton acts of plunder. They will institute a rigid scrutiny into all cases brought to their knowledge and arrest the offenders.

The greatest care must be taken to comply with the law, and officers on duty will be held to the strictest accountability for non-compliance with the same. All impressments by agents are positively prohibited. They must be made in all cases by a duly authorized commissioned officer.

Citizens, in all cases of illegal seizure of their property, are invited to make known their grievances. They should be careful to secure evidence and be able to identify the offenders, that the punishment may be inflicted and reparation made.

By command of General Bragg:
George WM. Brent, Assistant Adjutant-General [1]

Mission Ridge, November 19, 1863
General J. E. Johnston:
The deserters are an encumbrance to me and must be shot or they run off again. General Maury consents to take them on his forts for laborers. I ask no exchange. Sherman's army just arrived.

Braxton Bragg. [1]

Special Orders
Hdqrs. Army of Tennessee
No. 301
Missionary Ridge, November 19, 1863

Lieut. Col. H. W. Walter, assistant adjutant-general, is assigned to the special duty of gathering the absentees from this army. He will visit the quartermasters, commissaries, commandants of post, provost-marshals, and hospitals in the rear. Within this department he will send to the army all officers and soldiers thereof improperly or unnecessarily detailed and improperly in arrest or custody, and will substitute any disabled officer or soldier for a healthy detail, where the former can discharge the duties required.

In any other department he will (with the approval of the officer commanding the same) send to their commands all officers and soldiers detailed from this army and all improperly in arrest or confinement.

He will arrest and send to the army all officers and soldiers thereof found absent without authority from the commanding general. He will report weekly to these headquarters, and through them to regimental officers, the name of each officer and soldier sent to the army and the name of any one substituted for a detail and the length of time and the place for which the substitute is detailed.

Commanding officers of regiments will send to Lieutenant-Colonel Walter, through this office, a list of all absentees this side the Mississippi, stating their present locations as far as known.

By command of General Bragg:
George WM. Brent, Assistant Adjutant-General.[1]

During the siege of Chattanooga shelling enemy positions by Baxter's and other Confederate batteries became an almost daily chore. The men became accustomed to the howling and exploding federal shells fired at their position and to the sound of minie balls whizzing over their heads.

Baxter's men reported they were engaged in heavy cannonading and skirmishing which continued November 16th through 19th. On November 20 the company marched one and one-half miles in the rain. November 21, the men marched two and one –half miles into Georgia, turned and came back to the cave between Lookout Mountain and Missionary Ridge and spent the night. November 22 the battery moved one mile toward Lookout Mountain, and was assigned to Maj. General Carter Stevenson's Division. Stevenson's artillery battalion was commanded by Captain Robert Cobb. At the time of the Battle of Missionary Ridge, the battalion was temporarily commanded by Captain William W. Carnes of Memphis. In addition to Baxter's, other batteries in the battalion were: Captain Max Van Den Corput's Georgia Battery, Captain John B. Rowan's Georgia Battery (also referred to as 3rd Maryland Battery) and Carne's Tennessee Battery temporarily commanded by Lieutenant L. Y. Marshall, while Captain Carnes was commanding the battalion. Heavy skirmishing was reported all along the lines on the 23rd. The night of November 24, the battery withdrew from its position west of Chattanooga Creek, moved another mile and reported hearing the engagement on Lookout Mountain, which lasted until about midnight.

November 25 the battery left camp and marched across Missionary Ridge to join the rest of Stevenson's Division on the right wing of the line near the Tunnel Hill on the top of Missionary Ridge. Confederate Infantry were also in position in rifle pits at the base of Missionary

Ridge. General Patrick Cleburne's Division was posted on the end of the right wing. Walker's Division was stationed between Cleburne's and Stevenson's Divisions. General Benjamin F. Cheatham's Division was posted to the left of Stevenson's Division. Baxter's men moved two of it's four guns up the ridge into position at about 10 a.m. At about 2 p.m. Baxter's men engaged in a duel with a Federal battery located in a clearing northwest of their position and enfiladed the Federal lines assaulting tunnel hill and continued the action until the effort to possess that point was abandoned. The men kept their guns blazing for over two and a half hours, expending at least fifty-five rounds of ammunition. Private James Thompson reported that he carried forty-three rounds of ammunition up the ridge to one gun. They fired at a rapid rate to make the Federal think they were more heavily armed than they were. [22, 24]

About 4 p.m. the Federal Infantry advanced across the open plain toward the base of Missionary Ridge. Federal Major General Gordon Grainger recalled: " not less than fifty Confederate cannon opened fire on the advancing Federals, throwing a terrible shower of shot and shell. The Rebel salvos from high on the ridge were unusually intriguing because, due to some atmospheric peculiarity, each round fired could be seen from the moment that it left the cannon's muzzle. Solid shots plowed into the Federal ranks; shells screamed overhead, sometimes bursting too high above the men to cause casualties, but always a source of fear, even when failing to explode, as some did. Horses became frantic and unmanageable. Some soldiers were terrified, supposing the danger to be far worse than it was. Actually, the shelling inflicted very few casualties, and most of the soldiers, though unquestionably filled with a sense of urgency to cross the open ground, maintained their composure, moving ahead in good order." [1]

Baxter's Battery was in the thick of the fight in the Battle of Missionary Ridge, with artillery shells exploding around them and minie balls whizzing above their heads. In their vicinity, the Federals had made several charges up the ridge, being repulsed each time. Counter charges, hand to hand combat and bayonet charges were fought in the area. The right wing of the Confederate Army held fast. To the left some areas were too steep to depress the guns. Confederate soldiers rolled rocks down the ridge upon the Yankees. Some of the rebels lit the fuses of shells and rolled them down the ridge. The Union troops broke through the Confederate left wing and Rebels on the left were forced to retreat down the back side of the ridge under heavy fire. [1]

Private James B. Thompson relayed that he was standing near General Hardee and some other officers, who were yelling and laughing at the Federals retreating down the mountain. He said a shell exploded within twenty feet of them and "the tune changed, they all left and double quick time, too." [11]

In later years, many of the men in Baxter's Battery, in their Confederate Pension Applications listed shell shock, deafness and other injuries incurred at Missionary Ridge still haunting them after many years. Others reported in their pension applications of still suffering from diseases contracted while stationed in Chattanooga. [23]

In 1920, Captain W. W. Carnes recalled his battalion's role in the Battle of Missionary Ridge: "At that time I was in command of the battalion of artillery attached to the division commanded by Gen. C. L. Stevenson, the batteries being the Rome Artillery, commanded by Captain Max Corput; 3rd Maryland, Captain Rowan; Baxter's Battery, Captain Ed Baxter; Carnes's Battery, Lieutenant L.Y. Marshall. When it was thought that Lookout Mountain might be approached from the rear, Stevenson's Division was placed some miles to the south of the summit to guard the mountain in that direction, and Corput's Battery was sent with it, the other three batteries being together at the south end of Missionary Ridge, near Rossville. When General Hooker made his advance to drive back Walthall's Brigade, which defended the road to Chattanooga across the foothills of Lookout Mountain, a section of Corput's Battery was placed fronting west toward the approaching Federals, and a few trial shots were fired, which fell far short. When the two guns were moved over to the point where it was found impossible to depress the guns so as to reach the field of action below, and when it was apparent that the foot of the mountain could not be held against Hooker's superior force, I received orders before 4 p.m. to withdraw the battery, and with the other troops upon the mountain the guns came down the road to the valley and joined the other three batteries in camp. (The few trial shots fired by the two guns of Corputs' Battery have been made the cause for placing on top of Lookout Mountain tablets that tend to give color to the belief of the misinformed public that the Federal army actually charged and drove the Confederates from the mountain top, on which there never was a shot between hostile forces, the so-called 'Battle above the Clouds' having been in a heavy mist on Crane's farm, below the mountain.)

That night Stevenson's Division was ordered to march at daylight to reinforce the right of our line at Missionary Ridge. The infantry went ahead and the four batteries of artillery, following as fast as they could go over the terrible road along the ridge, did not arrive till after midday. I rode on ahead of the battalion and found Stevenson's Division posted on the left of Cleburne's Division, which was on the high ground north of the railroad tunnel, where assaults of the Federals had already been repulsed. It was seen that another attack was about to be made; and as our own batteries had not come up, I acted on General Stevenson's suggestion to get other guns to meet the attack, and I obtained Barrett's Missouri Battery, which I placed immediately over the tunnel in time to assist in repulsing the new assault. Soon after this Capt. Max Corput came up and reported of our battalion within call, and I placed at available points on our division front Rowan's Battery, Baxter's Battery, and Corput's Battery; but having no place for the guns under Marshall, they were left in the rear and well back of the ridge.

Standing on the heights south of the tunnel, I witnessed the result of the last assault on Cleburne's line north of us; and when the Federal assault had been checked a brigade (which I understood was composed of one volunteer regiment from each brigade in the division under command of General Cumming, of Georgia) charged over their breastworks and, following the enemy down the mountain side, captured and brought back a large number of prisoners and flags. (Our boys found that the canteens of the captured men contained whiskey, with which they were pretty well braced up to make the charge.)

Only one more effort was made to advance against our line, and that was broken up by our artillery, while their line was in the open field before it reached the ridge. After that repulse it seemed that it needed the offensive, and, having been without anything to eat all day, I got permission from General Stevenson to go back to find my cook and rations with my battery in the rear under Marshall. I rode at a gallop on the road in the rear of the ridge past Cheatham's Division, which was on Stevenson's left, and just beyond it I found coming down the summit of the Ridge in confusion, and a man in a Memphis regiment who knew me shouted to me to help him rally the retreating men. That was my first information of the attack on the Ridge west of us, and when he told me the line was broken and the men were in flight I spurred up the hill to give the news first to General Cheatham. I found that he had thrown his left brigade back to guard his flank and that no assault was being made in his front. I then rode rapidly to General Stevenson, and my news quickly brought to an end the supper he and his staff were taking under the impression that the fighting was over for the day.

The three divisions of Cleburne, Stevenson, and Cheatham remained in position on the Ridge until late that night. All crossed over on the railroad bridge, which had been planked to bring supplies of rations and ammunition for our troops. I do not know in what order the divisions moved, but I know that I was ordered to move after 9 o'clock, the three batteries on our line being joined by a battery of Walker's Division under command of Lt. Rene Beauregard crossing over the bridge about 9:30 p.m. My battery, under Marshall, got information of the break in front in time to withdraw by the regular road to the railroad station, where it joined us when we arrived there in the early hours of the morning.

The commands driven from the Ridge, being reassembled, were sent in advance on the retreat, and the unbroken divisions of Cheatham, Stevenson, and Cleburne brought up the rear. Cleburne's Division must have been the last to leave the Ridge, for it was the rear guard, and at Ringgold Gap it gave the pursuing Federals such a licking that further pursuit ended, and our march in retreat continued till we were encamped at Dalton, Georgia for the winter.[6]

Baxter's Battery was part of the orderly retreat from Missionary Ridge, departing at about 7:30 p.m. marching all night in rain and sleet, covering eight miles. The company marched twelve miles on November 26, reaching Ringgold, Georgia. November 27th, the company marched sixteen miles to Dalton.

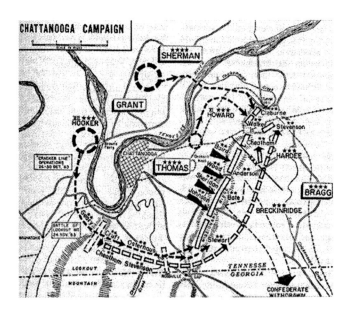

Baxter's Position during the Battle of Missionary Ridge
at the far right of the line with Stevenson's Division.

General Orders
Headquarters Stevenson's Division
No.-----
In the Field, November 27, 1863

The major-general commanding desires to return his sincere thanks to the brave officers and men of his command for the gallantry which they have exhibited during the recent operations of the army. It was Pettus' brigade, of this division, which first checked an enemy flushed with victory on Lookout Mountain, and held him at bay until ordered to retire.

On the next day, on the right of Missionary Ridge, the whole division (Brown's, Cummings, and Pettus' brigades, and the artillery) fought with courage which merited and won success. Cumming's brigade three times charged the enemy, routing him and taking several colors. Whatever may have been the issue as regards other commands, the officers and men of this division can look back to the battle of Missionary Ridge, can recall their repulse of every assault of the enemy, and their success in holding their position, with the pride of soldiers, whose strong arms and stout hearts have entitled them to the gratitude and admiration of their country.

By command of Major General Stevenson:
John J. Reeve, Assistant Adjutant-General [1]

Braxton Bragg's tenure as commander of the Army of Tennessee had long been mired by infighting between himself and his senior officers. Bragg's failure to pursue the Federals into Chattanooga after the victory at Chickamauga had been highly criticized. Other Generals had petitioned President Jefferson Davis for his removal, to no avail. After the defeat at Missionary Ridge and retreat to Dalton, Bragg was relieved of command. Lt. General William Hardee accepted temporary command of the army.[1]

Headquarters Army of Tennessee
Dalton, Ga., December 2, 1863
To the Soldiers of the Army of Tennessee:

General Bragg having been relieved from duty with this army, the command has devolved upon me. The steady purpose, the unflinching courage, and the unsullied patriotism of the distinguished leader who has shared your fortunes for more than a year, will be long remembered by this army and by the country he has served so well.

I desire to say, in assuming command, that there is no cause for discouragement. The overwhelming numbers of the enemy forced us back from Missionary Ridge, but the army is still intact and in good heart. Our losses were small and will be rapidly replaced. The country is looking to you with painful interest. I feel that it can rely upon you. Only the weak and the timid need to be cheered by constant success. The veterans of Shiloh, Perryville, Murfreesboro, and Chickamauga require no such stimulus to sustain their courage and resolution. Let the past take care of itself; we can and must secure the future.

W. J. Hardee, Lieutenant-General. [1]

HEADQUARTERS
Near Knoxville, December 2, 1863
General B. Bragg, Commanding:

General:

Your message reached me the night before last. I am much grieved to hear of the necessity for you to withdraw your lines to Dalton. I hope that you may be able to collect forces there, not only to make a successful stand, but to threaten the enemy's flank in such a way as to prevent his sending succor to the forces at Knoxville. The enemy being between us, I do not regard it as practicable for me to rejoin. My transportation is too limited to supply us by doubtful mountain route, and the only other route is occupied by the enemy. The best thing left for me to do is to capture the garrison here or force the enemy to great delays in other operations by sending a large force to its succor. I hope to have General Ransom with me in a few days, and shall then be strong enough to resist any ordinary succoring force. I shall hope that you will prevent any succor from Chattanooga. I am changing my depot from Loudon to some point in the direction of Virginia, and cannot spare the cavalry till that is safely executed.

I am, as you are aware, threatened on every side, without communication in any direction, so that cavalry is indispensable to me. I hope to be able to return it to you soon. I made an assault upon the enemy's works upon the 29th ultimo, and was repulsed with a loss of 800 in killed, wounded and missing. The assault was made by Wofford's, Humphrey's, and Bryan's brigades, of McLaw's division, and Anderson's brigade of Hood's division.

I remain, general, your most obedient servant.
J. LONGSTREET, Lieutenant-General [1]

Baxter's Battery set up camp about one and a half mile from Dalton on the Rome Road and remained there until November 30. Other batteries in the artillery camp were: Rowan's Georgia Battery, Gracey's Kentucky Battery, Smith's (Turner's) Mississippi Battery, Van den Corput's Georgia Battery, and Carne's Tennessee Battery. The artillerymen were ordered to construct shelters for the horses and mules before building their winter quarters huts. Baxter's Company was ordered to move out, it marched two miles toward Dalton and remained camped there until December 8. [1, 23]

Life in the artillery camps was regulated closely. At daylight, the men were awakened by the company bugler sounding "reveille". First duty of the day was stable call, for the grooming, feeding and watering of the horses. Breakfast was served at sunrise. Ten o'clock was time for inspection of the horses. The men assembled for roll call and dinner at noon. Artillery drills and afternoon stable duty finished the day. Dress parades were the norm for sunset, followed by supper. Men were required to be in their quarters by 8 p.m. and "taps" was sounded an hour later. A few men each day were allowed to go on foraging expeditions to purchase produce from area farmers. Sunday was designated as a day of rest. Artillerymen generally attended worship services with infantry regiments, which had full time Chaplains.

The ninety-six Confederate cannon engaged at Missionary Ridge fired 1,033 solid shot, 2,742 spherical case shot and 2,642 shell for a total of 6,417 projectiles, averaging 67 per gun. [1]

The loss of cannon, caissons, wagons and artillery horses at Missionary Ridge had been heavy. The Army of Tennessee had lost one-third of its artillery; thirty-nine field pieces, two 24-pound siege guns, twenty-eight caisson, twenty-five limbers, four battery wagons and 2,336 rounds of fixed ammunition. The Federals had incurred a similar loss at Chickamauga. Some of the Union cannon captured at Chickamauga had been assigned to Confederate batteries which had lost guns in the battle. Most of the cannon captured from the Federals at Chickamauga had been sent by rail to the Atlanta Arsenal for repair or for melting into new guns. Lt. General Hardee ordered a reorganization of artillery on December 6, taking away the guns, horses and ammunition of five batteries and redistributing them to other batteries. Men of the effected batteries were ordered to report to Colonel M. H. Wright, Commander to the Atlanta post, for post duty. The batteries chosen to be disarmed were said to have been those hardest hit at Missionary Ridge in the loss of guns and horses. This was not the case of Baxter's Company. According to the reports of General Stevenson and Captain

Carnes, they fought gallantly, made an orderly retreat from the ridge and arrived at Dalton with all their guns, horses and equipment. For the second time in his army career, Captain Baxter's command had been disrupted and he had been assigned post duty by Lt. Gen. Hardee. The other batteries sent to Atlanta were; Captain John Scrogin's Georgia Battery, Captain Thomas L. Massenburg's Georgia Battery, Captain John W. River's Arkansas Battery and Water's Alabama Battery commanded by Lieutenant William B. Hamilton. Scott's Tennessee Battery was disbanded with forty-two of the men transferred to Swett's Mississippi Battery. [1]

Copy

Hd . Qrt. Army of Tenn

General Orders

Dalton, Ga. Dec. 6, 1863

No. 218

I. The following is announced as the organization of the artillery of the army and will be carried into effect immediately.

Stevenson's Division, the following Batteries   Carnes, Rowans & Corputs Comm'd'g   Battl'n

II. The Officers and men of the following named Batteries will report to Col. M. H. Wright, Cmm'd'g, H at Atlanta, Ga. for duty. The horses, guns and ammunition eg belonging thereto, will be at once turned over to the Chief of the proper Staff Department at the Hd. Q's : Baxter's Battery

By Command of Official

Lt. Gen'l Hardee

Jno. J. Reeves , A.A.G.

-Sg- G. W Brent, A.A.G. [1]

Lieutenant General William Hardee

Captain Baxter was not pleased with Lt. General Hardee's orders to disarm his battery. He wanted to fight in the field rather than guard the post of Atlanta. Chief of Artillery, Lt. Colonel J. H. Hallonquist advised Baxter by correspondence on December 8, that he would try to quickly refit his battery for field service. Hallonquist was demoted from Chief of Artillery to commander of the reserve artillery, replacing Major Sam Williams who had transferred to the Army of Northern Virginia before he could arrange for refitting of Baxter's Company.

Office Chief of Arty.   Dalton, Geo.
Dec 8th 1863
Captain Edmund Baxter
Comn'd'g Baxter's Battery

Capt.
The reduction of the artillery of this army having made it necessary to send your Company to the rear, and the great want of Quarter Master and Ordinance supplies causes it to be temporarily dismounted. I take great pleasure in informing you that I will as early as possible re-equip it for field service.

There is no officer that I could be more sorry to part with than yourself, as there is no one whose reputation is higher than yours as an officer, and I earnestly desire to have your services, with that of your company at an as early a period as the want of necessary supplies would admit.

I am Captain Respectfully yours

J. H. Hallonquist, Lieut Col & Chief of Arty.

A.G. [1]

Dalton, December 8, 1863

President Jefferson Davis:

Reports this morning from division commands show an effective infantry force of about 33,000, rank and file; about 2,500 artillery, and between 3,000 and 4,000 cavalry. There are, besides, several thousand on the sick report who are not sick enough to be in hospitals. There are also 2,000 State troops at Rome, where fortifications are being constructed, 1,100 at Resaca, and a few hundred at Etowah. The ordnance officer reports 112 pieces of artillery on hand, with a sufficient compliment of horses; 20,000 smooth bore small-arms stored at Atlanta and other places, and plenty of ammunition. The commissary reports thirty days' rations on hand. Less than fifty wagons and ambulances were lost during the late battle. By equalizing the distribution of present field transportation, the whole army may be tolerably supplied. General Hardee considers that his force, if not attacked for two or three days, will be in good fighting order. During the past twenty-four hours 1,000 more men returned to the army from the rear. The wagon trains of two cavalry divisions have arrived safely from Knoxville; also the wagon trains of Vaughn from Loudon. Enemy's cavalry driven two miles beyond Ringgold last evening. The weather raining and roads bad. General Cleburne is strongly fortifying at Tunnel Hill.

J. C. Ives, Colonel and Aide-de-Camp [1]

Baxter's Company was again fortunate to survive the heaving fighting in the Battle of Missionary Ridge with no casualties. In the battle, the Union losses were 753 killed, 4,722 wounded and 349 missing in action. Confederate losses were reported as: 361 killed, 2,160 wounded and 4,146 captured or missing in action. Among the Confederate dead were several members of the 11th Tennessee Infantry Regiment from Dickson County including: Major William Green, Private John W. Davidson of Company K, and Corporal John E. Heath of Company E. Private Samuel B. Gray of Company H from Hickman County was also a casualty of Missionary Ridge. Among the captured were Privates Fred Beech and Paul Beech of Company H 20th Tennessee Infantry Regiment from Williamson County. [18, 19]

Confederate prisoners at the Chattanooga Depot.

In compliance with orders, the cannon, horses, ammunition and equipment of Baxter's Battery were turned in to the proper authority and the men of Baxter's Battery boarded a train for Atlanta on December 8 to report for post duty. [1]

While Baxter's men had been serving in Chattanooga, the war continued back home in Middle Tennessee. The Dickson County seat of Charlotte had been occupied by the Federals. Skirmishes were fought at the Hickman County seat at Centerville on October 29 and November 2. Franklin, the County seat of Williamson County continued to be occupied by Federal Troops. [1]

CHAPTER 4

ATLANTA

Baxter's Company arrived in Atlanta on December 9, 1863. Captain Baxter reported as ordered to post commander Colonel Moses H. Wright and the company was assigned to duty on the outer defensive line of Atlanta, stationed on the Atlanta and West Point Railroad line about two miles west of Atlanta on a major approach to the city. Though unhappy with his assignment to post duty, Baxter and his men went to work fortifying his position for a possible enemy attack.

Confederate defensive works on Atlanta's outer lines.

The company first got busy constructing winter quarters made of pine logs. Captain Baxter was placed in command of Batteries A and B in the line of entrenchments. The company was assigned to River's Battalion commanded by Captain John W. Rivers of Arkansas. The company was armed with: one 24-pound howitzer, two 3.62 inch Wiard rifles, two 6-pound bronze guns and one 12-pound howitzer. The weapons and the accompanying caissons came from the lot of the Atlanta Arsenal and were considered unfit for field service. With no horses with which to move the cannon, the guns were placed as a stationary battery. Baxter complained to Colonel Wright of not being supplied ammunition for the guns. In case of a surprise attack, his position would be defenseless. Colonel Wright insisted a supply of ammunition could be received from the laboratory on an hours notice.[23]

Atlanta was an important city for the Confederacy. With its arsenal, laboratory and shops, Atlanta was a major producer of supplies for the army, as well as a key transportation center. With the fall of Chattanooga, Atlanta became even more important to the survival of the Confederacy. The next objective of the Federals was to capture Atlanta and to further divide and conquer the South.

Atlanta, Ga. December 14, 1863
Col. George W. Brent
Assistant Adjutant-General, Dalton, Ga.:
Dispatch of the 13th just received. I have in all about 1,800 men, including the five artillery companies recently sent down and what number I can get from convalescents. I have but about 120 cavalry in the above number. With 500 additional good cavalry I would feel able to protect Atlanta against 5,000 men. Please advise me of any movements of raiding parties bearing on Atlanta. I write by evening mail.
M. H. Wright, Colonel, Commanding [1]

Atlanta, Ga. December 15, 1863
Lieut. Col. A.J. Smith, Chief Paymaster, &c.:
Colonel:
In reply to your letter of this date, I would state that the following named batteries of artillery have been ordered to and have reported here: Baxter's, Scogin's, Massenburg's, Water's, & River's,
Captain Pritchard's battery has been here some time. I am, colonel, respectfully, your obedient servant.
M. H. Wright, Colonel, Commanding [1]

Bean's Station, December 16, 1863 (Received 19th)
General S. Cooper, Richmond:
Your dispatch of the 14th is received. On the 14th instant I made an effort to intercept the enemy at this point. We were unsuccessful owing to bad roads and a rise in the Holston, which delayed our column of cavalry some twelve hours. The enemy have escaped in the direction of Knoxville. We captured sixty-eight of his wagons, about forty loaded with sugar and coffee and other stores. We had a sharp skirmish at this

place, losing about 200 men, chiefly Johnson's division. I regret to report General Gracie as having received a severe flesh wound. We shall be obliged to suspend active operations for want of shoes and clothing.

J. LONGSTREET, Lieutenant General. [1]

December 27, 1863 General Joseph E. Johnston arrived in Dalton to assume command of the Army of Tennessee. Johnston was popular with the troops and set about refitting the army. The morale of the army greatly improved under Johnston's command, as did the supply of food, clothing and equipment. [25]

A requisition for fuel for January 1864 listed seventy non-commissioned officers, musicians, and privates serving in the company, along with Captain Baxter and the three Lieutenants. Captain Baxter was supplied three cords of wood for the month. Each Lieutenant received two cords of wood. One-sixth cord of wood was allotted to each enlisted man. A requisition for forage on January 11 showed the company with only three horses, all privately owned. The horses were issued rations of corn and fodder. [23]

At age seventy-seven, Private James B. Thompson recalled life in the Atlanta entrenchments: "We were in the ditches at Atlanta for about nine months. Lived mostly on tough beef and biscuit, wore regular old gray uniforms, slept on a blanket on the ground, not exposed to cold, too far south. Got hungry many times and suffered from typhoid fever." [10]

Disease struck quickly in the trenches of Atlanta. Many of Baxter's men were still suffering from the effects of typhoid fever contracted in East Tennessee when they arrived in Atlanta. Diarrhea was a common illness in the trenches. Private Hiram Sears died from it January 20, 1864 in Catoosa Hospital in Griffin, Georgia. Private William Green W. Buttrey succumbed to diarrhea February 5, 1864 in a hospital in Covington, Georgia. Private Wesley Welch spent January and February 1864 in Blackie Hospital in Madison, Georgia. Private James Lewis was hospitalized April 16, 1864 in Empire Hospital in Atlanta The last service record of Private Benjamin Gilliam lists him as being sent to a hospital in Atlanta on December 14, 1863. [23]

After fourteen months of camping, marching and patrolling, the men were finally issued new uniforms and shoes in March 1864 in a requisition by Captain Baxter to Army of Tennessee Headquarters in Dalton. The requisition was approved by Major General Howell Cobb. [23]

Several new recruits were added to the company in the spring and early summer of 1864 in Atlanta. Many of the recruits had previously served in various Georgia Regiments, mostly infantry. Some had been wounded in early battles in Virginia and discharged. Others had been given medical discharges or discharged for being over age earlier in the war. Private Middleton Vickory was seventy-four years old at the time of his enlistment in Baxter's Company. He had been discharged from Company K of the 38th Georgia Infantry Regiment on December 31, 1861 due to old age and disability. Some of the recruits were boys sixteen years of age or under. The men were paid a fifty dollar bounty for enlisting. A few joined, collected the bounty and deserted. Private P. K. Colesman was found to belong to another unit after collecting his bounty and was captured by the Provost Marshall and held for trial. Private James Wright deserted less than two weeks after enlisting. Private John L. Foster did not stay with the company long enough to get paid. These men were the exceptions to the rule. Most of the Georgia and Alabama recruits remained with Baxter's Battery until the final surrender. The new recruits from Georgia and Alabama blended in with now veteran soldiers from Tennessee. Corporal Dan White's daughter recalled him speaking of his friend Rattree "The Frenchman" who served with him in Georgia.[15, 23]

MUSTER ROLL 1864 RECRUITS
BAXTER'S COMPANY TENNESSEE LIGHT ARTILLERY

Pvt. John J. Alexander Carroll Co., GA.
Pvt. James H. Buzbee Coosa Co., AL.
Pvt. John F. Cain Morgan Co., AL
Pvt. Seth Callahan Clayton Co., GA.
Cpl. Richard H. Carney Union Co., GA.
Pvt. Jefferson P. Christian Coosa Co., AL.
Pvt. P. K. Colesman Fulton Co., GA.
Pvt. James M. Duff Montgomery Co., TN.
Pvt. Guey Dukes   Fulton Co., GA.
Pvt. A. L. Emlen Fayette Co., GA.
Pvt. John L. Foster Union Co., GA.
Pvt. Francis M. Godwin Fulton Co., GA.
Pvt. James K. Gray Clayton Co., GA.
Pvt. Louis Griggs Fayette Co., GA.
Pvt. Minor Griggs Baldwin Co., GA.
Pvt. Robert Hadaway Clayton Co., GA.
Pvt. John M. Johnson Campbell Co., GA.
Pvt. John M. Kane Chatham Co., GA.

Pvt. Napoleon B. Kile Fulton Co, GA.
Pvt. Noah W. Kimberly Fayette Co., GA.
Pvt. Andrew Kite Fayette Co., GA.
Pvt. John S. Langley Gwinnett Co., GA.
Pvt. John B. Maddox   Coosa Co., AL.
Pvt. Joshua May Coosa Co., AL.
Pvt. William May Coosa Co., AL.
Pvt. James McCallister Meriweather Co., GA.
Pvt. James McCowan Clayton Co., GA.
Pvt. James R. Morrow Henry Co., GA.
Pvt. John Norris Campbell Co., GA.
Pvt. Lindrey Norris Campbell Co., GA.
Pvt. Reuben Norris Campbell Co., GA.
Pvt. William Parrish Walker Co., GA.
Pvt. Lewis H. Posey Edgefield Dist.,SC.
Pvt. James W. Powell Murray Co., GA
Pvt. George Randol Mississippi Co., MO.
Pvt. John Ratteree Paulding Co., GA.
Pvt. George Smallwood Wilkes Co., GA.
Pvt. James G. Speights Jasper Co., GA.
Pvt. Lewis T. Sudduth Fayette Co., GA.
Pvt. Middleton Vickory Bartow Co., GA.
Pvt. John T. Walker Clayton Co., GA.
Pvt. L. C. Whitmore Bartow Co., GA.
Pvt. James T. Wright Jasper Co., GA.

Note: Some of the soldiers recruited in Georgia by Captain Baxter in 1864 and 1865 may not be listed due to lack of service records. Some may have been listed as Georgia Militia, Georgia State Troops or Georgia Reserve Artillery.

On April 4, 1864, Private John Demumbreun of Williamson County wrote home to his wife in College Grove.

Cassville, GA.   April the 4, 1864

My Dear Wife and sweet baby,
As I have a chance to write a few lines to you my Dear, I can with the greatest pleasure in the world. I came down to see Doc Battle. I understood that he was going to Middle Tenn. I thought probably it would be a good chance to send a letter to you. Sallie I have no news at present every thing are quiet at the present. I sent a letter up to Dalton to Jim Haley to send to you by the first one that was passing through to Tenn. He said he would so. Sallie be certain to send me a letter by Dr. Battle. I want to hear from you and my sweet baby. I am in fine health

at present 185 lbs is my weight as the fair sex in and around Atlanta call me the Tenn. Fatman hog. I have been on furlow down south Ga. I enjoyed my self finely with the women. I merely pass my self off as a single man several promise they would follow me to Tenn. I was at great many parties. I have received several letters since I came back to my command from the fair sex down there insisting on me to come back again. Sallie it's some thing strange to me that I can't here from you. I generly here the news in and around the neighborhood but can not from you. I understand that people generally in that county loved Abe Lincoln rather liked him some better than they did old Jeff. I think old Jeff will bring them to their milk this fall. I think they have to---blue beef a while.   Tell Squire Gov. I understood that old Abe had taken his enrolling papers from him and was the enrolling offercer of the---and I also understand that hill was a candidate for constable in the 21, his honorable computitor Jack Bigers rather turned him down. I do not know how it is there, but down here they are not exempt. Sallie as I stated to you in my other letter, that Can is down at Atlanta. I saw him a few days ago, his health is as good as any one could wish. I have not seen his lady yet, she is staying up at Cartersville at her fathers. Sallie tell Mary also that Jim McClure is dead he died at Bristol, Virginia seval weeks ago with his wound so I was informed by one of his company Mr. Sim Woulds, the other day. I was very sorry to here it indeed. Sallie please tend to my dogs. I think probily I'll have the pleasure of following them this fall, if any of them is dead send me word which one it is. I have had a nice little first, but the cars run over him and killed him as dead as hector. I miss it very much. Sallie tell Dee I heard he was going to get married to Miss Angee, tell him please hold his courage until I get there, down here they take it for three years or during present war. I recon that is very good idea, tell him if wats to pull flat, Georga is the place for him, tell billy Allison I often think of past times we have had together. I hope to spend such times again with him. Sallie tell pa to send me some money by bob when he starts back, send me some greenbacks. Confederate money is payed out down here, the new issue is not much better than the old money. Tell him I am in for the war. You must send me a suit of close if you can possible do it.

My Dear give my love to all generly tell tham I am in better health and in better spirits than I ever was, tell them I hope to land in old Tenn once more. Sallie you write, send me all the news about every thing generally. You must kiss my sweet baby for me every day tell her that her pa will be at home this fall if its Gods will. My Dear you must rite.

Your everlasting lover.

Good bye My Dear wife and sweet baby.

Jno. F Demonbrin [7]

Private Demonbruen reported of having a good time during his furlough to south Georgia.   Other members of Baxter's company received furloughs during this quiet period in Atlanta.   Most went to areas in Georgia or Alabama which were under Confederate occupation.   Many of the men yearned to return to Middle Tennessee to visit sweethearts and families.   To do so would likely result in capture by the occupying Federals.

Other soldiers in the company deserted the army during this period, on March 19, 1864, Privates Hardy Bilbery, John Williams, Joseph Nall, and Samuel L. Davis. were listed on a roll of 10 rebel deserters released on oath of amnesty.   The oath was administered by Captain R. M. Goodwin, Assistant Provost Marshall, Department of the Cumberland at Nashville.   No records of their departure from Baxter's Company, as to whether they deserted or were on furlough, was listed in their Confederate service records. [23]

An inspection of the Atlanta Defenses conducted by engineers of the War Department in the spring of 1864 was critical of the condition of the artillery and equipment of Baxter's Command.   Captain Baxter had been led to believe by Lt. Colonel Hallenquist that his assignment to post duty was temporary until he could be refitted and equipped for field service. Baxter responded to the report by letter:

Hd. Qrs   Baxter's Battery
Defenses Atlanta, Ga.   June 1, 1864

Sir

In reply to the inquiries of the War Department, I have the honor to report I enclose a copy of the order and letter of the Chief of Artillery Army of Tennessee showing the purposes for which my command was ordered here.   I was assigned to the Command of Batts "A" &"B" on the entrenchments.   Col. M. H. Wright, then commanding this post sent me one 24-pound howitzer gun, two (3.62 in) Wiard rifles, two 6- pound bronze guns, one 12 pound bronze howitzer.   I put in a requisition and receipt afterwards.

Thin issues; but I had no voice in their selection and never saw these until they arrived at the entrenchments.

They had been taken from a large lot of artillery which had been turned over from the field to this Post for repairs and I understood from Col. Wright that he had selected for these stationary batteries the very carriages which were not fit for field services, and the carriages I have will answer all the purposes of a stationary battery.

I had us horses harness and caissons and had no idea I would be expected to have my carriages in condition for field service: one of the lines had no pole, another no splinter bar, some of the ammunition chests had no stay-piers, and some of the rails no pointing rings—these and all such defects. I had his tools and material to repair. I did service as soon as they came into my procession, but the principal injury which results for the wear and tear which they had received before they were sent to me and which could be repaired only in a regular arsenal.

Col. Wright was also in command of the arsenal and as he knew their condition and did not have them repaired. I did not suppose that I was expected to have it done. I have no forge or blacksmith tools having turned them over with my field battery and his iron work, I had done was by my artificers in private shops in this city and at no expense to the government.

The 24-pound and 2 rifle carriages are in good order, but have been pronounced too heavy for field service, and the field carriages had received all their injuries before they came in to my hands.

As to ammunition Col. Wright informed me that he would issue me none until there was some necessity for it, and accordingly I never received any until a few days since when he sent me a limited supply which I immediately had prepared for action.

The whole of the matter is I have from time to time had to secure just such ordinance and ordinance stores as were sent me and am in no way responsible for their conditions when delivered to me.

I am confident I can show they have suffered nothing while in my hands and that I have done every thing I could to explain their existing deficiencies.

Very Respectfully
Ed Baxter
Capt. Lt. Art'y Commd'g

To Major Lawrence L. Butler, A.A.A. Ga. [23]

Insp. Report W. 16
Hd. Q't. Baxter's Batt'y
Defenses Atlanta, Ga.
June 1st 1864
Capt Ed Baxter
Comm'd'g

Report upon engineers of the War Department in relation to this battery
C.S. Arsenal Atlanta
June 1, 1864

The statements herein made are all correct: In December (9th day) Capt. Baxter reported to me (then in command of the troops & defenses of Atlanta, Ga.) under orders from the General Commanding the Army of Tenn,: at the same time, four other Captains with their commands were ordered here- having lost their horses at the Battle of Missionary Ridge—Of course they were all put in the defenses four stretched armories. Atlanta- and the demand for artillery for the field was so heavy upon this arsenal after the battles in November when we lost much artillery, the arsenal was taxed to its fullest capacity to supply them with new work & in order to give the troops horses to put in the batteries here I was compelled to issue carriages as unfit for field service; but in every way invited to given the position where they were not exposed to the wear and tear of rapid movements.

No ammunition was given him for the very sensible reason given by the Captain- as I had a good magazine to keep it in & entirely convenient to carry battery & munitions I could thinly use all such supplies for the front & could put up at the laboratory at an hours notice, supplies for the guns when needed.

I again assert that the guns are all good-the carriages, entirely efficient for all purposes intended and I take pleasure testifying to Captain Baxter's capacity and skill as an Officer and beg to say that, in Command of the two batteries mounting 6 guns, on the principal approach to this city, I consider his services not only necessary, but intensified that in case we have trouble here, he will show that neither his guns nor his men, are unfit for service.

The command as stationed here, is not intended for field service- & of course Capt. B. could not be expected to have horses & a complete refit for field service.

Very Resp'y
M. H. Wright
Col. Cm'g Arsenal & defenses [23]

The main body of the Army of Tennessee spent the winter in camps in and around Dalton. The men engaged in snowball fights and other activities to pass the time. [25] Baxter's men spent the winter in the mud, boredom and drudgery of the outer defensive line of Atlanta. Though adequately supplied and sheltered, the men spent their second Christmas away from home and family in the misery of army life. Life in the trenches did at least give the men a rest from the almost constant marching they were subjected to during their first year in the army while stationed in East Tennessee. The warmer climate in Georgia was also welcome relief from the previous cold winter spent in the mountains.

This was the first time since joining the Confederate Army that Baxter's Company had been stationed in a pro-Confederate area.

After surviving the winter in camp in Chattanooga, the Federal Army was ready to pursue the Army of Tennessee and move on to Atlanta. The 110,00 seasoned Union troops were commanded by Major General William T. Sherman, divided into the Army of the Cumberland under Brigadier Gen. George Thomas, the Army of the Tennessee commanded by Brigadier General James B. McPherson and the Army of the Ohio commanded by Brigadier General John M. Schofield. Sherman had under his command 41 batteries with 207 guns and 18 reserve batteries at Chattanooga and Nashville. [1]

The Army of Tennessee consisted of 55,000 troops with 35 batteries armed with 138 guns. The army had been refitted, rations had been increased and ammunition supplies had been replenished. Some fresh horses had been procured for the artillery batteries.[1]

The campaign for Atlanta started as a continuous series of flanking maneuvers which began with the Federal attacks on the approaches to Dalton. The Federals attacked at Rocky Face Ridge and Tunnel Hill, Georgia on May 9, 1864. On May 13, Dalton was evacuated. The Confederate Army fell back twelve miles to Resaca, Georgia. and erected defensive positions. After a brief battle, the rebels retreated from Resaca on May 15. Confederate forces assembled for battle at Cassville and on May 20, fell back eight miles further south to Cartersville. The Federals continued pushing the Confederates closer to Atlanta in battles fought May 25 at New Hope Church, May 27 at Pickett's Mill, and the Battle of Dallas on May 28.[1]

In The Field, June 4, 1864
His Excellency Joseph E. Brown,
Governor of the State of Georgia, Atlanta:
    I have the honor to acknowledge the receipt of your letter of the 1st instant on the subject of impressments. The only orders I have given on the subject have been that as the army fell back and left territory to fall into possession of the enemy everything in the way of provisions should be impressed. I did this knowing that in so doing I was not oppressing the inhabitants, from whom the enemy, now suffering for want of provisions and forage would, take everything without compensation and use it to make his farther advance more easy. Around my army I have ordered all stock and forage to be purchased, not impressed. In some

cases my orders may have been exceeded by my agents, in others violated by lawless persons. I will take pains to remedy this.

And am, sir, very respectfully, your obedient servant.

J. E. JOHNSTON, General [1]

The Confederates had retreated almost one hundred miles in two months. The armies again clashed at the Battle of Kolb's Farm on June 22. The Rebels repulsed the Union push in the Battle of Kennesaw Mountain on June 27. The Federal where then less than twenty miles from Atlanta. Fighting around Marietta began June 9 and continued until the Federals were victorious on July 3. [1]

On July 5, 1864, the Battle of Pace's Ferry was fought near Atlanta. Union forces under command of Major General Oliver O. Howard seized a key pontoon bridge over the Chattahoochee River, enabling Federal troops to continue their offensive to capture the important rail and supply center of Atlanta.

The retreat from Chattanooga to Atlanta had been costly to the Confederates. Losses in the Army of Tennessee and Army of Mississippi combined were 1,358 killed and 8,614 wounded. Casualties suffered by the Confederate cavalry were not included in these totals. [1]

The City of Atlanta had been heavily fortified by the spring of 1864. The city had been encircled by ten miles of entrenchments, with nineteen redoubts on the main line, each capable of supporting five cannon. Five exterior batteries not connected to rifle pits and several interior batteries had been placed. Houses, barns, trees and everything in sight had been cleared for a distance of about a thousand yards from the entrenchments to open a clear line of fire in case of attack. With clearance from Major General Dabney Maury, commander of the Department of the Gulf, fourteen heavy cannon were transported from Mobile to Atlanta to bolster the defenses. With the addition of these guns, the city was defended with thirty-seven pieces of artillery. [1]

The six Army of Tennessee batteries sent to Atlanta in December had been consolidated into four: Scogin's, Baxter's, River's and Massenburg's and had been placed under the command of Major General Gustavus W. Smith, commander of the Georgia State Militia. Smith was a Kentucky native who had served in the Army of Northern Virginia. [1]

Major General Gustavus W. Smith

Richmond, Va., July 12, 1864
General Marcus J. Wright, Atlanta, Ga.:
Governor Brown proposes to furnish 5,000 old men and boys for the emergency. You will receive such numbers as are tendered, mustering them into service for local defense, and issue arms to them from the depot at Macon.

S. Cooper, Adjutant and Inspector General [1]

President Jefferson Davis had not been pleased with General Johnston's defensive fighting and wanted more aggressive action. On July 18, 1864 General John Bell Hood assumed command of the Army of Tennessee. Soldiers in the Army of Tennessee were disappointed in Hood's appointment. General Johnston had been a well respected, popular commander.

Special Orders
ADJT. AND INSP. GENERAL'S OFFICE
No. 168
Richmond, July 18, 1864
V. General Joseph E. Johnston, C.S. Army, is hereby relieved from the command of the Army and Department of Tennessee, and will turn over the same to General John B. Hood, Provisional Army, C.S.
By command of the Secretary of War:
SAML. W. MELTON, Assistant Adjutant-General. [1]

Headquarters Stevens' Brigade
In the field, July 18, 1864
General J. E. Johnston, C. S. Army

General:

Your order turning over the command of this army to General Hood has been read to the troops of this brigade. The announcement that you are no longer to be our leader was received by officers and men in silence and deep sorrow. I have the fullest assurance that I express the undivided sentiment of this brigade when I say that the abiding and unlimited confidence which we have felt in the wisdom of your judgment and leadership, has sustained us in the many trying hours of our very arduous campaign. We have ever felt that the best was being done that could be, and have looked confidently forward to the day of triumph, when with you as our leader we should surely march to glorious victory. This confidence and implicit trust has been in no way impaired, and we are to-day ready, as we ever have been, to obey your orders, whether they be to retire before a largely outnumbered foe, or to spend our last drop of blood in the fiercest conflict. We feel that in parting with you as our commanding general our loss is irreparable, and that this army and our country loses one of its ablest, most zealous, and patriotic defenders. Our most sincere well wishes will accompany you in your future career, and you carry with you the love, respect, esteem, and confidence of the officers and men of this brigade. We would hail with joy your return to command us.

I have the honor to be, very respectfully, your obedient servant,

C.H. STEVENS, Brigadier-General, Provisional Army, C.S. [1]

Atlanta, July 18, 1864
President Jefferson Davis:

The enemy being now in our immediate front and making, as we suppose, a general advance, we deem it dangerous to change commanders, now especially, as this would necessitate other important changes. A few days will probably decide the fate of Atlanta, when the campaign may be expected to close for a time, allowing a new commander opportunity to get his army in hand and make the necessary changes. For these reasons we would respectfully urge the order requiring a change of commanders be suspended until the fate of Atlanta shall be decided.

J. B. HOOD, General
W. J. HARDEE, Lieutenant-General
ALEX. P. STEWART, Lieutenant-General [1]

Headquarters Hardee's Corp
Circular. July 19, 1864
By direction of General Hood you will cause the banks of Peach Tree Creek to be thoroughly examined in front of your division; plan a strong skirmish line there, and cause the best defenses than can be made to be placed there. The object is to enable a small force to resist the enemy's crossing for some time. General Hood considers this of great importance, and Lieutenant-General Hardee wishes you to give it your prompt attention.

Respectfully
T.B. Roy, Assistant Adjutant –General[1]

On July 20 the Confederates planned to attack the left wing of the Union Army east of Atlanta at Peach Tree Creek. Federal forces had crossed Peach Tree Creek before the Confederates arrived and the bloody Battle of Peach Tree Creek ensued.

Near Atlanta, July 20, 1864
Hon. J. A. Seddon, Richmond, Va:
Late yesterday evening a force of the enemy, supposed to be a brigade, crossed Peach Tree Creek and attacked Reynold's brigade, Walthall's division, Stewart's corp.   That brigade charged them handsomely, drove them back, capturing about 150 prisoners and 2 stand of colors. The enemy still crossing Peach Tree Creek in our front.

J. B. Hood, General[1]

Atlanta, July 20, 1864-11 p.m (Received 21st)
Hon. J. A. Seddon:
At 3 o'clock to-day a portion of Hardee's and Stewart's corp drove the enemy into his breast-works, but did not gain possession of them. Our loss slight. Brigadier-General Stevens severely wounded. On our extreme right the enemy attacked Wheeler's cavalry with infantry and were handsomely repulsed.

J. B. Hood, General[1]

Headquarters
20, 1864-10:20 a.m.
Major-General Wheeler, Commanding Cavalry:
General:
General Hood directs me to say that you must retard the enemy as much as possible; that General Jackson has been ordered to send 1,000 cavalry to your assistance. Should you finally be forced back, form and

strengthen yourself upon the right of our infantry, which is now being extended to the railroad.

Very respectfully,
A.P. Mason, Major and Assistant Adjutant-General.[1]

HEADQUARTERS ARMY OF TENNESSEE
July 20, 1864-11 a. m.
Major-General Wheeler
Commanding Cavalry Corps:

General:

General Hood desires you to form a portion of your cavalry on the right of the infantry, holding the remainder in readiness to strike the enemy in flank in case they should attack General Cheatham. He sent you a note to this effect, and sends this to say that he does not wish your entire command formed on the right. He also desires you to keep them from General Cheatham's front as long as possible, and use every precaution to keep them from our flank. He wishes me to say also that your own judgment will prompt you when it may be best and at what point to strike the enemy in case they should attack General Cheatham.

Very respectfully, general, your obedient servant.
E. B. Wade, Aide-de-camp[1]

July 20, 1864-1:10 p.m.
General Wheeler:

Are you driven back or have you only fallen back to find a good position? What is your estimate of the enemy? Hold at all hazards. General Smith, with all the reserve artillery, occupies the works behind you.

Respectfully,
W. W. Mackhall, Brigadier-General[1]

Georgia Railroad Fortifications
Atlanta, July 20, 1864-4:35 p.m.
Major-General Wheeler,
Commanding Cavalry:

General:

I have 700 men here in the trenches upon the right and left of the railroad, supporting the reserve artillery. There is nothing to my right. Where is your right and left, and how far are the enemy from this position. Please notify me of anything of moment in regard to your position, that of the enemy, & c, and oblige.

Very truly, yours,
G. W. Smith, Major-General[1]

On the night of July 21, the Confederates abandoned their outer defensive line and withdrew to the interior lines to entice a Federal attack. On the morning of July 22 the Federals occupied the outer defensive lines and attacked the Confederates, opening the Battle of Atlanta. Baxter's position was attacked from the south side. Federal troops charged over the breastworks, firing a lead hailstorm into the trenches. Baxter ordered the men to open fire with their pistols and muskets. The return fire and hand to hand combat from the Georgia Militia troops and reserve artillery troops in the trenches drove the federals from the position. Private James Powell of Georgia was shot in the right leg with a minie ball. He was transported to the rear to Hood Hospital at Cuthbert, Georgia. He rejoined the company March 24, 1865. Private Noah Kimberly, also a Georgian was shot in the hip. [12,23]

The Confederates routed the Federals back to their former positions and repeatedly charged the works, capturing several pieces of artillery. Being unable to fire their guns without endangering their own troops, some of Baxter's men joined in the infantry charge attacking the Federal positions and aided in spiking two of the captured guns of DeGress' Illinois Battery.   Private Reuben Norris reported Baxter's Battery was almost annihilated while aiding in the capture of DeGress's Battery. [6] The Federals drove the Confederates back to their positions in the interior lines. Upon the return of the Confederates to their original lines, Baxter's and the other reserve artillery batteries opened fire on the Union batteries and a hot duel pursued. The Battle of Atlanta had been costly to both sides in killed and wounded, but the siege would continue for six more weeks.

ATLANTA BATTLEFIELD MAP

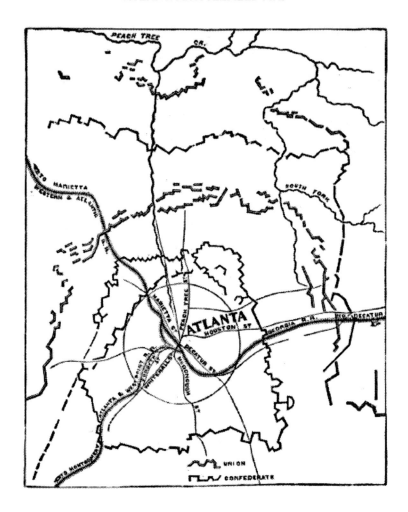

Baxter's position during the July 22, 1864 Battle of Atlanta
at the far left of the line near the railroad.

NEAR ATLANTA, July 22, 1864- 10:30p.m.
Hon. J. A. Seddon, Richmond:

The army shifted its position last night, fronting Peach Tree Creek, and formed line of battle around the city with Stewart's and Cheatham's corps. General Hardee, with his corps, made a night march and attacked the enemy's extreme left at 1 o'clock to-day; drove him from his works, capturing 16 pieces of artillery and 5 stand of colors. Major-General

Cheatham attacked the enemy at 4 p.m. with a portion of his command; drove the enemy, capturing 6 pieces of artillery. During the engagements we captured about 2,000 prisoners, but our loss not fully ascertained. Major-General Walker killed; Brigadier-Generals Smith, Gist, and Mercer wounded. Our troops fought with great gallantry.

J. B. Hood, General. [1]

Macon, July 22, 1864
General Bragg,
Columbus:

From what I know of the want of ammunition and arms at Atlanta, the stoppage of the arsenal here by your order to send details to the front may lead to great embarrassment.

BENJ. S. EWELL
Colonel and Assistant-Adjutant-General. [1]

Macon, July 22, 1864
General Braxton Bragg:

My supplies for the army are only from Macon and Augusta arsenals. If the detailed men from those arsenals be sent to Atlanta the work shall be stopped and I do not know how to supply the army.

H. OLADOSKI, Lieutenant-Colonel. [1]

Confederate defenses at the Potter House in Atlanta

Shell damaged Potter House after the Battle of Atlanta.

July 25, Baxter's Company left its position on the Atlanta and West Point Railroad and marched about three miles to the trenches and took position near the Rolling Mill on the State Road, July 27 was reported as all quiet, except picket firing.

On the afternoon of July 28, General Sherman stretched his army in an inverted U around the northern defenses of Atlanta and the armies clashed in the Battle of Ezra Church.

July 28, 1864-9 a.m. (Received 9:45 a.m.)
Lieutenant-General Hardee
Commanding, & c.:

The chief of artillery has instructions to open fire upon the enemy in certain contingencies. Please instruct your skirmishers in front to prepare cover, so that they may retain their positions. They must remain at all hazard

F. A. Shoup, Chief of Staff[1]. [1]

July 28 the enemy pressed Confederate pickets. Baxter's Battery opened fire and shelled the enemy camps with 55 rounds of ammunition. Shelling the enemy continued on July 29. July 30 and 31 were reported as the only action being picket firing in the vicinity of Baxter's position. Daily shelling of Union positions and the federal shells exploding around them and the whizzing sound of minie balls overhead were reminiscent of the siege of Chattanooga eight months earlier. Now the Federals were the ones laying siege and the rebels were on the receiving end.

July 28, 1864-10:30 a.m.
(Received at 11 a.m.)
Lieutenant-General Hardee:
General Lee is now moving against the enemy to our left.
F.A. Shoup, Chief of Staff [1]

July 28, 1864-10:30 a.m.
(Received at 11 a.m.)
Lieutenant-General Hardee:
General Hood directs me to again impress upon you the importance of relieving the troops of General Lee on the left of Peach Tree road.
F.A. Shoup, Chief of Staff [1]

July 28, 1864-12 o'clock
Lieutenant-General Hardee:
General:
General Hood has written twice to know if you can relieve the detachment of Lee's corps west of Peach Tree road. He also wrote you that he is moving on the enemy. I have sent to both to know how many men they can spare, and General Cheatham, who is here, has sent to see whether he can draw out a brigade and place it on the road to await your order.

Respectfully,
T. B. Roy Assistant Adjutant-General [1]

July 28, 1864-12:30 p.m.
(Received 1:10 p.m.)
Lieutenant-General Hardee,
Commanding Corps:

General Lee is directed to prevent the enemy from gaining the Lick Skillet road, and not to attack unless the enemy exposes himself in attacking us. Please inform your officers that all indications are that the enemy intends to attack us to-day or to-morrrow.

F. A. Shoup, Chief of Staff [1]

July 28, 1864-11:50 p.m.
Lieutenant-General Hardee:

Inclosed please find communication from Major-General Stevenson. The general desires that you order the co-operation, and arrange with General Stevenson that the movement may be simultaneous. He also directs me to acknowledge the receipt of your communication of 10:45 p.m., referring to the proposed night attack.

F. A. Shoup, Chief of Staff[1]

July 28, 1864-12 p.m.
(Received 1:05 p.m.)
Lieutenant-General Lee,
Commanding Corp:

Inclosed please find dispatch from General Jackson. If the enemy should make an assault upon our left the general directs you to strike him in flank.

F. A. Shoup, Chief of Staff[1]

July 28, 1864-2:20 p.m.
(Received 3:45 p.m.)
Lieutenant-General Lee:

General Hood directs that you hold the enemy in check. The object is to prevent him from gaining the Lick Skillet road.

F. A. Shoup, Chief of Staff[1]

July 28, 1864-4 p.m.
Lieutenant-General Lee:

General Hood directs me to inform you that he desires you not to allow the enemy to gain upon you any more than possible, and that General Stewart has directions to support you fully.

F. A. Shoup, Chief of Staff[1]

July 30, 1864-1:30 p.m.
Colonel Beckham,
Commanding Artillery:

The general desires you to use all the guns against the enemy's working parties on the Marietta road that can do execution. It is of great importance that the enemy do not gain a lodgment in front of that point.

F. A. Shoup, Chief of Staff[1]

August 1 picket fighting was reported to the left of Baxter's position and continued August 2 and 3. August 3 the Federals again attacked Baxter's position and were repulsed. Picket fighting continued in the area of Baxter's position through August 13. The men were exposed daily to exploding shells and musket fire.

HEADQUARTERS
Atlanta, Ga., August 4, 1864

To the MILITIA OF THE COUNTIES OF CAMPBELL, CARROLL, PAULDING, HARALSON, COBB, BARTOW, FLOYD, CHATTOOGA, WALKER, DADE, CATOOSA, WHITFIELD, MURRAY, GORDON, GILMER, PICKENS, CHEROKEE, MILTON, FORSYTH, AND DAWSON:

You who are between sixteen and fifty-five years of age are hereby ordered into the military service of the state of Georgia, and are directed to report to and obey till further orders from these headquarters such officers as General J. B. Hood, commanding the Army of Tennessee, now at Atlanta, may send into your respective counties to direct the service you are to render. You will not be kept constantly under arms, nor removed from the Cherokee country, but you will respond instantly to each call made by an officer sent by General Hood. It is very desirable that as large a number as possible from these and other counties in Northeast Georgia mount themselves on horses and form into cavalry companies and use shotguns, pistols, and such other weapons as they can command. All who cannot get horses, and who prefer it, can volunteer and form themselves into companies under officers of their own selection, and will report with their officers to the officer appointed by General Hood. All who refuse to join volunteer companies are required to report as militia under the laws of this State. The statute of the State declares that every man who refuses to respond to this or any other similar order shall be treated as a deserter. It will be but a short time till courts-martial can be ordered in the respective counties for the trial of all such, All are expected to use their own arms when they have them.

Those without arms will be supplied when they are required to render service. When in service or on active duty, under an officer having a commission from this state, or having an order from General Hood to assume such command, they will be entitled to all protection of prisoners of war, in case of capture by the enemy. The Confederacy has enough of Federal prisoners to enable us prompt retaliation, if necessary, to compel the Federal authorities to respect your rights as prisoners in case of capture. General Hood's army is now being rapidly re-enforced. The militia of the whole State not within the lines of the enemy are responding with a unanimity, promptness, and cheerfulness seldom equaled in the history of the world. It is hoped that General G. W. Smith's command, composed of State militia, who have thus far done the service of volunteers in every fight and have never once flinched, will soon amount to about 30,000 effective men. Georgia is determined at all hazards and every sacrifice to drive the invaders from her sacred soil. In this important consummation you are expected at the proper moment to act a useful part in freeing your homes, will be the only incentives necessary to induce proper action. Colonel Dobbs and Colonel Rogers, my aides-de-camp, are charged specially with the execution of these orders. They will communicate with and give orders to such officers as may remain in or be sent to the counties. If you are determined to be freemen, act promptly and vigorously, as your brethren in other parts of the State are doing, and the day of deliverance is near at hand.

JOSEPH E. BROWN [1]

On August 5, General Sherman's army made an offensive move to hit the railroad between East Point and Atlanta and clashed with the Confederates in the Battle of Utoy Creek. Union delays allowed the Confederate to strengthen their position before the fighting resumed on August 6. The Federals were repulsed with heavy losses inflicted by Brig. General William Bates' division and failed in an attack on the railroad. On August 7, the Union troops moved toward the Confederate main line and entrenched. Here they remained until late August. [1]

On August 9, Federal batteries fired more than 5,000 shells into the City of Atlanta. Only one third of the shells were reported to have exploded. A duel between eleven Union and ten Confederate batteries, including Baxter's lasted all day. [1]

GENERAL FIELD ORDERS
HDQRTS. ARMY OF TENNESSEE
No. 14
In the Field, August 12, 1864

I.   The lawless seizure and destruction of private property by straggling soldiers in the rear and on the flanks of this army has become intolerable. It must come to an end. It is believed to be chargeable to worthless men, especially from mounted commands, who are odious alike to the citizen and the well-disposed soldier. Citizens and soldiers are, therefore, called upon to arrest and forward to the provost marshal-general all persons guilty of wanton destruction or illegal seizure of property, that examples, may immediately be made. The laws of war justify the execution of such offenders, and those laws shall govern.

II.   Officers are held responsible that their men conduct themselves properly. In any case where it is shown that an officer, high or low, has permitted or failed to take proper steps shall be deprived of his commission.

III.   Hereafter all cavalry horses must be branded. Division and brigade commanders will determine the manner so as to best designate the commands to which they belong. No purchase or exchange of horses will be permitted except by authority of the company and regimental commanders to which they belong. In each case of such purchase or exchange the soldier must receive a written statement of the transaction. Any soldier otherwise introducing a horse into any command will be immediately arrested. General, field, and company officers are expected, and are earnestly requested, to give this matter their attention. Officers failing must be arrested. In procuring forage, the least possible damage must be done to the farmer. Too much attention cannot be given this. At best he is compelled to suffer.

IV.   Citizens are warned not to purchase or exchange horses with soldiers, except when the authority for the transaction is previously had from the company and regimental commanders. Otherwise they may lose their property and will fail to receive the support of the military authorities.

By command of General Hood
A. P. Mason, Major and Assistant Adjutant-General[1]

Headquarters Stewart's Corps,
Atlanta, August 17, 1864-11 p.m.
Major General French Commanding Division:

General:

The lieutenant-general commanding directs me to inform you that the artillery on your line has been ordered to open fire on the enemy tomorrow morning at sunrise, and to fire four rounds from each piece at intervals of ten minutes. You will notify your officers on the skirmish line, and direct them to observe closely the effect of the fire and report the result, which you will communicate to these headquarters.

Respectfully, your obedient servant.
Douglas West, Acting Assistant Adjutant-General[1]

On August 18, Federal troops destroyed tracks on the Macon & Western Railroad. On August 19, the Federals attacked the Jonesboro supply depot and burned great amounts of supplies. August 20 Confederate troops under command of General Patrick Cleburne defeated the Union troops in the Battle of Lovejoy's Station. Daily picket fighting and sporadic cannonading continued in the vicinity of Baxter's position through August 24.

August 25, the Federals evacuated their positions on the left and concentrated their forces on the right of the Confederates. Baxter's men reported all quiet until August 29, when the battery moved about two miles near Peach Tree Road. Reports on August 30 and 31 were all quiet in Baxter's ranks.

While all was quiet in the trenches, the armies again clashed at Jonesborough on August 31. The fighting continued into September 1.

Thursday, September 1, 1864 orders were given to evacuate Atlanta. Baxter's Company left the trenches at 6 p.m. and marched all night and did not stop until 2 p.m. on Friday September 2 on the bank of South River about sixteen miles from Atlanta. After two hours rest the men were again on the march, marching all night in the rain and mud. September 3, the company reached Griffin, Georgia, forty-four miles from Atlanta.

Lovejoy's Station, September 3, 1864
General Braxton Bragg, Richmond:

On the evening of the 30th the enemy made a lodgment across Flint river, near Jonesborough. We attacked them on the evening of the 31st with two corps, failing to dislodge them. This made it necessary to abandon Atlanta, which was done on the night of September 1. Our loss on the evening of the 31st was so small that it is evident that our effort was not a vigorous one. On the evening of September 1 General Hardee's corps, in position at Jonesborough, was assaulted by a superior force of the enemy, and being outflanked was forced to withdraw during the night to this point, with the loss of 8 pieces of artillery. The enemy's prisoners report their loss very severe. I send a bearer of dispatches to-morrow.

J. B. Hood, General [1]

September 3, 1864-2:05 p.m.
Major-General Smith
Commanding Georgia State Troops:

Let your command move quietly and steadily to Griffin, covering the artillery. In case of a raid against that place, or any other point within its vicinity, make such disposition as you may think expedient to resist it.

F. A. Shoup
Chief of Staff [1]

The evacuation of Atlanta was mass chaos. Warehouses of ordinance and supplies were set fire to prevent capture. Exploding shells, flames and smoke added to the confusion and disorder of the retreat. Hood's reserve ordinance train was stranded on the Macon Railroad Line due to tracks having been destroyed by the Yankees. The train was blown up.

Hood's ordinance train, burned to prevent capture by the Federals
during the evacuation of Atlanta.

It was reported the exploding shells in the fire could be heard from thirty miles away and that the bright flashes from the explosions lit up the night sky. Almost the entire reserve supply of artillery ammunition, over

14,000 rounds had gone up in smoke. Baxter's Company had no horses or harness with which to move their cannon. Horses had been promised, but never arrived. Colonel Melancthon Smith was ordered to remove the artillery from Hardee's Corp and the Georgia Militia to which Baxter's Company was assigned. Smith was able to salvage twelve of the twenty-eight Militia guns by having his teams of horses pull two cannon per team. Before the withdrawal was complete, mules were brought in to pull the remaining guns. All the guns except the siege guns were saved from capture. [1]

General Gustavus Smith reported the Georgia State Militia Troops served as rear guard on the retreat from Atlanta and guarded the reserve artillery until it reached Griffin. [1]

Baxter's Company remained in Griffin a few days and again were on the march heading one hundred mile to Macon. Where they had again been assigned to post duty. Part of the men rode the train to Macon with the artillery. [1]

Baxter lost nine men during the evacuation of Atlanta. Some became separated from the company, others were reported as having deserted. Private John M. Kane and Private Benjamin Terrell were captured September 1 in Atlanta. Kane was later exchanged. Terrell was sent to prison at Camp Douglas, IL. where he died of chronic diarrhea on February 2, 1865. Private Ira Castleman was captured near Atlanta September 4. Private James Barnhill was captured near Atlanta September 5. Both were sent to Camp Douglas where they died. Barnhill died on November 13, 1864 of typhoid fever and pneumonia. Castleman died on December 5, 1864. Private Elisha Varden and Jesse White were reported as deserted near Jonesboro, Georgia on September 7. both were taken to Camp Douglas. Varden "galvanized", joining the 5th United States Volunteers on April 6, 1865. White told his captors that: " he was conscripted and never wanted to join the rebel army, that he deserted to take advantage of the offer of amnesty." White remained in Camp Douglas the remainder of the war. He was released on May 12, 1865 and returned to Dickson County. Family members recalled him being very thin upon his return home.[23, 15]

Privates John and Lindrey Norris, brothers from Fayette County, Georgia were captured at Decatur, Georgia on September 9. John was imprisoned at Camp Douglas, where he died of chronic diarrhea on February 4, 1865. Lindrey took the oath of allegiance at a Military Prison Hospital in Chattanooga December 5, 1864. Their other brother,

Private Reuben Norris was wounded by a shell fragment near Jonesboro, ending his military service.   Reuben never knew the true fate of his brothers, thinking that both had been killed in action.   He survived the war and drew a Georgia Confederate pension for his service.[23,6]

Most of the Georgia recruits in Baxter's Battery were from the Atlanta area of: Fulton, Fayette, Campbell, Henry, Clayton and Paulding Counties.   During the retreat from Atlanta the men were passing through their home area and could have easily deserted and returned home, none did.   All the Georgia recruits, with the exception of the Norris brothers, proceeded with the battery to Macon.[23]

Private James Hall of Williamson County and Private Andrew J. May of Claiborne County, Tennessee had been left behind sick during the evacuation of Atlanta and were captured.   Private William Bethshears had visited Hall in the hospital the night before Atlanta was evacuated. Hall took the oath of allegiance October 26, 1864 in Nashville.   No record was found of May taking the oath.   The last service record on Private John F. Cain of Morgan Co., Alabama shows him hospitalized in Atlanta on August 15, 1865.   No record of his taking the oath was found.[23]

Baxter's Battery had been heavily engaged with the Federal Batteries from Illinois during the July 22 Battle of Atlanta.   Their accounts of the campaign:

No. 485

Report of Lieut. George Echte, Second Missouri Light Artillery, commanding Battery A, First Illinois Light Artillery.
HDQRS. COMPANY A, FIRST ILLINOIS LIGHT ARTILLERY
In the Field, Ga., September 6, 1864

Sir:

I have the honor to report to you the part taken by this battery in this campaign, commencing May 1, 1864, but it is impossible for me to give minute detail of the part taken May 1, 1864 to July 24, 1864, as I was not in command of the battery at that time, and no books or papers were found on my taking command.

The battery marched from Larkinville, Ala., under command of Capt. P. P. Wood, with the division commanded by Brig. Gen. M. L. Smith, to Chattanooga, Tenn., and took an active part in the battles of Resaca May 13, near Dallas from May 26 to 31; Big Shanty, June 10; Kennesaw Mountain, June 20, and fought more or less until July 2, 1864.   When the enemy evacuated Kennesaw Mountain the battery moved, with the division, through Marietta, Ga.   July 12, Batteries A and B were consolidated, and First Lieut. Samuel S. Smith assigned to command. The cause of this consolidation was the expiration of the term of service of most of the men of the two batteries, and they, with all the officers, were sent to Springfield, Ill., to be mustered out of the service of the United States.   July 22, the battery was engaged in battle near Atlanta, Ga.   The enemy made a successful assault on our left, which was held by the Fifteenth and Seventeenth Corps, succeeding in taking our line of works and with it the consolidated battery of company A, First Illinois Light Artillery.   This was a dear-bought victory for the enemy.   Battery A lost heavy in men and horses.   The casualties of the company were 32 men killed, wounded and captured, mostly killed; Second Lieutenant Raub was killed; First Lieut. Samuel S. Smyth was taken prisoner and reported killed, while being taken to the rear, by one of our own bullets. Shortly afterward our line advanced and drove the enemy from the works they had taken, and recaptured 2 of the six guns of the battery.   The enemy succeeded in drawing away four of them.

It was at this time, July 23, that I was assigned to the command of the battery by general orders from Fifteenth Army Corps headquarters, dated July 23, 1864. After having received, from the First Iowa Battery, two more guns, with horses and equipments, and from regiments of the First Brigade thirty-three infantrymen, the battery, July 24 was again in "fighting trim." On the night of the 26th of July marched from the extreme left to our extreme right, a distance of fifteen miles. Arrived at our destination July 28.   At noon the enemy's skirmishers were found and fighting began.   After our forces had driven the enemy about one mile they were found in strong force.   Preparations were immediately made to fight the enemy.   Only one section was withdrawn, by order of Major Maurice, chief of artillery of the Fifteenth Army Corps.

The battery was in different positions before Atlanta, Ga., doing good execution with shot and spherical case-shot, until August 26, when at night our army left the works and marched on the Sandtown road toward Jonesborough.

We arrived in the vicinity, near Flint River, and the battery was engaged in the battles on the 31st of August and 1st September; three horses were killed during the two days.

The battery was at this time in a very needy condition, and a quantity of ordnance and quartermaster's stores are required to fill up deficiencies in order to put the battery in complete condition.   At the same time I beg leave to report that sixteen men belonging to this battery are on detached service in different places within the department, and as these men are needed to complete the required number of a four-gun battery, I respectfully request that the same be returned to the battery or other men in place of them.

I am, sir, very respectfully, your obedient servant.

GEO. ECHTE
First Lieut. Company F, Second Missouri Light Artillery
Commanding Company A, First Illinois Light Artillery
Capt. G. Lofland
Asst. Adjt. Gen., Second Division, 15th Army Corps [1]

No. 486
Report of Capt. Francis De Gress, Battery H, First Illinois Light Argillery

HDQRS. BATTERY H, FIRST ILLINOIS LIGHT ARTY.
Near Jonesborough, Ga., September 1, 1864

Sir:

I have the honor to lay before you a report of the part taken by my battery during this campaign. My battery arrived at Larkinsville, April 30 from veteran furlough, and started on this campaign, May 1, poorly supplied with horses and material. Passing through Rossville on the 6th, we marched without opposition through Snake Creek Gap, and went into position at the cross-roads, about three miles from Resaca, and I was placed in position on Bald Hill, with the First Division, to fire at the railroad bridge. A rebel battery of eight guns, in a fort 1,100 yards off, opened on me, and after a lively duel I succeeded in silencing it; had 3 men wounded by pieces of shell-Private John Olson, in arm; Private August Johnson, in foot; Private William H. Case breast. Remained in position on the same hill, supporting our advancing infantry by firing at the rebel batteries, rifle-pits, and railroad bridge, until the morning of the 16th, when we went into Resaca, which the enemy had evacuated the night previous. Started again at 11 a. m. marching on Calhoun Road and crossed the Catahoula (Oostenaula) River at 4:30 p. m.; marched until the 19th of May, when we went into camp one mile and a half south of Kingston, where we remained until the 23rd.

Crossed the Etowah River, and marched without much opposition until we arrived at Dallas on the 26th; then after changing position several times during the day, and having 1 man (John A. Anderson) wounded in knee, on the 27th I was placed in position by Colonel Taylor, with the Fourth Division, to engage a rebel battery of eight guns 1,200 yards off. Fought several brisk duels during the day, and on the 28th the enemy charged along our whole front, but was repulsed with heavy loss. Had 3 men wounded-Corpl. John J. Buckland, in shoulder; Artificer Frederic Dohmeyer in shoulder; Private John Haggerstrom, shoulder. On the 29th 8 p.m. took battery to the rear, in a new line of works, to protect our corps, which was to swing back that night; but this was not done until 1st of June, when we marched to the left and relieved the Twentieth Army Corps. Went into position on 2nd in the center of our division. Withdrew on the 4th, and took up a position with the fourth Army Corps, relieving the Eleventh Indiana Battery.

The enemy evacuated during the night, and we marched for Acworth on the 5th, where we arrived on the 6th, and remained until the 10th, when we advanced on Kennesaw Mountain, passed Big Shanty 9 a.m. and went into position. Remained in reserve with division until the 15th, when I was ordered to assist the Seventeenth Army corps batteries. On the 16th went into position, with the Second Brigade, in front of Kennesaw Mountain and fought the enemy's batteries on top of Big Kennesaw. Fought duels every day; also fired at their camp at long range until the 30th, when I withdrew my battery and parked with our corps, then in reserve.

July 2, marched with the division to the extreme right of our line and went into position, relieving a battery of the Twenty-third Army Corps. July 3, went into position to engage rebel battery while the Second Brigade, of our division, charged their line at Nickajack Creek. July 4, moved to the front, with the division, to support the Sixteenth Army Corps, which charged about 5 p. m. July 5, marched on Sandtown road, and went into position on a high hill with the Seventeenth Army Corps; fired at a rebel fort and battery 3,500 yards off with good effect. July 6, seeing a dust suppose to be made by a column marching and crossing Chattahoochee River on a pontoon bridge, about 5,000 yards distant, we shelled them all afternoon, and as prisoners afterward said, with very good effect. July 7, went into position in the advanced line with the Seventeenth Army corps, and engaged the rebel batteries. Withdrew on the 8th in the evening and remained in camp until the 12th, when we marched, passing through Marietta on the 13th, and parked again near Roswell, on the Chattahoochee River. Crossed the river on the 14th and went into position. While our infantry threw up very strong works. Remained here until 17th, when we started for the Augusta railroad. Struck the road on the 18th and went into position at night. Advanced again the following morning and took up position in Decatur about 4 p.m. Advanced on the 20th, taking up position several times during the day and engaging rebel batteries. At 1 o'clock fired three shells into Atlanta at a distance of two miles and a half, the first ones of the war. On the 21st went into position (under protest) with a range of only ten yards, and in front of our line of works, by order of Brig. Gen. M. L. Smith. July 22, advanced again, and occupying the works evacuated by the enemy the night previous. I went into position at the extreme right of our division to engage three rebel batteries which were firing at our advancing columns; was ordered to keep up a continuous fire. There was a gap of at least 800 yards between my battery and the First Division, which fact I reported several times. The enemy charged our works about 4 p.m.; was repulsed in my front, but broke through our center, and changing front charged my battery, which I was obliged to leave after spiking the guns, and after all my support had left me. As soon as my battery was recaptured I had the guns unspiked and fired again at the retreating enemy. One of my guns, injured since the 25th of June, burst at the third round. My losses on that day were very heavy-14 men (3 killed, 3 wounded, 8 captured), 39 horses, 1 limber, ambulance and harness. Replaced lost horses and harness from Battery A, and had battery in marching order by 9 o'clock the following day. July 27, withdrew the battery and marched all night, with division, to the extreme right of our line; went into position in rear or our line, advanced into position July 31, firing at the rebel forts and city.

Took up position again in our new line of works August 3, and fired considerable at rebel batteries, rifle and skirmish pits; had 2 men wounded on the 13th. Remained in same position until the night of the 26th, when we withdrew, and marched all night, went into camp August 27. Started again the following day and went into camp about 2 p.m. on the West Point railroad. Started again on the 30th, and although our infantry was skirmishing continually, marched 12 miles. Battery crossed Flint River about 9 a.m. on the 31st and went into position to protect the flank; fired considerable at the rebel columns moving and rifle-pits. The enemy charged our line about 4 p.m., and moving one gun to the rifle-pits, fired twenty-seven rounds of canister; had 1 man wounded by shell, Private Henry Rahmeyer.

September 1, moved one section to the extreme left of our line to engage the enemy's batteries firing at the Fourteenth Army Corps, which was advancing; lost 1 man killed, Corpl. Frank Whistler. September 2, marched through Jonesborough, following up the enemy who had evacuated the night previous, and went into camp and returned to Jonesborough.

This campaign has been a very severe one on my battery, especially as I started out unprepared, caused by circumstances, and being continually in the field and in position, could not supply my horses with such forage as the country would furnish, and was often without forage altogether. [1]

HDQRS. LEFT WING, SIXTEENTH ARMY CORPS,
East Point, Ga., September 14, 1864

I have the honor to make the following report of prisoners of war captured by this command and deserters coming within the lines during the campaign from May 1 to September 14, 1864:   Total number captured, 727, number forwarded for exchange, 672; died in hospital of wounds, 27; transferred to hospital in Marietta, Ga., 26, left in hospital at Jonesborough, Ga., wounded, 2. Total number of deserters disposed of, 727.

Very Respectfully,
H. L. Burnham
Captain and Provost Marshall [1]

No. 722

Report of Majl Gen. Gustavus W. Smith, C. S. Army, commanding Georgia militia, of operations June 1-September 15

HEADQUARTERS FIRST DIVISION GEORGIA MILITIA

Macon, Ga., September 15, 1864

General:

I have the honor to make the following report of the part taken by the Georgia militia under my command during the operations at and near Atlanta:

My appointment was dated 1st June. I took command a few days thereafter, relieving Major-General Wayne, who returned to the duties of his office as adjutant and inspector general of the State. The force then in the field was composed entirely of State officers, civil and military. They had been formed into two brigades of three regiments each and one battalion of artillery, numbering in all a little over 3,000 men. The officers of the militia not needed for these regiments took their places in the ranks as privates with the civil officers. The command had reported to General J. E. Johnston for duty, and had been ordered to guard the crossings of the Chattahoochee River, from Roswell bridge to West Point, which duty they continued to perform until ordered by General Johnston to cross the Chattahoochee and support the cavalry upon the left wing of his army, the right wing then being at Kennesaw Mountain.

In the execution of this order the militia were twice brought in conflict with largely superior forces of the enemy's infantry. They behaved well-thoroughly executed the part assigned them, and when the army fell back to the Chattahoochee, they were the last infantry withdrawn to the fortified position. General Johnston in a letter to Governor Brown paid a handsome, and I think, well deserved, compliment to them for their conduct beyond the river and their services in beating back the enemy in their attempts upon the various crossings.

The day we reached the Chattahoochee we were assigned to your corps of the army. You soon placed us in reserve, which it was thought would give some opportunity for drilling and disciplining the command, no opportunity for this having previously occurred.

In the mean time the reserve militia of Georgia were ordered out by Governor Brown, and I was ordered to Poplar Springs, near the Atlanta and West Point Railroad, for the purpose of reorganizing, arming the reserves & c. We had had not been there three days before you found it necessary to order us into the trenches of the east side of Atlanta. You had in the meanwhile been assigned to the command of the army and instructed me to report to you direct, instead of through a corps commander. There were at this time about 2,000 effective muskets in the command. We guarded over two miles of lines, having on them, however, some eighty pieces of Confederate artillery.

On the 22 d July, while Hardee was attacking the enemy on our extreme right in the direction of Decatur, you ordered the troops on my left to advance. Without waiting for orders I closed the intervals in my line, formed line of battle in the trenches, and moved the militia forward over the parapet more than a mile against the enemy's strong works in our front. They were directed upon a battery which had annoyed us very much. Captain Anderson, who had served with my command beyond the Chattahoochee, volunteered to move his battery with us. He took position in clear, open ground within 400 yards of the embrasure battery of the enemy, supported by the militia upon his right and left. Within ten minutes the effective fire of the enemy was silenced in our front, and after this they only occasionally ventured to show themselves at the embrasures or put their heads above the parapet. My troops were eager to be allowed to charge the battery, but the brigade upon my left had given way, and though falling back, was extending still farther to the left. Hardee's fire, upon my right, had ceased just after we moved out of the trenches. I considered it useless to make an isolated attack, and therefore held the position, awaiting further developments. In about two hours I received orders from you directing me to withdraw to the trenches. We lost only about 50 men killed and wounded.

The officers and men behaved admirably. Every movement was promptly and accurately made. There was not a single straggler.

A few days after this affair of the 22d of July I was ordered again to Poplar Springs, but was scarcely established in camp there before we had again to be placed in the trenches on the left of the Marietta road, and from this time until the end of the siege continued under close fire night and day. We had to move from one portion of the lines to another, and had our full share of all the hardest places, extending from the left of the Marietta road across the Peach Tree road to our extreme right.

The militia, although but poorly armed—very few having proper equipments, more than two-thirds of them without cartridge-boxes— almost without ambulances or other transportation, most of the reserves never having been drilled at all, and the others but a few days—all performed well every service required during an arduous and dangerous campaign. They have been in service about 100 days, during at least fifty of which they have been under close fire of the enemy mostly night and day. They have always shown a willing spirit, whether in camp, on the march, working at fortifications, guarding trenches, or upon the open battle-field. They have done good and substantial service in the cause of their country, and have established the fact that Georgia is willing and able to do something effective in her own name beyond furnishing more than her quota to the Confederate armies proper. The greatest number of effective muskets in the trenches at any one time was about 5,000.

When Atlanta was evacuated the reserve artillery of the army passed out through my lines, my men were formed as a rear guard. The whole was safely brought to Griffin under your orders.

The march from Atlanta to Griffin satisfied me that men over fifty are not as a class fitted for military duty. I have therefore strongly advised the Governor to withdraw them from continuous active service. There being a lull in active operations the Governor has, with my recommendation and your concurrence, temporarily withdrawn the militia from Confederate service and furloughed them for thirty days. This report is hastily written without access to the detailed records and papers of my adjutant-general's office, but all omissions can be readily supplied by the returns, & c., already forwarded to your office.

Before closing I cannot refrain form alluding to a subject which, under ordinary circumstances, forms no part of reports of subordinates to their commanders. I allude to the outcry from the press and the people against yourself because of the evacuation of Atlanta.

Unsolicited by me, without my consent or knowledge, the civil and military officers of the State of Georgia, when called upon to take up arms in defense of their homes, almost unanimously elected me their leader, and as their leader I wish in this report to say to you and place officially on record this opinion, viz: Had your orders been properly executed either upon the 20th of July at Peach Tree Creek, the 22nd of July on our right, or on the 30th of August at Jonesborough, Sherman would have been foiled and Atlanta saved, at least for some time to come, and I am not alone in this opinion. Commanding a peculiar organization, the ranking officer in the forces of the State within which you were operating, I was invited to and participated in your councils. I had every opportunity of knowing what was going on. Your plans were fully explained to your lieutenant-generals, your chief of artillery, chief engineer, and myself. Opinions and views were called for, and then specific orders were given. I have never known one of them to express dissent to any plan of yours that was attempted to be executed, never a doubt expressed as to the meaning and intent of your orders, nor a suggestion made by them of a plan they supposed would be better than you ordered. If they are not now unanimous there is but one, if any, who dissents from the opinion expressed above, viz: Sherman would have been beaten had your orders been obeyed on the 20th and 22nd of July, or 30th of August. Whatever the press or the people may say, the militia of Georgia are more than satisfied with you as their Confederate general, and when they again enter that service in defense of their homes will be glad to hail you as their Confederate chief.

G. W. SMITH, Major-General [1]

The Left Wing of the 16th U. S. Army Corp reported expending the following ammunition during the Atlanta campaign: 3,674 rounds for 12-pounder light gun, 910 rounds in 10- pounder Parrot gun, 300 rounds for 3-inch Parrott gun, 1,174 rounds for 4 ½ siege gun, 714,130 rounds elongated 58 caliber ball cartridges, 88,500 rounds 44 caliber Henry rifle cartridges, and 11,088 rounds 52 caliber Spencer rifle cartridges. Approximate average of 350 rounds, per man for the actual force in the field. The Second Division of the 16th Army Corp suffered 2,752 casualties in the Atlanta Campaign. [1]

The Union Army occupied Atlanta on September 2, 1864 and the United States flag was raised over the city. General Sherman proposed to remove all citizens from the city. The order was strongly opposed by General Hood and Atlanta Mayor James M. Calhoun. The two Generals exchanged heated correspondence on the order. Sherman stuck by his decision and it was approved by Chief of Staff Halleck.

HDQRS. MILITARY DIVISION OF THE MISSISSIPPI
Atlanta, Ga., September 20, 1864
Maj. Gen. H. W. Halleck, Chief of Staff, Washington, D.C.:

GENERAL:

I have the honor here within to submit copies of a correspondence between General Hood, of the Confederate army, the mayor of Atlanta, and myself touching the removal of the inhabitants of Atlanta. In explanation of the tone which marks some of these letters I will call your attention to the fact that after I had announced my determination General Hood took upon himself to question my motive. I could not tamely submit to such impertinence, and I have seen that in violation of all official usage he has published in the Macon newspapers such parts of the correspondence as suited his purpose. This could have had no other object than to create a feeling on the part of the people, but if he expects to resort to such artifices I think I can meet him there too. It is sufficient for my Government to know that the removal of the inhabitants has been made with liberality and fairness; that is has been attended by no force, and that no women or children have suffered, unless for want of provisions by their natural protectors and friends. My real reasons for this step were, we want all the houses of Atlanta for military storage and occupation. We want to contract the lines of defenses so as to diminish the garrison to limit necessary to defend its narrow and vital parts instead of embracing, as the lines now do, the vast suburbs. This contraction of the lines, with the necessary citadels and redoubts, will make it necessary to destroy the very houses used by families as residences. Atlanta is a fortified town, was stubbornly defended and fairly captured. As captors we have a right to it. The residence here of a poor population would compel us to sooner or later to feed them or see them starve under our eyes. The residence here of the families of our enemies would be a temptation and a means to keep up a correspondence dangerous and hurtful to our cause, and a civil population calls for provost guards, and absorbs the attention of officers in listening to everlasting complaints and special grievances that are not military. These are my reasons, and if satisfactory to the Government of the United States it makes no difference whether it pleases General Hood and his people or not.

I am, with respect, your obedient servant,
W. T. SHERMAN, Major-General, Commanding [1]

HDQRS. MILITARY DIVISION OF THE MISSISSIPPI
In the Field, Atlanta, Ga., September 7, 1864
General Hood, Commanding Confederate Army:
GENERAL:

I have deemed it to the interest of the United States that the citizens now residing in Atlanta should remove, those who prefer to go south and the rest north. For the latter I can provide food and transportation to points of their election in Tennessee, Kentucky, or farther north. For former I can provide transportation by cars as far as Rough and Ready, and also wagons; but that their removal may be made with as little discomfort as possible it will be necessary for you to help the families from Rough and Ready to the cars at Lovejoy's. If you consent I will undertake to remove all families in Atlanta who prefer to go South to Rough and Ready, with all their moveable effects, viz, clothing, trunks reasonable furniture, bedding, &c., with their servants, white and black, with the privo that no force shall be used toward the blacks one way or the other. If they want to go with their masters or mistresses they may do so, otherwise they will be sent away, unless they be men, when they may be employed by our quartermaster. Atlanta is no place for families or non-combatants, and I have no desire to send them North if you will assist in conveying them South. If this proposition meets your views I will consent to a truce in the neighborhood of Rough and Ready, stipulating that any wagons, horses, or animals, or persons sent there for the purposes herein stated shall in no manner be harmed or molested, you in your turn agreeing that any cars, wagons, carriages, persons, or animals sent to the same point shall not be interfered with. Each of us might send a guard of, say, 100 men, to maintain order and limit the truce, to, say, two days after a certain time appointed. I have authorized the mayor to choose two citizens to convey to you this letter and such documents as the mayor may forward in explanation, and shall await your reply.

I have the honor to be, your obedient servant.
W. T. SHERMAN, Major-General, Commanding[1]

Washington, September 28, 1864
Major-General Sherman, Atlanta, Ga.

GENERAL:

Your communications of the 20th in regard to the removal of families from Atlanta and the exchange of prisoners, and also the official report of your campaign, are just received. I have not had time as yet to examine your report. The course which you have pursued in removing rebel families from Atlanta and in the exchange of prisoners is fully approved by the War Department. Not only are you justified by the laws and usages of war in removing these people, but I think it was your duty to your own army to do so. Moreover, I am fully of opinion that the nature of your position, the character of the war, the conduct of the enemy, and especially of non-combatants and women of the territory which we have heretofore conquered and occupied, will justify you in gathering up all the forage and provisions which your army may require both for a siege of Atlanta and for your supply in your march farther into the enemy's country. Let the disloyal families of the country thus stripped go to their husbands, fathers, and natural protectors in the rebel ranks. We have tried three years for conciliation and kindness without any reciprocation. On the contrary, those thus treated have acted as spies and guerrillas in our rear and within our lines. The safety of our armies and proper regard for the lives of our soldiers require that we apply inexorable foes the severe rules of war. We certainly are not required to treat the so-called non-combatants and rebels better than they themselves treat each other. Even here in Virginia, within fifty miles of Washington, they strip their own families of provisions, leaving them as our army advances to be fed by us or to starve within our lines. We have fed this class of people long enough. Let them go to their husbands and fathers in the rebel ranks, and if they won't go we must send them to their friends and natural protectors. I would destroy every mill and factory within my reach which I did not want for my own use. This the rebels have done, not only in Maryland and Pennsylvania, but also in Virginia and other rebel states, when compelled to fall back before our armies. In many sections of the country they have not left a mill to grind grain for their own suffering families, lest we might use them to supply our own armies. We must do the same, I have endeavored to impress these views upon our commanders for the last two years. You are almost the only one who has properly applied them. I do not approve of General Hunter's course of burning private houses or uselessly destroying private property-that is barbarous; but I approve of taking or destroying whatever may serve as supplies to us or to the enemy's armies.

Very respectfully, your obedient servant
H. W. HALLECK,
Major-General and chief of Staff. [1]

The Atlanta campaign had been another costly event in the number of soldiers killed and wounded. Among the casualties was Major Phillip Van Horn Weems of the 11th Tennessee Infantry Regiment. Weems, whose family owned the Bon Aqua Springs Hotel in Hickman County died from wounds received in the Battle of Atlanta while rallying his troops. He was buried in the Griffin, Georgia Confederate Cemetery. Family members moved his body in a vinegar barrel back to the family cemetery at Bon Aqua Springs after the war. Other casualties in the 11th Infantry at Atlanta: Sgt. Sterling Capps and Private Dickson Gentry, were killed at New Hope Church, as was Private George K. Freeman of Company C. Private James Pitts Hunter of Company E, and Privates James R. McClelland and Hugh J. McNeily of Company C and Private John Goodwin of Company K were killed July 22 at Atlanta. Private Silas Tidwell of Company K, older brother of Soloman Tidwell of Baxter's Battery, was killed at Lovejoy's Station. Captain F.F. Tidwell of Company K received his third wound of the war at Atlanta. [18]

The Hickman County men of Company H 11th Tennessee Infantry Regiment also suffered heavy casualties at Atlanta: Captain Jacob H. Johnson was killed July 22 at Atlanta. Privates S. H. Ballard, Floy Harris, and Daniel Montgomery were killed in the Battle of Jonesboro. Privates Harry Gordon and Jasper Rochell were killed at New Hope Church. Privates Armistead Martin and Thomas Benton Petty were killed at Atlanta. In the Battle of Peach Tree Creek Private Joseph Chandler was killed and Private John H. Barr was wounded. [21]

Companies B & F of the 42nd Tennessee Infantry Regiment from Hickman County also shed their blood in the heavy Atlanta fighting.

Captain George A. Lowe, Private Richard Cude and Private Asa Pell were killed at Atlanta. Captain Benjamin F. Coleman was killed at New Hope Church. Private Stephen E. Carothers had an eye shot out at Kennesaw Mountain. Cpl. Samuel Carothers and Private William Lynn were wounded at Kennesaw Mountain. Private James D. Murphree lost a leg from an Atlanta wound. Privates John Wilkins and James Blackwell were also wounded at Atlanta. [21]

The Williamson County boys in Company H 20th Tennessee Infantry Regiment also took a big hit in the Atlanta Campaign. Private John Murphy was killed at Atlanta. Lieutenant James H. White received a wound at Atlanta. Private John Jones was killed at Jonesboro. Lieutenant R. B. Hughes, Sgt. Jesse Short, and Private James Vowel were wounded at Jonesboro. Private Joe Fox lost an arm due to an Atlanta wound. Private Bryant E. Fox lost a leg in the Battle of New Hope Church. Privates Dub Smith and Phillip Southall were wounded at Resaca. Private Martin Stoval was wounded at Kennesaw Mountain and Private Nathan Morris was wounded at Peach Tree Creek. [19]

Colonel Harrison Lampley of the 45th Alabama Infantry, a resident of Louisville in Barbour County, Alabama, had been wound and captured at Atlanta on July 22, 1864. He died from his wounds a few days later while in Federal captivity. Colonel Lampley was a cousin to several of the men in Baxter's Company.[2]

Colonel Harrison Lampley 45th Alabama Infantry Regiment

The men in Baxter's Battery had again been lucky in having no men killed and only a few wounded during the siege and battles of Atlanta, after two months of almost constant exposure to enemy shelling and gun fire.

Many of the wounded from the Atlanta Campaign were sent to hospitals in Macon. Baxter's Company was assigned to post duty at Macon where they would spend the remainder of the war.

Atlanta Depot Before the Battle

Atlanta Depot after being burned by Sherman's men.

CHAPTER 5

MACON

Baxter's Company arrived at Camp Oglethorpe outside Macon on September 12, 1864. Camp Oglethorpe had been used as a prison camp for captured Union officers and had recently been closed. The company crossed the Ocmulgee River and was assigned to duty at East Macon on the Clinton Road. In East Macon, at the time Baxter's Company arrived, a defensive line with five redoubts was being constructed between the Ocmulgee River and Walnut Creek. In the defensive line was Fort Hawkins, a pioneer era fort built in 1806, which had been refurbished and armed with ten cannon. The Georgia Central Railroad track ran through the line. Just outside the line was a Great Temple Mound built by ancient Indians, inside the line was an earth lodge built by the Indians.

The post of Macon was commanded by Brig. General Marcus J. Wright. The Department of Georgia was commanded by Major General Howell Cobb. The post was manned principally by Georgia State Militia troops who had come to Macon after the fall of Atlanta and continued to be commanded in the field by Major General Gustavus W. Smith. Smith's command was estimated at 2,800 infantry, 3 batteries of artillery, and 250 local reserve cavalry. Many of Smith's soldiers were old men and young boys. There were a number of convalescent troops in Macon, along with the Army of Tennessee reserve artillery, which included Baxter's Battery. Lieutenant General Joseph Wheeler also had about 2,000 cavalrymen in Georgia. [1]

Major General Howell Cobb, Commander of the Department of Georgia

Four battalions of Army of Tennessee Reserve Artillery were sent from Atlanta to bolster the defenses of Macon: Palmer's, Martin's, William's and Waddell's. These battalions brought 42 guns with them to Macon. The horses in the best condition were sent with the main army and the horses in poorer condition were sent to the rear to be recuperated. Baxter's Battery was assigned to Martin's Battalion, commanded by Captain Robert Martin who also commanded Martin's (Howell's) Georgia Battery. Having no horses, Baxter was assigned four 12-pound howitzers to be manned as a stationary battery. Baxter's Battery was again under the command of Lt. Colonel J.H. Hallonquist who commanded the reserve artillery at Macon.[1]

September 12, 1864, 1st Lieutenant John Marshall, Jr. placed a requisition for fuel for the company. The requisition showed the company was manned with 151 non-commissioned officers, musicians and privates, 2 servants and laundresses, three lieutenants, and the captain. Requisition for forage showed the company with no publicly owned horses and only one privately owned horse, Captain Baxter's. This was the only supply requisition of the war which listed servants and laundresses as being part of the company.[23]

With little activity to occupy their time in camp, many of the men worked in the Macon Confederate Arsenal Laboratory manufacturing ammunition. The men were paid $3 per day for their labor. For the period from September 20 to September 30, 1864, Lt. Herrin received payment of $672 for 224 man/days of labor in the arsenal by the men in Baxter's Company. For services rendered the following named non-commissioned officers and privates of Captain Baxter's Battery of Artillery in making ammunition at Macon Arsenal Laboratory: Serg. Buttrey 9 days, Corp. Spencer 6, Sweeney 4 ½, White 6 ½, Green 8, Beard 8, Biggs 8, Beck 7 ¼, Buttrey 5, Clarke 8 ½, Callahan 7, Edwards 6 ¼, Forhand 7 ¼, Hooper 5, Johnson 9, King 4, Kimberly 6 ½, Langford 7 ¼, Lewis 8 ½, Laughlin 5, Nall 5, Parker 3, Richardson 6 ½, Sawyers 3, Sullivan 4, Tally 5, Tidwell 5, Hall 4, Houston 4, Ladd 6, Wray 6, McCowan 5 ½, Parker 8 ½, Tidwell 6, Thompson 7, Hadaway 5, Ladd 4, & McAllister 2.[23]

Macon Confederate Arsenal & Laboratory

Union Major General George Stoneman's cavalry had made an unsuccessful assault on the city of Macon in late July 1864.

No. 723
Report of Maj. Gen. Howell Cobb, C. S. Army,
of operations July 30 and 31 (Stoneman's raid).
Macon, Ga., August 1, 1864 (Received 2d)

General Stoneman, with a cavalry force estimated at 2,800, with artillery, was met two miles from this city by our forces, composed of Georgia reserves, citizens, local companies, and the militia, which Governor Brown is organizing here. The enemy's assault was repulsed and his force held in check along our entire line all day. Retiring toward Clinton, he was attacked the next morning by General Iverson, who, routed the main body, captured General Stoneman and 500 prisoners. His men are still capturing stragglers.

HOWELL COBB,
Major-General. [1]

Macon was a bustling town in September 1864. Many of the wounded soldiers from Atlanta had been moved to hospitals in Macon. Macon ranked second only to Richmond as the city with the most hospital space in the Confederacy. Ocmulgee Hospital was the largest in Macon, originally built to accommodate 300 patients, the capacity had been expanded to care for 600 patients. Macon's City Hall and the Georgia School for the Blind had both been converted to hospitals. The Floyd House Hospital was also a major medical facility. The overflowing hospital population had been supplemented with tent hospitals. Over 1,100 sick and wounded soldiers had been moved from Macon to hospitals in Columbus and Guyton, Georgia. Civilian refugees from Atlanta also flocked to Macon. The Confederate Arsenal in Macon, like the arsenals in Augusta, Georgia; Columbus, Georgia and Selma, Alabama were busy trying to take up the slack in the production of ordinance and supplies of the lost Atlanta Arsenal. Colonel Moses H. Wright, Baxter's adversary in Atlanta had been appointed to command the Macon Arsenal. [1]

Other than Stoneman's raid, Macon had been little effected by the war up to late 1864. Other than housing Union Prisoners at Fort Oglethorpe and many citizens having relatives away in the rebel army, life went on as usual.   Theatre and social functions continued, churches continued holding regular services. Factories and foundries in the city were busy. The cotton plantations and farms surrounding the city were flourishing.

Macon, September 7, 1864

General Bragg:

Dispatch received. Vigorous measures have already been taken here to arrest stragglers, and orders issued requiring every man to be in some organization. Your orders will be strictly enforced, and weekly reports made.   Accounts of stragglers from Army of Tennessee are much exaggerated. Governor Harris and other reliable parties from there report the army in good condition.

Marcus J. Wright
Brigadier-General, Commanding [1]

John Dillard wrote his family in Cheatham County:

Macon, Ga
September 18, 1864

Dear Mother

I my pen in hand one more time to write you a few lines to let you know how I am at this time I am well and doing well at this time dear father (scratched out).

Mother I receive your kind letter the 15 of the month witch give me grad pleasur to hear from you all and her that you all wea well and doing well. Farther I have nothing interesting to write to you. Wea have had a nother long march from Atlanta Ga. to Macon Ga a bout one hundred miles. Wea ar about 80 miles behind the main army now. Wea have plenty to eat and plenty to war. Sunch as it is I wold like to come home and see you all a gin if I culd stay with enemys with you all I don't know when I will leave have the change to come home if I get the chance to come I will. Wea hav not had many men ill in the company yet wea had the best luck in the world God has ben with the company. Wea come back to Griffin tar wea turn over our horses and goons then was order back to Macon Ga

Wea ar her now I don't know how long wea will stay her I hope wea will stay her all this winter wea hav had a good time eating fish since wea have bin her the water ain't good as it was at lantan.

Her wea have nothing munch to doo another tell my little sister that I wold send her something if I had it to send to her mother Give my love to grand mother and all of my friends and tell the girls I don't want them all to marry befor I get home a gin I wold like to see them agin be for thee al marry tell Mr. Thompson that Jams Thompson is Well and doing well at time and all the rest of the boys at this time I hear nothing mor to write at this time only

I remaind yo Son until Death So Good by until I see you a gin

John Dillyard

You said something a bout Tom Varding it has bin over a year sens I heard from him he was in Sarvanner I don't know where he is now I will tri to find wher he is if seen and I will write to you all about him Wea lost uon of our boys on the march wea lost Elisha Varding and Jesse White and heal (?) gasmon (?) and ben tannel and James Hall Gillam them is all the boys from our county I think thea well bee exchng before long thea tran went of on this morning with a load of yankes in bee exchange I have nothing more to write at this time. So I will com to a close for this

John Dillyard [9]

On October 31, 1864 Captain Baxter was ordered on a 60- day recruiting duty by Major General Howell Cobb. Where he went or how many recruits he procured was not recorded. Records of Private George C. Randol of Mississippi County, Missouri show he was enlisted by Captain Baxter on November 14, 1864 in Corinth, Mississippi. While records on all the new recruits were either not maintained or lost at the end of the war, the number of men listed in Baxter's supply requisitions increased by 65 after this recruiting trip. [23]

November 15, 1864 after burning the business district of Atlanta, Major General William Tecumseh Sherman departed for his infamous "march to the sea". Sherman departed Atlanta with 62,000 troops; 55,000 infantry, 5,000 cavalry, and 2,000 artillery manning 64 guns. His mission was to burn a sixty- mile wide path through the heart of Georgia, break the spirit of the southern people and capture Savannah. [1]

General John Bell Hood marched his Army of Tennessee northward for an invasion of Tennessee, hoping to capture Nashville with its abundant supply base and refit and add recruits to his army. [1]

Sherman split his army into two columns. The left column was commanded by Major General Henry W. Slocum. The right column was commanded by Major General Oliver O. Howard. The left wing departed Atlanta following the tracks of the Atlanta and Augusta Railroad. The right wing moved south toward Columbus and Macon. [1]

After burning the town of Blountville to the ground, General Howard was ordered by General Sherman to make a demonstration against Macon in an effort to confuse the Confederates and divide their forces. [1]

Howard sent a portion of the Third Cavalry Division under the command of Brigadier General Hugh J. Kilpatrick toward Macon to attack and capture the city if possible. Kilpatrick ordered Colonel Smith D. Atkins to make the assault on Macon with the Second Brigade. On the afternoon of November 20, 1864, Atkin's force of less than 2,000 cavalry and Captain Yates V. Beebe's Tenth Wisconsin Battery attacked East Macon. [1]

The Confederate works at East Macon were manned with between 1,000 and 1,200 troops consisting of Georgia State Militia, convalescent troops from Camp Wright, a volunteer company from the Georgia Blind School Hospital and Army of Tennessee Reserve Artillery including: Curry's, Bellamy's, Guist's, Howell's, Palmer's, River's and Baxter's Batteries. Having no horses with which to move their guns, Baxter's Company and other horseless batteries were deployed as infantry in the battle. [1]

At about 3:30 p.m., the Wisconsin Battery opened fire on the Confederate works, opening the battle known by the Confederates as the second Battle of Dunlap's Hill and by the Federals as the Battle of Walnut Creek Bridge. River's and Howell's Confederate batteries answered the fire. Colonel T. M. Colmes, Commander of the Fiftieth Tennessee Infantry Regiment and commander of Camp Wright led the Confederate forces. Colmes placed the entire force in line of battle and deployed a line of skirmishers. [1]

River's Arkansas battery in position in the road west of Walnut Creek on the East slope of Dunlap's Hill was attacked by the Tenth Ohio Cavalry and Ninety-Second Illinois Mounted Infantry. After crossing Walnut Creek, the Union troops charged up the road in columns of four. The Confederate artillerymen attempted to stop the Federals, but were hampered by faulty friction primers. The Federal Cavalry temporarily captured the redoubt and captured one 12-pound gun, but were unable to keep it due to the heavy fire from the rebels. The forward line of the

Rebels broke during the attack of the Tenth Ohio, but desperate fighting to stop the charge continued.[1]

Captain Howell's four-gun battery opened fire from Fort Hawkins in the rear of the Confederate works and poured a continuous and accurate fire into the right flank of the Tenth Ohio. Other Confederate batteries joined in the cannonading. Confederate reinforcements led by Lieutenant W.D. Hooper arrived on the battlefield and immediately joined the defensive struggle without taking time to form line of battle.

Faced with a more intense opposition than expected Atkins ordered his men to withdraw from the battlefield, giving the Confederates a defensive victory.[1]

General Joseph Wheeler and his Confederate cavalry arrived shortly after the charge was repulsed and placed two brigades of cavalry to fill in gaps in the line. The ten-man force guarding the Walnut Creek bridge had been driven away by the Ninety-second Illinois. Captain E. S. Hance of the Twenty-fourth Tennessee Infantry Regiment rushed to the bridge with a dozen troops, fired a few volleys at the Federals and pushed them back, saving the bridge from being burned.[1]

Upon leaving the battlefield, the Federals proceeded to destroy two miles of track of the Georgia Central Railroad and the adjacent telegraph wire. They also burned a pistol factory and a candle and soap factory.[1]

Captain Ed Baxter was absent on recruiting detail during the second battle at Dunlap's Hill. The battery was under the command of 1st Lieutenant John Marshall. Several of the men in the company were hospitalized in Ocmulgee Hospital during the battle. Lt. Marshall had been dismissed from the hospital on November 17.[23]

December 2, 1864 Brigadier General Archibald Gracie, Jr., the first General in command of Baxter's Battery was killed by Union artillery fire in the siege of Petersburg, Virginia. Gracie had been kind to the men of Baxter's Battery while serving as their commanding General. He had granted leave for some of the men to return home to sell their private horses, he had approved sick furloughs and kept the company well supplied with provisions. Many of the Union reports referred to him as "The Rebel Gracie". After the war, Gracie's body was moved from Virginia to Woodlawn Cemetery in his native New York City.

Headquarters Ninth Corps
December 4, 1864-10 a.m. (Received 11:25 a.m.)
General S. Williams
Assistant Adjutant-General

Everything remains about the same along our lines. The heavy firing of yesterday was caused by our people endeavoring to put a stop to the enemy's working parties. They were planting a new mortar battery on the Fort Rice and Sledgwick front. Two deserters came in last night and report that General Gracie was killed yesterday by a shell; also a captain and two men.

JNO. G. PARKE,
Major-General. [1]

HEADQUARTERS ARMY OF THE POTOMAC
December 5, 1864—1 p.m.
Lieutenant –General Grant:

Nothing of importance to report. A deserter confirms the reported death of Confederate general Gracie. Wheaton's division, of the Sixth Corps, has arrived and is relieving Crawford's of the Fifth. The divisions of the Fifth Corps, as they are relieved, will be moved outside of the rear line of works between the Weldon railroad and the Jerusalem plank road.

GEO. G. MEADE
Major-General [1]

December 12, 1864, Captain Baxter again took disciplinary action against some of his men for incompetence and neglect of duty. Sgt. Alfred McCaslin was demoted to private and replaced by Corporal William Hill. Corporal Joseph Sweeney was demoted to Private. Privates Malachia Beggs and John Forehand were promoted to Corporals to replace Hill and Sweeney. Private Richard Carney of Georgia was also promoted to Corporal to replace Corporal William Ellison who had died in Ocmulgee Hospital in October. [23]

Disease among the troops was rampant in the camps of Macon. While stationed at Macon, at least fifty-two of Baxter's men were hospitalized at Ocmulgee Hospital, several of them more than once. More of Baxter's men were hospitalized at Macon than any other location they had been stationed at during the war. Common diseases were: typhoid, recurring fever, spinal meningitis and diarrhea. Private James Gray of Clayton County, Georgia died of spinal meningitis on October 4, 1864 in Ocmulgee Hospital. Corporal William Ellison of Dickson County died in Ocmulgee Hospital on October 17, 1864. Both were buried in the Soldier's Square Section of Rose Hill Cemetery in Macon. [23]

Records show Privates William Sullivan, Tillman Lankford, William Fraisher, and Aaron Beard were hospitalized at Lumpkin Hospital in Cuthbert, Georgia in December 1864. Cuthbert is located about 120 miles from Macon. After being hospitalized at both the Floyd House and Ocmulgee Hospitals in Macon in Ootober, Private Wesley Welch was transferred to a hospital in Augusta, Georgia where he remained until rejoining the company at Macon on February 15, 1865.

Baxter's men spent their third Christmas away from home in the mild Middle Georgia climate of Macon. The main body of the Army of Tennessee, after suffering heavy losses at Franklin on November 30, had endured one of the coldest first two weeks of December on record in Nashville. Temperatures were sub freezing, with ice, snow and howling winds. The main Army spent Christmas day fighting the Federals near Pulaski, Tennessee on the retreat from being badly defeated in the Battle of Nashville fought on December 15 and 16. [1]

December 21, 1864 General Sherman's forces captured Savannah, Georgia. His march to the sea was complete. General Hardee and his 15,000 Confederate troops had escaped capture and moved into South Carolina. [1]

Vernon River, December 21, 1864
Major-General Foster:
Sir:
Savannah is ours. General Hardee has gone with his forces to Hardeeville. I heard General Sherman express some anxiety about your position on the Tullifinny, hence his note. Tatnall intends passing out of the Savannah River to-night with the iron-clad Savannah; at least this is reported by Generals Sherman and Howard. We will try and head him off. Please notify Captain Reynolds and the senior naval officer off Charleston, in case the latter port should be the Savannah's destination. We have Beaulieu, Rosedew, &c.

J. M. BRADFORD,
Fleet Captain, South Atlantic Blockading Squadron. [1]

SAVANNAH, Ga., December 22, 1864
(Via Fort Monroe 6:45 p.m. 25th)
His Excellency President Lincoln:
I beg to present you, as a Christmas gift, the city of Savannah, with 150 heavy guns and plenty of ammunition, and also about 25,000 bales of cotton.

W. T. SHERMAN
Major-General [1]

January and February 1865 in Macon were reported as being unusually cold and wet. Baxter's men spent the remainder of the winter in the doldrums of camp life. General Joseph Johnston had resumed command of the Army of Tennessee and had marched the army from Mississippi to South Carolina to join forces with General Hardee. Johnston was again fighting a defensive retreat with Sherman's troops in the Carolinas. [1]

April 9, 1865 General Robert E. Lee surrendered the Army of Northern Virginia to General Ulysses S. Grant at Appomattox Court House, Virginia. [1]

THE NASHVILLE DAILY PRESS & TIMES
NASHVILLE, TENN. APRIL 11, 1865

GRANT!
GLORIOUS NEWS !
SURRENDER OF GEN. LEE!
FULL PARTICULARS
END OF THE REBELLION !

War Department, April 9, 9 P.M.

This department has just received an official report of the surrender this day of Gen. Lee and army to Lieutenant –General Grant, on terms proposed by General Grant. Details will be given as speedily as possible.

E. M. Stanton, Sec'y of War.

HEADQUARTERS ARMY OF U. S. April 9, 1865

Hon. E. M. Stanton, Secretary of War:

General Lee surrendered the Army of Northern Virginia this afternoon, on terms proposed by myself. The following correspondence will show the conditions fully.

U. S. GRANT, Lieut.-Gen.

April 8, 1865

U. S. Grant, Lt. Gen. Commanding U.S.A.

I received your note on picket lines this morning, whither I had come to meet you to ascertain definitely what terms were embraced in your proposition of yesterday, with reference to the surrender of this army. I now request an interview, in accordance with the order contained in your letter of yesterday for that purpose.

Very respectfully your ob't Serv't,
R. E. LEE

On April 10, 1865 from Headquarters of Martin's Battalion at East Macon, Captain Baxter requisitioned for canteens, canteen straps and haversacks for 216 men under his command. Baxter signed the requisition as Battalion Commander. [23]

Federal Cavalry under command of Brevet Major General James H. Wilson were wrecking havoc in Alabama and headed toward Macon. The surrender of the Army of Northern Virginia and Sherman's campaign in the Carolinas signaled the end of the war was near. Questions on the handling paroled Confederates were being asked at many of the Federal Headquarters. The assassination of President Abraham Lincoln on April 14, 1865 greatly added to the confusion of ending the war.

EXECUTIVE DEPARTMENT
Milledgeville, Ga., April 15, 1865
Major-General Smith:

The movements of the enemy in Central Alabama indicate an intention on their part to make an early movement upon Columbus and other points in Georgia. To enable us to meet this successfully, it will require the united efforts of all who are able to bear arms, whether they belong to the State or Confederate service. You are, therefore, hereby directed to order out the militia of the State, subject to your command, to rendezvous at Columbus as fast as possible. All who are subject to your command under your former orders from these headquarters are embraced in this call, and all subject to militia duty under fifty years of age who fail to respond will be turned over to the Confederate service. I regret exceedingly to have to require them to leave their crops at this important period, but the movement of the enemy leaves no other alternative.

JOSEPH E. BROWN [1]

GENERAL ORDERS
HDQRS. FIRST DIV., GEORGIA MILITIA
NO. 1
Macon, Ga., April 15, 1865

1. In obedience to the above directions from the Governor and commander-in-chief, the militia of the State of Georgia, except those between fifty and sixty years of age, are hereby ordered to rendezvous without delay, at Columbus.

2. The publication of these orders will be considered sufficient notice to all subject to militia duty in this command. Officers and men will observe that not only those under fifty years of age, who have previously reported, but all others subject to militia

duty are embraced in this call, and must report accordingly or be dealt with as deserters.

3. Captains of companies will send their men forward immediately, and will themselves be allowed three days, if necessary, to gather and send to Columbus all who fail to start. General, field and staff officers and detachments will report at the rendezvous immediately. Captain Pruden's battery of artillery is included in this call

4. No excuse will be accepted from those who carried their arms home with them in case they fail to bring them back. All are enjoined not only to obey this order promptly, but they are authorized and directed to bring out all who owe service in the militia, and all public arms not in public use in their respective districts must be brought to the rendezvous.

5. The militia between fifty and sixty years of age in each county are required to hold themselves in readiness to respond at a moments notice to future orders of the Governor calling them into active service.

G. W. Smith
Major-General [1]

HEADQUARTERS DEPARTMENT OF THE CUMBERLAND
Nashville, April 15, 1865
President A. Johnson
Washington, D. C.

With profound sorrow for the calamity which has befallen the nation, permit me to tender to you as President of the United States assurances of my profound esteem and hearty support.

Geo. H. Thomas, Major-General, U. S. Army. [1]

HEADQUARTERS DEPARTMENT OF THE CUMBERLAND
Nashville, April 15, 1865 (Received 3:45 p.m.)
Hon. E. M. Stanton:

The news of the assassination of the President and Secretary of State was received here just before the ceremonies in commemoration of the fall of Richmond and surrender of Lee's army were about to commence. The whole community, military and civic, is profoundly affected at this terrible national calamity. The flags displayed at the different military offices have been draped in mourning, and minute guns will be fired until sundown.

Geo. H. Thomas
Major-General [1]

Hdqtrs, Dept of the Cumberland
GENERAL ORDERS.
Nashville, Tenn., April 17, 1865
No. 22

Whereas, certain rebels, former residents of the State of Tennessee and other portions of the Department of the Cumberland, having cast their lot with the Southern Confederacy in rebellion against the Government of the United States, and countenanced that rebellion by their presence within its limits, and frequently by their active assistance during the present war, and having recently become convinced that all attempts to establish such Confederacy must have proved vain and futile, and now wishing to secure themselves in the full possession of their property and all the rights of good and loyal citizens of the United States, have returned within the Federal lines and taken the amnesty oath, at places sometimes remote from their former places of residence, and where they are known, without the knowledge and consent of the major-general commanding the department, not, as is believed, from love of their country or repentance for their past recreantcy; it is hereby-

Ordered, That all amnesty oaths administered to any person or persons not bona fide deserters from the rank and file of the rebel army, and with the consent of the major-general commanding, no matter where or by whom, administered, since the 15th of December last, are hereby revoked and pronounced null and void, and hereafter no amnesty oath administered to persons coming to or living within this department, will be regarded or considered valid, unless taken with the knowledge and consent of the commanding general of the same.

By command of Major-General George Thomas:
WM. D. Whipple
Assistant Adjutant General[1]

Columbus, Ga., April 17, 1865
Col. O.H. LaGrange,
Commanding Second Brigade:

If you succeed in crossing the river instead of moving to Butler, as before ordered, you will move from LaGrange to Greeneville, crossing Flint river, between the shoals and Woodbury or Flat Shoals Texas; between these points will probably be the best crossing. You will then move toward Barnesville and from thence to Macon by the best and most direct route, communicating with the main column, which will move on the Columbus and Macon road. It is the desire of General Wilson that my division assault Macon first, and I will be in advance on the main road,

so that you may communicate with me. I hope you will use every effort
to make time, as you have farther to march than the rest.

> Very respectfully, & c.,
> E. M. McCOOK
> *Brigadier-General commanding.*[1]

HDQRS, CAVALRY CORPS, MIL. DIV. OF THE MISSISSIPPI
Fifteen Miles from Macon, April 20, 1865
General Upton:

GENERAL:

A communication just received for Maj. Gen. Howell Cobb states
that a truce for the purpose of a final settlement was agreed upon
yesterday between Generals Johnston and Sherman applicable to all
forces in their commands. The contending forces are to occupy their
present positions, forty-eight hours notice being given on event of
resumption of hostilities. It is reported that General Lee and his army are
captured. Move your command toward Macon to-morrow. The brevet
major-general moves to that place to-night.

> By command of Brevet Major-General Wilson:
> E. B. Beaumont,
> *Major and Assistant Adjutant –General.*

(Same to General McCook)
Forsyth, Ga., April 20, 1865—4:30 p.m.
MAJ. E.B. BEAUMONT,
Assistant Adjutant-General, Cavalry Corps :

I have the honor to forward the within communication, just received
from Lieutenant Colonel Frobel. I informed the colonel that I would
forward the communication to the general commanding, but would not
delay my march upon Macon. My column is still moving and will be
near there tonight. I will not assault until I hear from you, under the
promise from them that no property shall be removed or their defenses
strengthened. I would like to hear from you to-night on the Forsyth road
to Macon.

> Very respectfully yours, your obedient servant,
> E. M. McCook
>
> *Brigadier-General of Volunteers.*[1]

HEADQUARTERS
Near Foster's Farm, Five Miles West of Howard, Ga.,
April 20, 1865—11 p.m.
General E. M. McCook,
Comdg. Cavalry, Military Division of the Mississippi:
GENERAL:

Unless otherwise ordered I shall "go ahead" in obedience to your last order, and by 9 a. m. enter Macon or be engaged with the enemy. We shall probably pass Howard Station on the railroad. Directly down to that point appears to be your best route. The Second Division is reported as camped about three miles on our right. Most Respectfully, O. H. LA GRANGE[1]

HDQRS. CAVALRY CORPS, MIL. DIV. OF THE MISSISSIPPI
Macon, Ga., April 20, 1865
Col. R.H.G. MINTY,
Commanding Second Division Cavalry Corps:
COLONEL:

Detail a colonel from your command to act as provost marshal of Macon, to report to Captain Kneeland, corps provost marshal, for instructions. Detail also the best disciplined regiment in your command as provost guard, to report at a very early hour to-morrow morning.

By command of Brevet Major-General Wilson:
E. B. BEAUMONT
Major and Assistant Adjutant General.[1]

HEADQUARTERS FOURTH DIVISION OF CAVALRY CORPS.
April 20, 1865
(Maj. E. B. Beaumont)
Major:

I am camped twenty-two miles from Macon. If you want me to reach Macon in time for a fight to-morrow you must give me the right of way over everything. The negro brigade takes everything in the way of provisions. They ought to march in the rear of everything.

E. UPTON,
Brevet Major-General, Commanding.[1]

HDQRS, CAVALRY CORPS, MIL. DIV. OF THE MISSISSIPPI
.   *Macon, Ga. April 21, 1865—8 p.m.*
Maj. Gen. W. T. Sherman:
(Through General J. E. Johnston.)

Your dispatch of yesterday is just received. I shall at once proceed to carry out your instructions. If proper arrangements can be made to have sugar, coffee, and clothing sent from Savannah to Augusta, they can be brought hither by the way of Atlanta, or they can be sent by boat directly to this place from Darien. I shall be able to get forage, bread, and meat from Southwestern Georgia. The railroad from Atlanta to Dalton or Cleveland cannot be repaired in three months. I have arranged to send an officer at once, via Eufaula, to General Canby with a copy of your dispatch. General Cobb will also notify General Taylor of the armistice.

I have about 3,000 prisoners of war including Generals Cobb, Smith, Mackall, Mercer, and Robertson. Can't you arrange with General Johnston for their immediate release? Please answer at once. I shall start a staff officer to you to-morrow.

J.H. WILSON.
Brveit Major-General , Commanding[1]

On April 20 Macon was surrendered to Major General James Wilson's Federal Calvary. Fifty-three members of Baxter's Battery were captured. Captain Baxter, Lt. Marshall, Lt. Gault and a few of the men escaped capture and fled to Georgia's capital city of Milledgeville. A few other men fled Macon in other directions to avoid capture. Lieutenant William Herrin was the only officer with the enlisted men at the time of the surrender of Macon. The men were held under armed guard on April 21 and moved to the barracks, where they remained for a week before being paroled.[23]

Nashville, April 17, 1865—10 A.M.
(Received 1 p.m.)
Major General Halleck,
Washington:

I last night forwarded to General Grant General Wilson's official report of the capture of Selma, Ala., by his corps. I shall to-day send him orders to hold Selma and operate west of the Alabama river against Taylor's forces, with a view of aiding General Canby as much as possible. Have I authority to propose the same terms to General Taylor and all other confederate forces that General Grant proposed to General Lee?

Geo. H. Thomas
Major-General, U.S. Army[1]

Washington, D. C., April 17, 1865—4:10 P.M.
Major-General Thomas,
Nashville:

The Secretary of War authorizes you to give the same terms to rebel forces in the west and south as those given by General Grant to General Lee. Special permits will be required in all cases to go to any place in the loyal states.

H.W. Halleck
Major General-and Chief of Staff.[1]

In Middle Tennessee, guerrilla activity continued, even with the heavy Union occupation of the area. Questions also arose as to the terms of surrender to be offered to captured and surrendered guerrillas.

HDQRTS. FIFTH SUB-DISTRICT OF MIDDLE TENNESSEE
Clarksville, Tenn. April 20, 1865
Maj. B.H. Polk,
Assistant Adjutant-General, Nashville:

Major:

Application has been made to me, through citizens, by guerrillas in this district to know upon what terms they could lay down their arms and become peaceable citizens. As a decision in one case might form a precedent for others, I respectfully refer the question to district headquarters for decision.

I am, respectfully, your obedient servant,

A.A. SMITH
Colonel, Commanding

(First indorsement))
HEADQUARTERS DISTRICT OF MIDDLE TENNESSEE
Nashville, April 22, 1865
Respectfully forwarded to headquarters Department of the Cumberland for instructions.

LOVELL H. ROUSSEAU
Major-General

(Second indorsement)
HEADQUARTERS DEPARTMENT OF THE CUMBERLAND
Nashville, Tenn., April 25, 1865
Respectfully forwarded to the Adjutant-General of the Army for instructions.

GEO. H. THOMAS
Major-General, U.S. Army, Commanding

(Third indorsement)
May 3, 1865
Respectfully submitted to the Secretary of War.

W.A. NICHOLS
Assistant Adjutant General

(Fourth indorsement)
WAR DEPARTMENT
May 4, 1865
Respectfully referred to Lieutenant-General Grant for remark. By order of the Secretary of War.

JAS. A. HARDIE,
Inspector-General U.S. Army

(Fifth indorsement)
May 5, 1865
I would advise as a cheap way to get clear of guerrillas that a certain time be given for them to come in, say the 20th of this month, up to which time their paroles will be received, but after which they will be proceeded against as outlaws.

U.S. GRANT
Lieutenant-General[1]

HDQRS. Cavalry Corps, Military Division of the Mississippi
Macon, Ga., April 20, 1865—p p.m.
Maj. Gen. W. T. Sherman:
(Through headquarters of General Beauregard, Greensborough, N. C.)
My advance received the surrender of this city this evening. General Cobb had previously sent me under a flag of truce a copy of a telegram from General Beauregard declaring the existence of an armistice between all the troops under your command and those under General Johnston. Without questioning the authenticity of this dispatch or its application to my command. I could not communicate orders to my advance in time to prevent the capture of this place. I shall therefore hold its garrison, including Major-Generals G. W. Smith and Cobb and Brigadier General Mackall, prisoners of war. Please send me orders. I shall remain here a reasonable length of time to hear from you.

Fearing that it might be tampered with by the rebel telegraph operators, I had it put in cipher, in which shape I have reason to believe it reached its destination. The original was materially changed. I have seen in the newspapers what purported to be the reply of General

Sherman, directing me to withdraw from the city and release my prisoners. No such dispatch ever reached me, and had it done so in the most unquestionable form I should have obeyed it with great reluctance, and not until I had received every possible assurance that the following dispatch from General Sherman, and though not in reply to mine. I regarded it as convincing proof that an armistice had actually been agreed upon:

HEADQUARTERS
Greensborough, N. C. April 21, 1865---2 p.m.
Major-General Wilson,
Commanding Cavalry, Army of the United States:
(Through Major-General Cobb)

The following is a copy of communication just received, which will be sent you to-day by an officer:

HEADQUARTERS MILITARY DIVISION OF THE MISSISSIPPI
Raleigh, April 20, 1865
Major-General Wilson
Commanding Cavalry, U.S. Army, in Georgia:

General Joseph E. Johnston has agreed with me for a universal suspension of hostilities looking to a peace over the whole surface of our country. I feel assured that it will be made perfect in a few days. You will desist from further acts of war and devastation until you hear that hostilities are resumed. For the convenience of supplying your command you may either contract for supplies down about Fort Valley or the old Chattahoochee Arsenal, or if you are south of West Point, Ga., in the neighborhood of Rome and Kingston, opening up communication and route of supplies with Chattanooga and Cleveland, Report to me your position through General Johnston, as also round by sea. You may also advise General Canby of your position and substance of this, which I have also sent round by sea.

W.T. Sherman
Major-General, Commanding

Please communicate above to the Federal commander

J.E. Johnston [1]

HDQRS. MILITARY DIVISION OF THE MISSISSIPPI
In the Field, Raleigh, N.C., April 21, 1865
Col. R.H. G. Minty,
Commanding Second Division, Cavalry Corps:

Colonel:

A force of the enemy said to be 500 strong is reported across the river. General Wilson directs that you send a regiment over the bridge to bring it in.

By command of Brevet Major-General Wilson:

E.B. BEAUMONT
Major and Assistant Adjutant-General[1]

Macon, Ga. *April 21, 1865*
Brig. Gen. W.T. Wofford,
Commanding, & c.:

General:

I have the honor to inform you that an armistice has been agreed upon by Generals Sherman and Johnston, and that all military operations have ceased for the present, and will not be resumed except on forty-eight hours' notice. In my opinion they will not be resumed at all.

I am very respectfully, yours, & c.

Howell Cobb, Major-General

(First indorsement)

Official and correct. U.S. troops will observe. By command of Major-General Wilson

L.M. Hosea
Captain, sixteenth Regulars, and Acting Aide-de Camp.

(Second indorsement)

I believe General Wilson has been fooled.

Very respectfully, your obedient servant,
H.M. Judah
Brigadier-General[1]

HDQRS. CAVALRY CORPS, MIL. DIV. OF THE MISSISSIPPI
Macon, Ga., April 21, 1865
Maj. Gen. E.R.S. Canby.
Commanding Mil Div. Of West Mississippi, near Mobile, Ala.

General:

This place surrendered to me last night unconditionally. Major-Generals Cobb, G.W. Smith, and Brigadier-General Mackall, with 1,500 militia are prisoners. Since arriving here I have received through General Cobb a copy of an official dispatch from General J.E. Johnston declaring the existence of an armistice between the troops under his command and those under General Sherman for the purpose of arranging terms of agreement between the belligerents. General Cobb has also received a dispatch ordering him to communicate this information to General Taylor, who is requested to solicit an extension of its terms to your forces and his own. My own impression is that it is not contemplated by our authorities that a general armistice should be declared, or that its terms should apply to your or my forces. There is no doubt, however, that General Lee and his army are prisoners of war, and that General Johnston is in command of the confederate forces. I have telegraphic communication through the rebel lines and General Beauregard's headquarters to Goldsboro, N.C., and have sent a message to General Sherman.

I am, general, very respectfully, your obedient servant,

J. H. Wilson,
Brevet Major-General [1]

HDQRS. SEVENTEENTH INDIANA VOL (MOUNTED) INFTY.
Macon, Ga., April 21, 1865

Captain:

I have the honor to make the following report of this regiment, which I commanded the 20th instant:

On the morning of the 20th, the regiment being the advance regiment of the division (Second), the four companies with sabers were sent forward as advance guard of the division under Major Weiler. I had the remaining companies, as the regiment, in the proper order of the march in rear of the headquarters. From our camp of the proceeding night, from whence we started in the morning, it was forty-five miles to Macon. After marching about twenty-four miles, and when near Spring Hill, the advance guard first met a small force of the enemy and drove them off, capturing a few. I then moved forward with the other companies and assumed command of the advance. We rested near Spring Hill about an hour and then moved on. Near Montpelier Springs we again met the enemy and charged him up to and through a strong barricade of rails and brush across the road, charging it, driving the enemy from it, and capturing about a dozen of them, three officers, and a few horses. Resting a minute, I again moved forward at a fast trot in order to be in time to save the bridge over the Tobesofkee Creek, at Mimm's Mills. Here we found the enemy in line about 300 strong, and attacked them. The advance charged, mounted, over the burning bridge until stopped by the plank being torn up. They then dismounted, as did also the two advance companies E and H, and I double-quicked them across the bridge, and after a sharp fight of about five minutes drove the enemy off in confusion. In the meantime I had parts of the other companies at work extinguishing the fire on the bridge, the men carrying the water in their hats, caps and everything else available.

As we drove the enemy from the bridge, I sent two companies (G and I) across a ford below the bridge to pursue the enemy, and gave pursuit at the same time with the dismounted men. The road after crossing bridge makes a bend, and the enemy had to retreat around this bend, whilst my dismounted men double-quicking across the bend had the enemy under fire for about 200 yards, and took good advantage of it, firing very rapidly, demoralizing the enemy, causing them to throw away guns (over 100), blankets, haversacks, & c, and fly as for their lives. The fire on the bridge was sufficiently suppressed in about fifteen minutes to admit of horsemen crossing, and leaving men still at work against the flames, I crossed the command and pushed on.

About two miles from the bridge and about thirteen from Macon I was met by a flag of truce under the rebel Brigadier-General Robertson. The force we were pursuing passed the flag of truce and thus saved themselves.   I sent word to Colonel Minty, commanding Second Division, of the state of things, and awaited orders.   The flag of truce detained us about half an hour.   I then received orders from Colonel Minty to give them five minutes to get out of the way, and then to drive everything before me and save the bridge over Rocky Creek at Bailey's Mill. I placed Adjt. W.E. Doyle in charge of the advance guard of fifteen men, giving him instructions and sending him forward at a trot, supporting him closely with the regiment. After going about two miles he came in sight of the flag of truce party covering the rear of a force of about 250 men, said to be Blount's battalion. They were moving slowly, and evidently trying to delay us.   Seeing this the adjutant, as I had instructed him, charged them, causing the flag of truce to run into the woods, capturing three of the officers that were with it, and driving the rebel cavalry pell-mell along the road. They kept up a continual fire on us for some time, but with no effect. On getting within sight of Rocky Creek bridge, the enemy were discovered on foot attempting to fire the bridge. The advance drove them off, however, and pursued them closely to the palisades in the road. Before getting to the bridge the adjutant had sent to me for a small re-enforcement, and I sent him Major Weiler and Lieut. James H. McDowell with company E.   The major caught up before getting to the bridge.

On arriving at the palisades the advance got amongst the rebels and some firing ensued, the rebels breaking off the road through the gardens on the right in confusion. The advance tore down a few of the palisades, passed through, and rode up near the rebel works.   Here Major Weiler and Adjutant Doyle rode up on the works and demanded their surrender, telling them that we had two divisions of our cavalry in their rear. The colonel commanding not being present, the men believed that they were cut off; subordinate officers surrendered their commands, and the soldiery threw down their arms, and as directed marched down the road, where Lieutenant McDowell took charge of and formed them. The major and adjutant were at this time riding along the line of works, telling the men to throw down their arms and surrender; that they were cut off and were our prisoners; that flight was vain and that fighting would avail nothing, and the rebel soldierly were throwing down their arms and hastening to the road and the officers were following the men. I came up at this time with the regiment and found the rebel prisoners in line along the road under Lieutenant McDowell. I ordered Adjutant Doyle to the forts on the right of the road to receive their surrender. As soon as the regiment got inside the line of works the entire line surrendered, finding themselves cut off from town, and Colonel Cumming, who commanded the forces (one brigade) immediately on the road, came down with about 500 men and surrendered to me. I left two companies (G and I) In charge of the prisoners, and moved on toward town with the other companies At the edge of town I was met by some officers with a flag of truce from General Cobb, asking what terms I would give him if he surrendered the city and forces. My answer was unconditional surrender, and gave the flag five minutes to get out of my way. After passing into the town a distance of four or five squares, another flag of truce met me stating that General Cobb submitted to my terms, surrendering the city and everything in it. I marched into town and up to General Cobb's headquarters, thus taking formal possession of the city. I placed patrols on duty at once and camped the regiment in the court-house square and adjoining street. We captured in the city and in the works Maj. Gen. Howell Cobb, Brig. Gen. Gus W. Smith, Brigadier-General Mackall, and Brigadier General Mercer; 3,500 prisoners, including over 300 officers of all grades below brigadier general; 5 stand of colors, about 60 pieces of artillery of all calibers, and about 3,000 stand of arms. There were also large quantities of quartermaster's, commissary, medical, and ordnance stores captured in the city. The exact estimate of the stores I have not been able to find out. We had in action during the day 21 commissioned officers and 500 enlisted men. We lost 1 killed and 2 wounded. I have to return thanks to Maj. J.J. Weiler for the efficient aid given me in commanding the regiment, to Adjutant Doyle for the able manner in which he handled the advance guard whilst in command and to Lieut. J.H. McDowell, who ably assisted the major, for his promptitude and energy in getting the prisoners together and retaining them. I have also to return my thanks to every officer and man in the regiment for the cheerfulness with which they endured the hardships incident to the march, for the alacrity with which they obeyed every order, and for the gallant manner in which they have gone at the enemy wherever they have found him since the opening of the campaign. And I have also to return thanks to Capt. T.W. Scott and Lieutenant Culbertson, in taking of the city. I had omitted to state that we captured after getting in the city four 2-pounder breech-loading guns, known as Travis guns, made and intended for General Forrest, and a large number of horses and mules.

I have the honor to remain, captain, respectfully, your obedient servant,

Frank White
Commanding Regiment
Capt. O. F. Bane
Actg. Asst. Adjt. Gen., First Brig., Second Div., Cav. Corps.
Military Division of the Mississippi [1]

WAR DEPARTMENT
Washington City, April 22, 1865—2:30 p.m.
Major-General Thomas,
Commanding, & c., Nashville:

The proceedings and arrangement made between General Sherman and General Johnston are disapproved by the President and countermanded, and General Sherman has been directed to resume hostilities immediately. You are ordered not to act under that arrangement, but to prosecute any operations that may be going on, and push your military advantages.

EDWIN M. STANTON
Secretary of War [1]

HEADQUARTERS DEPARTMENT OF THE CUMBERLAND
Nashville, April 23, 1865—10 a.m. (Received 3 p.m.)
Hon. E.M. Stanton, *Secretary of War:*

Was the arrangement between Generals Sherman and Johnston the same as that between Generals Grant and Lee? I have by authority, offered Grant's terms to Dick Taylor and to the commanding general in Northern Georgia. Guerrilla bands also desire to surrender. Am I authorized to grant them any terms?

GEO. H. THOMAS,
Major-General U.S. Army, Commanding. [1]

War Department,
CONFIDENTIAL.
Washington City, April 23, 1865-9 p.m.
Maj. Gen. George H. Thomas, Nashville:

The arrangement between Generals Sherman and Johnston was not in accordance with that between Grant and Lee. General Sherman assumed authority not vested in him to arrange terms of peace and was disapproved upon many grounds. The agreement has been published in the newspapers. The following among other grounds for rejection, are made to General Sherman's arrangements:

1. It was an exercise of authority not vested in General Sherman, and on its face shows that both he and Johnston knew that General Sherman had no authority to enter into any such arrangement.
2. It was a practical acknowledgement of the rebel government.
3. It undertook to re-establish the rebel State governments that had been overthrown at the sacrifice of many thousand loyal lives and immense treasure, and placed the arms and munitions of war in the hands of the rebels at their respective state capitals, which might be used as soon as the armies of the United States was disbanded, and used to conquer and subdue the loyal states.
4. By the restoration of the rebel authority in their respective States they would be enabled to re-establish slavery.
5. It might furnish a ground of responsibility by the Federal government to pay for the rebel debt, and certainly subjects the loyal citizens of rebel States to the debt contracted by rebels in the name of the states.
6. It would put in dispute the existence of loyal state governments, and the new State of West Virginia, which has been recognized by every department of the United States government.
7. It practically abolished the confiscation laws, and relieved the rebels of every degree who had slaughtered our people from all pains and penalties for their crimes.
8. It gave terms that had been deliberately, repeatedly, and solemnly rejected by President Lincoln, and better terms than the rebels had ever asked in their most prosperous condition.
9. It formed no basis of true and lasting peace, but relieved the rebels from the pressure of our victories, and left them in condition to renew their efforts to overthrow the United States government and subdue the loyal States whenever their strength was recruited and any opportunity should offer.

The terms you have been authorized by General Grant to make, if you can do no better, will acceded to in respect to Dick Taylor. Guerrillas are entitled to nothing but powder and ball. Hancock is hunting down Mosby. But on the question of how much grace you can safely offer them upon unconditional surrender I would be disposed to leave to your judgment, within the limits of Grant's terms.

EDWIN M. STANTON. *Secretary of War* [1]

HDQRS. MILITARY DIVISION OF THE MISSISSIPPI
In the Field, Raleigh, N.C., April 24, 1865
General Wilson,
Macon:

The truce will expire on the morning of the 26th. You will renew your operations according to your original instructions.

W.T. SHERMAN, *Major-General, Commanding.* [1]

HDQRTS. CAV. CORPS, MIL. DIV. OF THE MISSISSIPPI
Macon, Ga., April 24, 1865.

The attention of division commanders is called to the communication from Co. J.G. Vail, Seventeenth Indiana (mounted) Infantry, commanding post at Macon, Ga.:

Major:

I would respectfully call your attention to the fact that a great number of depredations are being committed by parties of brigands dressed in our own and Confederate uniforms, on all the roads leading into the country. Houses are burned and the country desolated as far out as fifteen miles. The citizens are calling on me for protection, and I do not understand that my jurisdiction extends outside of the city, and at any rate have not a sufficient force at my disposal to afford protection to persons in the country. There seem to be no pickets on the roads, and negroes are coming into the city from every direction and will soon become a burden and endanger the city. I would respectfully ask that some measures be taken to prevent them from coming here.

I have the honor to be, very respectfully, your obedient servant.

J. G. Vail,, Colonel, Commanding Post.

Picket-posts, outposts, and vedettes must at once be properly posted to prevent the influx of negroes and depredations by our own troops within and beyond the lines. Patrols will be sent in every direction under the command of division and brigade provost-marshals to arrest all men engaged in marauding and out of camp without proper passes.

By command of Brevet Major-General Wilson:

E.B. BEAUMONT, *Major and Assistant Adjutant-General.*[1]

SPECIAL
HEADQUARTERS CAVALRY CORPS, FIELD ORDERS
MILITARY DIVISION OF THE MISSISSIPPI
NO. 24
Macon, Ga., April 24, 1865

Division commanders will at once forward to these headquarters all flags and other trophies captured from the enemy during the recent campaign from the Tennessee River to this place, with an account of the capture and by whom made. Recommendations for promotions on account of gallantry in action will also be forwarded without delay.   By command of Major-General Wilson.

E.B. BEAUMONT, *Major and Assistant Adjutant-General* [1]

DEPARTMENT OF TENNESSEE AND GEORGIA
Macon, April 25, 1865
Major-General Wilson,
Commanding federal Forces, Macon, Ga.:

General:

In answer to your verbal proposition of yesterday on the subject of the prisoners held by you, who have been captured in this department, I submit this communication: The officers and men captured by you in this department, which includes the prisoners taken at Columbus and West Point, shall be put upon their general parole not to go into service again during the war, unless regularly exchanged. The parole of the officers and men taken at Macon is subject to the condition that the parole is binding if the capture is held to be legal; but if my protest is sustained, and the capture of Macon held to be unauthorized, the officers and men are relieved from the obligation of the parole. A portion of the garrison here consists of convalescents and invalids, who cannot leave, and I feel bound to provide for their support during your occupation of this place. I am sure you will not hesitate to guarantee such provision for them as is demanded by the dictates of humanity and justice. Those officers and men who reside here, even temporarily, may desire to remain, at least until the armistice is at an end, and I mention the fact that there may be no misapprehension on the subject. I have no hesitation in saying that the general paroles of these officers and men, under the circumstances, will be recognized by our authorities.

I am, general, very respectfully, yours, & c.,

Howell Cobb
Major-General. [1]

HDQRS. CAVALRY CORPS, MIL. DIV. OF THE MISSISSIPPI
Macon, Ga., April 25, 1865
Maj. Gen. Henry C. Wayne.
Adjutant and Inspector General of Georgia, Milledgeville:
General:

I have the honor to acknowledge the receipt of your letter of the 24th instant, and in reply to say that the paroled prisoners from General Lee's army have been permitted to pass through my lines to their homes. All others that may arrive will be allowed the same privilege. I have no objection to your sending the train of which you speak to its destination, but to the contrary, a desire to have you do so. In view of the armistice and the probability of an early peace. I am anxious to do all in my power to prevent suffering among the people. I have directed the resumption of business of every kind, opening of the road, and a continuance of the mails. I will gladly co-operate with you in dispensing with all unnecessary restrictions. General Sherman has directed me to supply my command by contracting for provisions and forage in Georgia. General Cobb has kindly given me his assistance. Will you be good enough to lend your influence and advice to the people, in order that they may have confidence and sell to my supply departments. Captain Page will explain more fully my views upon the question alluded to herein. It would afford me great pleasure to meet you in person at any time and place convenient to yourself.

With high regard, general, very respectfully, your obedient servant,

J.H. WILSON
Brevet Major-General [1]

Augusta, April 25, 1865
Major-General Wilson, U.S. Army:

Lieut. Col. G.A. Henry, jr., of General Johnston's staff, telegraphs me from Charleston, S.C., yesterday that he is on the way with orders from Major-General Sherman to suspend hostilities, and that he will make all possible haste.

B.D. FRY
Brigadier-General, Commanding District. [1]

Macon, Ga.
SPECIAL FIELD ORDERS,
April 25, 1862
NO. 25

The provost-marshal of the Cavalry Corp, Military Division of the Mississippi, will at once parole all officers and men captured in the Department of Tennessee and Georgia. The conditions of the parole require that the officers and men shall not serve against the United States of America, or give any information, or do any military duty whatever until regularly exchanged. The parole of the officers and soldiers taken at Macon will be binding, provided the capture of the city is held to be legal, and if it is not, the officers and men will be relieved from the obligation of the parole. The officers captured at Macon will be allowed to retain their side-arms and horses. Major-general Cobb having pledged himself to use his influence with the Confederate authorities to have the parole of the officers and men of Lieutenant-General Forrest's command recognized, they will also be paroled under the conditions that they are not to serve against the United States of America, or give any information, or do any military duty whatever until regularly exchanged as prisoners of war. The utmost dispatch will be used in making out paroles in order that the officers and men may proceed to their homes as soon as possible.

By command of Brevet Major-General Wilson:

E.B. BEAUMONT
Major and Assistant Adjutant-General [1]

HEADQUARTERS DEPARTMENT OF THE CUMBERLAND
Nashville, April 25, 1865
Brig. Gen. R. W. Johnson,
Commanding Post of Pulaski:

General:

the bushwhackers are investing in the neighborhood of Rigg's Cross-Roads, upper end of Williamson County, out on the Nolen Pike, thirty-two miles from Nashville. The major-general commanding is informed that they are committing all kinds of depredations, and directs that you send to that neighborhood a sufficient force of cavalry to drive them out of the country. You will please refer to Mr. Alfred Ogilvie for further information.

Very respectfully, your obedient servant,

WM. D. WHIPPLE
Brigadier-General and Chief of Staff. [1]

CIRCULAR
HDQRS. CAV. CORPS, MIL. DIV. OF THE MISS.
Macon, Ga., April 28, 1865

For the purpose of restoring order in the neighboring country, the civil authorities are advised to take such measures as they may find necessary. The sheriff should call out the posse comitatus to assist in arresting guerrillas, stragglers, or men claiming to belong to the U.S.

forces who are engaged in pillaging, marauding, or other unlawful practices in violation of the armistice. All such persons should be punished by the civil authorities in accordance with the usages of civil law. The people must organize to protect themselves from disbanded soldiers and other lawless men. Where it is absolutely necessary they may call upon the military authorities for support.

By command of Brevet Major-General Wilson:

E. B. BEAUMONT
Major and Assistant Adjutant General. [1]

Pulaski, *April 28, 1865*
General W.D. Whipple
Assistant Adjutant-General and Chief of Staff:
I have 1,100 serviceable horses. To forage them I have had to deploy, and thereby I have been enabled to scout the country well. I have ordered a small regiment to concentrate at Franklin, where they can be rationed and foraged. I have ordered them to hunt down all the guerrillas in Williamson and adjoining counties. I have another regiment south of Athens. Will order that regiment to scout in the direction of Maryville, Paint Creek, New Market, & c.

R.W. Johnson
Brigadier-General. [1]

Chattanooga, *April 29, 1865*
Brig. Gen. W. D. Whipple
Chief of Staff:
There are large numbers of paroled rebel soldiers from Lee's army and Forrest's here and coming into our lines at all points, who are utterly destitute, and who will inevitably be driven to stealing and robbery, if not bushwhacking, unless they can be permitted to go to their homes or be provided for in some manner. What shall I do with them?

Jas. B. Steedman
Major-General. [1]

HEADQUARTERS DEPARTMENT OF THE CUMBERLAND
Nashville, April 29, 1865
Major-General Stoneman, *Knoxville:*
By decision of the Attorney-General no Confederate is entitled to come into a loyal state on his parole. He will have to take the oath of allegiance to the United States to enable him to remain. You are authorized to give a limited amount of subsistence to such rebel soldiers

who have to pass through East Tennessee to get to Georgia and Alabama. They must not be allowed to stop on the way.

GEO. H. THOMAS
Major-General, U.S. Army, Commanding. [1]

THE NASHVILLE DAILY PRESS & TIMES
NASHVILLE, TENN. APRIL 30, 1865

MIDNIGHT DISPATCHES
Surrender of Jo. Johnston's Army
The Richmond Bank Effects
The President on Rebel Leaders
Secretary Seward is Improving
The Steamer Sultana Blown Up
War Department
Washington, April 28—3 P.M.

To: Major-General Dir.

A dispatch from Gen. Grant, dated Raleigh, April 26, 10 P.M., states that Johnston surrendered the forces in his command embracing all the forces from here to the Chattahoochie to General Sherman, on the basis agreed upon between Lee and myself for the Army of Northern Virginia.

E. M. STANTON

Boston, April 28- A suit brought by Mr. Leonard Sturtevant against W. H. Allen, for illegal arrest and imprisonment, which has been on trial for some days in the Supreme Court, closed this morning, the jury rendering a verdict in favor of Mr. Sturtevant for $32,500. At the breaking out of the war he was doing business in New Orleans, and upon coming North was arrested and lodged in jail, upon charges of disloyalty preferred against him by Mr. William H. Allen.

New York, April 28—The Commercial's Washington special says the vaults of the Farmer's Bank, Richmond have been opened and the contents found intact.

A Cabinet meeting today considered the International question likely to arise, the consequences of which is alleged to have extensive attention.

President Johnson was loudly cheered today while passing through the streets. Booth's body has been placed where it will never be seen by Gertrace again.

The Post's special says a Pennsylvania delegation headed by Commissioner Lewis called on the President making the most radical address yet delivered. The President replied, repeating his conviction that the leaders should be punished and the masses of the people forgiven.

Sec'y Seward and son are doing well

Memphis, April 27, New Orleans, 21

Steamer Sultana arrived at Vicksburg with boilers leaking badly and remained there 30 hours repairing and taking on 1996 Federal soldiers and 45 officers, lately released from Cahawha and Andersonville prisons., arrived at Memphis last evening. After coaling and proceeding about seven miles up the river blew up and immediately taking fire and burning to the waters edge. Of 2,156 souls aboard, not more than 700 have been received. Five hundred and ten were received in the hospital. Two or three hundred more were received at the Soldier's Home. Capt. Mason, of the Sultana, supposed lost, survived.

John Greer who resided in the Turnbull Creek area after the war was one of the Union soldiers who survived the sinking of the Sultana. He survived the explosion and swam to the east bank of the Mississippi River. [23]

HEADQUARTERS DEPARTMENT OF THE CUMBERLAND
Nashville, Tenn., May 3, 1865—4 p.m.   (Received 7:50 p.m.)
Lieut. Gen. U. S. Grant:

Are paroled prisoners of war surrendered by Lee now to be permitted to come to their former homes in Tennessee ? Many have come here with orders granting them that privilege made from you headquarters in the field in Virginia. Have I authority to release on parole prisoners of war in prison and hospitals in this department upon their taking the oath of allegiance? These prisoners were all captured in battle. Among them are Brigadier -General Quarles, of Tennessee, and Brigadier-General Sears, of Louisiana, both severely wounded.

GEO. H. THOMAS,
Major-General, Commanding. [1]

SPECIAL FIELD ORDERS
MACON, GA., NO. 29
May 3, 1865

In pursuance of orders from the Secretary of War, a salute of 200 guns will be fired at noon to-morrow in honor of the victories gained by the armies under the command of Lieutenant-General Grant and the peace resulting to our country. Lieutenant Rodney, Forth U.S. Artillery, is charged with the execution of this order.

By command of Major-General Wilson:

E.B. BEAUMONT
Major and Assistant Adjutant General [1]

ROLL OF BAXTER'S COMPANY TENNESSEE LIGHT ARTILLERY PAROLED APRIL 28, 1865 AT MACON, GEORGIA

Private Vachel Barnhill
Private Aaron P. Beard
Private John T. Beck
Private William H. Bethshears
Private Benjamin F. Brown
Private James Buzbee
Sgt. James F. E. Buttrey
Private Seth Callahan
Private Thomas J. Carr
Private Harvey Clark
Sgt. John F. Cunningham
Private John F. Demonbruen
Private John B. Dillard
Cpl. John L. Forehand
Private William P. A. Fraisher
Sgt. William Gault
Private Albert Green
Lt. William Herrin
Sgt. William Hill
Private DeWitt Houston
Private John M. Johnson
Private Anderson King
Private William Ladd
Sgt. Arter Lankford
Private Dillard Lankford
Private Tillman Lankford
Private Thomas B. Laughlin
Private William May
Private Alfred A. McCaslin
Cpl. William McCrory
Private John W. McLaughlin
Private William Moore
Private Linden Nall

Private Andrew J. Parker
Private Thomas J. Parker
Private William S. Parrish
Private George Randol
Private James Richardson
Sgt. Eli Sherman
Private James Speights
Private Abraham Spencer
Cpl. Hiram A. Spencer
Private William M. Sullivan
Private Joseph Sweeney
Private David B. Talley
Private James B. Thompson
Private Aquilla Tidwell
Private Soloman Tidwell
Private Felix G. Truett
Private John Walker
Private Wesley Welch
Cpl. Daniel White
Cpl. James P. White

On April 29, the Tennessee boys in Baxter's Battery boarded a train for Atlanta. The Alabama troops were sent to Montgomery, Alabama. With the train tracks destroyed in Atlanta, the Tennesseans were again on the march covering thirty miles on April 30 arriving at Big Shanty, Georgia. May 1 thirty-three more miles of walking took them to Cassville, Georgia. May 2 after a 22- mile march, the men camped near the Chattahoochee River. May 3 the men marched 19 miles to Dalton and boarded a train for Chattanooga at 3 p.m. The men remained in Chattanooga until May 5. They took the Oath of Allegiance to the United States on May 4. They were told if they refused to take the oath, they would be sent North to Federal prison. Since the war was over, none of the men refused the oath. [23]

The men boarded a train for Nashville, headed home at last.

Captain Baxter and the men who escaped with him and avoided capture at Macon were captured near Milledgeville on May 5 and paroled. Records on those paroled at Milledgeville were incomplete but those known to have been captured with Baxter were: Lt. John Gault, Private James M. Buttrey, Private John J. Johnson, Jr., Private Joseph Cox, Private Jesse Edwards and Private James G. Lewis.

Several of the men were in Ocmulgee Hospital at the time of the surrender and were later paroled from the hospital. Those included: George Hogan and Noah Kimberly. Several of the men escaped capture at Macon and were later caught by the Federals: James Martin at Leesport, Mississippi and James M. Duff at Atlanta. Lewis Sudduth and Thomas Hooper were at home on furlough at the time of the surrender of Macon. Several other men in the unit were unaccounted for at the surrender, some possibly in the hospital, others possibly on furlough.

Parole paper of Private James M. Buttrey

CHAPTER 6

POST WAR

After two and a half years of enduring the hardships of war, the men of Baxter's Company were finally headed home. The train from Chattanooga arrived in Nashville at 6 a.m. on May 6. 1865. The Williamson County boys were ordered to report to Franklin. The Dickson and Cheatham County boys were ordered to report in Nashville. Private DeWitt Houston of Marshall County was ordered to report to Columbia. Private George Randol of Mississippi County, Missouri was sent to Louisville, Kentucky, where he again took the oath of allegiance and was paroled to go north of the Ohio River to return home, where he later entered into the practice of law.

After reporting in to the assigned Provost Marshall's office, the men were in for their last, and most pleasant march of the war, going home at last. Of the 107 original recruits who marched off to war from Bethesda on December 22, 1862, forty were on the return walk home, four other soldiers who had joined the company later in the war were with them. Fourteen of the original recruits had died of disease while in Confederate service, three while in Union Prison at Camp Douglas, Illinois. Private Jesse White remained imprisoned at Camp Douglas until the end of the war. He was released May 12, 1865 and returned to Dickson County in a thin and haggard condition. Three members of the battery had joined the Union Army to gain release from Union prison. Five of the original recruits had transferred to other units, twenty-four were reported as having deserted and six had been presumed captured while at home of furlough. Two were given medical discharges at Cumberland Gap. One of them, Private Robert S. Scales died at his home near Nolensville in Williamson County October 14, 1863. Two of the Georgia recruits of Baxter's Battery also died while in service, Private John Norris in Camp Douglas and Private James Gray in Ocmulgee Hospital in Macon. Private Wesley Welch of Dickson County remembered his walk home from Nashville; "I were bare footed and bare headed and my clothes half tore off of me."[10, 23]

Baxter's men were fortunate to have been captured in Georgia and given a train ride most of the way home. The Confederate soldiers from Middle Tennessee who surrendered with General Johnston at

Greensboro, North Carolina and with General Lee at Appomattox, Virginia were forced to walk home, many of them barefooted.

Private John Dillard had stated in a letter home to his family: "God has been good to our company." That Baxter's Battery had spent almost two and one half years in the Confederate army, were engaged in the bloody battles of Chickamauga, Missionary Ridge and Atlanta and had no men killed or seriously wounded in battle was truly a blessing. Artillery batteries stationed at other positions on the battlefields of Chickamauga, Missionary Ridge and Atlanta had suffered heavy casualties.[9, 23] Having been recruited fairly late in the war, Baxter's men missed the fighting in some of the early battles of the war at Fort Donelson, Shiloh, Perryville and Murfreesboro. Even so, the men had experienced enough death, mutilation, hardship, starvation, sickness and destruction to last them a lifetime.

Captain Baxter and the men who had been captured with him near Milledgeville were paroled there May 5, 1865 and sent to Nashville. Baxter did not take the oath of allegiance until June 16, 1865. His oath was administered by Captain Charles D. Colesman, Assistant Provost Marshall of the Department of the Cumberland. Private Joseph Cox, the company bugler also took the oath at Nashville and returned to his home in Lexington, Kentucky with the company bugle strapped to his shoulder. Lieutenant John Gault also took the oath at Nashville.[23]

The Alabama men in Baxter's Company took the oath and were paroled on May 19, 1865 at the Headquarters of the 16th U. S. Army Corp in Montgomery, Alabama.[2] Baxter's Georgia recruits, most of whom resided in the Atlanta area, were also paroled and sent home from Macon. No records were found as to where they were administered the oath of allegiance.

Being occupied by the Federal Troops early in the war, much of Middle Tennessee was not subjected to the mass burning and destruction of property as were other parts of the South, though some did occur. Since the men of Baxter's company had left home for the war in the fall of 1862, the Nashville and Northwestern Railroad had been completed by the Federals from Kingston Springs to Johnsonville. Johnsonville was a new town on the Tennessee River in Humphreys County named for Tennessee's Unionist Military Governor and later President of the United States, Andrew Johnson. Federal troops from the railroad camps in Cheatham and Dickson Counties had foraged heavily in the Turnbull Creek area during their tour of duty. While refitting his cavalry in the early winter of 1864, Major General James Wilson's Cavalry had scoured Middle Tennessee for horses, taking every steed fit for cavalry service from the pro-southern citizens of the region. [22]

Hickman County had been a battleground between Colonel Jacob Biffles 19th Tennessee Confederate Cavalry and Federal Cavalry under the command of Colonel Murphy in 1864. The Federals had converted the county courthouse in Centerville into a fort. The courthouse was burned by Confederates under the command of Captain Albert Hennon Cross to prevent further use by the Federals. The business district of Centerville and many of the homes in the town were burned by the Perry County Jayhawkers of the 10th Tennessee Federal Cavalry, leaving the Hickman County seat in ruins.[21]

Cross's men were implicated in the execution of 20 Federal soldiers belonging to the 130th Indiana Infantry Regiment. On November 26, 1864 the young soldiers were said to have been taken off in groups of four men each, shot, robbed and thrown in a ravine. The only three men identified in the incident were Captain Cross' brother, Brownlee Cross, and John Hammonds and Green Hammonds.

On November 30, 1864, four Confederate soldiers were tracked down by Federals and shot in the back near the Anglin Cemetery in the 1st District of Williamson County. The Beard family who lived near by heard the gunshots. Vachel Barnhill, Sr. is said to have built their caskets at night to prevent being seen by the Federals. Descendents recall one of the murdered men was a King. His body was said to have been taken by family members to a family cemetery in the Kingfield Community of Williamson County. Two of the others were identified as Hammonds, the other unknown. The three were buried near where they were killed in unmarked graves. No record was found on this incident, possibly because it happened the same day the bloody Battle of Franklin was being fought. [17]

The big battles fought at Franklin November 30, 1864 and at Nashville December 15 & 16, 1864 had brought more death and suffering to men of the area. In the 20th Tennessee Infantry at Franklin, Captain Todd Carter died in his home of wounds received while leading a charge on his father's farm. Corporal Buck Herbison was shot in the foot. Private Young McNeal was also wounded at Franklin. Of the Hickman County soldiers engaged at Franklin, Corporal James Cagle and Private John Wilkins of Company F 42nd Tennessee Infantry Regiment were killed. Lt. William Carothers, Lt. A. C. Donegan, Private Tillman Gray and

Private Hugh Carothers of the 42nd were wounded at Franklin. Privates Alexander Overby and Newt Anglin of Company H 24th Tennessee Infantry Regiment were wounded in the Battle of Franklin. Anglin's wound resulted in the loss of a leg. Corporal William Mayberry of Company B 49th Tennessee Infantry Regiment and Private Rafe Eubank of Company E 11th Tennessee Infantry Regiment were among Dickson County Soldiers killed at Franklin. Mary Spencer Lankford, wife of Sgt. Arter Lankford of Baxter's Battery, recalled to her children of hearing "the cannon balls busting" at home a distance of more than twenty miles away during the Battle of Franklin.[17, 21, 23]

At the Battle of Nashville, Colonel Bill Shy of the 20th was killed while defending the hill that now bears his name. Private Wes Mangrum of Company H 20th was wounded. Private Sam Hammon of Company K 11th Tennessee Infantry Regiment had been in the army only a month when he was captured at Nashville. He had survived the deadly charge of Brown's Division at the Battle of Franklin. He spent the remainder of the war in Union Prison at Camp Chase, Ohio.[23]

Several of the neighbors and kin of Baxter's men in Hickman and Dickson Counties had joined Company G of the 12th Tennessee Federal Cavalry in 1864. The unit was originally organized as a home guard unit to fight guerrillas and bushwhackers in the area and later entered into Federal service. At that time, Federal recruits were paid a $100 bounty in "Yankee green backs" and furnished a horse, uniform and rifle. Captain Andrew Jackson "Jack" Sullivan, a Mexican War Veteran, who had two brothers serving in the Confederate Army and another brother serving in his command, served as first Captain of Company G. While leading a Federal scouting party near Little Lot in Hickman County in April 1864, the party was ambushed by Dave Miller's Confederate Scouts. Sullivan was killed and it was reported he was tied to his horse and his face was dragged off to show what would happen to local citizens who sided with the Federals. Dickson County men who joined Company G 12th Tennessee Federal Cavalry included: David Tomlinson, James Tummons, and William Pendergrass.[23] Tomlinson survived the war and relocated from Dickson County to the Peytonsville community in eastern Williamson County.[17, 23]

The men of Baxter's Battery were happy to be home at last. For the twelve widows and children of Baxter's men who had died during the war, homecoming was not so happy. Several of the widows had brothers and other kin who did return with the company. The men were also reunited with some of their comrades who had been unable to return to the army from furloughs and those who had deserted. Some of the deserters and those who served throughout the war later testified for each other on the Confederate pension applications. The men were also reunited with friends and neighbors who had served in other Confederate units and learned of the casualties of their neighbors who had been killed, died and wounded in the war. [23]

Andy Stewart Lampley, brother of Radford and Bud Lampley, had moved to Henderson County, Tennessee in 1860. He had served as a Private in Company A of the 15th Tennessee Confederate Cavalry. He had been captured and imprisoned at Camp Chase, Ohio, where he died of small pox on December 9, 1864. Andy's nephew, James Monroe Lampley, had also relocated to Henderson County in 1860. He became a "Homegrown Yankee" and joined Company C of the 7th Tennessee Federal Cavalry. He was captured twice and died of diarrhea at the Confederate Prison at Andersonville, Georgia. [23]

Guerilla activity had been heavy in Hickman, Dickson, Cheatham and Williamson counties. Albert Henon Cross, Duval McNairy, Dick McCann, and Dave Miller all had irregular bands operating in the area. The guerillas foraged upon the citizens of the area as did the Federals. McNairy's Company was the last guerilla band operating at the end of the war. The command surrendered and was paroled May 16, 1865 at the Dean House on Lick Creek in Hickman County.[23]

THE DAILY PRESS & TIMES
Nashville, Tenn. May 8, 1865
CAPTURE AND EXECUTION OF GUERRILLA BAND-
We learn that the notorious guerrilla leader Duval McNairy and eight of his men were captured on Wednesday by a force of colored troops on Harpeth river, near the Northwest railroad. The entire gang were shot by the negroes after their capture, we are informed.

Upon enquiry we find the above to be incorrect.

THE DAILY PRESS & TIMES
Nashville, Tenn. May 18, 1865
PAROLED-
We learned from Mr. Truman, who was out in Franklin yesterday, that Duval McNairy and eight of his officers and forty-eight men were paroled yesterday a few miles from that town. There were also surrendered, as we learn by a dispatch at headquarters from General Rousseau, twenty inferior guns and some old pistols, and ten poor horses and equipments. The gentleman from Franklin states that there are quite

a number of McNairy's men who refuse to come in, not because they were opposed to a cessation of strife, but because they entertained fears that they would not be treated as other soldiers have been. Word has been sent to them however, that they will be treated as promised by General Thomas' proclamation.

The surrender of the guerillas did not bring an end to bushwhacking and lawlessness. Less than a month after returning home, Private John Dillard was one of several men who attended a meeting of citizens and paroled soldiers in Dickson County to address the problems.

NASHVILLE DAILY UNION
Nashville, Tenn. June 7, 1865

A public meeting was held in Dickson County at Hutton's Chapel on 3 June, 1865 and R.L.V. Schmittou presided. Parson Hutton addressed the group. This was a meeting of citizens and paroled soldiers. Resolutions were made by A. P. Nicks, J.H. Cullum, John McKechine, N.M. Hall and Charles S. Jones that they would aid and assist in restoring civil law and order in the county and that they regretted the assassination of President Lincoln and indorse the General Assembly of Tennessee in their act in regard to bushwhackers and horse-thieves, etc.

While the former Confederate soldiers were returning to their homes in Middle Tennessee and other parts of the South, Union troops were likewise being mustered out of service and returning to their homes in the North.

NASHVILLE WEEKLY TIMES & PRESS
Nashville, Tennessee July 2, 1865
MOVEMENT OF TROOPS

Friday night detachments of the following regiments left for home on the 6 o'clock train:

The 4th, 5th, and 7th Ohio regiments and the 4th Indiana infantry; also the 1st Illinois battery. In conversation, we learn from some of the men that a great many soldiers are being mustered out and sent home from around Chattanooga, Knoxville, Stevenson and other towns along the line of the railroad..

MUSTERED OUT—Saturday evening the 89th Illinois infantry passed through the city on their way home: They were about 400 strong and their banners were covered with the names of the engagements that they have participated in, such as Stone River, Chickamauga, Pilot Knob,

Resaca, Atlanta and Chattanooga and Lookout Mountain, besides some others which we were unable to find out. A fine brass band discoursed splendid music and the boys marched quite briskly.

Life was hard during the reconstruction period. Much of the South lay in ruins, the economy was destroyed and the former Confederate States remained under martial law. Tennessee Governor William "Parson" Brownlow, from Knoxville, had been a strong unionist and was unsympathetic to the former rebels. His Radical Republicans controlled state and local governments. Confederates had transported Brownlow out of the state to Kentucky early in the war. [1]

Some progress was being made shortly after the end of the war in opening schools and resuming postal service. Many Southern sympathizers remained in military prisons, lawlessness among the remaining Union troops persisted and guerrilla activity continued.

THE DAILY PRESS & TIMES
Nashville, Tennessee   July 19, 1865

MILITARY PRISON--The aggregate of all classes of persons confined in the military prison here is 534. Of these, four are prisoners of war. Of citizens, fourteen are under charges, sixteen are awaiting promulgation of sentence, and thirty-five are under sentence—sixty-five in all.   Six Federal deserters are under charges, and four are awaiting sentences, and three hundred and seven are awaiting execution of sentence. Of negroes, fourteen are under charges and twenty-seven are under sentence.

MAIL---The people residing along the old mail route on the Nolandsville Pike, at Nolandville, Triune and College Grove are very anxious for the resumption of mail facilities, and we understand that the former contractor is ready to accept his old contract and put a line of stages on the route. At College Grove the male and female Seminaries will be in operation in a few weeks, and it is anticipated will commence the term with at least one hundred and fifty pupils.

PATROL----Twenty-four arrests were made by the patrol up to A.M. o'clock last night.   Five soldiers of the 17th U.S.C. Infantry for drunkenness and disorderly conduct—sent to prison for 24 hours. Seven Government employees for same offense received same penalty. Eight soldiers belonging to different commands were sent up for 24 hours. Samuel Kessell, charged with being one of a party who robbed a discharged soldier of $125, was turned over to the civil authorities.

GUERRILLAS---When will the country be rid of the land pirates who murder and rob defenseless people in rural districts? We learn that a few days ago, some six or seven cut throats, near Carrollsville, Wayne, co., shot and killed an old man named Choate, and wounded his son-in-law, named James F. Dougherty, who however managed to escape. The villans were strangers.

Relatively few of the men in Baxter's Company or their families had owned slaves. Captain Baxter reported several of his former slaves remained with his family as servants after gaining their freedom. Sol Tidwell's former family slaves moved with him from Dickson County to the Sugar Creek area of Hickman and remained with the family as sharecroppers. The majority of the families of the men in Baxter's Company who owned slaves resided near Franklin and included the families: Paschall, Truett, Ellison, McLaughlin, Hill, Maury, Marshall, McKay, Sayers and Gault. The Scales family of Nolensville, Demumbreun family of College Grove and Sweeney family of Leipers Fork were also Williamson County slaveholders. In the First District of Williamson County, Benjamin and Joseph Terrell, who both died in the war, were slaveholders.

In addition to the Tidwells, other Dickson County families of Baxter's men who owned slaves were: Spicer, White, Beck, Carr, and Jackson. Davidson County families of Baxter's men who owned slaves included the McCrory and Hogan families. The Houston family of Marshall County and the Duff family of Montgomery County also owned slaves.

Most of the men in the company returned to their homes and resumed farming. Having been gone over two and one half years, much work was to be done in getting their property back in order and in reuniting with their families. Ben Brown's wife was pregnant when he enlisted in Baxter's Battery and he saw his eldest son, almost three years old, for the first time when he returned home.

The Turnbull Creek area was spared many of the hardships of the reconstruction era. Being an area of few slaves, the problems associated with the freed slaves and the Freed Man's Bureau were few. Being a sparsely populated rural area, there was less presence of Union troops than in the cities.

Since few of the men in the area had served in the Union Army, there was little bitterness between the former foes. In many areas, including parts of Hickman County, bitterness over the war lingered for years and resulted in several killings. [21]

Some Confederate Veterans chose to move to a new home to avoid the problems of reconstruction. Even though it was a Confederate State and was also undergoing reconstruction, Texas was the most popular destination.   Joseph Sears of Dickson County, who served in Baxter's Battery, relocated to Texas. Several Confederate Veterans from the First District of Williamson County moved their families to Texas: Malachia "Mack" Kerby, Jeffery Inman, Joseph Inman, Reuben Inman, Alfred Hutchinson and Franklin M. Givens. David Talley and Tom Laughlin of Baxter's Battery relocated to the rich farmland of Dyer County, Tennessee, in the western part of the state.

Most of the men remained on their home places. Arter and Billy Lankford, Abe Spencer, and Jesse Edwards moved from Dickson County to the First District of Williamson County. Aquilla and Soloman Tidwell moved from Dickson County to Hickman County. Albert Green relocated from the 1st District of Williamson County to Hickman County, where he prospered as a blacksmith and farmer. Joseph Sweeney returned to his home in Leiper's Fork and also became a prosperous blacksmith and carriage maker. Noah Kimberly moved from Georgia to Cleburne County, Alabama. James Buzby moved from Alabama to Coal County, Oklahoma. [2]

While many ex-confederates were leaving Middle Tennessee, others were moving in. Life for former Confederates in East Tennessee was especially rough, with them being in the minority and many moved away. Several of them relocated to Williamson County. Joseph A. Caldwell who had served as a Private in Company C of the 2nd Battalion of Thomas' North Carolina Legion moved his family from Blount County to the First District of Williamson County. At the time he applied for a Confederate pension, Caldwell listed his address as Jingo. In later years, he and his wife moved to Franklin where they died and were buried at Mount Hope Cemetery. [18, 23]

While many Confederate Veterans were leaving Tennessee, many Union Veterans were moving into the state. Tennessee, other southern states and many local governments were actively recruiting northerners to move to the south. The plan was to create a "New South" with an industrial based economy rather than an agriculturally based economy.

Northerners had industrial skills and money to invest in industry. Between 1860 and 1870, Dickson County had an in migration of over 1,200 new residents from both Northern and Southern states. The majority of the immigrants from the North came from Pennsylvania. Ohio ranked second in the number of immigrants to the county from northern states. A colony of Pennsylvanians also relocated to the First District of Williamson County during that time period. Unlike the "carpetbaggers" who came to the South at the end of the war to buy cheap land for back taxes, these settlers moved their families with them to start new lives in a warmer climate. Many of the immigrants established saw mills and took advantage of the abundant timber supply of Middle Tennessee. Others came to manufacture iron and other products. Most of them engaged in farming. These families blended in with their communities and their offspring intermarried with offspring of the local Confederate Veterans. Several of the union soldiers who had been stationed at the railroad camps at White Bluff and other areas in Dickson County settled in the county.[5]

J.W. Johnson relocated to Dickson County from Pennsylvania shortly after the end of the war. He had served in Company B 103rd Pennsylvania Infantry Regiment. He married a local girl and become one of the prominent farmers of the county. In later years, he was involved with several businesses in Dickson. He was proud to have been a Union Veteran, but stated that he had the highest respect for the men who wore the gray due to their valor and bravery on the battlefield. At his funeral, all of his pallbearers except one were former Union soldiers. The other was Robert J. Work who had served as a Lieutenant in Company H of the 11th Tennessee Infantry Regiment of the Confederate Army. One of Johnson's pallbearers was David Daubenspeck of Jingo in Williamson County. Daubenspeck had served with Johnson in Company B of the 103rd Pennsylvania Infantry Regiment. Daubenspeck had survived imprisonment at the Confederate prison at Andersonville, Georgia.

Tennessee was the first former Confederate state readmitted to the Union on July 24, 1866.

In 1871, former Confederate General John Brown of Pulaski was elected Governor of Tennessee. The ex-Confederates had been returned their right to vote and things were looking up for them. Other former Confederate to serve as Governor of Tennessee: James Davis Porter elected in 1875, Albert Smith Marks elected in 1879, General William B. Bate was elected in 1882 and Colonel Peter Turney elected in 1893.

Sgt. James F. E. Buttrey   Cpl. Hiram Spencer

Several of Baxter's former soldiers were active in the affairs of their communities. James F. E. Buttrey served as Chairman of the Democratic Party in the First District of Williamson County. Hiram Spencer served as a delegate to the Democratic Party from Dickson County in 1880. Thomas Carr served on the Dickson County Quarterly Court and Joseph Nall served on the Williamson County Quarterly Court. John F. Cunningham had served as Postmaster at Barren in the 1st District of Williamson County before the war. After the war, both James F. E Buttrey and Albert Green served terms as Postmaster at Naomi on the Williamson-Hickman County line.

Several of the veterans of Baxter's Battery belonged to the Tennessee Association of Confederate Soldiers, which later became part of the United Confederate Veterans. Captain Ed Baxter and George Hogan, Jr. belonged to the Cheatham bivouac # 1 in Nashville. John Gault, John Demunbreun, Eli Sherman and Vachel Barnhill belonged to the McEwen bivouac # 4 in Franklin. Daniel White, James P. White, Thomas J. Carr, John B. Dillard, William P. A. Fraisher and William H. Ladd belonged to the James Raines bivouac #14 in Dickson. Over the following years, several of the descendents of Baxter's men belonged to the United Daughters of the Confederacy and Sons of Confederate Veterans.

Thomas J. Carr   Cpl. Joseph L. Sweeney

Some of the early UDC members who were related to Baxter's men: Miss Betty B. Baxter and Mrs. Nannie B. Overton, daughters of Captain Ed Baxter; Katherine Kinzer Herrin Pursley, great-grandaughter of Lieutenant William Herrin; Mrs. Edna Synclaire Johnson, great-granddaughter of Private John Jefferson Johnson, Jr.; Miss Edna Porter Maury descended from Sgt. Matthew F. Maury; Mrs. Mabel Southall Hills descended from Corporal Joseph Sweeney; Mrs. Thelma Odel Truett Griswold and Mrs. Annie Mai Truett Payne Granddaughters of Private Felix Grundy Truett; Mrs. Floy Hopkins Bouldin descended from Private John T. Beck and Mrs. Ellen C. McClung Marshall widow of 1st Lieutenant John Marshall, Jr.. In later years, Private James B. Thompson had three granddaughters in the UDC: Mrs. Alice Blake of Dickson, Tennessee, Mrs. Margarite Duke of Burns, Tennessee and Mrs. Kathryn Brown Sanders of Franklin, Tennessee.

Private Felix Jones (second row, right, standing) attended a reunion of area Confederate veterans in Palmore, KY. Date unknown.

In 1891, the state of Tennessee began offering state funded pensions to indigent Confederate Veterans. In 1905 the state established pensions for indigent Confederate Widows. Pension applications were filed with the Tennessee Board of Confederate Pension Examiners for approval or disapproval. The veterans were required to provide a doctor's statement to prove their disability and the trustee of the county of their residence submitted a statement of their ownership of property and assets. Veterans who had served in their command or other citizens provided notarized statements as to the veterans' health, poverty, war time service and standing in the community. The pension board obtained the applicant's military records from the War Department in Washington, D.C. Soldiers whose records showed they deserted or served less than honorably were denied pensions.

Thirty-seven of Baxter's Middle Tennessee Veterans applied for Tennessee Confederate Pensions. Twenty-five of the applications were accepted. Two more were accepted upon applying a second time. Ben Brown's pension was approved on the third application. Those whose pensions were accepted: Vachel I. Barnhill, John T. Beck, William Bethshears, Benjamin F. Brown, James F. E. Buttrey, James Monroe Buttrey, Thomas J. Carr, Harvey Clark, John Bryant Dillard, Jesse Beck Edwards, John Lambert Forehand, William P. A. Fraisher, Albert Green, Tillman P. Lankford, James G. Lewis, Matthew F. Maury, Thomas J.

Parker, James Richardson, Abraham Spencer, William M. Sullivan, Joseph L. Sweeney, David Basil Talley, James B. Thompson, Aquilla Tidwell, Soloman M. Tidwell, Wesley B. Welch, Daniel White and James Polk White [23]

Pvt. William M. Sullivan   Pvt. Vachel I. Barnhill

Nine of the pension applications were rejected, most were due to desertion. For some applicants, no reason for rejection of the application was given. Those rejected were: James W. Allen, James Henderson Hall, Anderson King, Andrew Jackson "Jack" Lampley, Dillard H. Lankford, John C. Mangrum, James W. Martin and Jesse White. [23]

The major disability ailment listed in the applications was rheumatism, which was contracted during the war from sleeping on the cold ground. Other disabilities listed in the applications were: deafness contracted from firing of the cannon, shell shock, kidney trouble, heart trouble, lung problems due to measles contracted during the war, chronic diarrhea, blindness, war injuries, diabetes, and old age. Several of the veterans listed multiple disabilities in their applications. About sixteen physicians in Williamson, Dickson and Hickman Counties conducted the examinations of the veterans for their pension applications.

Dr. E. W. Ridings of Dickson performed the most veteran exams, conducting 7. Dr. James Park Hanner of Franklin, a Confederate veteran who had served as Captain of Company D of Feild's 1st Tennessee

Infantry Regiment (the Williamson Grays) and a surgeon for Morton's
Artillery, performed exams of three of Baxter's veterans.   Other
physicians who performed the exams included: Dr. J. O. Shannon, Dr.
Samuel Henderson, Dr. L.G. Hensley, Dr. J. E. Mathis, Dr. William T.
Clark, Dr. John T. Cox, Dr. J. C. Daniel, Dr. W. F. Black, Dr. M. Drake,
Dr. J. J. Sledge, Dr. A. Norris, Dr. J .A. Venable, Dr. W. H. James,
Dr. A.H. Abernathy and Dr. J. M. Bagwell.[23]

Twenty widows of Baxter's veterans applied for Tennessee Confederate
Widow's Pensions. Eighteen were approved: Elizabeth Barnhill (widow
of Vachel Barnhill), Tennessee Lampley Buttrey (widow of James
Monroe Buttery), Eliza Jane Buttrey (widow of William G. D. Buttrey),
Tennessee C. Porter Carr (widow of Thomas J. Carr), Eliza Jane Tidwell
Cunningham (widow of John F. Cunningham), Sarah Ann Merritt
Dembreun (widow of John F. Demonbreum), Mary Walton Polk Gault
(widow of John Gault), Mary Eliza Donnigan Green (widow of Albert
Green), Kiziah Hays Lankford (widow of Dillard H. Lankford), Lucy
Whitfield Lewis (widow of James G. Lewis), Evaline Cummins
McCrory (widow of James McCrory), Nannie Jane Taylor McCrory
(widow of William McCrory), Sue Jones Sherman (widow of Eli
Sherman), Judian Pewitt Spencer (widow of Abraham Spencer), Minerva
Jane Gatlin Sweeney (widow of Joseph L. Sweeney), Nancy Elizabeth
Stovall Talley (widow of David Basil Talley), Alice Richardson
Thompson (widow of James B. Thompson) and Parthena Lankford
White (widow of Daniel White) [23]

Two of the widow's pension applications were rejected: Emaline
Lampley Hall (widow of James H. Hall) because her husband was listed
as a deserter and Marivina Perry Bethshears (widow of William
Bethshears) because she was a second wife who had married the veteran
after 1908. [23]

James Buzbee of Alabama and Alfred McCaslin of Dickson County
moved to Oklahoma and drew Oklahoma Confederate pensions.
Buzbee's wife drew an Oklahoma Confederate widow's pension.
McCaslin had relocated in his later years to live with his son.   John
Dillard and Wesley Welch, still living in Dickson County signed
statements vouching for his service records in his application. Company
bugler, Joseph H. Cox, returned to his home in Kentucky after the war
and drew a Kentucky Confederate Pension.   Eli Sherman of Franklin
vouched for Cox's Confederate service in his pension application. [16, 20]

Franklin, Tenn. Oct. 22nd 1913
Mr. Joseph H. Cox
Frankfort, Ky.

Dear Old Comrade Joe:
    Enclosed find my certificate duly sworn to etc., which I do hope and trust will be of great benefit to you. Joe if you have got a parole it is worth all the witnesses you could possibly secure. Enclosed find a copy of my parole.
    Have you any more children Joe besides Miss Judith ? I have two sons living, by my first wife. The youngest living in Texas, the other here. And two daughters by my second and last wife, who are at work in Nashville, and come out home every evening.
    With my best wishes and kind regards for you and yours, I will close.
I remain yours truly,
Eli G. Sherman
Box 42 Franklin, Tenn. [16]

Nine of the Georgia recruits who joined Baxter's Battery late in the war drew Georgia Confederate pensions: Seth Callahan, Louis Griggs, Minor Griggs, John M. Johnson, Andrew Kite, James Rad Morrow, Reuben Norris, Lewis Sudduth, and Leonidas Whitmore. Whitmore's widow also drew a Georgia Confederate Widow's Pension. [12] Noah Kimberly who had moved from Georgia to Cleburne County, Alabama after the war drew an Alabama Confederate Pension and his wife drew an Alabama Widow's pension. [2]

In both Georgia and Alabama, pensions were filed with a local county pension board, rather than filing with a state board as in Tennessee. In Georgia pensions were renewed annually and could be transferred to another county if the veteran changed his county of residence.

In 1914 and 1915, questionnaire forms were sent to all known living Tennessee Civil War Veterans by Dr. Gus Dyer, who was then serving as Archivist of Tennessee. Dyer's form known as form No. 1 asked the veterans 44 questions. In 1920, Mr. John Trotwood Moore, Director of the Tennessee Historical Commission, sent a revised form No. 2 which asked 46 questions. Three of Baxter's men filled out the questionnaires: John Dillard, James B. Thompson and Wesley Welch.

CIVIL WAR QUESTIONNAIRES

1. State your full name and present Post Office address:
2. State your age now.
3. In what State and county were you born?
4. In what State and county were you living when you enlisted in the service of the Confederacy or Federal Government?:
5. What was your occupation before the war?
6. What was the occupation of your father?:
7. If you owned land or other property at the opening of the war, state what kind of property you owned, and state the value of your property as near as you can:
8. Did you or your parents own slaves? If so, how many?:
9. If your parents owned land, state about how many acres:
10. State as near as you can the value of all the property owned by your parents, including land, when the war opened:
11. What kind of house did your parents occupy ? State whether it was a log house or frame house or built of other materials, and state the number of rooms it had:
12. As a boy and young man state what kind of work you did. If you worked on a farm, state to what extent you plowed, worked with a hoe, and other kinds of similar work:
13. State clearly what kind of work your father did, and what the duties of your mother were. State all the kinds of work done in the house as well as you can remember-that is cooking, spinning, weaving, etc.
14. Did your parents keep any servants? If so how many?:
15. How was honest toil-as plowing, hauling and other sorts of honest work of this class-regarded in your community? Was such work considered respectable and honorable?:
16. Did the white men in your community engage in such work ?:
17. To what extent were there white men in your community leading lives of idleness and having others do their work for them ?:
18. Did the men who owned slaves mingle freely with those who did not own slaves, or did slaveholders in any way show by their actions that they felt themselves better than respectable, honorable men who did not own slaves ?:
19. At the churches, at the schools, and at public gatherings in general, did slaveholders and non-slaveholders mingle on a footing of equality ?:
20. Was there a friendly feeling between slaveholders and non-slaveholders in your community, or were they antagonistic to each other ?:

21. In a political contest in which one candidate owned slaves and the other did not, did the fact that one candidate owned slaves help him in winning the contest ?:

22. Were the opportunities good in your community for a poor young man-honest and industrious-to save up enough to buy a small farm or go into business for himself ?:

23. Were poor, honest, industrious young men, who were ambitious to make something of themselves, encouraged or discouraged by slaveholders ?:

24. What kind of school did you attend ?:

25. About how long did you attend school altogether ?:

26. How far was the nearest school ?:

27. What school or schools were in operation in your neighborhood ?:

28. Was the school in your community private or public ?:

29. About how many months in the year did it run ?:

30. Did the boys and girls in your community attend school pretty regularly ?:

31. Was the teacher of the school you attended a man or a woman ?:

32. In what year and month and at what place did you enlist in the Confederate or of the Federal Government ?:

33. State the name of your regiment, and state the names of as many members of your company as you remember:

34. After enlistment, where was your company sent first ?:

35. How long after your enlistment before your company engaged in battle ?:

36. What was the first battle you engaged in ?:

37. State in your own way your experience in the war from this time on until the close. State where you went after the first battle-what you did, what other battles you engaged in, how long they lasted, what the results were; state how you lived in camp, how you were clothed, how you slept, what you had to eat, how you were exposed to cold, hunger, and disease. If you were in the hospital or in prison, state your experience here:

38. When and where were you discharged ?:

39. Tell something of your trip home:

40. What kind of work did you take up when you came back home ?

41. Give a sketch of your life since the close of the Civil War, stating what kind of business you have engaged in, where you have lived, your church relations, etc. If you have held an office or offices, state what it was. You may state here any other facts connected with your life and experience which has not been brought out by the questions:

42. Give the full name of your father_____
born_____ at_____in the county of_____state
of_____. He lived at_____. Give also any particulars
concerning him, as official position, war services, etc., books
written by, etc.
43. Maiden name in full of your mother_____She was the
daughter of_____(full name) and his
wife_____(full name) who lived
at_____
44. Remarks on ancestry. Give here any and all facts possible in
reference to your parents, grandparents, great-grandparents, etc.,
not included in the foregoing, as where they lived, office held,
Revolutionary or other war services; what country the family
came from to America; where first settled, county and state;
always giving full names (if possible) and never referring to an
ancestor simply as such without giving the name. It is desirable
to include every fact possible and to that end the full and exact
record from old Bibles should be appended on separate sheets of
this size, thus preserving the facts from loss.
45. Give the names of all the members of your company you can
remember: (If you know where the Roster is to be had, please
make special note of this.)
46. Give here the NAME and POST OFFICE ADDRESS of living
Veterans of the Civil War, whether members of your company or
not
NAME   POST OFFICE   STATE

DILLARD, JOHN

Form No. 1
1. John Dillard burns, Tenn. R. 1 Box 45
2. Born 1842 Nov 22
3. Davison Co., Tenn.
4. Cheatom Co., Tenn.
5. farming
6. farming
7. none
8. $500.00
9. $500.00
10. log. One room
11. howed and plowed
12. disabled; cooking, spinning, weaving

13. none
14. yes
15. yes
16. no
17. they did
19. no
20. not much
21. no
22. yes
23. I don't know
24. Subscription school
25. not half- had to work
26. ½ mile
27. Subscription
28. private
29. four
30. yes
31. man
32. Nov. 27th in '62
33. Capt. Edd Baxter; 1st Lt. Marshal, Lt. Herron; Lt. Galt was our Lt. Artillery co. we consolidated with Col. Made a battalion of artillery we under Bragg at Chattanooga, Tenn.
34. Cumberland Gap
35. 2 months
36. in Kentucky was the first with Col. Hart
37. from there to Chickamauga Missionary ridge Lookout Mountain under Bragg. As to clothes we had plenty. I never done without eating over 3 days. I in hospital 1 month. I used to rain snow mud.
38. Macon, Georgia
39. left Macon On train one day come to Atlanta to citty was all destroyed and railroad was tore up and we walked to Dalton, Ga. there we stayed one night and went to Chatanog , from there to Nashville.
40. farming
41. held no office. Followed farming
42. Bryand Dillard; North Carolina; he lived in Cheatom Co.; none
43. Elizabeth Garland; Jessee Garland; Jenie Newsom; Davidson co.
44. this is unknown to me. This is as near as I can ans. You.

THOMPSON, J.B.

Form No. 2
1. James Bouldin Thompson
2. 77 years
3. Davidson Co., Tn.
4. Confederate
5. Edd Baxter Co.
6. Farmer
7. James Madison Thompson; Davidson, Tenn.; Kingston Springs, Tenn. Father was justice of peace 16 yrs.
8. Pollie Clark; Henry Clark; Betsey Clark; Davidson co.
9. My grandparents came from England and settled in Virginia. His name was Wm. Thompson. He was in Revolutionary war and was in battle of New Orleans
10. did not own any
11. no
12. 83 acres
13. between $300 and 500
14. Log house-4 rooms
15. yes, worked on a farm, used to plow and hoe and other implements they used at that time.
16. My father was a farmer and house carpenter. My mother did all the household work, such as cooking, weaving, spinning, washing ironing and caring and raising her ten children.
17. no
18. yes
19. Didn't practice such. Seemed to appreciate doing their own work.
20. Seemed to be on equals
21. They met at some gatherings but females seemed to have a distant feeling toward each other
22. friendly feelings between them except in young girls who seemed at times to shun poor girls.
23. Don't know too young to remember
24. yes
25. No influence whatever
26. Subscription school
27. about 6 mo.
28. three miles
29. what was known as Muddy Branch School
30. Private
31. about 3 mo.
32. no
33. man

34. 1863   about Oct. I think. Enlisted near Charlie Jones home on Turnbull
35. Cumberland Gap
36. fully a year
37. Missionary Ridge
38. Went back to Atlanta. Stayed there in ditches about 9 mo. No other hard battles. Lived mostly on tough beef and biscuit. Regular old gray uniform. Slept on a blanket on the ground. Not exposed to cold. Too far south. Got hungry many times, Suffered with typhoid fever.
39. Chattanooga May 8, 1865
40. They gave me transportation to Nashville and I walked from Nashville to Kingston Springs to my home
41. farming
42. farming has always been my occupation. No other occupation. Lived in Cheatham and Dickson Co. Member of the Christian Church
43. ………………..
44. Capt. Edd Baxter, John Marshal 1st Lt.; John gorter 2nd Lt.; George Herrin, Jeff Parker, Sol Tidwell, Tom Kerr, Jim White, Andrew Parker, Felix truitt, John Lansumber, Jim Buttrey, Billie Buttrey, Wash Carr, dick Jackson, Duck Lamply, Radford Lamply, Arter Lankford, Till Lankford, Dee Lankford
45. Nute Cathey, Burns, Tenn.; Mose Garton, Burns, Tenn.; Wm. White, Burns, Tenn. and Henry Blackburn, Burns, Tenn.

(Extra page)   During service in war at Missionary Ridge I met Generals Hardee, Cayce, Williams and nearly all the Head men of the Army of Tennessee. I remember at one time they were all standing together laughing and shouting and watching the federals retreat down the mountain when a shell hit in fifteen or twenty feet of them and then the tune changed they all left and in double quick time too.

WELCH, WESLEY

Form No. 1

1. Wesley Welch, Bon Aqua, Tenn.
2. 77 years
3. Tenn., Dickson County
4. State of Tenn. Dickson County

5. Farmer

6. Blacksmith

7. x

8. No

9. Not any land

10. The value of the livestock were about $450 and not any land

11. My parents lived in a log house it had two (2) rooms in it

12. As a boy I plowed and worked with a hoe mostly. White men that had slaves did not do very much work and them did not have any slaves done all the farm work.

13. My father was a blacksmith by trade. My mother reared the family and done cooking, sewing, spinning and weaving and the duties of every home.

14. No

15. Any kind of farm work were considered honest an respectable.

16. Yes white men generally done such work in my community.

17. There were a few white men that did not do anything and had others to do the work for them

18. The men that owned slaves did not mingle freely with those that did not own slaves. Yes they felt themselves better than them that did not own slaves

19. No they did not mingle on a footing of equality

20. Not unless they were some relation to each other

21. Not any one are the other that helped either one very much

22. Not good before the war.

23. Yes poor honest were discouraged by slave holders

24. I did not attend school at all

25. x

26. About three miles

27. Free school. The name of the school Laws School

28. Public

29. Two to four months

30. No.

31. They were all men teachers

32. 1862 June 1 Spencer Mill, Tenn.

33. I belonged to Baxter's Co. an Artilery Co. (Baxter's Light Art. Co.) Capt. Baxter, 1st Lt. John Marshall, 2nd Lt. William Heron, 3rd Lt. John Gant, Sgt. John Cunningham, Dick Gant, Q.M. Sgt. John Sherman, 1st Sgt., George Hogan, 2nd Sgt. Mack McCaslin, 3rd Sgt. High Spencer, 4th Sgt.

34. It were sent to Bethursday (Bethesda ?) Maury Co., Tenn.

35. Nearly twelve months before I engaged in battle.

36. The battle of Chicamauga.

37.   I went to Missionary Ridge and went into the ditchesses The other were Missionary ridge lasted about one day. I cant tell how many were killed. The Yankes took the day. I lived in Camp 3 yr. 6 mo. 5 days I had not very much clothing. I slep on the ground. Mostly I had beef horse beans sugar crackers and corn bread. That is what I had to eat. I were exposed to cold by not having sufficient clothing an eatables I were in hospital 31 days
38.   Nashville is the place I were discharged 1865 in May
39.   I walked from Nashville home. I were bare footed bare headed and my clothes half torn off me and worn pretty bad.
40.   Cutting cord wood
41.   I am a farmer and a butcher. I am a Missionary Baptist and a Democrat.
42.   John Welch; Centerville; Hickman Co.; Tenn.; Dickson Co., Tenn.
43.Betty Luther; George Luther; Polly Bowden; they came from North Carolina to Tenn.
44.   My grandfather and grandmother were Irish-came from No. Carolina. [10]

Like many of the veterans, Soloman Tidwell had problems getting his pension approved and enlisted a lawyer to assist him.

John H. Claggett
Telephone No. 1
W. L. Pinkerton
CLAGETT & PINKERTON
LAWYERS
First National Bank building
CENTREVILLE, TENN.
October 18, 1921

Hon. John P. Hickman
Nashville, Tennessee
Dear Friend Hickman:
    Mr. Tidwell has been in to see me and handed me the enclosed letter, which seems to worry him a great deal. Mr. Tidwell has not received any legacy and evidently some person who does not like this old man has sent you this report simply to worry him. The idea of his having received any legacy is a huge joke. If any one writes you that Mr. Tidwell has received any legacy, I suggest that you have them make oath to the fact.
    Mr. Hickman if any one will swear that Mr. Tidwell has received any property from any source, we can show that ever who swears it swears a

plain falsehood. Now I tell you that this is not true, and you can rest assured that I would not uphold Mr. Tidwell in such a fraud. Mr. Tidwell could not pay his debts at this time and is in very hard luck to my personal knowledge, but like most people has some enemies, and they send you these reports just to annoy this old man. If any one files proof on this charge, kindly give me a chance to be heard, as I will expose these parties. They will not come out in the open and say this about Mr. Tidwell.

I hope the board will not allow these tales to prejudice it against Mr. Tidwell, who is very honest and good old man. I have known him personally all my life.

Very truly,
W. L. Pinkerton [23]

James Polk White applied for a Confederate Pension March 9, 1905 and his application was rejected. He re-applied and the application was accepted July 11, 1927. He died three months later.

Burns, Tenn.
10-17-1927
Mr. John P. Hickman
Nashville, Tenn.

Dear Sir

I am writing to inform you of my Father's (J. P. White) death, which occurred on the 6th of this month: so that you could adjust his pension accordingly.

Best wishes to you and the rest of the old boys of the south.

W. R. White
ADM. [23]

Jackson, Tennessee
October 15, 1940
The Board of Confederate Pensions,
Nashville, Tennessee

Dear Madam Chairman:

My mother the late Mrs. Mary W. Gault, was the widow of a Confederate soldier, my father. She had drawn a pension for a good many years, and on account of a very serious and protracted illness was forced to use what little funds she had outside of this pension. Her only other child, my brother died in 1937.

Last April we were forced to come to Jackson, from Franklin, Tenn., our home, and make this our residence, due to the fact that I could not hold a position and nurse her and we had no means of paying a nurse and living expenses. After six months of severe illness she died Sept. 22d. My son Bates L. Green, Jr. accompanied her remains to Franklin, I was too ill at the time to go, and he went to your office in Nashville Sept. 27 and notified the young lady there of his Grand-mother's death, and inquired if we could secure any part of her pension check that would have come to her Oct. 1st. He was given a paper that I was to fill out and have Notorized as her sole heir and was told that instead of the check for the pension of $25.00 that $100.00 was given for funeral expenses.

Of course this amount would not defray expenses, but it certainly would help. My son had to borrow part of this on a thirty day note and he hates to ask the Bank to allow him to renew it, if he could pay part of it off we could pay more to the Doctors and Druggist. Will you kindly let me know how soon we can expect this money, so we can plan accordingly. If any reference other than the affidavit or rather form signed by the Notary, I have lived practically all of my life in Franklin, and am well known both there and in Nashville. I shall much appreciate any assistance you can give me, for until I can rest sufficiently to regain my strength and go back to work, I am dependent upon my Son for support and he has a wife and two little boys.

Very truly yours,
Mrs. Bates L. Green [23]
680 Neely St., Jackson, Tenn

Mrs. Green's check was mailed October 17, 1940.

In addition to providing veteran and widow's pensions, all eleven former Confederate States and the states of Missouri, Oklahoma, Kentucky and Maryland operated old soldier's homes for their aging, indigent Confederate veterans. John Bryant Dillard died at the Tennessee Confederate Soldier's Home in Hermitage in 1928. Minor Griggs was listed as being an inmate at the Georgia Confederate Soldier's Home in Atlanta in 1930.

As with all wars, many of the veterans of Baxter's Battery were reluctant to talk about their wartime experiences. Descendents of Arter Lankford recalled that when asked about the war he would have what they called a "looking up spell". He would look up at the sky for the longest time and never say a word. He did tell his children of being above the clouds at Chattanooga and a few other things about the war that didn't relate to battle and death. He did relay to the family of going for three days with nothing to eat but a piece of moldy bread. Family members recalled Lankford coming home from camp on leave and infesting them with lice. Lankford was granted a furlough from Cumberland Gap in February 1862 to return home to sell his horses. Lice were known to be rampant in camps on both sides during the war. Another tale handed down in the Lankford family was: at one point in the war when the men in Baxter's Company were almost starving, they knocked Captain Baxter unconscious and stole a cow; either from the "beef on the hoof" traveling with the army or from a local farm. The cow was butchered and barbequed over the camp fire. The men had a feast. The next morning the Captain was said to have come out of his tent rubbing the back of his head and said: "Some s.o.b. knocked me in the head last night and he looked a lot like Sergeant Lankford." [17]

By the 1890's the aging Confederate Veterans had become respected senior citizens. Arter Lankford's family recalled that he enjoyed putting on his "Sunday go to meetin' " clothes and travel to Nashville to visit with other veterans. The classy thing to do was to have a newspaper under your arm. One day an acquaintance walked up to him and asked what was in the news. He looked at the paper and replied: "I see here where a ship has sunk." He could not read or write and was holding the newspaper upside down and was looking at a picture of a boat. [17]

Sol Tidwell relayed many war stories to his family. He was proud of his Confederate service and wanted to be buried in his uniform, but it was too small. All of his children wanted his uniform, but he requested that it be buried with him and his request was granted. Tidwell also told his family of spending three days after the Battle of Chickamauga loading corpses on his wagon and hauling them from the battlefield to the burial trenches. He relayed that the odor of the decaying corpses made him sick to his stomach, that he would have to stop loading, vomit and return. He also relayed at one time of having only seven grains of corn to eat for seven days. [17]

Aaron Beard kept a diary during his four years of service both in Baxter's Battery and in Company B of the 24th Tennessee Infantry Regiment. The diary he kept and the musket he carried during the war were passed on in his family. [17]

Albert Green was another who shared war experiences with family members. In addition to serving as a blacksmith (artificer), he served as the company dentist. The pliers with which he pulled teeth during the war were preserved by his family[17]

Radford T. Lampley is said to have acquired the nickname "Duck" when the battery first came under enemy fire and the other soldiers shouted: "Duck, Lampley, duck." [17]

Pvt. Radford T. Lampley   Pvt. James B. Thompson

In 1935, James B. Thompson gave testimony of his wartime experiences to his granddaughter, Marguerite Brown Adams, who wrote them down and had them notarized.[24]

Private William George Demarkes Buttrey died in 1881 and was buried in his wife's family cemetery, the White Cemetery in Dickson County. It is said a monument of cannon balls was placed in the cemetery in honor of the veterans buried there. William's brother, James Felix Ewing Buttrey, is said to have come to the cemetery and removed the cannon balls and thrown them in nearby Turnbull Creek. When asked about his deed, he is said to have replied: "We saw enough of those things during the war and don't need to be buried with them." [17]

Over the years, many wartime tales were passed down through the families of Baxter's men. Some were lost in the succeeding generations. Some of the family lore was in error. The most common misconception among the descendents of the men of Baxter's Battery was that the battery was engaged in the Battles of Franklin and Nashville, when the battery was actually stationed at Macon, Georgia during that time.

Descendents most likely assumed that since the Confederate Army fought at Franklin and grandpa was in the Confederate Army that he fought at Franklin.

By 1930 only a handful of Baxter's men were still living. Franklin Attorney Thomas P. Henderson assisted several of the families of Baxter's men in acquiring government gravestones for the deceased veterans, in most cases, several years after their deaths. Henderson was a World War I Veteran, having served as Captain of Battery F of the 114th Field Artillery in France. Some of those who received stones with Henderson's help were: James F. E. Buttrey, William Sullivan, Abraham Spencer and John Lambert Forehand.

T. P. HENDERSON
ATTORNEY
FRANKLIN, TENNESSEE
October 31, 1938

Mrs. Mary B. Gamble
Nashville, Tennessee
Dear Mary:
 The grandchildren of William Sullivan, a Confederate veteran from this County who was born August 26, 1826, died February 10, 1920 and who they say served as a Teamster in Baxter's Battery during the Civil War, are trying to get a Federal Monument for him.
 They say he drew a Confederate pension, and if so you must have his record in your office. I would appreciate it if you would send it to me.
 You are probably not interested in the dates of his birth and death; these were put in this letter for my files.
 I think that we will have quite a number of requests for Federal Monuments for Confederate soldiers from this County, and I will probably be worrying you from time to time for records.
 The Grandson who is sponsoring this is Gilbert Sullivan, Franklin, Tennessee.

Your friend,
Tom Henderson [23]

Captain Baxter died at his summer home at Ridge Top, Tennessee of kidney failure in 1910. 1st Lieutenant John Marshall, Jr. was killed in a railroad accident in 1874. Both Baxter and Marshall were buried in

Mount Olivet Cemetery in Nashville. Lieutenant William Herrin died in Nashville in 1883 and was buried at the Herrin Family Cemetery in Cheatham County. Lieutenant Gault died in Saint Thomas Hospital in Nashville in 1905 and was buried at Mt. Hope Cemetery in Franklin. [18]

With the death of Benjamin F. Brown on March 21, 1837, Dickson County lost its last surviving Confederate Veteran. Brown was the last surviving member of Baxter's Middle Tennessee Recruits. Of the Georgia recruits, Minor Y. Griggs was living in the Georgia Confederate Soldiers Home in Atlanta in 1930.

Pvt. Benjamin F. Brown

Eliza Jane Tidwell Cunningham, widow of Sergeant John Francisco Cunningham was the last surviving widow of Baxter's Middle Tennessee Recruits. She died at her home in Fairview on October 20, 1943.

Sallie Vinson Whitmore of Habersham County, Georgia, widow of Private Leonidas Whitmore, applied for a Georgia Confederate Widow's pension February 19, 1940. She had married Whitmore in 1905 at age 27. He was 76 years old at the time of their marriage. [12]

While much personal information on the soldiers was lost over time, some remained and was shared with other descendents over the country many years after the war:

January 19, 1955
Mrs. Prudence White Holt
RFD #1
Burns, Tennessee

Mr. John Gordon White
Oakland, California

I'm not very well yet and hope you are not so bad as I am. And having passed the time of day, let's get down to brass tacks. Let's cheer up.

Daniel White, the youngest child of Josh & Patty White, born about 1840 or there-a-bouts, he was my daddy. I being the seventh daughter of Caroline Parker White. Born in the year of our Lord A.D. 1880, July 14, which makes me about 75 ½ years young and that's me.

Now Josh had a son O'the name of David White, who after the death of Josh, betook himself and his earthly belongings to the West. This included a wife, a negro "mammy" and other oddments that might be useful in the unknown land. Things being what they were and mail and transportation uncertain, slow in those days, the family did not keep in very close touch one with another. However the news that David's wife had borne him a lovely son (1850), which same he named Daniel in honor, shall we say, for his baby brother, Dan (my daddy).

Time went by and Daniel, son of David, became a dingdong grand-daddy. And somewhere there abouts you came in. And that's the whyness of all the whatness of our kinship. Make of it what you can. Daniel of David, came in his mid-life to visit Daniel of Josh and Patty his 60's or thereabouts.

Now time came to go out and resist the dam-yankies and give them the larruping of the ages. My daddy, Dan, and his brother Jesse, went forth to victory or die on the field---they neither died nor did they win, but stayed until the last roll was called. Limped home, and without a "gim-me---gimee" or G.I. loan, began to till the soil. Rebuilt the ashes like the Phoenix rose from the ashes, bigger, better, finer, men, and left a heritage unsullied; lived their time out at about 85 each; but the good State of Tennessee put markers at their heads in recognition of the time and effort they had given to the lost cause, (or XXX it?)

A cousin, William White, son of Joseph, also went.

My daddy's commander was and his place of action was BAXTER'S BATTERY, if that's the way to spell it, enlisted at Franklin, Tenn. I do not know if Uncle Jesse was with him or not but do know he was in a (D__Y) prison a long time and came home long after Dan did, almost starved. He lived to rear his two daughters, Mary & Martha; begat a son

Ballard and twins Amanda and Melvina, What names: But that was then and this is the day of Brendas and Paulets, etc., etc.

Cousin Will White, his monument is in the White graveyard; was under Captain Fulton Tidwell. Jesse's monument is in the Stuart graveyard and my daddy lies in the Parker graveyard. All within a radius of 6 miles of Burns, Tenn.

Well Burns is a little country town on the NC &St L. RR, 37 miles from Nashville, Tenn. That is the road that reaches from Chat. Tenn. to St. Louis by way of Nashville. Burns is 37 miles almost west of Nashville, Tenn. There has been a P.O. there eons of time. There's also a 2 RFD; There are 3 churches: Primitive Baptist, Methodist; Church of Christ of which I am a member. Once there was a telegraph office and a depot. Hiways and busses and cars have taken the place and only specials stop at Burns. But life goes along the little town is scattered over considerable area but not incorporated even after being a hundred or so years old---------THAT'S BURNS.

Some of the places they (confederates) were;--Peach-tree creek in Ga.; Missionary Ridge; Chickamauga; Look-out Mountain; and others Please make what you can of this I'm too ill to go back over it. Will be better soon, I hope.

Some of their comrades were: Mose (Gid) Garton, (Shad) Welch, sure-shot, never wasted a bullet; A.J. Parker (Andrew); T.J. Parker (Jeff); J.T. Parker (Jim wounded in Ga.); T.P. Lankford (Tillman Parish), Dee Lankford, Arter or Arthur Lankford; ? ? ? Rat-a-u-rel, a Frenchman, Wash Car, died near Chat.; Marshal Allison. Some of these may be helpful in your look see. But your kin, direct are: Jesse White, commander Baxter Bat.; Daniel White??? William White under Fulton Tidwell.

As I've told you, I'm too ill to go over all this truck. When I'm well, if I ever am, I'll try to get the tree typed. There is more, lots more. Love to all the folks.

Mrs. Prudence Holt
Burns, Tenn. R. 1 [15]

The following is part of a letter written by Mrs. Prudence White Holt to Suzie White of Cedar Rapids, Iowa in 1959, shortly before Mrs. Holt was killed by a train (possibly suicide).

I was surprised to hear from you. That is, if you are who I think you are, that is Ballard White's daughter. I thought they kept a record.

To begin with. In those days, just exactly what days we can't say at present, but I'll get busy and find out. But suffice to say:

"Bout" 1800 (before or after) many people came from the Carolinas, Georgia, Virginia and a round about to make homes in this goodly free land.

There came the Whites Uncle William by name and he took unto himself to wife ---- as he said his aristocratic North Carolina lady. He begot and she bore him many sons and daughters Nancy (Mansel) Tidwell headed the list and Colonel William (Bill) White married a Stuart and she bore him Lundy White and Docia Brown, was last. More about him later.

Also came a bachelor brother of William, Jr. His name was Joshua White, his mother and sister Susan White who married a Morris. And if I have it right there were the parents of Milly Sellers of whom we shall hear more. They went to Texas and some of them died here and some there.

Now Joshua and his mother had some 640 acres of land from Old Turnbull Meetin house down branch to Turnbull Creek, down the creek to the baptisin hole there is a fine bridge there now, back to the ridge where it joins Uncle Williams, thence to the present Turnbull meetin-house, there is the third house built there. The White burial section is there also. This is goodly land rich and well timbered. They had many slaves to run the plantation.

The call came for Joshua to come to the army and help put down the rebellion (not civil war). He mounted his stud hoss left the mother and slaves to make the best of it. I remember the barns that stood for years. As Josh rode south he stopped at the spring of a Lampley family to refresh his beast and get a drink of water for himself. Now a teen-aged gal was doing the daily wash, She had bright eyes, black hair and a goodly form. Enter Dan Cupid. She lowed it's a pretty day and he rejined that she was also a pretty gal or something to that effect. She asked where he was going on his pretty beast and he told her that there was war and the unmarried men were called to duty, He did not think it would take long, he'd come back and they'd marry if she was willing; she said she'd be waiting. Now she was Martha Patricia Lampley. Patey for short, sister of Uncle Dode or Joseph Lampley; he married a Buttrey, Joe did.

They married and he rid her behind him to his home and she became Mistress of the plantation. Somewhere along the way Josh's Ma died and Patey took over. And they were man and wife. Josh, a mature man and Patey a teen-age girl, she bore him children as follows: David married a Reynolds girl, they went to Texas. They were the great-grand parents of the preacher (Jack) White; and James, I believe it was, went to the gold fields of California. Records lost of him. Benjamin, Alec's daddy. Uncle Ben to us. He got a second wife and wound up by committing suicide. His second wife was a corker.

Jesse, your grandpa, married Adeline Mitchell, she owned the property and wore the britches. He was modest and retiring and smiled and made little nice jokes with the girls. But it was up snakes and come to thaw, oh he could take only so much. Then he shut up like a clam. [15]

Monument to Tennessee Confederate Artillerymen
on the Chickamauga Battlefield.

The Chickamauga-Chattanooga National Military Park was the first and largest of the National Military Parks created by Act of Congress in the 1890's. In the Chickamauga battlefield section of the park a statue honoring the Tennessee artillerymen was erected. Baxter's Battery is listed on the statue. On Missionary Ridge in the Chattanooga section of the park is a historical marker showing the location of Baxter's Battery during the Battle of Missionary Ridge.

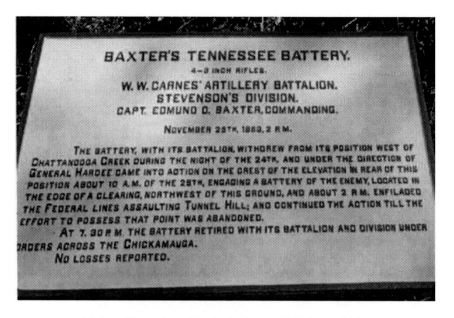

Marker of Baxter's position in the Battle of Missionary Ridge
in Chattanooga, TN.

In March 2001 a monument honoring the Confederate soldiers of Dickson County was erected at the Courthouse in Charlotte by Captain William H. McCauley Camp 260 Sons of Confederate Veterans in Dickson.   A dedication ceremony was held May 12, 2001.   The monument listed the Confederate units from Dickson County and listed: Baxter's Company Tennessee Light Artillery and Baxter's Battery Tennessee Light Artillery.

On December 9, 2003 Captain E. D. Baxter Camp 2034 Sons of Confederate Veterans was chartered in Fairview, Tennessee with 26 members.   The camp was named in honor of the Captain who had recruited many of his men in the area which later became the Fairview area.

On May 22, 2004 the camp placed a military stone on the captain's grave and held a memorial service at Mount Olivet Cemetery in Nashville. The Commander of the Tennessee Division Sons of Confederate Veterans, Mr. Edward M. Butler of Cookeville and President of the Tennessee Division of the United Daughters of the Confederacy, Mrs. Deana Bryant of Franklin, were both present for the event.   Seven SCV camps and five UDC Chapters were represented at the event, which ended with a 21-gun salute fired by Confederate re-enactors.

In addition to the grave stone placed for Captain Baxter, members of Camp 2034 placed markers for many other members of the unit who did not already have military markers: James G. Lewis, Dillard H. Lankford, William J. Lankford, Radford T. Lampley, Harvey Clark, Benjamin Terrell, Joseph Terrell, William G. D. Buttrey, William G. Buttrey, James M. Buttrey, Andrew J. "Jack" Lampley, Joseph Nall, John T. Groves, Albert Green, William Hood, Hiram Spencer, William Bethshears, James P. White, Jesse White, John B. Dillard, and Aaron P. Beard.

Family members and others had previously placed military stones on the graves of: James F. Cunningham, Arter R. Lankford, James F.E. Buttrey, James B. Thompson, John L. Forehand, Tillman Lankford, William McPherson, William Sullivan, Vachel Barnhill, Thomas J. Parker, Jesse B. Edwards, William Herrin, Benjamin F. Brown, Thomas J. Carr, John Demonbruen, Aquilla Tidwell, Soloman Tidwell, Wesley Welch and Daniel White.

In 2004 a Confederate Artillery Re-enactment unit named Baxter's Battery was organized in Goodlettsville, Tennessee.

In 2007 a historical marker commemorating the recruitment of Baxter's Battery was placed by the City of Fairview, Tennessee.

A dedication ceremony was held on June 3, 2007, Confederate Decoration Day.

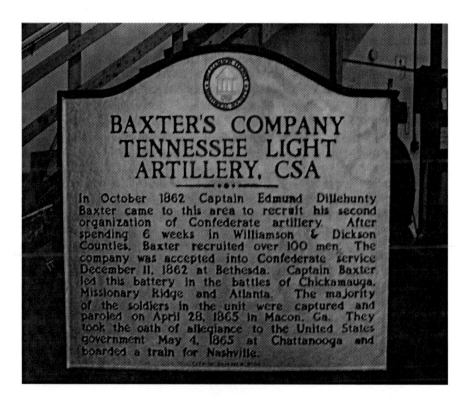

Marker commemorating the recruitment of Baxter's Battery in front of city hall in Fairview, TN.

THE FORGOTTEN REBELS OF TURNBULL CREEK ARE NO LONGER FORGOTTEN.

CHAPTER 7
ED BAXTER

After being paroled and taking the other of allegiance on June 16, 1865 in Nashville, Ed Baxter returned to his Nashville home to reunite with his wife Eliza and daughter Katie. As the men in his company returned to their farms and trades, he resumed his occupation, the practice of law. Baxter energetically entered his practice of law and soon became well known in Nashville and built a large practice. With the end of the war and the recovering southern economy, railroad transportation was booming. New tracks were being built and smaller lines were being bought by the larger rail lines. Baxter was hired to represent the Louisville and Nashville Railroad, the largest in the area, and soon became its Attorney General for the state of Tennessee. He held that position for over twenty years. At that time, Baxter was a member of the firm of Baxter, Smith, and Allison. The firm was composed of Baxter, Colonel Baxter Smith and Judge Andrew Allison.

As his career grew, so did his family. He and Eliza had two more children, P. Perkins Baxter and Nancy Baxter. Baxter built a home for his growing family in the Rutledge Hill area on the south side of Nashville. He named the home Rose Hill. He also owned a summer home in Ridge Top, Tennessee, north of Nashville. Baxter was a member of Elm Street Methodist Church in Nashville.

Rose Hill, home of Ed Baxter in the Rutledge Hill section of Nashville. Added onto over the years, the left entrance and rear of the house is the original portion built by Baxter.

In 1875 Baxter became a faculty member of the newly formed Vanderbilt University School of Law. The faculty consisted of William B. Reese, Thomas H. Malone and Baxter. All three were Confederate veterans and practicing lawyers. Reese had served as a Private in Company C of the 11th Tennessee Cavalry Regiment and Malone had served as Lieutenant in Company A of the 1st Tennessee Infantry Regiment (Feilds). Baxter served as Professor of the Law of Domestic Relations, Agency, Partnership, Corporations, Evidence, Wills and Executors. His students addressed him as "The Captain" rather than professor. In later years, he told his students that he spent more time preparing for a lecture for his classes at Vanderbilt than he did in preparation for arguing a case before the United States Supreme Court.

Mrs. Eliza Baxter died on December 17, 1876. In 1879 Baxter married Mrs. Sarah Elizabeth Perkins Baxter. She was the widow of his late half brother Jones Baxter and a sister of his late wife. Edmund and Sarah Baxter had three children together: Sloss D. Baxter, Hamilton Baxter, and Bettie B. Baxter.

Baxter's private practice and railroad work continued to grow. With the passage of the Interstate Commerce Act in 1887, transportation litigation continued to increase. In 1896 Baxter was chosen general counsel for an association of southern railroads and steamship lines. The association was based in Nashville and Baxter held the position until his death. He became an expert on the Interstate Commerce Act and rate litigation. He appeared often before the Interstate Commerce Commission and argued many cases before the United States Supreme Court. He was said to have argued more cases before the United States Supreme Court than any other lawyer of his era. Much of his courtroom work was done in Washington, Philadelphia, Chicago, Cincinnati and other northern cities. He became better known in those areas than at home in Nashville.

While Baxter's legal specialty was railroad and Interstate Commerce Law, in 1893 he was hired by the United States government to prosecute several officers of national banks in the Commercial National Bank cases. Baxter won the case for the government. The Circuit Court Judge who tried the cases was Judge William Howard Taft, who would later become President of the United States, Taft stated that Baxter was the best criminal lawyer he had ever known.

Baxter was known as a meticulous attorney, never going to court unprepared for a case. He was said to always have used notes when pleading his case

With his workload and travel increasing, Baxter gave up his faculty position at Vanderbilt in 1890. He was appointed by Governor William B. Bate, a former Confederate General, as a Substitute Justice on the Tennessee Supreme Court.

While maintaining a busy career, Baxter was much the family man. He was known as a modest, unassuming man who loved spending time with his family and friends while not working.

Baxter never forgot his Confederate service. He was a member of Cheatham Bivouac #1 of the Tennessee Association of Confederate Soldiers (predecessor of the United Confederate Veterans) and gave the keynote address at the associations reunions in 1889 in Nashville and 1892 in Franklin. He also spoke at the dedication ceremony of the National Cemetery in Nashville. A replica of his company flag was presented to him by the Ladies Auxiliary of Memphis in 1901. Baxter never forgot the men who had served in his command. Several of his former soldiers, when needing help in getting their Confederate pensions contacted Ed Baxter. In July 1903 Baxter called on the Tennessee Confederate Pension Board on behalf of William M.Sullivan.[23]

Replica of Baxter's company flag sewn by Mrs. Rene Bowser of Fairview, TN. presented to SCV Camp 2034 April 10, 2007

In 1907 four of Baxter's former soldiers wrote him asking for support for the Confederate pension application of former comrade, Thomas Hooper. Hooper had been at home on sick furlough at the time of the surrender.[23]

Burns, Tenn.
August 23, 1907

Capt. Ed Baxter

Sir this is for the purpose of informing you with regard to T.J. Hooper's service in your co. in Civil War.   To wit-He was in the company and if there ever was any complaint-against- him I knew nothing of it I am satisfied that –He served to the close of the war.

B. F. Brown [23]

Stayton   Dickson Co., Tenn.
August 23, 1907

Capt. Ed. Baxter

My knowledge and recollection of T. J. Hooper's Service in your co. in Civil War is that –He was Faithful and true til close of war.

Respectfully   A. A. McCaslin [23]

Bon Aqua   R 3   8/22 1907
To all it may cosern

Capt. Ed Baxter   in regard to T. J. Hooper I was messing with him at the time when he left the camps. I think it was about the last of March 65 But I don't know the Day of the month and he had a sick furlow for 30 days and as to his service-he was about like the balance of us he don what he was ordered to do and eat his rations as the balance of us Did.

Yours truly,
H. A. Spencer [23]

Bon aqua
August 24th 1907
Ed Baxter

Dear sir

With Regard To T. J. Hooper I remember him as a Faithful Soldier and one that Staed with us through the War

A. Q. Tidwell [23]

ED BAXTER   W. G. HUTCHENSON   PERKINS BAXTER
BAXTER & HUTCHESON,
ATTORNEYS AT LAW
NASHVILLE, TENNESSEE

Subject No. 5003
Letter No. 1960

Jno. P. Hickman
Nashville, Tenn.
Dear Sir:
    At the request of P. E. Cox, Attorney, Franklin, Tenn., I here enclose application of J. W. Martin formerly of Baxter's Battery, for pension.

Yours truly,
Ed Baxter [23]

ADDRESS TO THE TENNESSEE ASSOCIATION OF
CONFEDERATE SOLDIERS
OCTOBER 3, 1889 NASHVILLE, TN.
CAPTAIN Ed BAXTER
The True Status of the Confederate Soldier

"All men are born free and equal, and have certain natural, essential and untenable rights; among which may be reckoned the right of enjoying and defending lives and liberties; that of ACQURIRING, POCESSING AND PROTECTING PROPERTIES, and of the institution, maintenance, and administration of government is to the existence of the body politic, to protect it, and furnish the individuals to oppose it with the power of enjoying, in safety and tranquility, their natural and blessings of life; and whenever these great objectives are not obtained PEOPLE HAVE A RIGHT TO ALTER THE GOVERNMENT, and take measures for the safety, prosperity and happiness."
Government is instituted for the common good, for the protection, safety, prosperity, and happiness of the people, and not for the profit, honor, or private interests of any one man, family or class of men; therefore the people alone have an untestable, unalienable, and indefeasible right to institute government, and to REPEAL, ALTER OR TOTALLY CHANGE THE SAME, when the protection,, safety, prosperity, and happiness require it."
CONSTITUTION OF MASSACHUSETTS, 1780

"Whenever any form of government becomes destructive of these ends, IT IS THE RIGHT OF THE PEOPLE TO ALTER OR ABOLISH IT, and to

institute new government, laying its foundation on such principles, and
organizing its powers in such form as to them shall seem most likely to effect
their safety and happiness."
DECLARATION OF INDEPENDENCE OF THE UNITED STATES,
1776.

Ladies, Gentlemen, and fellow Comrades:

Nearly a quarter of a century has elapsed since the war ended, and
the South has accepted, in good faith, and without mental reservation, all
the legitimate results of the war.

I have come here today, not to pronounce a panegyric upon the
Confederate soldiers, for I think they need none; nor to abuse the
Federal soldiers, for I do not think they deserve it; but I have come here
today to see that in making up the record of the Confederate cause, the
facts are put down fairly, so that we may all understand clearly what
were the legitimate results of the war, which the South ought to accept,
and has accepted.

I wish to appear as a lawyer, when his opponent is making up a bill
of exceptions, to carry a cause to the Supreme Court; and to see that my
opponent fairly states the facts as they were proven in the court below,
and fairly presents the issues of law which are to be submitted to the
court above.

I wish to see that the facts of the Confederate cause are put down
fairly and correctly; so that when we are judged by posterity, as we will
be, posterity will have an opportunity of knowing the view that we, who
went into the war, took of the questions that were involved in it; and
whether the judgment of posterity shall be for, or against us, I wish to do
my part in enabling posterity to come to an intelligent decision.

For one, I am not willing that my children, and my grand children,
and others who are to come after me, shall look back upon my memory
as though I were a base-hearted traitor, whose hands were dyed in the
blood of his countrymen; nor, am I willing that my children, and
grandchildren, when they go North, East, or West, and meet the men of
other states, shall hang their heads in humiliation, and acknowledge that
they are the descendents of a conquered race.

Therefore, I propose to devote my remarks to a discussion of three
propositions:

First, I intend to argue to you, just as I would argue before the
Supreme Court of the State, or the Supreme Court of the United States,
that the South was fully justified in going into the war.

My second proposition will be that the South having engaged in conflict, acted humanely, and bravely, throughout the war.

And my third proposition will be, that the South was not conquered in the war; and that the people of the South are not today, in any correct sense, a conquered people.

In support of my first proposition, I have preferred to quote from the Constitution of Massachusetts, and the Declaration of Independence of the United States; because, I feel sure that the Northern people will agree that they contain a correct enunciation of the principles of republican government.

They establish, beyond controversy, that among the unalienable rights of men are life, liberty, and the pursuit of happiness; which latter includes the right to acquire and own such lawful subjects of property, as are necessary to our happiness.

And they establish, the proposition, that whenever any form of government becomes destructive of these ends, it is the right of the people to alter, or abolish it.

If, therefore, I can show that the people of the South had a valuable property right, and that they had a reasonable ground to believe that it was about to be destroyed under the form of government of the United States, then I will have shown that it was the right of the people of the south to endeavor to alter, or abolish, that form of government.

At the commencement of the war, the confederate States, viz.: Virginia, North Carolina, South Carolina, Georgia, Florida, Alabama, Mississippi, Louisiana, Texas, Arkansas, and Tennessee, contained an area of 733,144 square miles, a white population of 5,672,272 and a slave population of 3,607,057.

1st Putnam, Rebellion Record, p. 130 (R.I.)

Add the slaves in the other Southern States, place a fair average valuation upon them, and it will be seen that the slave property of the South represented an actual value of not less than $2,000,000,000- a sum so large that it is almost impossible for the human mind to clearly comprehend it.

We owned those slaves in the same sense that you now own your lands, or personal effects; and the injustice of depriving us of those slaves, was precisely as great, as if the attempt were now made to deprive us of our lands, and personal property.

Whether slavery was originally right, or wrong, had nothing more to do with the title to our slaves, than the question, as to whether the Indians were rightfully expelled from this country, has to do with our title to our lands.

We did not enslave the colored people.   We inherited them as property from our fathers and forefathers, just as we inherited our lands; and our title to our slaves, like our title to our lands, could be traced back, by an unbroken chain, to the Colonies, by whom the government of the United States was founded, and established.

A large portion of the slaves were imported into the Colonies by the mother country, and in twelve, out of the fifteen original States, negro slavery existed and the right of property in slaves was protected by law.

The census of 1790 shows, that in Vermont there were 17 slaves; New Hampshire, 158; Rhode Island, 952; Connecticut. 2,759; New York, 21,324; New Jersey, 11,423; Pennsylvania, 3,737; making a total of 40,370 slaves in the Northern States. In Massachusetts, slavery was not abolished until 1780.

It will be seen, therefore, that the Northern people cannot justly taunt the South as having been the only people who were the owners of slaves under the government of the United States. On the contrary, it will be seen, that the North, as well as the South, when the government of the United States was first established, recognized that slaves were lawful subjects of property.

On December 28, 1837, Mr. Calhoun introduced into the Senate of the United States the following resolution:

"Resolved, That domestic slavery, as it exists in the Southern States and Western States of this Union, composes an important part of their domestic institutions, inherited from their ancestors, and existing as the adoption of the Constitution; by which it was recognized as constituting an important element in distribution of powers among the States, and that no change of opinion or feeling , on the part of the States of the Union in relation to it, can justify them as citizens, in open and systematic attacks thereon, with the view of its overthrow, and that all such attacks are in manifest violation of the mutual and solemn pledge to protect and defend each other, given by the States respectively, on entering into the constitutional compact which formed the Union, and, as such, are a manifest breach of faith, and a violation of the most solemn obligations."

Upon that resolution the vote in the Senate stood 34 for it and only 5 against it; and the vote by States, stood 18 for it and only 2 against it; two were divided and four did not vote.

Stevens' History of the United States, pp; 359, 360.

In December, 1838, Mr. Atherton, of New Hampshire, introduced into the House of Representatives the following resolution: "Resolved, that this government is a government of limited powers, and that, by the Constitution of the United States, Congress has no jurisdiction whatever over the institution of slavery in the several States of the Confederacy." The vote upon this resolution was 194 in favor, and only 6 against it.

He also introduced the following resolution: "Resolved, That petitions for the abolition of slavery in the District of Columbia, and the Territories of the United States, against the removal of slaves, from one state to another, are a part of a plan of operations set on foot to affect the institution of slavery in Southern States, and thus indirectly to destroy that institution within their limits." The vote upon this resolution stood 136 in favor, and only 65 against it.

Stevens' History of the United States, pp 361, 362.

It will thus be seen that as late as 1838, it was almost the unanimous opinion of the people of the North, as well as of the South, that slaves were the lawful subjects of property; that slavery was recognized and protected by the Constitution of the United States; that Congress had no power to interfere with it, either in the States, or the Territories, or with removal of slaves from one State to another; and that the operations which were set on foot, to affect the institutions of slavery in the Southern States were intended, indirectly, to destroy that institution within those States.

In 1856, the Supreme Court of the United States, decided, "that the Constitution of the United States recognizes slaves as property, and pledges the Federal government to protect it. And Congress cannot exercise any more authority over property of that description, than it may constitutionally exercise over property of any other kind."

19 How., 395 Dred Scott vs Sanford

As we all know, the Supreme Court is the highest judicial tribunal known to our form of government and upon all questions relating to the Constitution of the United States, the decision of that Court is final. It is the duty of every citizen, of every section, to yield prompt obedience to the decrees of that august tribunal; but I ask the people of the North whether they did, or did not, submit with true loyalty, to the arbitrament of that Court of last resort?

If the violation of the Constitution of the United States, as construed by the people of the North, on the question of secession, was an offense by the people of the South, what is to be said of the conduct of the people of the North, who openly violated the Constitution, as construed by the Supreme Court of the United States, on the question of slavery?

The South had the right to differ from the North in construing the Constitution on the subject of secession, because, the question of secession had not been decided by the Supreme Court; but, the North had no right to differ from the South on the question of slavery, after that question had been put at rest by the Supreme Court.

As late as march 1, 1861, President Lincoln, in his inaugural address used this language: "I have no purpose, directly or indirectly, to interfere with the institution of slavery in the States where it exists. I believe I have no lawful right to do so, and I have no inclination to do so."

In the same address, he distinctly recognizes the right of the Southern people to reclaim their fugitive slaves from the Northern States, and the duty of Congress to provide the means of reclaiming them by national laws.

1st Putnam Rebellion Record; 36, 37 (Doc.)

The Congress of the United States, which assembled on the 4th of July, 1861, passed a resolution in which it was declared that the war was not prosecuted on the part of the government "for the purpose of overthrowing or interfering with the rights, or the established institutions" of the Southern States.

Steven's History of the United States, p. 431.

I have thus shown that the right of property, in slaves, was recognized by the people of the North, as well as by the people of the South, in the days of the Colonies, and before this government was established; that it was recognized in the Constitution, as decided by the Supreme Court of the United States; that it was recognized by both houses of Congress, not only in 1838, but as late as 1861, after the war had in fact commenced; and that it was also recognized by President Lincoln, who conducted the war.

The South thus had the recognition of the Executive, Legislative, and Judicial Departments of the government, from the foundation of the government down to a point of time after the late war had commenced.

Who, then can deny that the South had a lawful property right in her slaves?   And who that acknowledge the principles of republican government, as announced in the Constitution of Massachusetts, and the Declaration of Independence, can deny the right of the South to protect that property.

The next question under my first proposition is, whether the South had reasonable grounds to believe that she could defend her right of property in slaves, only by a resort to war.

I assume that the law of self-defense is the same for a people as for an individual. A man has no right, even in what he supposes to be the defense of his life, to inflict great bodily injury upon another, unless he has reasonable grounds to believe at the time that he can protect his life in no other way. It is his duty to resort to the courts of the country, whenever the circumstances of the case will permit him to do so. But if the facts surrounding him are such as to justify a reasonable man in believing that he cannot protect his life otherwise than by slaying his adversary, then he may lawfully do so; although it may afterward appear that his adversary was wholly unarmed, and did not in fact meditate any assault.

And so with the people of the South. Though they may have felt that the institution of slavery was endangered by the action of the people of the Northern yet, they had no right to resort to war, if there were any other means of redress, by appealing either to the courts, or to the intelligence of the people of the country, But the South had appealed to the courts, and the Supreme Court of the United States in the Dred Scott case, to which I have referred, had decided the question in favor of the South. The North, however, refused to abide by the decision, and so demonstrated that the people of the South could not be protected by any remedy which the courts of the country were competent to afford.

The South had also appealed to the public opinion of the country; and in 1838, and even in 1861, Congress as voicing the sentiment of the country, had recognized the right of the South in her slaves, and her right in protection in regard to them.

But, notwithstanding these declarations of Congress, the agitation continued, and the South saw that there was no more relief to be obtained from Congress, than there was from the courts. The South was then fully justified in believing that sooner or later the issue must be met, and that she must either cowardly surrender $2,000,000,000 of property without a struggle, or that she must resort to the dread alternative of war.

The only question about which there can be any doubt, is as to whether the South was justified in going to war just when she did; and upon that point there was a great diversity of opinion, even among the people of the South.

Mr. Stevens, Vice-President of the Confederate States, on Nov. 14, 1860, used this language; "The first question that presents itself, is shall the people of the South secede from the Union, in consequence of the election of Mr. Lincoln to the Presidency of the United States? My Countrymen, I tell you frankly, kindly, and earnestly, that I do not think they ought."

His advice was, that the South should wait until Mr. Lincoln committed some violation of the Constitution, before resorting to war.

1st Putnam, Rebellion Record, p.220 (Doc.)

General Lee was of the same opinion. In a letter dated April 20, 1861, he used this language: "The whole South is in a state of revolution, into which Virginia, after a long struggle, has been drawn; and though I recognize no necessity for this state of things, and would have forborne, and pleaded to the end , for redress of grievances, real or supposed, yet, in my own person, I had to meet the question whether I should take part against my native State. With all my devotion to the Union, and the feeling of loyalty, and duty as an American citizen, I have not been able to make up my mind to raise my hand against my relatives, my children, my home."

Thousands of other people in the South, took the same view as Mr. Stevens and General Lee, and I was among them. I thought that the South ought to wait until Mr. Lincoln should commit some overt act. I believed he was sincere, when he said in his inaugural address, that he had no purpose, directly or indirectly, to interfere with the institution of slavery in the states where it existed; and I believed he had sufficient influence, with the conservative masses of the Republican party, to control the radical Abolitionists, and to prevent them form taking any action under the form of government, that would interfere with the property right of the South in slaves.

But the subsequent events proved that Mr. Stevens and General Lee, and all Southern people who believed in them, were mistaken; that however sincere Mr. Lincoln had been, he was powerless in his party to thwart the designs of the anti-slavery agitators, whose power had wonderfully increased, in a comparatively short period of time.

Under the influence of those men, Mr. Lincoln, on Sept. 22, 1862, issued the emancipation proclamation, freeing all slaves of the South; and from that day forward, the abolition of slavery, was one of the undisguised objects of the North, in prosecuting the war.

The incident shows the wonderful wisdom which resides in great masses of men; and that they possess a common sense, or instinct, vastly superior to the aggregate powers of the individuals of the individuals of which the mass is composed. I do not know where this wonderful power of masses comes from, but it exists, as certainly as we are here; for both Mr. Stevens and General Lee were mistaken, and the people of the South were right in their estimate either of Mr. Lincoln's sincerity, or of his power to control the abolition faction, by which he was surrounded.

Slavery had practically disappeared from Vermont and New Hampshire by the year 1800, and from Rhode Island, Connecticut, New York and Pennsylvania it had disappeared by the year 1840.

In 1844, just four years after the last four named States had abolished slavery, the Abolitionists appeared, for the first time, as a regularly organized party, and put in nomination James G. Birney, of Michigan, for the office of President.

At that time, the party was so small, that Mr. Birney received no electoral vote, and local returns showed that out of a popular vote of over 2,500,000, he received but 64,653 votes.

The party, however, comprised some of the boldest, most active and aggressive men, the country has ever known; and starting with the public sentiment overwhelmingly against them, they continued to wage a relentless war upon the institution of slavery, in utter disregard for the Constitution of the United States, as construed by the Supreme Court. They claimed that Congress had the right to prevent the South from carrying slaves into the Territories, while they practically admitted that all other property could be taken there. Under the operation of their plan, the Territories would all come into the Union as free states; and as soon as three-fourths of the States were free, the Constitution of the United States could be amended, so as to abolish slavery in states where it already existed. They denied that the Constitution of the United States secured to the Southern people, the right to reclaim fugitive slaves from the Northern States, and the Governors of several of those states, refused to issue their warrants for the arrest, and delivery of fugitive slaves, thus, in effect, nullifying that clause of the Constitution, which requires that a person held to service, or labor, in one State, escaping to another, shall be delivered up on the claim of the party, to whom such service, or labor may be due.

This aggressive party inscribed upon its' banner, "No more slave states." "No more slave territories." "No return of the fugitive to his master"- an "irrepressible conflict between the free and slave states; and whether it be long or short, peaceful, or bloody, the struggle shall go on, until the sun shall not rise upon a master, or set upon a slave."

These prophetic words have been verified; but we are now endeavoring to see who was responsible for the bloody struggle which ensued.

It will be noticed that the Abolitionists proposed to proceed with their plans strictly in accordance with the forms of the Constitution, as construed by them, though directly in opposition to the construction which had been placed upon it by the Supreme Court; and whenever three-fourths of the States should become free States, the Constitution would be amended, so as, in form, to legally abolish slavery, in the States where it had always existed.

It was to meet just such a contingency, that it was announced in the Declaration of Independence, that if any form of government becomes destructive to the ends for which it was created, the people have the right to alter or abolish it.

Such changes as are attempted to be made in opposition to the form of government, are for that reason void, and of no effect; they require no active resistance, because they are mere nullities. But when a change is made in the structure of government, in strict accord with all the forms of the government, and yet it results in destruction of the rights of a large portion of the people, they have the right under the Declaration of Independence, to insist that the form of government having been altered, to their determent, they have the right to establish another government, under a form that will sufficiently protect them; and this is all the South desired to do.

Instead of waiting until the changes were actually made in the form of government, which the Abolitionists proposed to make, the South, believing that those changes would soon be made, and that no good could come from further delay, determined to secure her rights, by adopting a form of government, under which they could not be assailed.

In a word, the South determined to fight for her property right in slaves; and in order to do so, it was necessary for her to resist the change which the Abolitionists proposed to make under the Constitution of the United States as construed by them, and to insist upon construction which had been placed upon it by the Supreme Court; and therefore, in the 4th paragraph, of the 9th section, of the first Article of the Constitution of the Confederate States, it was expressly declared that no "law denying , or impairing the right of property in negro slaves shall be passed."

This was simply asserting in express terms, in the Constitution of the Confederate States, what the Supreme Court had already decided was the true construction to be placed upon the Constitution of the United States.

Upon this issue the South went to war.

I repeat that the people of the South had a right to fight for their property. It was best for them, and best for the Government, and best for all the other people in the Government, that the South should have made the fight.

If she had basely surrendered her right to $2,000,000,000 of property without a struggle, she would have deservedly gone down in history, as the most cowardly nation that ever existed upon the face of the earth; and though she eventually lost the property, to protect which she went to war, the heroic resistance which made in its behalf, will be of invaluable service, to generations of people yet unborn.

Its benefits will accrue to the people of the North, and of the East, and of the West, as well as of the South. The losses, and long privations to which the South was subjected, in that long and bloody war, will teach the people in all sections of the country, that they should carefully consider the consequences of arraying themselves in hostility to the federal government; and therefore, revolutions, or rebellions in the future, will be few, and far between. But on the other hand, the frightful losses which the South inflicted upon the government in that war, will teach the Federal Government that the courage of the American people will never submit to any serious encroachments upon their rights of life, liberty, or property; and I hope that centuries may elapse, before the Federal Government will ever again undertake, to deprive any considerable portion of the people, of any section of this country, their vested rights.

My second proposition, is that the South acted humanely and bravely during the war.

It was charged at one time, that federal prisoners were treated inhumanely by the Confederates; but since the publication of the official records upon the subject, it has been discovered, that 220,000 Confederates taken prisoners by the Federals, 26,436 died in their hands; while 270,000 Federals taken prisoners by the Confederates, only 22,576 died in their hands. In other words, with a larger number in Southern prisons, fewer died, than in Northern prisons, and we have remember the inadequate means, which the Confederates had at their disposal, to take care of prisoners, and the excessive warmth of the southern climate in the summer months, the figures which I have just given, are truly astonishing.

See Stevens' History of the United States, p. 467

It must also be remembered, that the South made the first offer to exchange prisoners; that the offer was continued throughout the war; and that such federal prisoners as remained in the hands of the Confederates at any time, were kept there, because of the refusal of the Federal authorities to exchange.

We did not have the money to provide elegant apartments for prisoners; and, at times, it was difficult to furnish them with suitable food and medicine; but it must be remembered that our own armies were at times in great distress, and we gave to the men who were so unfortunate as to fall into our hands, the best accommodations, the best food, and the best medicine, we could secure- all charges to the contrary, notwithstanding.

It cannot be said with truth, that the Confederates ever struck an unarmed foe; or injured, or oppressed any man, who was a prisoner, or who begged mercy at their hands.

The South was brave as it was humane. The records show that the Federals had, from first to last, 2,600,000 men in the service; while the Confederates, all told, in like manner, had but little over 600,000.

Stevens' History of the United States, p. 466.

If all those men had been engaged in a single battle, the 600,000 Confederates could have been surrounded by four Federal armies of 600,000 men each, in front, in rear, and on the right and left flanks; and a Federal army of 200,000 more could have been held in reserve. Think for a moment, of the fearful odds, which would have been against the Confederates, in such a battle.

I am aware that some over-sanguine people in the South expressed the opinion at the commencement of the war, that one southern man could whip ten Yankees; but that idea was soon dissipated, even in the minds of the very few by whom it was entertained. You may think that one man can whip ten little boys; and it is true, that, if they will come at him, one at a time, he can slap them over like kittens; but the trouble is, that they won't come at him that way. Some will cling to one arm, some to another, some to one leg, some to another, some will be in front of him, and some will be upon his back; and he finds himself at last, overpowered by the mere force of numbers.

A distinguished Alabamian is said to have remarked at the commencement of the war, that he could whip the whole Yankee army with a squirt gun; and when the remark was called to his attention at the close of the war, he said with great readiness that "the Yankees had declined to fight that way."

If any considerable number of the people of the South ever seriously doubted the courage of the Federal officers and soldiers, that doubt was removed within the first six months of the war; and no men stand more ready to speak in the highest praise of the courage, and skill, of the Federal officers and soldiers, than do the Confederates, who so often witnessed their valor, upon the field of battle.

Some of our friends seem afraid to allow Northern historians to write the history of the Confederate army and navy. I confess that I do not share the alarm. We are perfectly safe to leave the history of our army and navy in the hands of those who fought them. They dare not, if they would, question the courage of the Confederate army and navy, because to do so, would brand as the worst cowards, the 2,600,000 Federals, who could not overcome 600,000 Confederates inside of four long years of war. Such prejudiced publications as may have been made in guise of northern histories since the war, are mere advance proof sheets of what is yet to become the real history of it. Mistakes, or falsehoods which may have appeared, will all be corrected, and the South may rest with confidence upon the final edition, which will be stereotyped for the use of posterity. The records of the War Department of the United States government, and of the Confederate States, cannot at this day be mutilated, or falsified.   They will necessarily show the number of soldiers enlisted on each side, and the northern historian cannot account for the prolonged, and desperate fighting, between such unequal forces, except by according to the officers and soldiers of the Confederate army, their full meed of praise.

The desperate financial straits into which the United States government was forced during the war, and the extreme danger to which it was exposed by the comparatively small Confederate army and navy, has been placed upon the record, in the opinions of the Supreme Court of the United States; and the northern historian cannot account for it, when he considers the disparity of numbers, without yielding, at least reluctantly full justice to the Confederate army and navy. Let me read you just here what the Supreme Court has said upon this matter:

"Suffice it to say, that a civil war was then raging, which seriously threatened the overthrow of the government, and the destruction of the Constitution itself. It demanded the equipment, and support of large armies and navies, and the employment of money, to and extent beyond the capacity of all ordinary sources of supply. Meanwhile the public treasury was nearly empty, and the credit of the government, if not stretched to its utmost tension, had become nearly exhausted. Moneyed institutions had advanced largely of their means, and more could not be expected of them. They had been compelled to suspend specie payments. Taxation was inadequate to pay even the interest on the debt already incurred, and it was impossible to await the incoming of additional taxes. The necessity was immediate and pressing. The army was unpaid. There was then due to the soldiers in the field nearly a score of millions of dollars. The requisitions from the War and Navy Departments for supplies, exceeded fifty millions and the current expenditure was over one million per day. The entire amount of coin in the country, including that in private hands, as well as that in banking institutions, was insufficient to supply the need of the government three months, had it been poured into the treasury. We say nothing of the overhanging paralysis of trade, and of business generally, which threatened loss of confidence in the ability of the government to maintain its continued existence, and therewith the complete destruction of all remaining national credit."

12 Wallace, 540-541, Legal Tender cases

At the commencement of the war, the aggregate Federal population was above 22,000,000, while the white population of the Confederate States was less than 6.000.000; the Government of the United States was recognized by all the nations of the earth, while the Government of the Confederate States was not recognized by any of them; the United States had a high national credit in all the money centers of the world, while the Confederate States had no credit, except among their own people; the United States had a regular army and navy to serve as a nucleus for the concentration, and instruction of new levies, while the Confederate States were forced to rely entirely upon an untrained militia;   the

Northern people had been largely engaged in mechanical pursuits, and were prepared to manufacture all the materials and munitions of war, while the Southern people had been engaged almost exclusively in agriculture, and knew but little of the mechanical arts; the Northern ports remained open throughout the war, so that the United States could procure supplies of men, money, and munitions of war, while the Southern ports were blockaded; and even the food, clothing and medicine which the South needed for the Federal prisoners had to run the blockade of their own navy. And yet, with all these disadvantages to contend against, the Confederate army of only 600,000 men, though opposed by more than four times their number, reduced the Federal Government to the verge of bankruptcy, and caused it to totter, to its very foundation stone.

As for the Confederate navy, what can the Northern historian say in derogation of, when it is remembered that the few cruisers of which it consisted, in defiance of the Federal navy, swept from the face of the ocean, every United States merchantman; that could be found.

The people of the South who were not in the army or navy, displayed a high degree of devotion, and self sacrifice to the cause. They economized in every possible way to supply the forces in the field, with all means of conducting and prolonging the conflict; and when the final result came, they found themselves bankrupted, in all save honor

The ladies of the South deserve the most honorable mention. They organized themselves into a recruiting force, more powerful and efficacious than ever was the conscript law of the Confederacy: and many a young man who found himself in the front of battle, owed his position to the influence of some fair one, whom he had left behind. Some of the ladies sold their jewels to supply the Confederacy with means; and all of them denied themselves the luxuries, and even the comforts of life, so as to curtail the family expenses, in order that those in the field might be provided for. The ladies also organized relief associations of various kinds, and in the gloomy hospitals of the South, they hovered like ministering angels, over friend, and foe alike.

My third proposition is, that the Southern people are not a conquered race.

Under the form of the United States Government, it is impossible for the Federal Government to conquer a State, or the people of a state. It may suppress an insurrection, or rebellion; but it cannot conquer a State, or the people of a state.

Conquests can obtain only between separate and independent nations; and the United States never did, and never could have afforded to, recognize the Confederate States, as an independent nation.

The consequences of such a recognition, would have been calamitous to the United States. It would at once have ended the war in favor of the Confederacy; for every other Nation would immediately have followed the example of the United States, and would have recognized the Confederacy as one of the great powers of the world. If it had assumed the attitude of a conqueror, it would have been necessary for the United States, after the war to have recognized as valid, all of the acts of the Executive, Legislative, and Judicial Departments of the Confederate States, and of the various states composing the Confederacy. This would have compelled the United States to have recognized the validity of the bonds issued by the Confederate States in aid of the war; and of the bonds issued by the various states of the Confederacy, for the same purpose. These bonds were held by the citizens and subjects of foreign nations, who would have demanded their payment from the United States, if it had assumed to play the role of a conqueror of the Confederacy.

The United States would have been forced to recognize as valid, the confiscation acts of the Confederate States, and of the various States composing it, by which the property of Northern citizens, found in the South, had been confiscated, and by which debts due from the Southern people to the Northern people had been extinguished. In short, the United States, would have been bound to accept the status in quo as it existed at the close of the war, and to have treated as perfectly valid, all acts done under Confederate authority while the war existed.

The Congress of the United States declared in 1861, that the war was not prosecuted for any purpose of "conquest or subjugation", and the Supreme Court of the United States, since the war, have decided that it was prosecuted for the suppression of a rebellion, and not for conquest or subjugation.

7 Wallace, 726, Texas vs. White

If then the United States Government, through its highest Legislative, and Judicial Departments, has expressly admitted, in every form in which the admission can be made, that the war was not prosecuted for conquest or subjugation, upon what ground do some of the people of the North now taunt us with being a conquered race?

Mexico, in her war with the United States, surrendered a territory large enough for an empire; and France surrendered Alsace and Lorraine, in her war with Prussia; yet, the South did not surrender one foot of her territory, at the close of our war.

France was compelled to pay an immense war indemnity to Prussia; but no such exaction was submitted to by the South; on the contrary, no tax can be levied on the South, that does not fall equally upon the North,

Under the International Law, a conquered people are compelled to surrender the laws and institutions of their own country, and they are forced to submit to the laws of the conqueror; and the conqueror may subject them to laws and regulations much more onerous and oppressive than those which he imposes on his own subjects.

But the Southern people have every right under the Constitution of the United States, which the Northern people have; and no laws or institutions can be imposed upon them, that are not, at the same time, imposed upon the people of the North.

While the United States never claimed the right to conquer the South, it did claim the right to suppress insurrection; and on July 17, 1862, Congress passed what was known as the Confiscation Act, which, after providing in its 1st Section that treason should be punished by death, it provided in the 5th Section, that the President should cause the seizure of all the estate and property of the officers of the Confederate army and navy, and of all persons who gave aid and comfort to the rebellion; and the said property, or its proceeds should be applied to the support of the army of the United States.

18 Wallace, 156 Day vs Micou

But under the terms of the surrender of General Lee on April 9, 1865, it was stipulated that upon the officers of the army giving their individual paroles for themselves, and for the men of their commands, "each officer and man will be allowed to return to their homes, not to be disturbed by the United States authorities, so long as they observe their parole, and the laws in force where they may reside."

Lee and His Generals, p. 158

The terms of surrender of General Johnston on April 26, 1865, and of the other Confederate Commanders, were substantially the same, as the terms agreed upon between Generals Lee and Grant.

Stevens' History of the United States, p. 465.

Under these terms, the United States yielded the right to inflict any punishment for past offences, and provided the officers and soldiers of the late Confederate army and navy should thereafter obey the laws in force where they respectively resided.

As an effect of the surrender, the South yielded the institution of slavery, and the Government yielded the right to punish those who had participated in the rebellion; and agreed that they should be restored to all their rights under the Constitution of the United States, except the single right to own slave property.

So far as the South being conquered, she did not even make an unconditional surrender of her armies; but she secured for her people all the rights in the Union, to which the Northern people were, or are, entitled.

As to the right of secession; the word "secession" does not appear in the Constitution of the Confederate States.

See Putnam, Rebellion Record, p. 321 (Doc.)

I have never believed that any State had the right under the Constitution of the United States, to secede from the Union, or to nullify the laws of the Union; though many of the most distinguished men in the country believed in that doctrine.

I justified the action of the South in the war, upon the right to revolution, which is distinctly recognized in the Declaration of Independence.

It is useless, however, to draw refined distinctions between secession, nullification, and rebellion; for the Government of the United States will never allow the exercise of either of those rights, without a resort to arms. They all necessarily result in war; and therefore it always seems to me, that as the right of rebellion was expressly recognized in the Declaration of Independence, the South ought to have predicated her action upon that right, and thrown upon the government, the responsibility of its violation, rather than to have claimed the right, under the Constitution, to secede from the Union.

It is said that the question of secession has been forever settled by the war, and that no state can ever again claim the right to peaceably secede from the Union. As I do not believe that the right of peaceable secession ever existed, I am, of course, perfectly willing to concede that it does not now exist; but the Northern people must remember, that if the war settled the question of secession against the States of the South, it also settled it against the States of the North. The time may come in the future, as it has come in the past, when the people of some of the Northern States, may be quite as anxious to invoke the right of secession, as were the people of the Southern States during the late war.

In 1791-2 great discontent prevailed in Pennsylvania, caused by an act of congress imposing an excise tax on distilled spirits. It was known as the "Whiskey Insurrection," and to suppress it, the Government of the United States was forced to call out an army of fifteen thousand men.

The Alien and Sedition Acts of Congress, at its session of 1797, were regarded as palpable violations of personal rights, as guaranteed by the Constitution; and popular indignation was quite as high, and quite as demonstrative in the North, as it was in the South.

In 1814, Massachusetts and Connecticut, throwing themselves upon their reserved rights under the Constitution, refused to allow their militia to be sent out of their own states to aid the Government of the United States in its war with England; and in the same year the celebrated Hartford Convention was held, composed of delegates from Massachusetts, Rhode Island, New Hampshire, Vermont, and Connecticut; the purpose of which was to force a change of policy on the part of the Government of the United States, or for those States to provide for their own well being as they thought best, by seceding from the Union.

I do not allude to those events in any reproachful spirit; because I believe that the people of those States thought that they were being unjustly oppressed under the forms of Federal Government; and if so, they had the same right to resist its tyranny, as the Colonies had to resist the tyranny of the King of England. I allude to those events only to show that if the Southern States lost anything of value when the surrendered the right of secession, the Northern States lost at the same time, and to the same extent. If, on the other hand, the destruction of the doctrine of secession, was a benefit to the States of the North, it was equally so to the States of the South. The South had no special interest in the doctrine of secession, not common to the other States of the Union, except in so far as it was a means by which she sought to protect her property right in slaves; and now that the institution of slavery has disappeared forever, and the South has no other peculiar institution to protect by resort to secession, there is no reason why the South, in the future, should ever desire to exercise that right, that might not apply equally to any of the States of the North, The South now has no more special interest in the doctrine of secession, than she has in a last year's bird's nest.

Under the terms of General Lee's surrender, the South demanded and secured all of her rights in the Union, as guaranteed to her by the Constitution of the United States except the right to hold slaves; she has gone diligently to work to repair the ravages of war; and has succeeded in doing so, in a remarkably short space of time. The wonderful development of her varied resources, has more than compensated for the loss of her slave property; and the generous rivalry which now obtains between her and the North, in advancing their material prosperity, while it may have excited the envy and jealousy of the Northern people, furnishes the strongest guaranty that in the future, the voice of the South will at all times be for peace.

All of her interests will be subserved by peace. None of them can be promoted by war, either foreign or domestic. She still asks "to be let alone" and to be allowed to work out in her own peaceful way, the glorious destiny which awaits her in the Union.

One word in conclusion, as to the parole which was given by the Confederate officers and soldiers when General Lee surrendered. They gave their words of honor as soldiers and gentlemen, to return to their homes, and to obey the laws in force where they might reside; and General Lee, in accepting the Presidency of the Washington College, placed a construction upon the parole, which, I think, is obligatory upon every Southern man. He said: It is the duty of every citizen in the present condition of the country, to do all in his power to aid in the restoration of peace and harmony, and in no way to oppose the policy of the State or general government directed to them." And "It is particularly incumbent on those charged with the instruction of the young to set an example of submission to authority."

Lee and His Generals, p. 165

I have always felt that all Confederates were, in honor, bound to observe good faith, and sincerity, in the terms of that parole: because, it was given upon their behalf, and furnishes the basis of their right to protection.

The parole should be observed, not only in form, and in accordance to its letter, but it should be observed according to its spirit, from the heart outward, and without any mental reservation whatever. We should not only obey the Constitutional laws of the Union, but we should obey them cheerfully, and having voluntarily claimed our places in the Union, we should feel that it is our country, and that its flag is our flag; that its honor is our honor, and its destiny is our destiny. And in justice to the people of the South, it must be said, that they have observed the obligations of the parole, in the spirit in which I have said that it ought to be observed.

It is true that they object to being denounced as cowards, or traitors, or being reproached or taunted as a conquered people. Because all such charges are utterly false. They have the right to deny with just indignation, all such aspersions upon their fair name. Their parole imposed on obligation of self-degradation upon the people of the South; they have the right to hold their heads up, and look the world squarely in the face, with the proud consciousness of having acted throughout the war from the purest motives, and with the highest courage. But they may do all this, and yet demean themselves, as I hope they will ever do, with true loyalty to the Constitution of the United States, and to all laws passed pursuant thereto. [3]

On June 24, 1922 a copy of the above address was presented to attorney John W. Gaines of Nashville by fellow attorney Perkins Baxter, son of Ed Baxter. Gaines later donated the copy to the Tennessee State Library and Archives.

JOHN W. GAINES
Attorney at Law
603 Stahlman Building
Nashville, Tenn.

May 3/23

Jno. Trotwood Moore
State Historian:

Dear Sir: I've for your library this great speech of Ed Baxter at Nashville Oct. 3, 1889.
I like to read about his great mind, but this should be preserved by the state.

Yours truly,
Jno. W. Gaines [3]

EXCERPTS FROM ED BAXTER'S 1892 ADDRESS TO THE TENNESSEE ASSOCIATION OF CONFEDERATE VETERANS REUNION AT MCGAVOCK GROVE (CARNTON PLANTATION) FRANKLIN, TN.

September 14, 1892. Mr. John C. Wall spoke in behalf of the Sons of Confederate Veterans. After which Col. Ed. Baxter, the orator of the day, was introduced and made a most interesting speech, which was received with frequent outbursts of applause. The Colonel's theme was to show that "rebels" had often been among those whose deeds shone most resplendently in history, like the Barons who brought King John to terms at Runnymead, and the patriots of the American Revolution who followed Washington to a glorious independence.

"The history of the English people is a history of rebels struggling to maintain their rights and liberties against the tyranny and oppression of the governing powers. To the American citizen who has carefully read the history of the race from which we sprang, the term rebel conveys no suspicion of dishonor or reproach. It is a term which tyrannical governments have at all times applied to people who have the courage to resist their oppression, and while tyrannical governments may intend to use the term, rebel, as one of reproach, every true lover of liberty who knows his history must regard it as a title of honor; history proves that it is a title of liberty which is older and more honorable than the king's prerogative; it is a title which was originally won by the sword, it has been maintained by the sword, and unless it is defended by the sword, liberty will perish from the face of the earth. All the rights, privileges, and immunities now enjoyed by the American people were acquired by rebels and will be bequeathed to them by rebels. There cannot be found to-day in all the world a man in whose veins does not flow the blood of a rebel, whether of English descent or not. Allow me to add that any man deserves this honorable title who is ready to fight, regardless of doubts or consequences for the rights of life, liberty, and property. These are the things for which we fought, and we counted not the cost when we bade defiance to the enemy's forces that undertook to despoil us of them." [4]

<hr>

CONFEDERATE VETERAN
Nashville, Tenn.
Volume II NO. 6   June 1894
CONFEDERATE AT A FEDERAL CEMETERY

Elsewhere there is printed a speech of United States Judge George R. Sage at the National Cemetery here (Nashville).

After the conclusion of the address of Judge Sage, Mr. Ed Baxter, a comrade of whom all who know him are proud, in response to an earnest invitation made a brief extempore address.

Mr. Baxter said, in substance, that though he was an ex-Confederate soldier, he was glad the government of the United States had established and maintained the National Cemeteries, which beautify and adorn the country. He was glad that the government had recognized the debt of gratitude which it owed to the gallant soldiers who followed its flag. Those who confronted the Union soldiers for four long years of battle were the best witnesses of their valor and devotion to the cause for which they fought.

He honored the Union soldiers. He felt the highest respect for the gallant men who lay buried around him. They were American citizens of the highest type; for they lost their lives in the defense of what they thought to be the constitutional principles of their country.

It is easy to talk; but when a man risks his life in defense of his convictions of right, he presents the best specimen of manhood, whether he wore blue or gray.

Though the war had resulted in the abolition of slavery, Mr. Baxter felt no regret at the loss of his former slaves. When he entered the army he left his wife and child at home, and his former slaves remained with them. Several of those who were once his slaves are now his servants; and for all of them he cherished the most kindly feelings. If any one of them harbored the least ill feelings toward him, he had never heard of it.

The soldiers in the opposing armies, even in the heat of conflict, always treated each other with personal consideration and respect. No instance has been recorded where a soldier of either army refused to share his canteen of water with his wounded foe.

At the close of the war the devastated condition of the South rendered it impossible for her people to provide suitable cemeteries and monuments for the Confederate dead; but, with such means as were at their disposal, they gathered together, in the public cemeteries, the treasured relics of their heroic dead, and tenderly cared for them as best they could.

While the Confederate dead have not received the honors due to their courage and devotion, the fact that the Union soldiers who fell in battle have received the honors justly due them excites neither envy nor regret. There is no leaf too green, no bud too bright, to be laid on the graves of heroes.

The day will yet come when some great-hearted man of the North will say, in the halls of Congress, of his own volition, and without solicitation from the South, "the Confederates were brave American citizens, who died in the defense of their ideas of constitutional principles. Let the nation gather up their relics, and accord to them the honors which they so richly deserve."

There is not a foot of territory belonging to this Union which has not been acquired or defended by the aid of Southern valor. During the war the South fought in good faith, and at its close she returned her allegiance with equal good faith.

The flag of the Union is now, as before the war, the only flag to which the South yields her allegiance; and where she gives her allegiance, there also will she give her loyalty. [6]

Ed Baxter was not the only member of his family to have a successful career. Younger half-brother Nathaniel Baxter, Jr. who had enlisted in Baxter's Battery 1st Organization at age sixteen and remained with it through out the war, serving under Captains Freeman and Huggins, was also a successful Nashville Attorney. He served a term as Speaker of the Tennessee State Senate and was a member of the Board of Trustees of Vanderbilt University.

Ed Baxter's other youngest half brother, Jere Baxter, became a Nashville business tycoon. He founded the Tennessee Central Railroad and several other businesses. He ran unsuccessfully for governor of Tennessee in 1890 on the democratic ticket. A middle school in Nashville and the town of Baxter in Putnam County, Tennessee are named in his honor. Being a principal of the Tennessee Central Railroad, Jere Baxter had strongly opposed the L&N Railroad's monopoly of rail lines in the mid-south, pitting him against his half-brother Ed, who represented the L&N.

Jere Baxter recalled from his childhood: In his handsome home on Belmont Avenue in Nashville, there stood a fine old mahogany table with an apparently solid base, ornately carved in the elaborate fashion of the sixties. Around the table clung many memories of a happy childhood, and one particularly interesting. When the Yankees came to Nashville, a detachment of soldiers rode out to the Baxter place. The mother of little Jere sat sewing on the trousers of a Confederate uniform. Seeing the approach of the soldiers, she feared for the safety of her work, as it was a much needed garment designed for an elder son, and she was at a loss to know where to hide it. Jere, who was near, and who was at that time eight or nine years old, grasped the situation at once, and springing up, turned over the heavy table, revealing the base was hollow, and exclaimed: "Tuck 'em here, mother; tuck 'em here!" The childish advise was followed, the Federals never traced the garments, and they afterwards made a safe journey across the line to the soldier for whom they were made. [6]

Ed Baxter's three sons: Perkins, Sloss and Hamilton Baxter, all followed his footsteps in the practice of law. Perkins and Sloss practiced in Nashville. Hamilton practiced in Washington, D. C. His son-in-law W. G. Hutchenson, husband of his beloved eldest daughter Katie, was also his partner in the practice of law.

The Captain died at his summer home in Ridge Top of kidney failure on June 12, 1910. Ed Baxter's death made front page news in the June 13, 1910 edition of the *NASHVILLE TENNESSEAN,* the lengthy obituary included his photograph. A similar article with his photograph was published on the front page in that day's edition of the *NASHVILLE BANNER.* Baxter's death also made the news in his hometown of Columbia in the *COLUMBIA HERALD.* His national reputation and support for Confederate causes were acknowledged in a death notice in *CONFEDERATE VETERAN* magazine.

Nathaniel Baxter, Jr., younger half brother of Ed served with him in Baxter's Battery 1st Organization and continued to serve as a Lieutenant in the Freeman-Huggins Battery.

Jere Baxter, youngest half-brother of Ed. Became a railroad and business tycoon in Nashville.

CHAPTER 8

OBITUARIES, ETC.

NASHVILLE TENNESSEAN
Nashville, Tenn. Monday June 13, 1910   TWO CENTS

JUDGE EDMUND BAXTER DIES AT SUMMER HOME
Illness of Four Days Causes Death of Prominent Attorney
WON A NATIONAL REPUTATION
Recognized as Authority on Interstate Commerce Questions
WAS 72 YEARS OLD
*Served Valiantly Throughout the Civil War Under Gen. Bragg's
Command*

Judge Edmund Dillahunty Baxter, who was recognized as one of the highest authorities in the general railroad laws in the United States died Sunday morning at 4 o'clock at his summer home in Ridgetop, after a very critical illness of four days. Judge Baxter was in his seventy-second year and had been in poor health for about a year.

The announcement of his illness a few days ago was the occasion of apprehension among Judge Baxter's friends in this city and throughout the entire south. On Saturday morning he lapsed into unconsciousness and the members of his family were hastily summoned to his bedside. The end came quietly while the sick man was still unconscious. The news of the death when known throughout the city cast a decided pall over his friends and acquaintances. Hamilton Baxter, his son, who is located in Washington, was summoned to the city a few days ago.

RAILROADS
Judge Baxter was at the time of his death the representative of an association of southern railroads, which included in its membership every road of any importance in the entire south. This high position of trust and honor was won through the careful and thorough work that had marked the efforts of the deceased in each and every case of even the most minor importance. It was a characteristic of the man that he never went to trial trusting to events or luck, but always had the idea of breakers ahead and was prepared to defend himself. Every public opinion or argument made by Judge Baxter is said to have been carefully planned and written, and he seldom spoke without the use of notes.

Beginning with the simple foundations of a great suit, Judge Baxter was noted for his logical and careful arguments, which were read from his notes, and by which he usually built up a defense that was impregnable. He was known to be an indefatigable worker, who had a complete mastery over his body and mind and was as systematic as he was tireless. It has been said of him that he had such a confidence in the evidence that he was to bring out in a suit that he never objected to submit to an opposing attorney his briefs. It was such talents and power that brought him among the foremost lawyers in the country.

BORN IN COLUMBIA

Edmund Baxter was the oldest son of Nathaniel Baxter and was born at Columbia, Tenn. in 1838. He also had four brothers, only one of whom, Nathaniel Baxter of Nashville is now living. At a very young age he graduated from the old Nashville University, having completed an academic course.

During the course of his duties as clerk in the office of the circuit court clerk and deputy sheriff under Sheriff Edmundson he made up his mind to begin the study of law and began a systematic course of reading, without the aid of any teacher. When hardly 20 years of age he passed the state bar examination with a high grade and resigned from his other duties to begin the practice of law.

The civil war broke out shortly after this time and Edmund Baxter joined in company with Col. Baxter Smith and was promoted to the office of lieutenant in a battery of artillery. Both he and Col. Smith were made captain shortly after, in which position he served until the end of the war. His service was under Bragg in the western army. He was active in many of the fiercest battles of the war. After the war he returned to Nashville and resumed the practice of law with great energy and success.

LARGE PRACTICE

Before he had reached his thirtieth year he enjoyed a very large practice and had established himself at that early age as one of the leading lawyers of the state. About that time he was employed as chief attorney for the Nashville & Decatur Railroad Company and later the Louisville & Nashville, he became attorney for the later. In this position he continued until some eight or ten years ago, when he was employed by an association of the southern railroads as their representative before the interstate commerce commission. From the time he accepted employment from the railroads he gave up his general practice almost entirely, although he still had the patronage of many large corporations. At the time of his illness Judge Baxter's keen wits were in no way impaired, and he had engagements to meet some of the prominent lawyers in Louisville this week.

When the Vanderbilt law school was organized he became professor of the law of evidence, pleading and procedure serving in company with Thos. H. Malone and Col. W. B. Reese. At one time he was dean of this department.

IN CIRCUIT COURT

He never held public office excepting for a very brief time in the office of the circuit court, at which time he was still a boy, only seventeen years of age. He had been repeatedly urged to make the race for different offices but had refused positively. On several occasions when the judges of the supreme court were sick or otherwise disabled, Judge Baxter was appointed by the governor to take their place and held these positions with distinction.

As a young man in general practice he became very much distinguished as an orator and was considered one of the most forceful in the state, but on account of his heavy duties he had no time to cultivate this great talent.

Among the contemporaries of Judge Baxter were many of the most prominent and successful lawyers of this generation in this city. Among them were: Thos. H. Malone, Col. W. B. Reese, Judge DeMoss, Andrew and Edwin Ewing, John Reed, Neil S. Brown, Morton B. Howell, Col. Baxter Smith and others. He was one of the few members of this number who still lived and practiced law here.

Judge Baxter is survived by one brother, Nathaniel Baxter and a sister, Miss Mary Louise Baxter of Nashville. He also leaves seven children, Mrs. W.G. Hutchison of Ridgetop, Perkins and Sloss Baxter of Nashville, Hamilton Baxter of Washington, Mrs. Dabney and Mrs. Malcom Poage of Nashville.

Family prayers will be conducted at the home at Ridgetop Monday morning at 9:30 and the body will later be taken to Mt. Olivet in a hearse, where Rev. R. Lin Cave will have charge of the services at 3 o'clock. All members of the bivouac are requested to meet at headquarters at 1:30 o'clock form where they will go to the cemetery.

COMMANDING FIGURE
Judge Baxter Distinguished Most in Field of Rate Litigation

For a half century Judge Baxter was a member of the Nashville bar. He was the son of Judge Nathaniel Baxter, who was a very able lawyer and was at one time judge of the circuit court, serving with distinguishing ability.

Mr. Baxter returned from the civil war after serving four years through the great struggle and resumed the practice of law, in which profession he had made a star. He was at that time regarded as a man of ability and appeared as counsel for the defendant in the application made by John M. Bass and other citizens to put Nashville in the hands of a receiver.

VERSITAL AS A LAWYER

As an indication of the variety of his gifts his remarkable work resulting in the conviction of Porterfield and Spurr in the bank cases in 1893 and 1894 is in point. It was after he had been out of this line of practice for many years that he did this work, which is striking evidence of his versatility and ability to participate in cases in a court from which he had removed his practice for so many years.

The years following the war were before the legal profession became so specialized and gave Mr. Baxter a full opportunity to display his all round ability in any branch of his chosen profession.

Not only was he recognized as an able practitioner, but for many years he was a member of the faculty of the law department of Vanderbilt University. When that department was organized he with Judge Thos. H. Malone and Col. W. B. Reese constituted the faculty, this being in 1874 or 1875. He continued in this association until the death of Col. Reese in the early 90's. However, Judge Baxter remained a member of the faculty for several years longer, when his engagements were such as to make it necessary to sever his connection with the institution.

PROFOUND IMPRESSION ON STUDENTS

His special branches might be denominated as pleading, practice and evidence. No man ever made a more profound impression upon his students than Judge Baxter, all over the south being at present men who attended the law department of Vanderbilt University in its early days who can testify as to the lasting influence of Judge Baxter upon them, not only by his ability as a lawyer and teacher but by his many splendid personal qualities and character.

Perhaps Mr. Baxter in late years had been known more by reason of his connection with corporate litigation, especially in reference to railroads. Many years ago when Judge Russell Houston was made general counsel of the Louisville & Nashville at Louisville, he appointed Judge Baxter as attorney for the road at Nashville. Judge Baxter was then a member of the firm of Baxter, Smith & Allison, composed of himself, Col. Baxter Smith and Judge Andrew Allison.

DISTRICT ATTORNEY FOR L.& N.

In the early 80's Judge Baxter was made district attorney for the Louisville & Nashville for the state of Tennessee, with headquarters in

Nashville. He was the first man to hold this position in the state remaining with the road in this capacity until 1897. During the time he was district attorney for Louisville & Nashville, he was engaged in counsel in all the more important litigation which went to federal courts and the bulk of the cases were ultimately decided by the Supreme Court of the United States.

SHAPED LEGAL INTERPETATION

Little doubt exists the he participated in the argument of more cases involving the interstate commerce act before the supreme court than any other one lawyer of his time. It is also true that he won a much larger percentage of his cases than he lost, and it is a safe statement that no other lawyer in the whole country has had the same influence in forming the judicial opinions by arguments that bore upon this act than Judge Baxter. He could well be said to have occupied the same position in reference to this particular branch of litigation that Daniel Webster occupied in reference to the interpretation of the constitution in the early days of the country.

MORE RENOWNED ABROAD

Judge Baxter is one man whose reputation was even more extended abroad than at home. In the last years of his life he only dealt with big suits, but few of which were argued in this section of the country. His most able arguments were heard in distant cities by only a few interested persons and the Nashville public knew of his work chiefly through press dispatches telling of his argument before high federal courts.

Before the supreme court of the United States no man stood higher. The foundation of great success in this line of work was due not only to the wonderful grasp of his mind and his profound knowledge of legal principles and the capacity to apply them forcibly and clearly, but he had in this field the greatest opportunity for the use of that other great quality in which he excelled almost any man, the quality of developing fully and handling powerfully, the facts of any case.

SPECIAL COUNSEL FOR SOUTHERN LINES

In 1897 the interstate commerce branch of litigation among the roads of the southeast became so large that a legal department was constituted by the roads and steamship companies engaged in interstate operations in these sections of the country. Judge Baxter was offered the position of special counsel of the combined railroad and steamship lines, with headquarters at Nashville. Among the roads included were the Louisville & Nashville, the Nashville, Chattanooga & St. Louis, the Illinois Central, the Central of Georgia, and other, of the most important roads in the south and southeast. This position Judge Baxter accepted and held until his death.

It was while in the position which he held for the last years of his life that Judge Baxter had best opportunity to develop his powers in the field of litigation, that he had already begun to develop when he was district attorney for the Louisville & Nashville road.

Notwithstanding the fact that Judge Baxter had an enormous practice in his position, which carried him over a large part of the country, so great was his capacity for labor that he found time to engage in much more important litigation of other character. He was frequently employed specially by railroads to represent them in special cases. He was also often employed by other large corporations in important cases, notably representing the Nashville Street Railway in litigation with the city of Nashville, precipitated in 1899 and involving the franchises of the entire system. He was also counsel in some of the most important litigation before the supreme court in recent years in the interpretation and construction of wills.

MODEST IN ALL THINGS

Through all of these years Judge Baxter was characterized by the greatest modesty. He never assumed anything in his manner, and never liked to hear anybody speak in his praises. He was always deferential and respectful to his antagonist and courteous and considerate to his junior counsel. He never assumed a duty that he did not feel he had time to prepare for, and he never appeared in a case until he had so thoroughly mastered it that when he had finished his presentation it was felt that nothing remained to be said or done for the protection of the interests of his client. No legal principle was too obtruse for him to elucidate, no fact bearing upon the issue so minute as to be overlooked.

As a lawyer he towered above the body of his fellows, and was recognized at home and abroad as a man of masterly ability and power to handle the greatest questions.

EXPRESSIONS ON DEATH OF JUDGE BAXTER

John Bell Keeble—"In the death of Mr. Baxter the greatest lawyer of the Nashville Bar of this generation, and one of the greatest who ever practiced in the courts of this country, has passed away. He was not only the most eminent lawyer of our own bar, but no man in the South in recent years has occupied such a commanding position in the American bar at large. As one of his old students, I lament his death, am grateful for the fact that I had the opportunity of studying under him, and his career has been an inspiration to me many times."

Judge W. M. Hart: "Judge Baxter has been for a number of years recognized as the leading member of the Nashville bar in his specialty of railroad and corporation work. His death is a great loss not only to this state, but to the nation as well, for he had many friends throughout the union."

District Attorney A. M. Tillman: "The bar of this state as well as the bar of the south and its citizenship as well sustained a great loss at the death of Judge Baxter."

Judge John Allison: "I regard Judge Baxter as one of the most distinguished lawyers of the south. He is respected as a great lawyer from the inferior courts to the supreme court of the United States. He was one of the most industrious and painstaking men and in his family relations was an indulgent parent and a devoted husband. He was a good neighbor and good citizen. The south sustained a great loss in his death."

G. S. Moore: "He was one of the finest lawyers in the United States and in railroad law, he is without a peer. He was the head of the Nashville bar, and besides being a profound lawyer he was an excellent gentleman."

Frank Simmons: "One very remarkable trait which I have noticed in Judge Baxter was his extreme simplicity. He was always courteous to every one and had greatly attracted people by his frankness and openness. He was a good neighbor and I have enjoyed many pleasant hours in his company, His death will be a great loss to the legal profession and his place will be hard to fill. I have heard it said that some members of the United States Supreme Court have said that he was the greatest authority on interstate question who ever appeared before that body."

Col. Baxter Smith: "Ed Baxter and I were own cousins and we have been very intimate almost since infancy. I have always regarded him as a brother. We went into the army at the same time and for the last forty-five years we have both been living in Nashville. In 1870 he and I formed a law partnership, Smith & Baxter, and later on the firm became Smith, Baxter, & Allison. He was one of the ablest lawyers I have ever known and he could do more work than anyone I ever saw. He was simply indefatigable and was always on the lookout for breakers. I have never known him to go into a case without being fully prepared for it.

Lyton Taylor: "The demise of Ed Baxter is a loss not only to our community and state, but to the nation. He had by industry and energy, coupled with distinguished ability, attained the foremost rank in his profession and was America's greatest lawyer. No one knew him but to love him; he was an inspiration especially to those of his own profession who ever will cherish his memory."

Capt. John P. Hickman: "Ed Baxter was the most sensible man I have ever seen and he was the most gentlemanly. He was certainly one of the best lawyers in the south. He was a most indulgent and loving father."

Jordan Stokes: "Judge Baxter was one of the ablest lawyers not only of this state but of the nation. Possessed by nature with a big brain and indomitable energy, he won the high esteem of lawyers everywhere. The thoroughness with which he mastered every detail of a question was possibly his most pronounced characteristic."

E.E. Barthell: "Judge Baxter's impress on the bar not only of Tennessee, but of the whole country, has been second to that of very few men. His career as a teacher in the Vanderbilt law school was a brilliant one, and he left that to make a specialty of cases under the interstate commerce act. From that day to this he has been the highest authority in the United States on that branch of law. The bar of course suffers a very distinct loss in his death."

Col. A. M. Shook: "Mr. Ed Baxter was not only a remarkable man but also a very great man. His home and his profession were his life. Up to fifteen years ago he never had a bank account here. When he collected a fee or drew a salary, if he required any part of it for his personal use, it was taken out and the balance given to his wife and family."

"He was an indefatigable worker. He knew no such word as rest. I spent a week once with him in Philadelphia, when he was preparing an important lawsuit. He was always up and at work before breakfast and worked continuously all day; then worked until midnight every night."

"While he was known as a good general practitioner, of late years he had made a specialty of corporation law, and practiced before the interstate commerce commission. As attorney for the Louisville & Nashville road, he enjoyed the confidence of President Smith to a greater degree than any other lawyer who was ever employed by the company. As evidence of his great legal ability he has for the past ten years represented twenty-one of our leading railroads before the interstate commerce commission."

"He has left a very high mark on the scroll of fame for the legal profession and his life is a shining example for the young men of this profession for the whole country."

W. D. Witherspoon: "Judge Baxter was one of the greatest lawyers in the south. He was particularly noted for his learning in corporation law. He was very methodical and went into the minutest details. He always showed that he had studied the case. His life as a lawyer was very laborious."

Bradley Walker: "Judge Baxter was a leader among the lawyers of the city. His death was a great loss to the profession."

Judge M. H. Meeks: "I regarded Judge Baxter as one of the most profound lawyers in the south. He took hold of the difficult questions that he encountered in his profession with a thoroughness of comprehension, which was very extraordinary, and in their elucidation he exhibited a wealth of legal learning and intellectual power which placed him in the front rank of his profession."

John H. DeWitt: "Judge Baxter was a great lawyer, of much intellectual powers, an honest man. He was as great an expert in railroad rate regulation law as lived in this country. He was one of the finest lawyers that the state has ever produced. His life showed how splendid could be the achievement of a combination of intellectual power and prodigious energy."

Gen. E. A. Price: "I had the honor of being a student in the law department of Vanderbilt University under Mr. Baxter. I have known him ever since, and have regarded him as one of the greatest lawyers of the country. His death is a distinct shock to the state and nation."

Thomas J. Tyne: "Cherishing the recollection of our relations as professor and student at Vanderbilt University, and subsequently as members of the Nashville bar, I feel a distinct personal loss in the death of Judge Baxter. Our bar and the country have lost one who unconsciously possessed all of the facilities of a good man. He was distinguished among the great lawyers of our time, and respected as a citizen of the highest impulses and purest actions. He was a man whose conduct in life edified and inspired for good all who came under his influence."

J. H. Zarecor: "I regard him as the equal of any lawyer in the south. He possessed an unusual strength of intellect and his capacity for mastering differences in detail seem to have been consecrated unreservedly to his profession. Neither as a reader of law or as practitioner had he a superior or and equal in this part of the country. He magnified his calling."

Attorney-General Jeff McCarn said: "The profession has lost one of its greatest lawyers and the state one of its best citizens in the death of Judge Baxter. He was one of the professors of law in Vanderbilt University when I was a student there, and the student body left with an affection for him as strong as its admiration for his ability. Both as a man and a lawyer he had no superior in the south."

J. C. McReynolds said: "Judge Baxter was one of the most affable of all men. I regarded him as one of the very foremost lawyers in the United States, and he was esteemed as such by people all over the union who knew him. As an authority in interstate commerce law, his specialty, he perhaps had no equal and certainly no superior in the United States."

NASHVILLE BANNER
Monday evening, June 13, 1910

JUDGE BAXTER PASSES AWAY

PROMINENT ATTORNEY REPRESENTING
ALL RAILROADS IN THE SOUTHERN STATES.

EX-CONFEDERATE SOLDIER

COMMANDED BAXTER'S ARTILLERY COMPANY A
LAW PROFESSOR AT VANDERBILT UNIVERSITY

END COMES AT SUMMER HOME

Judge Ed Baxter, one of the most prominent attorneys in the South, and whose ability as a practitioner, had been recognized by the United States government on occasions, died at his summer home at Ridge Top, near Nashville at 3:30 o'clock yesterday morning, surrounded by the members of his family.

Prayers were said at the family residence at Ridge top this morning by L.F. Chapman. The funeral services were conducted by Dr. R. Lin Cave at the grave at Mt. Olivet, immediately upon the arrival of the remains at the cemetery.

In his passing the City of Nashville loses one of her most prominent citizens, the south loses a friend, and the profession of law one of its most able exponents, and the news of his taking causes a gloom over the entire section in which he had lived for seventy-two years. He had been in ill health for several months, but an attack of kidney trouble came upon him recently, which caused his condition to become gradually more critical until death relieved his suffering. Judge Baxter was one of the original professors of law at Vanderbilt University and many of the graduates of this department of the great Southern school owe their training to his teachings. He was in command of Baxter's Artillery Company A throughout the Civil War and while he never went to school after he was 14 years of age, he read law while in the office of Mr. Andrew Ewing at Nashville and upon his return from the war he entered upon the practice of his profession, being admitted to the Davidson County bar in 1867.

PROMINENT RAILROAD LAWYER

In the year of 1875 Mr. Baxter was chosen as counsel for Tennessee of the Louisville & Nashville Railroad, which position he held for over twenty years, his law firm Baxter, Smith & Allison, having formerly represented the road. During that time he not only looked after the legal business of the road in Tennessee, but had a great deal to do with the reorganization and extension of the system between 1879 and '82. He drew up the charters of the organization and was familiar with every detail of the work: under which the system was extended through to New Orleans and Pensacola in the South and to St. Louis in the West, which more than doubled the previous mileage of the system.

After the act of 1887 to regulate interstate commerce passed he was active in presenting arguments and procuring guidance to support the position of the L & N and other railroads in their plea for a suspension of the long and short road provisions of the act.

His distinguished ability and success before the commission resulted in the formation of an association in the southern roads and two steamship lines,, of which he was chosen general counsel under a five-year contract, beginning July 1, 1896.

When the contract expired it was renewed for another period of five years and again in 1906 it was renewed for another seven years. This latter contract had about three years yet to run. At the last renewal of Mr. Baxter's contract, owing to the greatly increased litigation under the new act to regulate commerce, he was given two assistants, one located in Nashville and the other in Washington. Hon. Sidney F. Andrews, formerly general attorney of the Illinois Central Railroad Company, has since that date been his Nashville assistant, while Hon. R. Walton Moore, a distinguished Virginia lawyer and President of the Bar Association of Virginia, has been his assistant in Washington City.

During his period of service with the Louisville & Nashville and later with the association, Mr. Baxter did more to mould the construction and interpretation of the interstate commerce laws of the country than any other man. During his service with the railroads he carried to the Supreme Court of the United States eight leading cases, involving the construction of the act. His services in interstate litigation were not confined to the Southern railway systems, his regular clients. In 1904 he was called upon to represent twelve Chicago railroads in litigation involving the entire system of rates on cattle from the West and Southwest to that market.

One of the most famous interstate cases in which Judge Baxter was ever engaged was the famous Chattanooga case, in which that city sought to have the rates from New York and other Eastern points to Chattanooga reduced to the level of the rates to Nashville from the same points. This cause aroused a great deal of interest while pending many prominent local merchants going to Chattanooga to testify in the case as to the logical effect on rates of the Cumberland River competition.

The construction of the "long and short haul" clause was involved in the noted Social Circle case. Another famous case in which Judge Baxter was leading counsel was the Cincinnati Freight Bureau case in which the Interstate Commerce Commission attempted to fix for the future an entire line of rates from Cincinnati to Atlanta and Augusta, Ga. He successfully contended that under the then existing law the commission was without power to fix future rates. Fourteen years later the law was amended so as to confer this power upon the commission.

In presenting the legal phases of the road's position before the first Interstate Commerce Commission he secured a decision which has had a helpful effect on the railroads in the South and has also proved of much benefit to various commercial centers in this section, including Nashville.

He subsequently represented the railroads in successful defense of the basis of rate adjustments to and from Nashville, carrying the case through the United States courts, which adjustment had been so vigorously attacked by other cities upon the ground that the rate adjustment at Nashville was a discrimination against other cities. His success in handling the cases presented to the Interstate Commerce Commission for consideration was so thoroughly understood and appreciated by the roads in the South that, in 1894 he was induced to tender his resignation to the Louisville & Nashville and accept the position as General Counsel for all the railroads of the Southern States, which position he held at the time of his death, and in which he demonstrated his great ability and peculiar fitness as a strong and forceful lawyer.

VAST INFORMATION

He was not only a great lawyer, but through his vast experience in these matters became thoroughly familiar and conversant with railway management, especially all that related to the traffic departments, so that there was scarcely any question that might arise which he was not able to handle with a marked degree of intelligence and efficiency.

For the past several years besides Col. Sidney F. Andrews, he had associated with him in his local office, his son, Mr. Perkins Baxter, and his son-in-law, Mr. W.G. Hutcheson. The work multiplied to such an extent that every member of the firm had been continuously employed in the work for the large number of roads which Mr. Baxter represented.

Mr. Baxter's success was not alone confined to his legal work in connection with railroads. He was a great attorney in questions pertaining to any and every phase of the law. Even in criminal cases he ranked high, standing at the front. It was he whom the United States Government appointed to prosecute the Commercial National Bank cases, and in which conviction followed largely through his efforts. He was a Chancery practitioner, esteemed as one of the best by the leading attorneys before the chancery courts of the country.

All in all, it is doubtful if there was ever in Tennessee a lawyer who ranked higher and was more.

SOMETHING OF HIS LIFE

Judge Baxter was the eldest son of Judge Nathaniel Baxter, and was born in Maury County, where he attended the schools of this section until he was 14 years of age. When he came to Nashville and entered the office of Andrew Ewing in Nashville where he began reading law.

He filled various positions in the offices about the courthouse and at one time was a deputy in the Criminal Court Clerk's office, some of the records of the office in his own hand being on file in the office to-day. When in retrospective mood, Judge Baxter was wont to relate some of his early experiences which were very interesting. He has related on occasions his first law case in which he claimed he learned more law than he knew before. In that case, a farmer took a turn of corn to a little water-powered mill and the creek went dry and the corn was eaten up by the rats. The man came to Judge Baxter, then a young attorney and wanted to bring suit for the recovery of the price of the turn of corn. Judge Baxter said he didn't know whether to sue for corn or for meal, as he didn't know if the corn had been ground before the creek went down or not. In looking up the question, he says he found out more about the law than he ever knew before.

In 1859 he was married to Miss Eliza T. Perkins. She was 15 and he 20. Seven children were born to them, three of whom survive, being Mrs. W.G. Hutcheson of Ridge Top, Perkins Baxter, and Mrs. A.S. Dabney of Nashville. When the civil war began Judge Baxter enlisted as Captain of Baxter's Artillery, Company A, and served throughout the war with his command. The first gun fired by his command was named in honor of his daughter, Katie. Upon his return from the war he entered upon his practice as an attorney.

MARRIED SECOND TIME

In the fall of 1879 Judge Baxter married Mrs. Bettie P. Baxter, the widow of his half-brother, Jones Baxter, who survives him. Three Children were born to them, Sloss Baxter, an attorney of Nashville; Mrs. Malcolm Poage of Nashville, and Hamilton Baxter of Washington. Judge Baxter is also survived by Miss Louise Baxter and Nat Baxter, Jr., his half-brother of Nashville. Jere Baxter who built the Tennessee Central Railroad, was also a half-brother, Mrs. Benj. B. Allen, of Nashville; Mrs. A.M. Baldwin, of Montgomery, Ala.; Miss Loulie Ewin of Nashville; Mr. Overton Ewin, of Florence, Ala. And Mr. Ben D. Ewin of Franklin, are his sisters and brothers-in-law.

He was one of the original professors of law at Vanderbilt University, and was a member of the Elm-Street Methodist Church and the Frank Cheatham Bivouac.

As a husband and father he was indulgent and generous to a fault. He always had the interest of his state and city at heart and was a man who will be sadly missed in the community.

NASHVILLE TENNESSEAN
June 14, 1910
COURTS ADJOURN IN JUDGE BAXTER'S HONOR

In respect to Judge Ed Baxter the prominent railroad attorney, who died at his home at Ridgetop Sunday morning, all courts in the city were adjourned Monday at noon in order to allow the judges and members of the bar to attend the funeral at 3 o'clock at Mt. Olivet. Judge Baxter's death is received not only as an irreparable loss to the bar of Nashville, but also to the entire commonwealth.

NASHVILLE TENNESSEAN
June 14, 1910

JUDGE ED. BAXTER IS LAID TO REST
Services Over Nashville's Great Lawyer Held at Mt. Olivet Monday
R. LIN CAVE PRESIDES
Services are Conducted by the Frank Cheatham Bivouac of U.C.V.

The remains of Judge Edmund Baxter, one of the south's greatest attorneys, and one of Nashville's most prominent lawyers and citizens who died at his summer home at Ridgetop Sunday morning were laid to rest with appropriate exercises Monday afternoon at Mt. Olivet Cemetery. The services were conducted by Rev. R. Lin Cave.

Mr. Cave read at the services the fifteenth chapter of the first Corinthians and following this the Frank Cheatham Bivouac, of which Judge Baxter was an honored member took charge of the services. The regular burial ritual was read by President W. M. Long. The services were concluded with a prayer by Rev. Cave and the body was placed in the family burial grounds. A great many beautiful flowers, the expressions of sympathy from the many friends of the family were laid upon the grave.

Before bringing the remains from Ridgetop prayers were held in the family residence by L. F. Chapman. Following these prayers, carriages were taken from Ridgetop to Mt. Olivet cemetery, where the procession arrived about three o'clock.

TO ADOPT RESOLUTIONS

Memorial services to the memory of Judge Baxter, the distinguished lawyer and citizen of this community will be held Wednesday afternoon in the board of trade rooms of the Stahlman building. Resolutions will be adopted on his death and addresses delivered on his noble life and splendid service for the commonwealth. The official announcement of the meeting has been sent out by Mayor Howse after a conference with a number of prominent citizens of Nashville

The call issued is as follows:

"To the City, State and County Officials, and the People of Nashville: The city, the state and the nation have in the death of Judge Edmund Baxter lost a distinguished son of a renowned family. The Baxter family has accomplished great things toward the material development of Tennessee and Judge Edmund Baxter has for half a century been a shining light in the legal profession of the nation."

"Tennesseans, always foremost in their devotion and loyalty to the memory of their distinguished sons, are requested to meet at the board of trade rooms, second floor of the Stahlman building, Wednesday, June 15, at 3 p.m. at which time resolutions of sympathy will be adopted and eulogies on the life and achievements of our lamented friend and benefactor will be delivered. All of our people that can possibly do so are requested to be present.

.....................".H.E. Howse, Mayor"

There will also be a meeting of the Nashville Bar Association held Tuesday morning at 10 o'clock in the chancery court room at the courthouse to adopt appropriate resolutions in honor of his memory.

NASHVILLE TENNESSEAN
June 14, 1910

PERSONAL NOTES

Senator Alfred Jones of Marshall County is in the city. He came to attend the funeral of Judge Baxter.

NASHVILLE BANNER
June 14, 1910

TRIBUTES TO JUDGE BAXTER
PAID AT MEETING THIS MORNING BY HIS ASSOCIATES OF THE NASHVILLE BAR.

A memorial meeting for Judge Edmund Baxter was held by the Nashville Bar at 10 o'clock this morning, attended by practically the entire membership of the bar. The committee to draft resolutions asked time to prepare the matter carefully, which request was granted. For the purpose of hearing the resolutions, an adjourned meeting will be held at 10 o'clock Saturday morning. At the meeting this morning a number of men closely associated with Judge Baxter, both professionally and socially, paid tributes to his memory.

The meeting was called to order by Mr. J. C. Bradford. Judge Matthews moved that Mr. Bradford be made chairman, which motion was unanimously carried.

"I am sure," said Mr. Bradford, "that in my time I have never known a lawyer who was the equal of him in whose memory we have met. An unobtrusive man, he did not cultivate as much as he would have liked to do the social amenities, but we who knew him recognized in him a kindly, genial man."

Mr. Albert G. Ewing, Jr., was appointed Secretary.

The Chairman appointed as a Committee on Resolutions: Judge Thomas F. Matthews, Mr. K.T. McConnico, Judge J.M. Gant, Mr. J.S. Pilcher and Col. D.S. Wilkin.

While the committee was engaged in the preparation of the resolutions, remarks from members of the bar were heard. Col. Baxter Smith, a first cousin of the deceased was the first speaker. He told of his childhood friendship with Col. Baxter and of his scholarly habits even in his childhood. "From that time to this," he continued, "I took no important step without first consulting with him. Both of us were newly married when the war cloud broke, we decided it was our duty to go into the army. His record as a soldier is too well known to need comment here."

"He never in his own estimation, measured up to what he really was. When the Southern Railway would have paid him $25,000 a year, he declined to ask it, because he did not believe his services were worth that much. He would never ride in a special car. It was his habit to set apart a portion of every fee to his own use, to provide for the necessary expenses of the family and divide the remainder among his children. The portion retained for himself was hardly more than enough to pay his street car fare. He dispensed the most generous hospitality, and wanted all of his friends to come to see him. I have never seen any other man take such pains in the preparation of cases," He referred to the great railroad bond case in which Chief Justice Matthews and other lawyers of national fame appeared, and said that Mr. Baxter's argument was the most able made in that case.

Judge Matthews read the report of the Committee Resolutions asking sufficient time to prepare suitable resolutions and requesting that the meeting, after hearing tributes, adjourn until Saturday at 10 o'clock. The request was granted by vote of the bar.

Mr. James L. Watts spoke of Judge Baxter, not of a lawyer, but as to his other qualities. He told of a number of incidents in their early association, one of which was sledding on the Cedar Street hill, with Judge Baxter and Gen. B. F. Cheatham. Others were of like human interest, showing the character of the man.

Judge John M. Gaut said that if any country produces in a generation one such lawyer as Edmund Baxter, it is highly honored, "I do not believe," he said, "that any other lawyer in the state withheld himself as he did from all other channels that he might make himself a lawyer." He told of the unusually systematic manner in which Judge Baxter arranged his information. "No man," he concluded, "can claim a higher degree of professional fame."

Judge Thomas E. Matthews next spoke. He was a member of the first law class taught by Judge Baxter in Vanderbilt University. "He would put," said Judge Matthews, " a dozen times as much study on the preparation of a lesson as any student did. He was blessed with a wonderful physique, giving him a great advantage over the average man. I have never seen any other lawyer press a jury case as he did. He once said that politics was the haunting temptation of his life, and I have often wondered what might have been had he been in the Senate for the past thirty years.

At 11:15 o'clock the meeting adjourned until Saturday.

NASHVILLE TENNESSEAN
June 15, 1910
RESOLOUTIONS ON JUDGE BAXTER
WILL BE DRAWN UP BY THE NASHVILLE BAR ASSOCIATION

For the purpose of drawing up resolutions, a memorial meeting of the Nashville bar association took place on Tuesday morning at 10 o'clock in honor of the late Edmund Dillehunty Baxter, almost the entire membership of the association was present, and many tributes were paid to the life and the ability of Judge Baxter. A committee was appointed to draw up the resolutions, and these will be submitted to the body on Saturday morning at 10 o'clock.

The committee selected to draft the resolutions is composed of Judge T.E. Matthews, K. T. McConnico, Judge J. M. Gaut, J.S. Pilcher, and Col. D.S. Wilkin. The meeting was presided over by James C. Bradford, who called the association to order and who, upon motion of Judge Matthews, was made permanent chairman.

BAXTER SMITH

Col. Baxter smith, who was a first cousin of the deceased, told of the early life of Judge Baxter, and told how he had never done anything in his younger days of importance without first consulting Judge Baxter, and that the advice thus received was always just what it should be. In speaking of his association with Judge Baxter in these early days, Col. Smith said:

"I took no important step without first consulting him. Both of us were newly married when the war cloud broke out, but we decided it was our duty to go into the army. His record as a soldier is too well known to need comment here."

"He never, in his own estimation, measured up to what he really was. When the Southern Railway would have paid him $25,000 a year, he declined to ask it, because he did not believe his services were worth that much. He would never ride in a special car. It was his habit to set apart a portion of every fee for his own use, to provide for the necessary expenses of his family and to divide the remainder among his children. The portion he retained for himself was hardly more than enough to pay his street car fare. He dispensed the most generous hospitality, and wanted all of his friends to come to see him. I have never seen another man take such great pains in the preparation of a case."

While the various members of the bar were talking of Judge Baxter, the committee on resolutions retired, and when they returned, more time was asked in which to draw up the resolutions. Judge Matthews read the results of the meeting of the committee and a motion was passed by the request of the committee, allowing them until Saturday morning to complete drafting the resolutions.

Among the others who spoke in the highest terms of the life and legal ability of Judge Baxter were John M. Gaut, James L. Watts and Judge T.E. Matthews.

Everyone who spoke of Judge Baxter stated that he was the greatest lawyer the south ever produced, and that he was one whom everybody loved and admired who came in contact with him.

The meeting adjourned shortly after 11:15 o'clock, to meet again Saturday morning.

NASHVILLE BANNER
June 16, 1910

RESOLUTIONS AND EULOGIES

HEARD IN PUBLIC MEETING ON THE PASSING OF JUDGE BAXTER.

FRIENDS AND ASSOCIATES
Tell By Word of Mouth of the High Esteem in Which the Man and
Lawyer Was Held.
UNCONSCIOUS OF GREATNESS

Resolutions and eulogies on the passing of Judge Edmund Baxter in which his friends and associates participated were heard yesterday afternoon at the rooms of the Board of Trade. "I've attended many memorial exercises," said Adjutant-General Tulley Brown at the conclusion of the various talks, "to many departed great men, but never in my life have I heard such expressions of love and esteem as these to which I have just listened."

That Judge Baxter was a great man, a loyal citizen, a learned attorney, a friend to the South and the city in which he lived, and beloved by all who knew him, is admitted. He was unconscious of his greatness and his modest nature shrank from a compliment; in fact, he held himself in less regard than did his friends and associates who recognized his worth and appreciated his magnificent qualities of mind and heart.

In addition to the speakers on the programs, Mr. W.H. Bumpas, G.P. Thruston and Mr. E. L. McNeilly made brief talks upon the sterling worth of the man as a friend and an instructor, the latter having sat at his feet when he was a professor of law at Vanderbilt.

As one of the speakers said, it was a meeting at which every young man in Nashville should have been present, so that the life and character of the man as related by those who knew him best should have been an inspiration to the present generation.

SERVITOR OF THE STATE
The meeting was called to order by President E.A. Lindsay of the Board of Trade and the first speaker was Adjutant-General Tully Brown, representing the state. "I feel that I have a right to say for the state that Mr. Baxter was a servitor of the state and everybody in the state feels a distinct loss in his taking," said Gen. Brown. "He left his young wife to fight the battles of his country and deserves to be honored by the state for he has helped to make the state great. He was a good citizen and measured up to the mark of the South's greatest citizens," Gen. Brown

told of his trip with Mr. Baxter to recruit men for an artillery company and said after he had made his little speech to the men at a barbeque, he had the pleasure of hearing a man talk. "Mr. Baxter said to those men on that occasion," continued Gen. Brown, "The conflict is already begun, Why stand ye idle." A man who never saw Mr. Baxter in action as a lawyer can form no estimate of the tremendous capacities of the man. He seemed never to tire. God almighty made Ed Baxter a great lawyer. He was eminently a gentleman and in his conduct of a lawsuit was courteous and generous to his competitor. His motto was work, work, work." Gen. Brown concluded by giving a brief resume of Mr. Baxter's work as a lawyer.

"There was not a citizen in the country or city more highly esteemed than Judge Baxter," said Mayor Howse, who represented the city, "and too much honor cannot be paid the memory of such a citizen. I remember the first time I met Mr. Baxter," he continued. "It was when a committee went to see him about a right-of-way through his farm for the Interurban Railway. He told us that we were welcome to any part of the farm we desired and that there would be no charge. This shows what he was in the work of assisting to build up the section. He was a great citizen and the community should cherish his memory."

WORKED FOR NASHVILLE

President F.A. Lindsay of the Board of Trade said that Mr. Baxter had worked for Nashville interests and that in his passing he felt a sense of personal loss as did also the organization which he represented. "It was said of him," continued Mr. Lindsay, "that he was never found unprepared in a case. He didn't rely on tricks or short-cuts in his presentation of a case and Mr. Justice Matthews of the Supreme Court has been heard to remark that Judge Baxter was one of the four or five great lawyers of the United States." Mr. Lindsay referred to several decisions which had been given which were of great benefit to the city through the arguments of the great attorney.

"He was one of the great lawyers of the nation," said John Bell Keeble, who represented the railroads at the meeting yesterday. "I was recently at a meeting of the railroad lawyers at Atlantic City and every man in the meeting asked about Mr. Baxter. There were lawyers there who didn't know anything about Nashville except that it was Mr. Baxter's home, but they all knew Mr. Baxter and counted him their friend."

Mr. Keeble referred to the great work accomplished by Mr. Baxter during his association with the railroads of the South and said that when Mr. Baxter first became connected with the roads there were very few systems in the South with any considerable mileage.

INTERSTATE COMMERCE ACT.

"If the interstate commerce act of '87 had not been passed," said Mr. Keeble, "probably Mr. Baxter would have died with but very little reputation. He accomplished a great work for the railroads in connection with that act, however, and greatly benefited this section, but in his work in this connection he also benefited himself and developed into one of the biggest lawyers in the nation. He met such men as Evaris, Carter and Choate in his practice before the Supreme Court of the United States and the records of that court will show frequently many such minds arrayed against Mr. Baxter who, single-handed, has met them and often-more often than not-in victory.

"But for the Titanic efforts of Mr. Baxter," he continues, "the interpretations of the interstate commerce act would have been different from what it is, especially the long and short haul clause, which has proved of more benefit to this section than its citizens realize. No man has contributed as much to Nashville in the matter of freight rates as Judge Ed Baxter. He was the greatest wielder of facts I ever knew: he was a constructive lawyer and possessed a analytical mind. He marshaled his facts as a general handles his men in preparing for a conflict; he was the colorbearer of the profession and there is not a great railroad system in the country but what is to-day pondering over the question, 'what can be done to supply the place of Mr. Baxter ?'"

AN INTELLECTUAL GIANT

In representing the citizens at large Maj. E.B. Stahlman said that Nashville had lost an intellectual giant, a great lawyer and a friend in the passing of Col. Baxter. "The average layman not familiar with transportation problems," he said, "might assume that Col. Baxter's relations with the railroads as counsel was designed in some way to hurtfully affect the masses, and that he was selected to do helpful work for the railroads at the expense of the people, but this is entirely erroneous. The questions which confronted the railroads and the people after passage of the Interstate Commerce act was as to whether certain communities and shippers were receiving favors to the detriment of others. When Col. Baxter was engaged in the work his aim was to show that certain conditions had become necessary, had been made so by reason of geographical conditions, that it would be hurtful to take away from the people rates which they were enjoying-not because the railroads favored them with these advantages, but because nature had favored their section with river or ocean transportation facilities even before the railroads were constructed. The contention was and was maintained that it would be wrong to take away from Nashville and other cities with similar natural advantages rates, which they were entitled to and give them to other cities less favored by natural advantages.

"Judge Baxter's presentation of the facts and the law before the first Interstate Commerce Commission made such a profound impression that scarcely any other argument was necessary, and the Commission's decision sustained his contention. The report of his argument appears in the first report of the Commission to Congress. He was a great man, he was a giant, he was a giant among giants of the legal profession. I make no extravagant assertion when I way that this man to whom we are paying tribute not only understood the legal phases of railroad work, but understood the traffic details and transportation questions better than many of the men by the big railroads to manage these departments.

"When he took an office in my building," continued Maj. Stahlman, "It was on condition that he be allowed to come to it at any time, night or day. He worked incessantly and kept it up to the last. I wish we had 5,000 young men of the city, county and state present to hear these tributes. What an example to the rising generation.

"I was intimately associated with him for many years. I was very fond of him-I really loved the man and shall revere his memory."

FRIENDS AND ASSOCIATES

Maj. E. C. Lewis who spoke for his friends and associates said that when all that was mortal of his friend and associate was placed in Mt. Olivet he was impressed most with the thought that at his head was a monument not made with the hands-a big sycamore tree- which was typical of the man. "His friends had furnished the flowers," said Maj. Lewis, "but God Almighty had furnished the monument." I never saw Judge Baxter without approaching and I never met him without taking off my hat. He was as ingenuous as a child. He was modest and would run away from a compliment and stop you if you attempted to flatter. He was timid and didn't know that he was a great man. Not in a generation have we had such a man as Baxter-not since John Bell. Bell was a sterner man, while Baxter was as gentle as a woman. It was a great privilege to be his friend; a very great honor to be his associate.

On motion of Maj. F. P. McWhirter, Mr. Lindsay appointed a committee of seven on resolutions and the following resolutions were submitted and adopted:

"When a community loses by death, a great man, an upright individual and an illustrious citizen, whose life was spent in adding renown to that community and setting a shining example so worthy to be emulated by future generations, it is becoming to assemble and express to the world somewhat of appreciation of his life and sorrow at his death.

"Edmund Dillahunty Baxter was all his life of and for Nashville. He was born August 22, 1838 and died June 12, 1910."

"His eminence was pronounced and accepted by each and every one in all the lines of life. His virtues embraced those held highest by mankind. His faults were few and so buried beneath the good he did and the virtues he possessed that no man held a light against him, and now all bow in sorrow at his death. Be it therefore.

"Resolved by the citizens of Nashville and of Tennessee in memorial meeting assembled, that in the death of Edmund Dillehunty Baxter the state, the city, and country have lost a man so great in his attainments, so true in his virtues and so charming in his personality that we are bowed in our bereavement at the irretrievable loss, and are painfully reminded that for the possibilities of betterment to mankind and for the labor and example of such a man, the three score years and ten all too soon exhausted: that we uphold to the youth of Tennessee the life and service of this man, to be esteemed in his character, valued as an example and emulated as a citizen. Be it.

"Resolved further, that the people of Nashville and of Tennessee extend to his family the tenderest expressions of sincere sympathy in their sorrow.

F.P. McWhirter, E. B. Stahlman, E. C. Lewis, Baxter Smith, G.P. Thurston, E.E. Barthell, A.W. Akers.

"Committee"

NASHVILLE BANNER
Nashville, Tenn. Saturday Evening June 18, 1910

MEMORIAL TO JUDGE BAXTER
ADOPTED BY HIS PROFESSIONAL BRETHREN OF THE NASHVILLE BAR.
FULL BAR IN ATTENDANCE
Will Be Presented To All courts in Which He Practiced, Including United States Supreme Court

At an adjourned meeting of the Nashville bar, held at 10 o'clock this morning in the Chancery Court room a memorial and resolutions to Judge Edmund D. Baxter were read and adopted. The committee which prepared the memorial was appointed at a meeting of the bar held last Tuesday, which was adjourned to give that committee time to prepare its work. At the meeting this morning practically the entire bar was present. After the adoption of the memorial, Mr. J. C. Bradford, Chairman, appointed the following gentlemen to present it to the various courts: Supreme Court, Maj. D. F. Wilkins, Court of Civil Appeals, Judge J.M. Anderson; First Circuit court, Mr. K. T. McConnico; Second Circuit

Court, Mr. Albert G. Ewing, Jr.; Chancery Court, Mr. J. S. Pilcher; Criminal Court, Gen. W. H. Washington; United States circuit Court, Mr. G.T. Smith. No appointment was made for the United States Supreme court, the Chairman preferring to wait until a conference with Justice Lurton.

The memorial and resolutions will be published in full Monday

EXPRESSIONS OF SYMPATHY

The following telegram of sympathy signed by the entire Interstate Commerce Commission, so full of expression of the big character and splendid ability of Mr. Baxter, fully serves to justify and emphasize the tribute paid to Mr. Baxter by his host of friends and admirers at home.

"Washington, D.C.   June 14, 1910   Mr. S. F. Andrews, Special Railroad Counsel, Nashville, Tenn.:   The members of the Interstate Commerce Commission desire to express their sincere sorrow in the death of Mr. Baxter, and tender to his family their unaffected sympathy. His appearance as counsel before the commission began with its creation and continued to be frequent until his recent illness. During those years he argued many important cases and became widely known for his expert knowledge of interstate commerce law. No abler lawyer has appeared before the commission, and none has been more highly regarded by its members. His arguments always illuminating and helpful, his understanding of the subject, most thorough and comprehensive, his fairness and candor beyond question, while his modest dignity and engaging personality made all he said interesting and profitable. All of us felt for him the greatest respect, and the most genuine liking, and his passing away in the fullness of his powers comes to each of us as a personal bereavement.

Martin A Knapp, Hudson C. Clements, Chas. A. Prouty, Francis M. Cockrell, Franklin K. Lane, Edgar E. Clark, James E. Harlan.

THE COLUMBIA HERALD
FRIDAY, JUNE 17, 1910

JUDGE ED BAXTER IS CALLED HOME
Able Jurist Dies at his Summer Home after a Long Illness

Nashville, Tenn.   June 12.   Judge Edmund Baxter, one of the foremost lawyers in the Nation and a gentleman without a superior anywhere, died yesterday morning at 3:30 o'clock at his summer home at Ridgetop. The end was not unexpected. For several weeks, Judge Baxter's condition has been regarded as critical, and Thursday his family was summoned to

Ridgetop. All of his children were at the bedside when the end came. He had been ill for about a year.

Prayers will be said at the family residence at Ridgetop this morning by L. F. Chapman. The funeral services will be conducted by Dr. R. Lin Cave at the grave at Mt. Olivet immediately upon the arrival of the remains as the cemetery.

Judge Baxter was a truly great man, as well as a distinguished councilor. "He was the greatest man I ever knew," said one of the leading members of the local bar, speaking of him yesterday.

Judge Baxter was nearly 72 years old. He was born on August 22, 1838. His father was Judge Nathaniel Baxter, who for a number of years was Judge of the Circuit Court of Davidson County and subsequently was Clerk of the Supreme Court for Middle Tennessee. His mother was a Miss Hamilton. Judge Baxter was one of a number of children. Jones Baxter was his half-brother; Jere Baxter was his half-brother; Nathaniel Baxter, who survives him, is his half-brother, and Miss Louise Baxter his half-sister.

Judge Baxter was born in Columbia and was one of the most distinguished men produced by this county. He was held in high esteem by members of the local bar, many of who consider him the leading Southern lawyer. He was named for the famous jurist, Edmund Dillehunty, who was widely popular here. Mr. Baxter has one niece, Mrs. Sue Sanders; a nephew, Dr. Baxter, and other relatives in this county

---

NASHVILLE BANNER
Nashville, Tenn. June 20, 1910

MEMORIAL TO JUDGE BAXTER
WILL BE SPREAD ON MINUTES OF ALL COURTS IN WHICH HE PRACTICED
REVIEW OF HIS CAREER
Contained in Comprehensive Document Prepared By Committee of His Associate

INTERSTATE COMMERCE ACT
At the adjourned meeting of the Nashville bar held Saturday morning, an account of which was published in the Banner, the following memorial and resolutions of the life and labors of Judge Edmund D. Baxter were reported by the committee appointed at the previous meeting and adopted by the bar.

"Mr. Chairman and Gentlemen of this Bar.---Your committee, to whom was assigned the duty of drafting resolutions commemorative of the life and character of Judge Edmund Baxter begs leave to submit the following:

"Edmund Dillahunty Baxter, who was born at Columbia, Maury County, Tennessee on August 22, 1838, died at his summer home at Ridge Top, near Nashville, on Sunday morning, June 12, 1910. When he died one of the greatest American lawyers of this or any other period in our history, and one of the best and most loveable men our state has ever produced, passed into the beyond."

"His father, Nathaniel Baxter, was an accomplished lawyer and judge, while his mother, whose maiden name was Hamilton, whose superior and intellectual woman, and this, as the result of the laws of heredity, the first foundations of Mr. Baxter's greatness were well and solidly laid. Early in life while he was yet only 20 years old, and his bride only 15 years of age, Mr. Baxter was married to Miss Ella T. Perkins and seven children were born to them, three of whom survive. After the death of his first wife, and on November 25, 1879, Mr. Baxter married Mrs. Bettie P. Baxter, the widow of his half-brother, Jones F. Baxter, and she, together with three children of this union also survive him."

"Mr. Baxter finally left school while he was still under 20 years of age, and for a period read law in the office of Andrew Ewing at Nashville and with this preparation, was admitted to the bar as a practicing attorney. More truly can it be said of him, than perhaps of any other of the great lawyers of our country, that by his own methods of study, and his own choice of books, he superbly educated himself, and trained as the result of his own handicraft, the great endowments which nature had bestowed upon him.

ENLISTED AS A CONFEDERATE

"In his very early manhood, Mr. Baxter enlisted as a volunteer in the Confederate army. His service as a Southern soldier was in the Western army; he was active and gallant in many of the fiercest battles of the great civil war, and rose to the rank of Captain of Company A, Baxter's Artillery. It was in 1867, shortly after his surrender at the close of the war, that he began to practice the profession over which he later achieved such a mastery, and in which he was destined to gain for himself such distinction and renown."

"While still a young man, by the time he was 30, he was already recognized as a lawyer of great power and attainment, and had acquired a large general practice at this bar. As early as 1876, Mr. Baxter was appointed by Judge Russell Houston, a former resident of Nashville and then General Counsel of the Louisville and Nashville Railroad Company, to the position of attorney for that railroad for the state of Tennessee. While acting nominally, in this position for years, Mr. Baxter became in reality the chief legal advisor of that road, and as such represented it during one of its main construction periods, and while it was acquiring many of its branch roads in the South. He was even urged to accept the position of Chief Counsel during the closing years of Judge Houston's life, but his delicate regard for Judge Houston, who had been his friend for years, ever constrained him to refuse the honor. While representing this and other clients, Mr. Baxter was already recognized as one of the great men and lawyers of this section of the country, and was, at this period of his life more than at a later period, busily and actively engaged in the State and Federal courts sitting in Tennessee.

REFUSED THE HONOR

"In 1887 the act to regulate interstate commerce was passed by the Congress of the United States and the attention of railroad lawyers throughout the country was drawn to the proper construction and application of the various sections of this statute. This was the first time the Federal Government had undertaken to any extend the regulation of the railroad rates and traffic and railroad affairs generally. It was a new field for the lawyers of the country and one which demanded the highest talents and the greatest labor from those who would undertake to assist the courts in reaching proper construction of this great new act, and a proper application of its provisions to the great commercial carriers of the country. The railroads of the South and Southeast felt that while the provisions of the act theoretically fell strictly alike upon all the roads of the country, practically the act, unless properly construed would fall more heavily upon the railroads in this section. Mr. Baxter first represented the Louisville & Nashville railroad in this connection and after having made a study for months of the new act and its bearing upon traffic, he entered this field of litigation having been selected for this particular duty by the President of that company.

"It was not long, however, before it became apparent that Mr. Baxter was perhaps the most eminently qualified man in the entire country for this line of practice. The result was that he frequently became counsel for other railroads in cases involving the interpretation of the interstate commerce act, and the rulings of the commission there under. This litigation carried him largely into the Federal courts and it transpired that many of the great cases which he was handling in this new field were carried for their ultimate decision to the Supreme Court of the United States. He participated in more of the great cases involving the interstate commerce act before this, the highest court of the nation than any other lawyer of his time. He was marvelously successful in convincing the greatest of courts that it ought to adopt that construction of the act which, in his opinion, should represent for all time to come the law of the land.

BECOMES GENERAL COUNSEL

"It is a safe statement that no other lawyer in the whole country has had anything like the same influence in the forming, by his arguments, of judicial opinions bearing upon the construction of this act. It has been said of him that he occupied the same position in reference to the construction of this act that Daniel Webster occupied in reference to the interpretation of the Constitution of the United States in the earlier days of the republic.

"In 1897 the interstate commerce litigation of the roads of the South and Southeast became so large that a legal department was constituted by all the principal roads and steamship companies engaged in interstate operations in these sections of the country. Mr. Baxter was offered the position of special counsel of the combined railroads and steamship lines of these sections with his headquarters in Nashville. He accepted the position, and from then until his recent death was actively engaged in representing all these various vast enterprises in perhaps their most important litigation in the courts. The bar of the entire nation has long realized and recognized that Mr. Baxter was the very head of this branch of the legal profession. The frequency with which Mr. Baxter was called to represent those clients in the higher tribunals of the country operated to make his reputation even more extended abroad than at home. In the last years of his life he personally dealt only with great suits, but few of which were argued in this section of the country. His most able arguments were heard in distant cities, by only a few interested persons, and his home people knew of his work chiefly through press dispatches telling of his great arguments before the high Federal tribunals.

"At an earlier stage of his career, Mr. Baxter, in the highest courts of this state, represented clients in many of the greatest and most important cases tried during his generation in Tennessee. And during this period of the state's legal history, a period prolific of great and strong lawyers, he ever occupied a position at the very top. An enumeration of his many large and successful contests in the courts in this connection would require a space beyond the compass of this testimonial.

SIMPLE AND LOVABLE LIFE

"While Mr. Baxter was living his great professional life and winning national renown in his frequent appearances before the highest courts of the country he was living his simple and lovable social life among his family and friends, in this, his home. It was perhaps the greatest charm of his personality that he was the most genial, and at the same time, the most modest and unassuming of gentlemen. He was the only person in all the field of his acquaintances who never, to the slightest extent realized his own greatness. His heart was warm and loyal as we people of the South would have it. His disposition and temperament were genial and happy, and when in moments and hours of leisure, he would rest from his vast professional labors and responsibilities, he could be, and was, one, of the most genial, entertaining, and lovable companions and friends.

"Mr. Baxter was the most devoted and indulgent husband and father. He was absolutely unselfish. He never thought of accumulation wealth, and while he earned vast sums of money in his practice he would never hoard any part of it for himself, but would divide it among the members of the family from time to time. His home life and his association with his intimate and beloved friends were to him the source of his greatest pleasure and happiness.

"More than any lawyer of whom we have any knowledge, Mr. Baxter was industrious, thorough, painstaking and exact. Endowed by nature with a splendid physique and great strength, he permitted the burden of no weight of work to prevent him from giving to each and every case and question the most exhaustive and illuminating effort.

"His style of speech, like that of all the really great, was marked for its chaste simplicity and exquisite precision and accuracy. It had been said of him that he used more short, strong words, more pure Anglo-Saxton than almost any other great debater.

CONVINCING LOGIC

"His arguments in court were models of convincing logic. He could by his genius present to unskilled juries the most intricate questions of fact in their proper relation and bearing to abstruse questions of law, and make the whole presentation absolutely charming in its simplicity and order. As an orator, while discarding the ornate and ignoring any of the studied efforts to captivate, he was capable, upon demanding occasions, of the most impassioned eloquence that could bend the hearts and minds of the greatest Judge or the plainest juror to the right and justice of his case. He was full of sentiment for everything lovable and ennobling and whether exchanging a friendly word or a bit of humor and good-fellowship with a friend, or charming by a great speech the highest court of the nation, he was always as modest, simple and unassuming as are ever the truly great.

"While as much as any man could safely do it, Mr. Baxter could have risked to the inspiration of the moment and the ingenuity of the present, in the presentation and trial of his cases; yet he was never known to do this to any appreciable degree at all. Each and every point in every case in which he ever appeared had claimed from him moments and hours of patient thought and labor, which his friends would often think had been unnecessary, but which he, in his modesty and his desire to ever do his best, had been seen fit to lavish upon his client's cause. He actually seemed to accept and value each and every day as a field of preparation to meet the problems that to-morrow would present. The result was that at the close of his great life, he possessed the accumulation of ability and character that only such a patient toiler could acquire.

TEACHER AND EDUCATOR

"It would not be proper to conclude this testimonial without paying a deserved tribute to Mr. Baxter as a teacher and educator in the field of the law. For many years he was a member of the faculty of the Law Department of Vanderbilt University. When that department was organized, he with the late Judge Thomas H. Malone and the late Col. William B. Reece, constituted the faculty. This was in 1875. Mr. Baxter continued in this association until the death of Col. Reece, in the early nineties, and indeed remained a member of the Law Department of this university for several years longer, until his engagements and professional obligations to the vast interests which he represented made it necessary for him to sever his connection with this institution. The branches of law which he taught in this university were those of Pleading and Practice and Evidence—those branches of the law most charming to the mature lawyer, and at the same time most difficult and hardest to master. He was a great inspiration to work, and a great source of light and education to every student who had the blessed opportunity to sit before him as a pupil, to be instructed in the law. He never placed upon any student any task, no matter how laborious in the way of study and preparedness for any lecture, when he did not, give more time and patient study upon the subject of that same lecture than did the unlearned intimate. One day, in a mood of simple and modest confidence, he told his class that he gave more care towards preparing for his lectures for them than he did to preparing a case for trial before the Supreme Court of the United States.

"No student whom he ever taught could doubt the absolute accuracy of this statement. He said that he realized that the highest court would be composed of eminent lawyers, who could protect his client's rights if he were guilty of any shortcoming; but that he realized that, in teaching his students, the responsibility was resting upon him to guide them, at the expense of every possible labor, into the paths which they should tread. While inspiring more work from his pupils than any other could inspire, they were never conscious of any burden, and had no other thought than to do their very best for him, even though in their youth, they might not yet have realized the burden and responsibility of the profession they were presumptuous enough to seek to master. He so lived his life as a teacher that every student with whom he came in contact not only loved him, but fully realized and knew that in him they had a true and loyal friend whose hand would be stretched out to them in all their after life as long as they were worthy, and knew that his charity was such that he would regard them as worthy as long as would and knew his charity was such that he would regard them worthy as long as would any living man.

GREAT LOSS

"The citizens of Tennessee and the nation have suffered a great loss in Mr. Baxter's death. Let us ever cherish his life and character as a source of inspiration, and as presenting a standard and model for all of us to humbly try to approach so nearly as we can. Perhaps we shall not see his like again.

"Therefore, be it resolved by the members of the Nashville bar in special meeting assembled. That the death of Edmund Dillehunty Baxter the bar of the South and of the nation has lost a great lawyer and champion of justice, who will be sadly missed in the high places of this profession in which he climbed by such patient and unrelenting labor; and that his life and character will ever be honored and revered by the entire circle of lawyers with whom he has come in contact in his long and invaluable professional career.

CONFEDERATE VETERAN
Nashville, Tenn.
Vol. XVIII   August 1910
EDMUND D. BAXTER

The recent death of Edmund Dillehunty Baxter at his summer home, near Nashville, has been published extensively. He was a lieutenant in the Harding Artillery, C.S.A., early in the war, and later was Captain of Baxter's Artillery. He made an able address for the South years ago before the Frank Cheatham Camp which was published in pamphlet form, a copy of which the VETERAN has sought in vain to procure.

Judge J. M. Dickinson, Secretary of War, wrote from Washington on June 18 of Mr. Edmund Baxter, with whom he was associated for many years as follows:

"Probably no man ever won so early in life a front rank at the Tennessee bar. Almost immediately after the war he was recognized as a competitor for the first honors. This statement carries great significance when we recall the names of those whom he met in the arena. There were in Nashville then Francis B. Fogg, John Trimble, Neil S. Brown, Henry S. Foote, Edwin H. Ewing, Robert L. Caruthers, Edmond H. East, William F. Cooper, Thomas H. Malone, and other strong men. No bar in any city of like size in the United States could have presented an equal number of able lawyers. By the time he was thirty Mr. Baxter had achieved a place by the side of the foremost.

"For more than forty years he was a recognized leader of the Tennessee bar. Having had a good opportunity for knowing, I do not hesitate to say that no man ever excelled him in his devotion to his clients and his profession, that he performed more constant and arduous labor than any man I ever knew, no matter in what calling, and he was in more important cases than any lawyer of Tennessee throughout its entire history. I venture the opinion that if the reports were examined it would appear that he argued more cases before the Supreme Court of the United States than any other lawyer in America. I have often heard various members of that court speak of the great ability with which he presented his cases and their pleasure and profit of hearing him. His success was great, and was as uniform as could be expected of a man whose reputation caused him to be employed in desperate cases.

"His clients were not limited to his own state. When the railroad companies centering in Chicago wanted a lawyer of exceptional ability in two cases of great importance, both on account of the amounts involved and the complicated nature of the litigation, they selected Mr. Baxter. It has been stated that he rarely practiced in the criminal courts. This is true; but on account of his reputation he was employed by the United States government to prosecute several officers of national banks. Recently I heard President Taft, who as circuit judge tried those cases, say that Mr. Baxter was the best criminal lawyer he ever knew.

"With all of his professional greatness, he was modest. In conference with even the merest fledglings of the law, who knew but little and whose paucity of knowledge he was well aware of, he treated them as equals, listening politely to their views, and never showed impatience or discourtesy, however little he may have been impressed by them. He never made a junior feel small by any show of his own superiority. He practiced his profession honorably. He did not need any code of legal ethics. His own sense of right conduct always kept him on the highest professional plane. He has left by his career a rich legacy to the bar of the State one that should be kept before the younger members of the bar as an inspiration. If all lawyers pursued their profession in the way that Mr. Baxter did, it would need no apologist, for no one would have the hardihood to assail it."

(Judge Nathaniel Baxter. Father of Ed Baxter)
CONFEDERATE VETERAN
Nashville, Tenn.
Vol. III No. 2   February 1895

Judge Nathaniel Baxter, a father of Veterans, deserves extended notice here. Recently he retired in usual health, and on Sunday morning messages were sent to his sons in different parts of the city that he had fallen asleep. The writer was favored with apartment in private car by Judge Baxter to the Birmingham reunion, on which occasion the Judge was especially agreeable. He told many stories of interest. One is here given about Jas. K. Polk when going to Washington as President of the United States. Mr. Baxter was a young lawyer at the time and he rode near the head of a long procession to Nashville, and he happened to have change for the President's toll at the turnpike gates, as the keeper could not change Mr. Polk's bill. Long afterward, Mr. Polk called at his office, saying he wanted to pay what he owed him. Mr. Baxter was embarrassed, not having expected reference to be made of the trifling amount, and so was Mr. Polk, but he added: "It will relieve me very much if you will accept, for I don't owe another cent in the world."

When the reunion at Birmingham was over, the venerable gentleman tarried to visit the locality near Elyton, where fifty-seven years before he had enjoyed a rest, while a volunteer for the war in Florida. Those who know the upright, kind-hearted man, are ever anxious to give expressions in his honor. He was of North Carolina stock, but born in Tennessee in 1812. The life of fourscore and two years went out as peacefully as the setting sun.

Sergeant Aaron Pink Beard
THE REVIEW APPEAL
Franklin, TN.   April 7, 1904

Aden: Elder Pink Beard of the First District, visited Franklin last week for the first time since 1889. He is seventy-seven years of age, enjoys good health and as one of the most notable characters within the confines of this county, in as much, as he has a record that is probably not equaled by any other man living in the State; a veteran of two wars, a preacher of the gospel for half a century and a politician. Respected and honored by his friends here he was given a royal welcome.

The remarkable career of Mr. Beard began at an early age. When a youth he, together with a brother and several neighbor boys, joined the Tennessee troops for the invasion of Mexico, which were with the first regiments of the American army to land in the enemies' country. The early arrival of his company gave Mr. Beard and his comrades an opportunity to take part on several engagements before the capture of Mexico City, they being present and participating in the battle. For his services in that war he is now receiving a pension. At the cessation of hostilities he returned to his home in the first district and turned his attention to farming and later entered the ministry.

When the war clouds gathered in 1861, he took his stand for the Union, and was the only man in this district that voted against secession, his two brothers voting for it. However, when the announcement came that his state had seceded, he at once enlisted in the Confederate service and served gallantly for four years in the defense of his Southland. Singular enough, the two brothers, who had voted to secede, joined the Federals. After the war he became a Democrat and his brothers Republicans.

On his return he entered upon the peaceful pursuits of life, as a farmer and minister, with the same courageous spirit which prompted him on two occasions to offer his life, if need be, in the defense of his country. During his ministerial work he has preached at the same church, Primitive Baptist for thirty-five years, baptizing 788 converts and officiating at over 400 marriages besides conducting services over the remains of hundreds of his neighbors and friends.

Private Benjamin Franklin Brown
(Last surviving member of Baxter's Middle Tennessee Recruits)

THE DICKSON COUNTY HERALD
DICKSON, TENNESSEE, FRIDAY, MARCH 26, 1937

LAST OF COUNTY'S CIVIL WAR VETERANS IS DEAD

Benjamin Franklin Brown, last surviving Confederate veteran of Dickson county, died Sunday, March 23, at his home four miles south of Burns.

"Uncle Ben", as he was familiarly known to his host of acquaintances, was born December 8, 1841, being 95 years, three months and thirteen days of age. He was born on the same place where he died and had lived at the same place his entire lifetime.   His grandfathers, both on his father's and mother's side, were among the pioneer families who settled in Dickson county.

The deceased married Miss Louisiana Garton on September 27, 1861, and a short time afterward enlisted in Baxter's Tennessee Artillery Battery, serving throughout the Civil War.   When he returned home in 1865, his first son had been born and was a good sized boy, whom he then saw for the first time. His first wife died on December 7, 1884, and he afterward married Miss Susan D. Campbell. From these two unions there were born the following children: Miles Brown, Liberty Brown, Asa Brown, Sydney Brown, Dalton Brown, Mrs. C.V. Vandiver, Mrs. Clay Dozier, Mrs. W.S. Totty, Mrs. Hattie Dennison, Mrs. Charles Underhill and Mrs. R.D. Stinson.   He also has living twenty-eight grandchildren and nine great-grandchildren.

So far as is known, "Uncle Ben" was not only the last surviving Confederate soldier of Dickson County, but also the last surviving member of Baxter's Tennessee Artillery Battery. His principal business was dealing in livestock, and in this capacity he came in to contact with practically all of the people of not only Dickson county but throughout the surrounding counties throughout Middle Tennessee and was extensively well known over a large part of this section. By his passing there is removed one of the last landmarks connecting this generation with the antebellum days.

Funeral services were held Monday afternoon, conducted by Elder J. A. Pope and interment followed in the family graveyard in the Turnbull section.

(Widow of Private William G. D. Buttrey)

THE DICKSON COUNTY HERALD
Dickson, Tennessee   Friday December 22, 1933
MRS. ELIZA BUTTREY

Mrs. Eliza White Buttrey, aged 92, died at the home of her son, R.T. Buttrey, on Jones Creek, Friday, December 15, 1933. She was married to William Buttrey 76 years ago, he having preceded her to the grave 52 years. To this union was born ten sons and one daughter. Six of the sons together with 40 grandchildren and 60 great-grandchildren survive her. She was a highly esteemed and faithful member of the Turnbull Primitive Baptist Church for 68 years. She was loved and honored by all who knew her.

Funeral services were held by Elder J.A. Pope and C.L. Thomason and interment took place in the White graveyard on Turnbull last Saturday afternoon.

Sergeant James Felix Ewing Buttrey
THE REVIEW APPEAL

Franklin, TN. January 18, 1912

Pasadena: Two of our oldest citizens have passed away since the last items published from here. The first was James F. Buttrey who died at the residence of his son-in law, G. W. Carter, Dec. 21. He was a Confederate soldier; a member of Baxter's Battery; a highly respected citizen, a life-long democrat. For many years he was chairman of the democratic committee of the First District. He was charitable and gave liberally to deserving needs. He was about seventy-eight years of age. He left several children and grandchildren and other relatives and a host of friends to mourn his departure. His remains were laid to rest in the family burying ground.

The other was Paul B. Beech, who died at the residence of his son-in-law, Will Smith near Fernvale, Friday evening Jan. 12. He had been in feeble health a long time, but his last serious illness that terminated in death was only three or four days duration. He was a Confederate soldier, having served with honor in the Twentieth Tennessee Infantry in DeGraffenreid's company. After the battle of Chicamauga he was taken prisoner and spent the winter of 1863 and 1864 in Rock Island prison, the horrors of which, when he told them, would make a strong man shudder. He was a good neighbor, a kind father, and an affectionate husband. He leaves one son, five daughters and several grand-children and many friends to mourn his demise. He was about eighty years old. Interment took place at the family burying ground at the Branch B. Beech place.

Sgt. John F. Cunningham
(Widow of Sgt. John F. Cunningham, Last surviving widow of Baxter's
Middle Tennessee Recruits)
NASHVILLE TENNESSEAN
Nashville, Tenn. October 21, 1943

Mrs. Cunningham To Be Buried today
Fairview Resident was 98 Years Old

Franklin, Tenn.   Oct. 20.   Funeral Services for Mrs. Eliza J. Tidwell Cunningham, 98, of the Fairview community, who died early this morning at her home after a long illness, will be held Thursday afternoon at the home. Burial will be in the family burying ground.

Mrs. Cunningham suffered a fall four months ago and had been confined to her bed since. She was the daughter of the late Mr. and Mrs. Mansell Tidwell, who were among the first settlers in Williamson County. She was married to the late John F. Cunningham in 1865, after his discharge from the Confederate Army. She lived at the time of her death in the house where they moved when they were married.

A great student of the Bible she had been a member of the Baptist Church all her life. She was the oldest of 12 children, all of whom died before her.

She is survived by seven children, Oscar and Robert Cunningham of Fairview, John Cunningham of Phoenix, Ariz., Mrs. Mattie Lankford of Bon Aqua, Mrs. Nellie Spencer of Burns, Mrs. S. A. Gentry of Montgomery, Ala., and Miss Margaret Cunningham of Nashville; 38 grandchildren; 75 great-grandchildren and 23 great-great-grandchildren.

Her grandsons will serve as active pallbearers at the funeral and her granddaughters will be honorary pallbearers.

888

(Note : The same obituary was printed in the October 20, 1943 issue of the *NASHVILLE BANNER* and a similar obituary was printed in the October 21, 1943 edition of *THE REVIEW APPEAL*)

Private John Bryant Dillard

THE DICKSON COUNTY HERALD
Dickson, Tennessee December 14, 1928
BURNS NEWS

The remains of Mr. John Dillard were brought to the home of his daughter, Mrs. A.L.M. Johnson Friday. Funeral service was held Saturday and burial took place in the Garton graveyard. Mr. Dillard was 86 years old, and had been a member of the Old Soldier's Home for several months.

(Widow of Private William P. A. Frashier)

THE DICKSON COUNTY HERALD
Dickson, Tennessee Friday May 31, 1918

OBITUARY

Rebecca H. Parker was born Feb. 22, 1835 and was married to W. P. A. Frashier June 22, 1862. She joined the Primitive Baptist Church and was baptized the Second Sunday in March 1865 and lived an exemplary Christian life and devoted member of said church till her death on May 1, 1918, being 83 years, 2 months and 9 days old. Turnbull, the church of her membership was 112 years old last April. She was dutiful, she enjoyed her church privilege and god's sweet blessings and presence so much.

Whereas, it pleased God to remove her from the church militant to the church triumphant, she and her husband journeyed through life happily until it pleased the dear Lord to call her hence. She leaves a devoted husband and children and many other relatives and friends to mourn the loss of this good woman, all of whom esteemed her highly and loved her dearly.

In the ranks of Zion's children able stood, and with there she stepped in the footprints of her blessed Savior. Her faithfulness as a wife and mother is best known by her aged, heart-broken husband and their children. Her patient, loving service in the home circle will ever linger in the memory of the family. Great as her loss is, it is not to be compared with the eternal gain that has come to her. She now bathes in the fountain of infinite peace, the streams of which blessed her soul as she journeyed here.

(Widow of Lt. John Gault)

THE JACKSON SUN
Jackson, Tennessee
Monday September 23, 1943

SERVICES FOR MRS. GAULT ARE HELD ON SUNDAY
Mrs. Mary W. Gault, 77, died Sunday morning at 8:05 o'clock at the home of her grandson, B.L. Green, Jr., 680 Neely, after an extended illness.

She had resided in the home of Mr. Green since April 18. She was a member of St. Luke's Episcopal Church. Surviving is one daughter, Mrs. Mary Gault Green, of Jackson, in addition to her grandson.

Funeral services were conducted at the residence Sunday afternoon at 2:30 o'clock by the Rev. W.J. Loaring-Clark, rector of St. Luke's Episcopal Church and the body was carried to her former home at Franklin, Tenn., for burial.

Griffin Funeral Home in charge.

(An obituary for Mrs. Gault was also printed in the September 26, 1940 edition of *THE REVIEW APPEAL.*)

Sgt. George W. Hogan, Jr.

NASHVILLE TENNESSEAN
Nashville, Tenn. Tuesday Morning October 4, 1921

Hogan.—Saturday evening, October 1, 1921, at 8 o'clock, George W. Hogan, in his eightieth year of age. Survived by sons, W. Murray of Nashville, Hooper P. of Pittsburgh, Pa., and H.H. of Kansas City, Mo. Funeral from the residence of his son, M. Murray Hogan, No. 2308 Belmont Boulevard, at 10 o'clock Tuesday morning, services being conducted by Rev. George W. Stoves and Micah S. Combs. The following friends are requested to attend as pallbearers: Leon Geny, John McGraw, E.M. Polk, Lillard Waggoner, Lem Warner and Paul Stumb. Company B, Confederate Veterans, will meet in the transfer station at 9 o'clock, without arms, to attend the funeral. Interment in Confederate Circle, Mt. Olivet.

M.S. Combs & Co., directors.

Private Felix M. Jones

DAILY MESSENGER
Mayfield, Kentucky   August 21, 1907
Death's Work

One of the county's best citizens died August 7, 1907, at his home near
Palmore. He was none other than F.M. Jones, and was born December
16, 1840 and at the time of his death he was 66 years, 7 months and 22
days old. He was baptized in the Christian Church at Knob Creek, Aug.
15, 1878 and moved his membership to Mt. Pleasant in 1880. He was an
ex-Confederate soldier, a brave and good man and was the son of Mr.
Jeff Jones and a brother of Mrs. A. D. Cosby of this city.
He left a wife, two daughters and one son. His funeral was preached by
Rev. S.H. Long and assisted by Mr. J. T. Daughaday. He was a good and
popular man.

Mrs. Kiziah Hays Lankford
(Widow of Private Dillard H. Lankford)
THE DICKSON COUNTY HERALD
Dickson, Tennessee   Friday February 26, 1915

PARKER'S CREEK
M. J. Lankford of Bellview was in this vicinity recently, the guest of his
mother, Mrs. Kizzie Lankford.
Mrs. Kizzie Lankford died Tuesday. Feb 23 and was buried at the family
graveyard.

(1st Lieutenant John Marshall)

NASHVILLE REPUBLICAN BANNER
Nashville, Tenn. Sunday June 7, 1874

FOUND DEAD

The body of a man was found between Camden and Johnsonville, on the Northwestern Road, Friday, he having apparently been run over by some passing train.

CONFEDERATE VETERAN
Nashville, Tenn.
Vol. XXVIII January 1920

MATTHEW F. MAURY

Mr. Matthew Fontaine Maury, one of the oldest citizens of Williamson County, Tenn., passed away at his home, in Franklin, on December 5, 1919.

Sgt. Matthew F. Maury

Matthew F. Maury was born in Williamson County January 19, 1829, and had thus nearly completed his ninety-one years. His father, who was a brother of the famous Commodore Matthew Fontaine Maury, the "Pathfinder of the Seas," for whom the nephew was named, came to this county from Virginia at the opening of the last century, and the family has always been prominent in the county. He went into the Confederate army with Baxter's Artillery from Williamson County, but was later detailed by General Johnston in the Engineering Corps.

Mr. Maury spent some years in Washington as a youth when his distinguished uncle, by whom he was educated, was in official life at the national capital, and the nephew had a rare fund of first-hand reminiscences and anecdotes of the great men of that time. He was a man of keen intelligence, high principles, and generous sentiments, strong in his convictions and firm to maintain them. He leaves an honored memory as a heritage to his children. His wife, who was Miss Eliza Buford, daughter of a prominent citizen, died several years ago.

Surviving is one sister, Miss Bethena Maury, of Franklin, the last of a large family. Of his children, five sons and five daughters survive him.

(Widow of Sgt. Eli G. Sherman)
THE REVIEW-APPEAL

FRANKLIN, TENNESSEE FEBRUARY 18, 1926

MRS. SHERMAN DIED HERE LAST FRIDAY
LONG ILLNESS PROVES FATAL TO FRANKLIN WOMAN; SERVICES SATURDAY

Mrs. Sue Jones Sherman died Friday Feb. 12 at 4 A.M. at her home on 3rd avenue North after a long illness.

Funeral services were conducted from the residence Saturday at 10:30 A.M. by Elder F.W. Smith and her remains were interred at Mt. Hope Cemetery.

The deceased was born and reared in this county and was widely known and esteemed. She was the wife of the late E.G. Sherman and the daughter of the late C.O. Jones and Mrs. Frances Meacham Jones. She was a consistant member of the Christian Church. Mrs. Sherman was a woman of retiring nature and a great lover of home where she was the center of an affectionate home life.

She is survived by two daughters, Misses Frances and Susie Lee Sherman, and granddaughter, Anne Sherman, all of Franklin, two brothers, C.O. Jones and Jas. H. Jones of Nashville.

The following nephews were pall bearers, Lee H. Jones, Paul Jones, Ridley Jones, C.O. Jones, Jr., Emery Jones, and Lee H. Hardison.

Regen and Cotton were the funeral directors.

(Widow of Corporal Joseph Sweeney)

THE REVIEW-APPEAL
FRANKLIN, TENNESSEE, THURSDAY FEBRUARY 22, 1934

HILLSBORO WOMAN DIED THURSDAY
Mrs. Minerva Jane Gatlin Sweeney Had Been Ill Two Years

Mrs. Minerva Jane Gatlin Sweeney, aged 84, died Thursday morning at her home at Hillsboro, following an invalidism of two years.

Funeral services were conducted by Elder Oscar Parham, at the Hillsboro Church of Christ, Saturday at 2 p.m. Interment was in the Hillsboro Cemetery.

The deceased was buried in a handmade casket, fashioned and carved by her husband, the late J.L. Sweeney from black walnut, cut in 1918. Her husband was buried 16 years ago in a casket which he made to receive his own body, similar to the one he made for the burial of his wife.

Mr. Sweeney was a carriage maker. The caskets were made at the shop near Mr. Sweeney's home, at Hillsboro, with the greatest care and skilled workmanship. He was the grandfather of J. H. Sweeney, funeral director, in Nashville.

Mrs. Sweeney had been a resident of Hillsboro during her long and useful lifetime. She was a member of the Church of Christ. She was a woman, who was ever active in deeds of kindness and mercy, and looked well to the ways of her own household.

She is survived by two daughters, Mrs. John W. Moss of Tuscumbia, Ala., and Miss Ada Sweeney of Hillsboro; five sons, L. F. Sweeney of Joelton, Tenn., Latt Sweeney of Hollywood, Calif., Bonnie Sweeney of Coffeyville, Miss., Ed and Charley Sweeney of Hillsboro, and three brothers, John, Jim, and Will Gatlin of Hillsboro.

The pall bearers were H. H. Davis, Gus Carl, Runyun Parham, P. A. Rose, W. H. Bixwell and J. M. Overbey.

Henry M. Cotton was the funeral director.

Samuel Spencer
(brother of Abe & Hiram Spencer)

THE SEMI-WEEKLY HOME ENTERPRISE

Dickson, Tennessee   December 31, 1895

DIED

At his home at Spencer's Mill, Sunday morning, Dec. 29, 1895, Rev. Samuel Spencer. A burial outfit was furnished by J. Davis & Son, and interment took place near his home yesterday.

Private Amos Spicer

DICKSON COUNTY HERALD

August 23, 1918   Dickson, Tennessee

AMOS SPICER'S BODY FOUND IN WOODS
Had Been Missing From His Home on Turnbull For Several Months

The finding of the body of Mr. Amos Spicer, Wednesday morning under an old tree-top two miles from his home on Turnbull, clears up a mystery that has been the talk of the neighborhood for the past several months. The body was discovered by Lonnie Buttrey about 300 yards from the White Bluff road, while he was hunting a strayed cow, according to information received.

Mr. Spicer lived at the home of his daughter, Mrs. Mason Buttery, at the time of his disappearance several months ago. She and other members of the family were absent from the home only a short time the day he disappeared, and from that day until the finding of the body, no clue had been found that gave any promise of unraveling the mystery of the disappearance, as no one in the neighborhood had seen Mr. Spicer leave the premises. A reward was offered by Mason Buttrey and his wife for the finding of the latter's father.

The skeleton and tattered clothing as found clears up the mystery as to Mr. Spicer's whereabouts. It is surmised that Mr. Spicer, who was old and almost blind, had attempted to walk to White Bluff, and in doing so, wandered away and became lost in the woods, and finally becoming exhausted sought the covering protection of the fallen tree-top, where he expired. A coroner's jury, however, will be empaneled today, we understand, to make investigations.

DICKSON COUNTY HERALD
Friday April 25, 1941

IN MEMORIAM
Mrs. Alice R. Thompson

Funeral services for Mrs. Alice Richardson Thompson were conducted at her home near Burns Sunday afternoon, April 6, 1941 by the Rev. Earl Woods of White Bluff and Elder C. L. Thompson of Nashville.

The deceased was born near Erin, Houston County, Tenn. June 25, 1858 and married to the late J. B. Thompson of Kingston Springs, a soldier in General Baxter's Artillery, on October 8, 1879. They spent their entire lives at the same place where they first started housekeeping having celebrated their fiftieth Anniversary in September 1929. Mr. Thompson proceeded her in death in September 1935.

Nine children were born into their union, of which five survive, namely Mrs. J. C. Brown, Mrs. P. E. Moon and Battie Thompson of Nashville and Mrs. Milton Daniel and Mrs. T. B. Howell of Burns. Also one stepdaughter, Mrs. Sydney Brown, of Bellevue, Tenn., ten grandchildren and two great-grand children survive.

Private Soloman Marsh Tidwell
HICKMAN COUNTY NEWS HERALD
Centreville, Tennessee   February 1925

GRAY UNIFORM SHROUDS CONFEDERATE VETERAN
SOL. M. TIDWELL 85-YEAR Old Confederate Veteran, Rests in Uniform Worn in Civil War Service

Sol. M. Tidwell of the Sugar Creek community in the western section of this county, died at his home on Friday after a short illness complicated with infirmities of age. Funeral services were held Saturday and burial was at the family cemetery, where rest the remains of members of the family which has long been prominent in affairs of that section. The remains were shrouded in the uniform of Gray, treasured memento of valiant service as a soldier of the Confederacy throughout the Civil War, and by request of deceased.

Mr. Tidwell was not a member of any church organization, although firmly believing in principles of faith of the Primitive Baptist Church, attending its services and being active in church worn. He had borne affliction patiently, expressing hope of eternal salvation and his passing came as a benediction on a long life well spent in service to home and loved ones, to his country in its great need, and to the cause of the Master.

Deceased was 85 years of age having been born in Dickson County on January 29, 1844. During early manhood he conducted a mercantile business in Dickson County, also dealing in livestock, and later moved from that county to the Eighth civil district of this county, in which the greater part of his life was lived. He was first married to Miss Lou Garton about 60 years ago. Following her death, he was married to Mrs. Hannah Wilkins Baugua and to this union eleven children were born, a number of whom died in infancy. He is survived by wife, and three children, Arlie and Noah Tidwell and Miss Mary Tidwell; sister Mrs. Missie Reeves of Nashville, and more distant relatives.

Private James Polk White
THE DICKSON COUNTY HERALD

Dickson, Tennessee October 14, 1927

DEATHS OF WEEK

Mr. James P. White, aged 83 years, died Thursday, October 6, at his home near Burns. Funeral Service was held Saturday at the residence conducted by Elder J. A. Pope and interment took place in the family graveyard. He is survived by three sons, W. B. White, Farmer White, of the Burns neighborhood and R. S. White, of Taft, Calif., and one daughter, Mrs. Eliza Buttrey of Burns.

Cpl. James P. White

CONFEDERATE VETERAN
Vol. XIII Nashville, Tenn. 1905

J. H. Elder writes from Atlanta, Ga.: "An old comrade, Reuben Norris of Baxter's Tennessee Battery, wishes to hear from any surviving comrades in arms. He and his two brothers, Lindsey and John , of Campbell

County, Ga. joined the battery while it was stationed at West End, Atlanta, in March 1864. At the battle of Atlanta, on July 22, 1864, while his battery was aiding in the capture of Degress's Battery, his two brothers were killed. In fact, Baxter's Battery was almost annihilated. Mr. Norris was wounded by a piece of shell at the battle of Jonesboro, Ga., and was disabled for the balance of the war."

THE NASHVILLE TENNESSEAN
Nashville, Tenn.   June 27, 1920
PERSONALS
Mrs. Edmund Baxter and her granddaughter, Miss Elizabeth Thomas, have returned from New York and Washington, D.C.

THE DICKSON COUNTY HERALD
Dickson, Tennessee   June 10, 1932

U.D.C DEDICATES SOLDIER MARKERS
Confederate Memorial Day, June 3rd, means much to the members of "Old Hickory" Chapter, U.D.C. The business meeting in the assembly room of the First National Bank was presided over by Mrs. G.A. Slayden, president. The minutes of the May meeting were read and reports heard, the outstanding one being that of the chairman of the Ft. Donaldson committee, Mrs. Ray Hogin, who stated that the date for the occasion of the benefit card party would be announced soon and that Mrs. Frank Hall had graciously offered her home for the occasion. It was voted by the Chapter to send Mrs. Baker, who is ill in Vanderbilt Hospital, a basket of flowers. The Chapter voted to disband for the two hottest months, July and August, and after a detailed report of the District meeting at Centreville by Mrs. Claude Hooper, the members drove to the cemetery where the ritual was read by the Chapter President and the song, "How Firm a Foundation," sung. After prayer, many beautiful flowers were strewn on the Confederate soldiers' graves, and the new markers which had recently been placed by the committee, with Mrs. R.P. Beasley, chairman, were reverently dedicated.

The Confederate veterans buried in Union Cemetery, include: W.M. Hogin, J.K. Davis, J.M. Talley, W.H. McCauley, F.F. Tidwell, John F. Alexander, E.A. Andrews, John C. Buford, B.A. Clifton, Thomas Davidson, J.E. Fussell, S.P. Larkins, J. T. Murrell, W.H. Patterson, James Nall, W.W. Smith, Dr. L.D. Wright, A.B. Williams, Eugene Kelsey, Andrew Easley, John Easley, Bob Easley, W.H. Lowery, R.T.

Work, J.R. McNeil, R.F. McCaslin, T.J. Carr, Green Davidson, Rev. E. W. White, I.N. Shannon, T.M. Childress, Pete Miller, Jas. Lunn, J.A. Thomas, A.L. Dozier, T.D. Pinkerton, and John Brown.

Mickens Barter Carr
(Brother of G.W. & T.J. Carr)

THE DICKSON COUNTY HERALD
Dickson, Tennessee Fri. July 2, 1937

OVER-EIGHTY CLUB
I was just a boy during the Civil War, being only about 15 when it started, so I didn't go. However I was fixing to shoulder a musket and go when it ended. I had two brothers who fought for the Confederate side. My oldest brother died in the service.

W.F. (Frank) Moore
(Son of John B. Moore)

THE DICKSON COUNTY HERALD
Dickson, Tennessee Fri. November 19, 1937

OVER-EIGHTY CLUB
Ruth Johnson   Interviewer

Dear Mr. Editor,

I wish to join with other boys over eighty. I was born January 19th, 1856 on Turkey Creek. My father was John Moore and my mother was Lucy Redden. Father and his brother, J.B. Moore were both killed in the War Between the States.

I was six years old when my father got killed. My mother was a very poor woman, left with five little children, three boys and two girls. My uncle, Wiley Redden, moved us to a little house on his farm on Piney. My mother's uncles and other kinfolks kept us from starving until we got big enough to work.

THE FAIRVIEW OBSERVER
Fairview, Tennessee December 30, 2003

FAIRVIEW'S NEW SCV CAMP RECEIVES CHARTER
Captain E.D. Baxter Camp 2034 Sons of Confederate Veterans received its charter at the December 9th meeting. Tennessee SCV

Division Commander, Milton "Skip" Earle of Franklin presented the Charter. The camp was chartered with 26 members.

Membership is open to all males 12 years of age and older who are descended form Confederate Soldiers who served honorably.   An associate member program is available to men who cannot document an ancestor.

Camp 2034 meets the 2nd Tuesday of each month at 7 p.m. at the Fairview Recreation Center, Room 3. all meetings are open and the public is always welcome to attend. For more information, call 799-0916 or email lampleydj@aol.com.

THE FAIRVIEW OBSERVER
Fairview, Tennessee   March 2, 2004

LOCAL HISTORY TOPIC AT SCV MEETING

Dennis Lampley will present a history of Baxter's Company Tennessee Light Artillery, CSA at the March 9 meeting of Captain Ed Baxter Camp 2034 Sons of Confederate Veterans.

Baxter's Company was comprised mainly of men from Williamson and Dickson Counties. Most of the soldiers have descendents living in the area today.

The meeting will be held at 7 p.m. in Room 3 of the Fairview Recreation Center and the public is invited to attend.

This will be an excellent opportunity for area residents to learn about their ancestors roll in the Civil War. For more information, call 799-0916 or visit the new camp website at: http://tennessee-scv.org/camp2034.

THE FAIRVIEW OBSERVER
Fairview, Tennessee June 8, 2004

MEMORIAL SERVICE HELD FOR CAPTAIN BAXTER

A military grave marker was placed and a memorial service was held on May 22 for Captain Edmund D. Baxter at his grave in Mt. Olivet Cemetery in Nashville. The event was sponsored by Captain Ed Baxter Camp 2034 Sons of Confederate Veterans in Fairview.

Seven Sons of Confederate Veterans Camps and five chapters of the United Daughters of the Confederacy participated in the event.

Ed Butler of Cookeville, Commander of the Tennessee Division of SCV, welcomed the participants, Dennis Lampley, Commander of Camp 2034, gave a biography of the life of Baxter. Reverend Thomas Sullivan of Old Path Baptist Church in Fairview, who serves as Chaplain of Camp 2034 gave a prayer in memory of the Confederate soldiers buried at Mt. Olivet.

The grave marker was unveiled with a 21-gun salute fired by Confederate re-enactors. Baxter recruited his artillerymen in what is now Fairview and surrounding areas and led them in battles at Cumberland Gap, Chickamauga, Missionary Ridge and Atlanta.

After the war, Baxter became a nationally renowned lawyer, State Supreme Court Judge and Professor at Vanderbilt University.

SCV Camp 2034 meets the 2nd Tuesday at 7 p.m. in Room 3 of the Fairview Recreation Center. The public is always invited to attend.

(Note this article was also printed in the June 2, 2004 edition of the *DICKSON HERALD* and the June 21, 2004 edition of the *HICKMAN COUNTY TIMES*)

Memorial service for Captain E. D. Baxter held May 22, 2004 at Mt. Olivet Cemetery in Nashville, TN. Participants front row l to r: Irene

Lampley, Teresa Luther, Rene Bowser, Ann Schlemm & Dennis Lampley. Re-enactors l to r: Mike Bond, Bryan Sharp, Joe Bailey, Lee Lankford, Ricky Luther & Jeff Hughes.

CHAPTER 9

SERVICE & PENSION RECORDS

BAXTER'S COMPANY TENNESSEE LIGHT ARTILLERY
2ND ORGINAZATION

Private John J. Alexander Born: 1837 Died: ? Residence at time of enlistment: Carroll Co., GA.
Enlisted: March 8, 1864 in Fulton Co., GA. by Capt. E. D. Baxter. Received $50 bounty for enlistment.
Paid: April 30, 1864 by Maj. Ragan and October 31, 1864 by Maj. Higgins. Previous service in Company H Cobb's Georgia Legion.

Private James W. Allen   Born: April 26, 1830 Williamson County, TN. Died: ? Buried: Allen Cemetery Forest Glen Rd. Williamson Co., TN. (unmarked grave?)   Residence at time of enlistment: Williamson County, TN.

Private James W. Allen

Enlisted in Baxter's Battery: November 3, 1962 in Maury County, TN. by Captain E. D. Baxter. Height: 5' 7" Complexion: Dark   Eyes: Dark Hair: Dark Occupation: Farmer. Paid: December 31, 1862 by Capt. Hord, February 2, 1863 by Capt. Hord, March 30, 1863 by Maj. Hord, and June 30, 1863 by Capt. Fowler. Deserted near Knoxville, TN. August 6, 1863.

Tennessee Confederate pension application 7234   Rejected   Filed: July 22, 1905   Disability: rheumatism.   Physician signing application: Dr. J.O. Shannon   Witnesses: E. G. Sherman and John M. Gault. Notary: Thomas B. Haynes.   Residence at time of application: Jingo Route No. 2 (Williamson Co.).   Application stated he surrendered at end of war and took oath "only as others took it."   Assets listed in application: About 300 acres of poor land worth about $2 an acre, mare & mule, three head of cattle & 8 head of hogs.   Eli Sherman swore: " J. W. Allen made a good soldier, always ready for duty. He was always a weak man not of full health. He served the entire war surrendering with the battery at Macon, Georgia at the time of the general surrender of the army.   J. M. Gault, whose name appears as a witness has lately died." Married Elizabeth Pomeroy   January 29, 1865 in Williamson Co., TN.

Private James G. Barnhill   Born: 1832   Hickman County, TN. Residence at time of enlistment: Williamson County, TN.   Died: November 13, 1864 in Union Prison at Camp Douglas, IL of typhoid fever and pneumonia. Buried: Block 2 Chicago City Cemetery Chicago, IL.   Moved to mass Confederate grave in Oak Woods Cemetery in Chicago in 1867.   Enlisted in Baxter's Battery: November 6, 1862 in Williamson County, TN. by Captain E. D. Baxter.   Height: 6' 1" Complexion: Fair   Hair: Dark   Eyes: Dark   Occupation: Farmer February 27, 1863 detached near Knoxville, TN. by Brig. Gen. Archibald Gracie to forage for horses. August 1863 reported sick sent to Asylum Hospital in Knoxville, TN.   Captured by Federals September 5, 1864 near Atlanta, GA.   Transported to Louisville, KY.,   then to Camp Douglas, IL.   Paid: December 31, 1862 by Capt. Hord, February 28, 1863 by Capt. Massengale, April 30, 1863 by Maj. Hord, June 30, 1863 by Capt. Fowler, October 30, 1863 by Lt. Neal, December 31, 1863 by Maj. Ragan, February 29, 1864 by Maj. Ragan & April 10, 1864 by Maj. Ragan.   Married Sarah (Sally) King date unknown.

Private Vachel Isiah Barnhill Born: March 3, 1841 Hickman County, TN.   Died: September 2, 1917. Buried: Beard Cemetery Williamson County, TN. VA Marker. Residence at time of enlistment: Williamson County, TN.   Height: 6'   Complexion: Light   Hair: Light   Eyes: Gray   Occupation: Farmer. Enlisted in Co. C 9th TN. Cavalry Battalion (Gantt's) in May 1861. Escaped capture February 16, 1862 at the fall of Ft. Donelson and returned home.   Enlisted in Baxter's Battery: November 5, 1862 in Williamson County, TN. by Captain E. D. Baxter. February 18, 1863 detached near Knoxville, TN. to forage for horses by order of Brig. Gen. Archibald Gracie.   Hospitalized at

Ocmulgee Hospital in Macon, GA. October 9-12, 1864 for intermittent fever. Paroled April 28, 1865 in Macon, GA. Took oath of allegiance May 4, 1865 in Chattanooga, TN. Ordered to report to Franklin, TN. Paid: December 31, 1862 by Capt. Hord, April 30, 1863 by Maj. Hord, June 30, 1863 by Capt. Fowler, October 30, 1863 by Lt. Neal, December 31, 1863 by Maj. Ragan, February 29, 1864 by Maj. Ragan, April 30, 1864 by Maj. Ragan & October 31, 1864 by Maj. Higgins.

Tennessee Confederate Pension application 5242 Filed: July 25, 1903 Accepted. Disability: old age and heart trouble. Physician signing application: Dr. L.G. Hensley. Witnesses: John Gault & Eli Sherman. Notary Public: Arthur B. Watkins. Residence as time of application: Craigfield (Williamson Co.) Assets listed in application: A piece of barren land taxed at $400 I have made a scant living on it. Some household & kitchen furniture worth $10. Williamson County Trustee, Henry E. Perkins states he owned 442 acres of land valued at $450. Statement of witnesses: " Mr. Vachel Barnhill was a member of Baxter's Battery. Mr. Barnhill joined said Battery about October 1862 and served faithfully until the surrender, was paroled at Macon, GA. I served as Lieutenant of said Artillery Company and E.G. Sherman was member of the same and endorses the above statement." John Gault.
He was a member of McEwen Bivouac #4 Association of Confederate Soldiers, Tennessee Division, Franklin, TN.

Tennessee Confederate Widow's Pension Application 6873 Filed: October 10, 1907 Accepted. Elizabeth Hutchinson Barnhill Born: December 6, 1844 in Williamson Co., TN. Died: July 24, 1918 Married: April 1, 1869 in Williamson Co., TN. by Rev. Henry D. Hogan. Had 12 children. Witnesses: J. W. Overby & J. W. Forrest. Notary Public: J. W. Hendricks. Williamson Co. Trustee B. B. Roberts.

Captain Edmund Dillahunty Baxter "Ed" Born: August 22, 1838 Columbia, TN. Died: June 12, 1910 at his summer home at Ridgetop, TN. Buried: Mt. Olivet Cemetery Nashville, TN. VA Marker. Occupation: Attorney, Judge and Professor of Law at Vanderbilt University. Enlisted in Harding Artillery May 1861. Residence at time of Enlistment: Davidson Co., TN. Complexion: Light Hair: Light Eyes: Blue Height: 5' 8" Surrendered May 5, 1865 at Milledgeville, GA. Oath of allegiance taken June 16, 1865 at Nashville, TN. by Captain Charles D. Colesman, Assistant Provost Marshall Department of the Cumberland. Previously served as Captain of Harding Artillery (Baxter's Battery 1st Organization)

Married Eliza T. E. Perkins (Born 1845 Died December 12, 1876) August 6, 1859 in Davidson Co., TN. Married Sarah Elizabeth Perkins Baxter (sister of his late wife and widow of his half brother, Jones Baxter) in 1879. He was a member of Cheatham Bivouac #1 Association of Confederate Soldiers, Tennessee Division in Nashville, TN.

Sergeant Aaron Pink Beard "A.P."   Born: March 26, 1827   Died: May 31, 1916   Buried: White Cemetery Dickson County, TN. Enlisted in Baxter's Battery: November 27, 1862 in Williamson Co., TN. by Captain E. D. Baxter.   Residence at time of enlistment: Williamson County, TN.   Complexion: Dark   Hair: Dark   Eyes: Gray   Occupation: Farmer & Preacher (preached for 50 year, 35 years at Turnbull Primitive Baptist Church in Dickson County).   February 1863 detached to Strawberry Plains, TN. to care for sick and forage. Paroled April 28, 1865 in Macon, GA. Oath of allegiance taken May 4, 1865 in Chattanooga, TN. Ordered to report to Franklin.

Sgt. Aaron P. Beard

On June 29, 1861 enlisted in Company B 24th Tennessee Infantry Regiment at Nolensville, TN. by Joseph G. Pickett, Unit was accepted into Confederate service August 24, 1861 for 10 months at Camp Trousdale, TN. by Lt. G. H. Smith. Company was first stationed at Bowling Green, KY. and was engaged at Battle of Shiloh. Served as Corporal up to March 20, 1862 promoted to 1st Sergeant served to May 1, 1862 then a Private. Discharged July 16, 1862 under Conscription Act of Congress passed April 16, 1862 being over 35 years of age. Final statement given. Paid: December 31, 1862 by Capt. Hord, February 28,

1863 by Capt. Hord, June 30, 1863 by Capt. Fowler, October 31, 1863 by Lt. Neal, December 31, 1863 by Maj. Ragan, February 29, 1864 by Maj. Ragan, April 30, 1864 by Maj. Ragan, & October 31, 1864 by Maj. Higgins. Paid $14.20 for use of horse. July 1, 1863 resigned as Sergeant. Beard also served in the Mexican War in Company K of the 3rd Tennessee Regiment of Volunteers and received a pension for that service. Married Mahala Green October 18, 1849 in Williamson Co., TN. Later married Izory White.

Private David Crawford Beck   Born: 1837 Dickson Co., TN.   Died: ?   Buried: Stuart Cemetery Burns, TN. (unmarked grave ?) Appointed to the Dickson County Home Guard of Minute Men June 10, 1861. Enlisted in Baxter's Battery: December 23, 1862 in Maury County, TN. by Major J. L. House   Reported to company January 26, 1863.   Residence at time of enlistment: Dickson County, TN. Height: 5' 8"   Complexion: Fair   Hair: Light   Eyes: Gray. December 14, 1864 furloughed 45 days by Brig. Gen. Cockrill, did not return, reported deserted. Oath of allegiance taken January 7,1865 in Nashville, TN. by Lt. William H. Bracken, Assistant Provost Marshall Department of the Cumberland. Reported having family. Paid: February 28, 1863 by Capt. Hord, April 30, 1863 by Maj. Hord, June 30, 1863 by Capt. Fowler, October 31, 1863 by Lt. Neal, December 31, 1863 by Maj. Ragan, February 29, 1864 by Maj. Ragan, April 30, 1864 by Maj. Ragan & December 31, 1864 by Maj. Higgins.
Married Mary F. Shelton December 23, 1856 in Dickson Co., TN.

Private John T. Beck Born: April 29, 1836 in Dickson Co., TN. Died: Fall of 1917 White Bluff, TN.   Buried: Hutton Cemetery   White Bluff, TN. (unmarked grave?). Enlisted in Baxter's Battery: December 4, 1862 in Dickson Co., TN. by Capt. E. D. Baxter Residence at time of enlistment: Dickson Co., TN.   Complexion: Light   Hair: Light Eyes: Blue Paid: October 31, 1863 by Lt. Neal, December 31, 1863 by Maj. Ragan, February 29, 1864 by Maj. Ragan, April 30, 1864 by Maj. Ragan & October 31, 1864 by Maj. Higgins. Paroled April 28, 1865 at Macon, GA. Oath of Allegiance May 4, 1865 at Chattanooga, TN. Ordered to report to Nashville, TN. Has family.

Tennessee Confederate Pension Application 6540   Filed: December 1, 1904   Accepted   Disability: chronic diarrhea & rheumatism. Physician signing application: Dr. G. P. Dobson   Witnesses: T. J. Carr, B. F. Brown, & J.J. Johnson   Notary Public: T. H. Whitifeld.

Residence at time of application: White Bluff (Dickson Co.). Assets listed in application: I haven't a thing real or personal. Witnesses statement: " We was a member of J.T. Becks Company & was with him every day. He is a worthy soldier & was discharged with us at Macon, Giargie in April 1865 & is old & unable to perform manual labor & ought to have his pension." Married M.G. Shelton November 2, 1858 in Dickson Co., TN.

Corporal Malachia Beggs   Born: 1845   Residence at time of enlistment: Cheatham Co., TN.   Died: ? Enlisted in Baxter's Battery: December 22, 1862 in Dickson Co., TN. by Recruiting Officer B. T. Gilliam.   Reported to Company January 4, 1863.   Appointed Corporal December 12, 1864 upon promotion of Hill to Sergeant.   Paid: February 28, 1863 by Capt. Hord, April 30, 1863 by Maj. Hord, June 30, 1863 by Capt. Fowler, October 31, 1863 by Lt. Neal, October 31, 1863 by Maj. Ragan, February 29, 1864 by Maj. Ragan, April 30, 1864 by Maj. Ragan & October 31, 1864 by Maj. Higgins.

Private James E. Bentley   Born: 1839 Wilson Co., TN.   Died: 1911 Davidson Co., TN. Enlisted in Baxter's Battery: November 20, 1862 in Williamson Co., TN. by Capt. E. D. Baxter   Complexion: Light   Hair: Red   Eyes: Blue   Occupation: Carpenter. Detached as government cooper by Special Order # 19   of Gen. Braxton Bragg dated Murfreesboro December 9, 1862.   Married Mollie Furguson October 1, 1874 in Williamson Co., TN.

Private William H. Bethshears   Born: January 15, 1845   Rutherford County, TN.   Died: September 12, 1913   Buried: Jane Jones Cemetery Fairview, TN.   VA Marker.   Residence at time of enlistment: Williamson Co., TN.   Enlisted in Baxter's Battery: November 5, 1862 in Maury County, TN. by Capt. E. D. Baxter.   Height: 5' 10" Complexion: Fair   Hair: Light   Eyes: Dark   Occupation: Farmer February 15, 1863 detached at Knoxville, TN. to forage for horses by order of Brig. Gen. Gracie . Paid: December 31, 1862 by Capt. Hord, February 28, 1862 by Capt. Massingale, April 30, 1863 by Maj. Hord, June 30, 1863 by Capt. Fowler, October 30, 1863 by Lt. Neal, December 31, 1863 by Maj. Ragan, February 29, 1864 by Maj. Ragan, April 30, 1864 by Maj. Ragan, & October 31, 1864 by Maj. Higgins.   October 16-27, 1864 patient at Ocmulgee Hospital Macon, GA. for intermittent fever.   Paroled April 28, 1865 at Macon, GA. Oath of Allegiance May 4, 1865 at Chattanooga, TN. Ordered to report to Franklin, TN. No family reported.

Tennessee Confederate Pension Application 6119   Accepted   Filed:
March 29, 1905.   Disability: rheumatism and kidney trouble.
Physician signing application: Dr. Samuel Henderson.   Witnesses:
E. G. Sherman, A. P. Beard & John Gault   Notary: Thomas Haynes
Residence at time of application: Aden (Williamson Co.). Assets listed
in application: one hundred and fifty acres, all real and personal.
Witnesses Statement: " We served in the army with Mr. Bethshears and
know him to have been a good and true Confederate soldier, as well as a
good and sober citizen since the war."
Married Harriet Terrell January 24, 1867 in Williamson Co., TN.

Tennessee Confederate Widows pension application 5629   Filed:
October 12, 1914   Rejected (pension law denied pensions to widows
who married veterans after 1890, Bethshears' marriage was in 1891)
Mrs. Marivera Perry Bethshears   Born: October 18, 1843 in Dickson
Co., TN.   Married: May 24, 1891 in Williamson Co., TN. Witnesses:
J. B Edwards & V. J. Barnhill.   Notary Public: J. W. Hendricks.
Williamson Co. Trustee: W. T. Robinson.

Private Harding Bilbrey "Hardy"   Born: 1842 Overton Co., TN.
Died: ?   Height: 5' 7"   Complexion: Light   Hair: Light   Eyes:
Brown .

Pvt. Harding Bilbrey

Enlisted in Company D 4th Tennessee Cavalry Regiment November 23,
1861 in Livingston, TN. by W. H. Turner for 1 year. Records show
transferred to Company H 8th Tennessee Cavalry Regiment on November

23, 1862 (apparently was assigned to Baxter's Battery at that time)   Oath of allegiance administered on March 19, 1864 in Nashville by Capt. R. M. Goodwin, Assistant Provost Marshall, Department of the Cumberland.   Name appears on: Roll of 10 rebel deserters released on oath of amnesty at Nashville, TN. March 19, 1864.

Private John S. Black   Born: 1845   Maury Co., TN.   Died: >1880 Weakley Co., TN. ? Enlisted in Baxter's Battery: November 8, 1862 in Williamson County, TN. by Capt. E. D. Baxter   Height: 5' 4" Complexion: Fair   Hair: Dark   Eyes: Gray   Occupation: Farmer December 31, 1862 absent sick furlough for 15 days. Believed deserted. Never paid.   Married Mary A. Howell January 17, 1864 in Williamson Co., TN.

Private Benjamin F. Brown "B. F.", "Uncle Ben" Born: December 8, 1841 Dickson Co., TN.   Died: March 21, 1937   Buried: Brown Family Cemetery Dickson Co., TN. VA Marker. Appointed to Dickson County Home Guard of Minute Men June 10, 1861.   Enlisted in Baxter's Battery: February 13, 1863 (some records show enlistment date March 3, 1863, March 23, 1863 & March 25, 1863) in Columbia, TN. by Major Nicholson. Residence at time of enlistment: Dickson Co., TN. Height: 5' 10   Complexion: Dark   Hair: Dark Eyes: Gray. Paid: June 3, 1863 by Capt. Fowler, October 31, 1863 by Lt. Neal, December 31, 1863 by Maj. Ragan, February 29, 1864 by Maj. Ragan, April 30, 1864 by Major Ragan & October 31, 1864 by Maj. Higgins. Hospitalized at Ocmulgee Hospital Macon, GA. from October 13-27, 1864 for recurring fever.   Paroled April 28, 1865 Macon, GA. Oath of allegiance taken at Chattanooga, TN. May 4, 1865. Ordered to report to Nashville, TN. Reported having family.

Tennessee Confederate Pension Application 3475   Accepted after 3 submittals.   Residence at time of applications: Spencer's Mill (Dickson Co.)   First filing: July 1, 1901. Disability: rheumatism and reported being wounded in right ankle while camped at Atlanta, GA.   Physician: Dr. J. E. Mathis   Witnesses: Thomas J. Parker and F. F. Tidwell (Captain Co. K 11th Tenn. Infantry) Notary: W. B. Williams.   Second filing: November 2, 1903   Disability: chronic rheumatism and piles. Physician: Dr. J. E. Mathis   Witnesses: T. J. Carr and W. H. Hogan. Notary: W. B. Williams.   Third Filing: October 5, 1906   Disability: Chronic rheumatism and piles.   Physician: Dr. E. W. Ridings

Witnesses: J.B. Thompson, T.J. Carr, John Dillard, Daniel White & J. P. White   Notary: Samuel Hammon (Pvt. Co K 11th Tenn. Infantry) Assets listed in pension: sixty-four acres of land valued at $200. Stated he took Oath of Allegiance at end of war to get out of prison. Witnesses statements: Personally appeared before me, James W. Herrin, an acting Justice of the peace for said county, John Dillard who made oath in due form of law, that B.F. Brown served as a member of Baxter's Battery in the Confederate Army and that he was disbanded from said command at Macon, GA. on the 28 of April 1865 at the same time that the said command was disbanded and the he the said John Dillard was also a member of said command and was disbanded at the same time and place. 16 Day November 1905.   July 28, 1906 State of Tennessee Dickson County, personally appeared before me, Lester Garton, a Notary Public for said county, J. B. Thompson and T.J. Carr who verify that they are personally acquainted with B. F. Brown the above mentioned applicant for pension that they knew him as a comrade in Capt. Ed Baxters Battery that said Brown was honorably paroled at Macon, GA. April 28, 1865 and that they have known personally ever since the close of the war and his character as a citizen and soldier is good sworn to and subscribed before me. Lester Garton, Notary Public. Married Louisiana Garton September 22, 1861 in Dickson Co., TN.   Later married Susan D. Campbell.

PRIVATE BROWN WAS THE LAST SURVIVING CONFEDERATE SOLDIER IN DICKSON COUNTY AND THE LAST SURVIVING MEMBER OF MIDDLE TENNESSEE RECRUITS OF BAXTER'S BATTERY.

Private Carter T. Brown   Born   1830   Died: >1880   Buried: Mt. Hope Cemetery   Franklin, TN. Section F-64.   Enlisted in Baxter's Battery: March 13, 1863 (some records show enlistment date as March 3, 1863) at Columbia, TN. by Major Nicholson. Residence at enlistment: Hickman Co., TN.
Left sick in Dickson County May 24, 1863 by order of Lt. Herrin. Believed deserted time and place unknown.   Never paid.

Private Charles L. Brown   Born: November 16, 1839 Dickson Co., TN.   Died: December 10, 1886   Buried: Brown Cemetery Dickson Co., TN.   Enlisted in Baxter's Battery: March 13, 1863 (some records show enlistment date as March 3, 1863) in Maury Co., TN. by Maj. Nicholson.   May 24, 1863 left sick in Dickson County by order of Lt. Herrin. Believed deserted time and place unknown. Never Paid.

Private George M. D. Brown   Born: January 20, 1843   Dickson Co.,
TN.   Died: March 28, 1928   Buried: Mt. Hope Cemetery   Franklin,
TN.   Section F-64.   Enlisted: March 13, 1863 (some records show
enlistment date as March 3, 1863) in Maury County, TN. by Major
Nicholson.   Left sick in Dickson County May 24, 1863 by order of Lt.
Herrin.   Not heard from since believed deserted, time and place
unknown. Never Paid.

Private James H. Busby (Buzbee)   Born: December 2, 1844 St. Clair
Co., AL.   Died: February 28, 1921 Standing Rock, Oklahoma (Coal
County).   Enlisted in Baxter's Battery July 12, 1864 in Fulton Co., GA.
by Lt. Herrin.   Residence at time of enlistment: Coosa County, AL.
Height: 5' 4"   Complexion: Fair   Hair: Light   Eyes: Blue.
Hospitalized at Ocmulgee General Hospital at Macon, GA. October 7-
20,1864 by Surgeon Murphy for recurring fever. Surrendered April 28,
1865 at Macon, GA.   Paroled and oath of allegiance taken May 19,
1865 at Montgomery, AL. at Headquarters of 16th U. S. Army Corps.

Oklahoma Confederate Pension # 1952   Application # 240 Filed: June
23, 1915   Rejected   October 7, 1915   Accepted   July 3, 1917
Disability: old age & unable to farm, weak kidney and general debility.
Physician Signing Application: Dr. F. E. Sadler   Witnesses signing
application: J. T. Buzbee (his brother) and M. J. Morgan (his sister)
Coal Co., OK. Judge P. E. Wilhelm.   Witnesses statement: "We are
brother and sister to the applicant and as such know that he enlisted in
the army as stated and we received letters from him during his service in
the army and know he came home after the surrender."

Sergeant James Felix Ewing Buttrey "Big Jim"   Born: January 27,
1834 Davidson County, TN.   Died: December 21, 1911   Cheatham
County, TN.   Buried: Joe & Sack Lampley Cemetery Dickson Co.,
TN. VA Marker.   Residence at time of enlistment: Williamson
County, TN.   Enlisted in Baxter's Battery: November 8, 1862
Williamson Co., TN. by Capt. E. D. Baxter Height 6' 2" Complexion:
Fair   Hair: Sandy   Eyes: Blue   Occupation: Farmer & Blacksmith.
March & April 1863 absent at Lewis Springs, TN. in charge of sick and
baggage by order of Brig. Gen. Gracie. Appointed Sergeant July 1863
upon resignation of G. W. Hogan. Hospitalized at Ocmulgee Hospital
Macon, GA. October 13-27, 1864 for recurring fever. Paroled April 28,
1865 at Macon, GA. Oath of allegiance taken at Chattanooga, TN. May

4, 1865. Ordered to report to Franklin, TN. Reported having family. Paid: December 31, 1862 by Capt. Hord, February 28, 1863 by Capt. Hord, June 30, 1863 by Capt. Fowler, October 31, 1863 by Capt. Fowler, December 31, 1863 by Maj. Ragan, February 29, 1864 by Maj. Ragan & May 30, 1864 by Maj. Ragan.

Tennessee Confederate Pension application 4964   Accepted.   Filed: May 6, 1906. Disability: heart trouble & near blindness. (Application states he was hospitalized for heart trouble in Knoxville, TN. while in the army). Physician signing application: Dr. W. T. Clark.   Witnesses: J. H. Hall & W. H. Bethshears. Notary Public: J. M. Griffin. Residence at time of application: Naomi (Williamson Co.)   Assets listed in application: farm value $200. Statement of witnesses; " We, J. H Hall & W.H. Bethshears do testify that this said J. F. Buttrey was with us in the Confederate army and that he was to our knowledge paroled and that this the same J. F. Buttrey."   Married Sarah Hall March 15, 1855 in Dickson Co., TN.   Franklin Attorney, Tom Henderson, assisted family in acquiring government grave marker in 1941.   Buttrey served as Chairman of the Democratic Party in the 1st District of Williamson County and served as Postmaster at the Naomi Post Office in Hickman County.

Private James Monroe Buttrey "Little Jim"   Born: April 1, 1844 Williamson Co., TN. Died: September 28, 1920. Buried: Jack Lampley Cemetery Dickson Co., TN. VA Marker. Residence at time of enlistment: Williamson Co., TN. Enlisted in Baxter's Battery: November 5, 1862 in Williamson Co., TN. by Capt. E. D. Baxter. Hospitalized in Ocmulgee Hospital Macon, GA. in October & November 1864 for intermittent fever. Paid: December 31, 1863 by Capt. Hord, February 28, 1863 by Capt. Hord, April 30, 1863 by Maj. Hord, June 30, 1863 by Capt. Fowler, October 30, 1863 by Lt. Neal, December 31, 1863 by Maj. Ragan, April 30, 1864 by Maj. Ragan. Captured May 5, 1865 near Milledgeville, GA.

Tennessee Confederate Pension Application 2758   Accepted.   Filed: May 14, 1900. Disability: rheumatism and near blindness. Physician signing application: Dr. John T. Cox. Witnesses: J. B. Edwards & A. S. Spencer. Notary Public: J. W. Hendricks. Residence at time of application: Naomi, Williamson Co. Assets listed in application: I have a small piece of land. I paid fifty dollars for. Witnesses statement: "That the applicant was with them in the army in the same company and that he was captured at Milledgeville, Georgia and paroled. That he was a good soldier, of good habits & that he is destitute and needs help, not being able to work half of his time." Application states he never took oath of allegiance.

Tennessee Confederate Widow's Indigent Pension 7477   Accepted. Filed: October 22, 1920.   Tennessee Lampley Buttrey   Born: 1852 Dickson Co., TN.   Died: December 4, 1934.   Married: December 17, 1868 in Dickson Co., TN. by Rev. A. P. Beard.   Had 6 children. Witnesses: J. B. Edwards & Eld. J. W. Sullivan   Notary Public: V. J. Barnhill. Williamson County Trustee B. B. Roberts.   Residence at time of application: Jingo (Williamson Co.)

Private William George Demarkes Buttrey   "Billie"   Born: August 12, 1836 in Williamson County, TN.   Died: September 22, 1881.   Buried: White Cemetery Dickson Co., TN. VA Marker.   Residence at time of enlistment: Dickson Co., TN. Enlisted in Baxter's Battery: November 11, 1862 in Dickson Co., TN. by Capt. E. D. Baxter.   Height: 5' 10' Complexion: Light   Hair: Light   Eyes: Blue   Occupation: Farmer. Sent to Fairgrounds Hospital in Knoxville, TN. from Cumberland Gap by W. J. Abraham, Chief Surgeon.   Granted 20 day sick furlough by Surgeon W, L. Hillard.   June 1863 reported he never returned from sick furlough, presumed deserted.   Paid: December 30, 1862 by Capt. Hord, February 28, 1863 by Capt. Hord, & April 30, 1863 by Capt. Kate.

Tennessee Confederate Widow's Indigent Pension 2609   Accepted Filed: May 3, 1909   Eliza Jane White Buttrey   Born: September 25, 1841 Dickson Co., TN.   Died: December 15, 1933. Married: January 26, 1857 in Dickson Co., TN. by Rev. Sanders.   Had 11 children. Witnesses: J. T. Beck & J. F Buttrey.   Notary Public: T.J. Carr. Residence at time of application: Burns (Dickson Co.)   A paroled prisoner's pass filed with the application showed William G. D. Buttrey paroled at Dean's House in Hickman Co., TN. on May 16, 1865 as a member of Capt. A. Duval McNairy's Company of Harvey's Battalion of Scouts as part of the Army of Miss, Ala, & East Louisiana.

Private William Green W. Buttrey   Born: 1843 Williamson Co., TN. Died: February 5, 1864 in hospital at Covington, GA. of chronic diarrhea.   Buried: Covington Confederate Cemetery.   Memorial stone in Jane Jones Cemetery   Fairview, TN.   Enlisted in Baxter's Battery: November 8, 1862 in Dickson Co., TN. by Capt. E. D. Baxter.   Height: 5' 11"   Complexion: Fair   Hair: Dark   Eyes: Dark   Occupation:

Farmer.   Paid: December 30, 1862 by Capt. Hord, February 28, 1863 by Capt. Hord, June 30, 1863 by Capt. Fowler, October 30, 1863 by Lt. Neal & December 31, 1863 by Maj. Ragan.

Private John Franklin Cain   Born: February 18, 1847   Died: June 7, 1915   Buried: Chestnut Cemetery Decatur, AL.   Enlisted in Baxter's Battery: July 6, 1864 in Fulton Co., GA. by Lt. William Herrin. Residence at time of enlistment: Morgan Co., AL.   Sent to hospital from Atlanta on August 15, 1864.   Paid: October 31, 1864 by Maj. Higgins. Married Nancy Jane Walden July 18, 1867 in Morgan Co., AL.

Pvt. John F. Cain

Private Seth Callahan   Born: 1832   Died: November 6, 1917 in Clayton Co., GA.   Enlisted in Baxter's Battery: April 27, 1864 in Fulton Co., GA. by Capt. E. D. Baxter. Residence: Morrow, GA. (Clayton Co.) Hospitalized at General Hospital in Macon, GA. October 9-20, 1864 by Assistant Surgeon Stuart for recurring fever. Paroled April 28, 1865 at Macon, GA.   Previous service in Co. D 44th GA. Volunteer Infantry Regiment. Married Miss M. E. Norman October 8, 1874 in Clayton Co., GA. by Reverend D. E. Starr.

Georgia Confederate Pension Application   Filed August 3, 1910 in Clayton County. Disability: not stated. Assets: 30 acres of land worth $20 per acre. Witness to application: John T. Walker.

Georgia Confederate Widow's Pension Application   Mrs. M. E. Callahan. Filed 1920 Clayton County. Witnesses: J. M. Avery & B. W. Avery. Clayton County Ordinary W. H. Reynolds.

Corporal Richard H. Carney   Born: 1823.   Died: ? In 1870 resided in Blairsville (Union Co.), GA.
Enlisted in Baxter's Battery: January 17, 1864 in Fulton Co., GA. by Capt. Baxter.   Formerly served in Anderson's Company of Georgia Infantry.   Sent to hospital from Atlanta August 12, 1864.   Appointed Corporal December 12, 1864 upon reduction in rank of J.L. Sweeney. Married Catharine Queen January 6, 1847 in Union Co., GA.

Private George Washington Carr "Wash"   Born: 1839 Dickson Co., TN. Died: June 8, 1863 of typhoid fever in camp in Grainger Co., TN. Buried: unmarked grave near Bean Station, TN. He had been left behind sick when the company moved out of Bean Station and was being treated by a private physician, with no military personnel present at the time of his death to inventory personal effects, letter of administration was granted to Lt. Herrin by Knox County Court to remove personal effects.   Enlisted in Baxter's Battery: December 6, 1862 in Dickson Co., TN. by Capt. E. D. Baxter.   Height: 5' 7"   Complexion: Dark Hair: Dark   Eyes: Blue   Occupation: Farmer. Paid: December 30, 1862 by Capt. Hord, February 28, 1863 by Capt. Hord & April 30, 1863 by Maj. Hord.   Married Harriet P. McCrory   October 10, 1862 in Williamson Co., TN.

Private Thomas Jefferson Carr "Jeff"   Born: July 23, 1842 Dickson Co., TN.   Died: November 20, 1914 in Burns, TN. Buried: Union Cemetery Dickson, TN. VA Marker.   Enlisted in Baxter's Battery: October 6, 1862 in Dickson Co.,TN. by Capt. E. D. Baxter Residence at time of enlistment: Dickson Co., TN.   Height: 5' 8 " Complexion: Dark   Hair: Dark   Eyes: Dark   Occupation: Farmer. Detached February 15, 1863 at Knoxville, TN. to forage for horses by order of Brig. Gen. Gracie. Paid: December 30, 1862 by Capt. Hord, February 28, 1863 by Capt. Massingale, April 30, 1863 by Maj. Hord, June 30, 1863 by Capt. Fowler, October 30, 1863 by Lt. Neal, December 31, 1863 by Maj. Ragan, February 29, 1864 by Maj. Ragan, April 30, 1864 by Maj. Ragan & October 30, 1864 by Maj. Higgins.   Hospitalized in Ocmulgee Hospital Macon, GA. October 10-13, 1864 and January 3-25, 1865.   Paroled April 28, 1865 at Macon, GA. Oath of Allegiance taken at Chattanooga, TN. May 4, 1865. Ordered to report to Nashville. No family reported.

Tennessee Confederate Pension Application 2496   Filed: February 8, 1900   Accepted.   Disability: effects of typhoid contracted in army, eulonged prostrate gland, chronic nephritis with a floating kidney and bladder disease.   Physician Signing application: Dr. E. W. Ridings. Witnesses: John Dillard & J. P. White   Notary Publics: S. T. Larkins & Samuel Hammon (Co. K 11th Tenn. Infantry)   Residence at time of application: near Burns (Dickson Co.)   Assets reported on application: about 69 acres of land with mortgage foreclosed on land.   Land valued at $200, mortgage $185.   Statement of witnesses: " That we served in the Confederate army with the applicant.   That since said attack of typhoid fever at Tate Springs in May 1863, said applicant has suffered from effects of same at different times & has not been well at any time. For last 7 or 8 years he has not been able to do any work or manual labor of any kind."

Tennessee Confederate Widow's Indigent pension   5767   Filed: February 3, 1915   Tennessee C. Porter Carr   Accepted. Witnesses: Moses Garton (Co. E 11th Tenn. Infantry) & T. F. Austin.   Notary Public: J. A. Myatt.   Residence at time of application: Burns (Dickson Co.)   Born: July 23, 1850 in Dickson Co., TN.   Died: October 27, 1936.   Married: December 26, 1867 in Dickson Co., TN. by William Hammon, Justice of the Peace.   In letter of October 29, 1936 to the pension board Mrs. John Spencer, daughter, reported death of Mrs. Carr and requested application for burial fund.

He was a member of James E. Raines Bivouac #14 Association of Confederate Soldiers, Tennessee Division, Dickson, TN.

Private Ira Castleman   Born: 1823   Davidson Co., TN.   Died: December 5, 1864 of typhoid in Union Prison at Camp Douglas, IL. Buried: Block 2 Chicago City Cemetery.   Moved to mass Confederate grave in Oak Woods Cemetery Chicago in 1867.   Enlisted in Baxter's Battery: December 10, 1862 in Hickman Co., TN. by Capt. E. D. Baxter. Height: 5' 11"   Complexion: Dark   Hair: Dark   Eyes: Blue Occupation: Shoemaker.   Paid: December 30, 1862 by Capt. Hord, February 28, 1863 by Capt. Hord,   April 30, 1863 by Maj. Hord, June 30, 1863 by Capt. Fowler, October 30, 1863 by Lt. Neal, December 31, 1863 by Maj. Ragan, February 29, 1864 by Maj. Ragan & April 30, 1864 by Maj. Ragan.   Captured September 4, 1864 at Atlanta, GA.   Sent to Nashville, TN., to Louisville, KY., to Camp Douglas, IL.

Private Jefferson P. Christian   Born: 1846   Georgia   Died: >1880
Enlisted: March 8, 1864 in Rockford, AL. by Capt. Hancock. Residence
at time of enlistment: Coosa Co., AL.   Hospitalized at Ocmulgee
Hospital Macon, GA. October 20 to November 18, 1864 for intermittent
fever. Entitled to $50 bounty. Paid: April 30, 1864 by Maj. Ragan. In
1880 Resided in Columbiana, Shelby Co., AL. Married Annonette L.
Horton April 15, 1869 in Shelby County, AL.

Private Harvey Clark   Born: 1826   Harrison Co., IN.   Died: 1898
Jingo, TN.   Buried: Tomlinson Cemetery   Dickson Co., TN.   VA
Marker. Residence at time of enlistment: Williamson Co., TN. Enlisted
in Baxter's Battery: November 27, 1862 in Williamson Co., TN. by Capt.
E. D. Baxter.   Height: 5' 10"   Complexion: Light   Hair: Light
Eyes: Gray   Occupation: Farmer. Paid: December 30, 1862 by Capt.
Hord, February 28, 1863 by Capt. Hord, April 30, 1863 by Maj. Hord,
June 30, 1863 by Capt. Fowler, October 30, 1863 by Lt. Neal, December
31, 1863 by Maj.Ragan, February 29, 1864 by Maj. Ragan & October 31,
1864 by Maj. Higgins.   Paroled April 28, 1865 at Macon, GA. Oath of
allegiance taken May 4, 1865 in Chattanooga, TN. Ordered to report to
Nashville. Married Amanda Buttrey August 8, 1875 in Williamson Co.,
TN.

Tennessee Confederate Pension Application 1492   Filed: June 19, 1894
Accepted   Residence at time of application: Naomi, TN. (Williamson
County)   Disability: Rheumatism   Physician signing application: Dr.
William T. Clark   Notary Public: J. W. Hendricks   Witnesses: A. R.
Lankford, Wh. H. Bethshears, J. F. Cunningham, & A. P. Beard.
Application states he owned 265 acres of land worth $200 and property
worth about $75.   On re-application states he owned 265 acres of land,
mostly worn out, and one mule worth $10, one cow and calf value $10
and 14 head of hogs worth $14. He states in application: "I had a very
bad rising in October 1864, it did not stop running till July 1865 and I
then taken the rheumatism and am not yet well."   Statement of
witnesses: "We were members of the same company with the said
applicant and know that he was a good soldier, performed all the duties
required of him so long as he was able and was of sober habits."

Private P. K. Colesman   Enlisted in Baxter's Battery: May 3, 1864 in
Fulton Co., GA. by Capt. E. D. Baxter. Deserted May 28, 1864 at
Atlanta, GA. Captured by Provost Marshall, Capt. Fidon, held until trial.
Belonged to another unit.

Private (Bugler) Joseph H. Cox   Born: October 1827 Richmond, KY. (Madison Co.) Died: > 1913 Frankfort, KY.   Enlisted in Baxter's Battery: March 7, 1863 in Claiborne Co., TN. by Capt. E. D. Baxter. Residence at time of enlistment: Fayette Co., KY. Paid: April 30, 1863 by Maj. Hord, June 30, 1863 by Capt. Fowler, October 31, 1863 by Lt. Neal, December 31, 1863 by Maj. Ragan, February 29, 1864 by Maj. Ragan, April 30, 1864 by Maj. Ragan & October 31, 1864 by Maj. Higgins.   Served as company bugler. When enlisted was employed in orderly   department   at   Cumberland   Gap   until   April   22,   1863. Hospitalized in Ocmulgee Hospital Macon, GA. October 7-11, 1864 for recurring fever.   Escaped capture at fall of Macon, GA. Fled to Milledgeville, GA. captured April 1865. Oath of Allegiance taken at Nashville, TN.

Kentucky Confederate Pension 2074   Filed: June 11, 1912   Accepted. Disability: old age Physician Signing application: Dr. W. V. Williams Notary Public   J. B. Nash of Frankfort, KY. Witnesses: N. B. Smith, Ben Marshall & W. E. Bosworth. Eli Sherman of Franklin, TN. sent a sworn certificate to the Kentucky Board of Pension Examiners on his behalf verifying service in Baxter's   Company.   The certificate was notarized by E. E. Green, cashier at the National Bank of Franklin. W. E. Bosworth's Witness statement: In the matter of an application for a pension pending before the Kentucky board of Pensions for Confederate Soldiers, by Joseph H. Cox, the affiant being W. E. Bosworth of Franklin County, Ky. States that Private Joseph H. Cox is his half brother, that in the fall of 1862 said Cox left Lexington, Ky. and went out with Bragg's Confederate   troops   and   joined   Baxter's   Battery,   a   Tennessee organization with which he continued as a regular Confederate soldier, (he being its Bugler) until the end of the war. That Joseph H. Cox left Lexington, Ky., his home in the fall of 1862 and did not return again before the 1st of May 1865. That from all his knowledge and belief said Cox served in his position as Bugler to Baxter's Battery continuously from the fall of 1862 until the surrender ended the war, and then returned to Lexington not earlier than 1st May 1865, when he came into appointed place of business in Lexington, Ky. still wearing his Confederate clothes and had his bugle strapped on him.

Orderly Sergeant John Francisco Cunningham   Born: March 18, 1843 Hickman Co., TN.   Died: November 23, 1903   Buried: Aden-Cunningham Cemetery   Fairview, TN. VA Marker.   Residence at time of enlistment: Williamson Co., TN.   Enlisted in Baxter's Battery: November 9, 1862 in Dickson Co., TN.   by Capt. E. D. Baxter. Height: 5' 8"   Complexion: Fair   Hair: Light   Eyes: Blue Occupation: Shoemaker.   Paid: December 31, 1862 by Capt. Hord, February 28, 1863 by Capt. Hord, April 30, 1863 by Maj. Hord, June 30, 1863 by Capt. Fowler, October 30, 1863 by Lt. Neal, December 31, 1863 by Maj. Ragan, February 29, 1864 by Maj. Ragan, April 30, 1864 by Maj. Ragan, & October 31, 1864 by Maj. Higgins.   Promoted to Orderly Sergeant May 8, 1863 upon Sgt. Matthew Maury being detailed from company.   Paroled April 28, 1865 at Macon, GA.   Oath of allegiance taken at Chattanooga, TN. May 4, 1865. Ordered to report to Nashville. No family.

Tennessee Confederate Widow's Pension Application 165   Filed: July 8, 1905   Accepted.   Eliza Jane Tidwell   Cunningham   Born: February 9, 1846 in Dickson Co., TN.   Married: September 18, 1865 in Dickson Co., TN.   Died: October 20, 1943 Fairview, TN.   Had 12 children.   Witnesses: A. P. Beard & W. H. Bethshears.   Notary Public: J.W. Hendricks.   Williamson Co. Trustee H. E. Perkins.   Residence at time of application: Jingo RFD # 1(Williamson Co.)
MRS. CUNNINGHAM WAS THE LAST SURVIVING WIDOW OF MIDDLE TENNESSEE RECRUITS OF BAXTER'S BATTERY.

Private Samuel L. Davis   Born: 1843   Died: ?   Buried: ? Residence at time of enlistment: Williamson Co., TN.   Oath of Allegiance taken at Nashville on March 19, 1864 administered by Capt. R. M. Goodwin, Assistant Provost Marshall, Department of the Cumberland. Listed on roll of 10 rebel deserters taking oath.

Private Thompson Davis Born:1830 Williamson Co., TN. Died: March 20, 1870   Buried: Greenbrier Cemetery Williamson Co., TN.   Enlisted in Baxter's Battery: December 7, 1862 in Williamson Co., TN. by Capt. E. D. Baxter. Height: 5' 6" Complexion: Dark   Hair: Dark   Eyes: Hazel   Occupation: Farmer.   Paid: December 31, 1862 by Capt. Hord & April 30, 1863 by Maj. Hord.   Confederate report dated June 1, 1863 shows he deserted at Cumberland Gap.   Federal reports show: captured at Richmond, KY. On May 6, 1863.   Received at Camp Chase, Ohio from Lexington, KY. on June 13, 1863. Transferred to Johnson's Island Prison at Sandusky, Ohio on June 20, 1863. Sent to Point Lookout, MD.

Prison November 30, 1863. Joined Union Army April 8, 1864. Married Sarah Jane Davis September 29, 1852 in Williamson Co., TN.

Private John Foresythe Demonbruen Born: May 8, 1841 Williamson Co., TN. Died: January 25, 1904 near College Grove, TN. Buried: Demonbruen (Demumbrane) Cemetery Arno-College Grove Road in 20th District of Williamson Co., TN. VA Marker.   Residence at enlistment: Williamson Co., TN.

Pvt. John F. Demonbruen

Enlisted in Baxter's Battery: December 11, 1862 in Williamson Co., TN. by Capt. E. D. Baxter. He had previously enlisted in Company D 20th Tennessee Infantry Regiment on May 27, 1861 in Williamson Co., TN. by Capt. Scudder. Discharged for disability on September 19, 1861. Height: 5' 7" Complexion: Fair Hair: Light   Eyes: Blue Occupation: Farmer. AWOL from December 11-31, 1862. Believed deserted January 1, 1863 in Williamson Co., TN. Rejoined company April 13, 1863. Paid: April 30, 1863 by Maj. Hord, June 30, 1863 by Capt. Fowler, October 30, 1863 by Lt. Neal, October 31, 1863 by Maj. Ragan, February 29, 1864 by Maj. Ragan, & April 30, 1864 by Maj. Ragan. Paroled April 28, 1865 at Macon, GA. Oath of Allegiance taken at Chattanooga, TN. May 4, 1865. Ordered to report to Franklin, TN. Reported having family. He was a member of McEwen Bivouac #4 Association of Confederate Soldiers, Tennessee Division in Franklin, TN.

Tennessee Confederate Widow's Pension application 5492   Filed: July 14, 1914   Accepted.

Sarah (Sallie) Ann Merritt Demumbrane   Born: April 13, 1842 in 13th District of Williamson Co., TN.   Residence: College Grove, TN. Married: February 7, 1861 in Williamson Co., TN. by M. L. Andrews. Died: January 17, 1919.   Buried: Demonbruen Cemetery   College Grove, TN.   Had 7 children.   Witnesses: Robert H. Haley & Dr. John J. Covington.   Notary Public: W. J. H. Covington.   Williamson Co. Trustee W. T. Robinson.

Private John Bryant Dillard   Born: November 22, 1842   Cheatham Co., TN   Died: December 7, 1928 at Confederate Veterans Home in Hermitage, TN.   Buried: Martin-Garton Cemetery Dickson Co., TN. VA Marker.   Residence at time of enlistment: Cheatham Co., TN.

Pvt. John B. Dillard

Enlisted in Baxter's Battery: November 27, 1862 in Williamson Co., TN. by Capt. E. D. Baxter.   Height: 5'8" Complexion : Dark   Hair: Dark   Eyes: Dark   Occupation: Farmer. Paid: December 31, 1862 by Capt. Hord, April 30, 1863 by Maj. Hord, June 30, 1863 by Capt. Fowler, October 30, 1863 by Lt. Neal, December 31, 1863 by Maj. Ragan, February 29, 1864 by Maj. Ragan & April 30, 1864 by Maj. Ragan. Hospitalized at Ocmulgee Hospital Macon, GA. October 16-27, 1864 for recurring fever. Paroled April 28, 1865 at Macon, GA. Oath of allegiance taken at Chattanooga, TN. May 4, 1865. Ordered to report to Nashville. Reported no family.

Tennessee Confederate Pension Application 5502   Accepted   Filed: August 22, 1903   Disability: rheumatism and head injury received during war.   Physician signing application: Dr. E. W. Ridings. Witnesses: W. M. Hogan , T. J. Carr, & T. P. Lankford.   Notary Publics: L. D. Myatt & Samuel Hammon (Co. K 11th TN. Infantry). Residence at time of application: Spencer's Mill (Dickson Co.)   Assets listed on application: small lot in North Nashville one hundred dollars and 50 acres of very poor land $150.   Witnesses statement: D.H. Lankford & T.J. Carr made oath that they are personally acquainted with John Dillard.   "That said Dillard was sworn into Captain Ed Baxter Artillery company November 27, 1863 that said Dillard contracted catarrh of the head from a severe attack of typhoid fever while in the Confederate service and in line of duty from which said Dillard has never recovered and continues to grow worse.   Said Dillard is indigent is not physically able to earn a support and has no children able to support him. Said Dillard was a good faithful and obedient soldier is a good citizen and neighbor.   Said Dillard was honorably paroled at Macon, GA. April 28, 1865."   This February 5, 1904.

He completed Tennessee Civil War Veterans Questionnaire in which he states: He was first engaged in battle in Kentucky with Colonel Hart about 2 months after joining the army.   As to clothes we had plenty, I never done without eating over 3 days, I in hospital 1 month.   I used to rain, snow & mud.   At the end of the war, he reported: left Macon one day, come to Atlanta to city was all destroyed the railroad was tore up and we walked to Dalton, GA.   There we stayed one night and went to Chattanooga and from there to Nashville.   He was a member of James E. Raines Bivouac #14 Association of Confederate Soldiers, Tennessee Division, Dickson, TN.   Married Mahuldah Garton January 3, 1866

Private James M. Duff   Born: 1827   Died: ?   Residence: Montgomery Co., TN.   Enlisted: November 13, 1862 at Savannah, GA. in Guerard's Battery Georgia Light Artillery by Capt. John M. Guerard. Height: 5' 10"   Complexion: Fair   Hair: Light   Eyes: Blue   Paid: December 31, 1863 by Major Hirsch.   Transferred to Baxter's Battery August 23, 1864 by Special Order Number 199/46 of the War Department.   Last paid October 31, 1864 by Maj. Higgins.   Hospitalized at Ocmulgee Hospital Macon, GA.   October 24-29, 1864 with dyspepsia. Surrendered May 5, 1865 at Atlanta, GA.   Oath of allegiance taken May 12, 1865 in Nashville, TN.

Private Guey R. Dukes   Born: 1846 Georgia   Died: >1900   Enlisted in Baxter's Battery: April 23, 1864 in Fulton Co., GA. by Capt. E. D. Baxter. Previously served as 1st Sergeant in Co. C 61st Georgia Infantry Regiment. Entitled to $50 bounty. Paid: April 30, 1864 by Maj. Ragan. Resided in Grayson Co., TX. in 1900.

Private Robert S. Earl   Born: 1843 Virginia   Died: ?   Residence at time of enlistment: Sullivan Co., TN.   Enlisted in Company C 63rd Tennessee Infantry May 17, 1862 in Mooresburg (Hawkins Co.), TN. by Lt. G. H. Neal for 3 years or duration of war. Hospitalized August 24, 1863 by order of Surgeon McDonough.   Detached detail in Baxter's Artillery on September 18, 1863 by order of Brig. General Gracie. Deserted April 27, 1864 place unknown. Paid: October 30, 1864 by Lt. Neal, December 31, 1863 by Maj. Ragan & February 29, 1864 by Maj. Ragan.

Private Jesse Beck Edwards   Born: January 20, 1844 Dickson Co., TN. Died: December 13, 1930. Buried: Anglin Cemetery Pinewood Road Williamson Co., TN   VA Marker. Enlisted in Baxter's Battery: October 30, 1862 in Dickson Co. by Captain E. D. Baxter. Residence at time of enlistment: Dickson Co., TN.   Height 5' 8"   Complexion: Light   Hair: Light   Eyes: Blue   Occupation: Blacksmith. Paid: December 31, 1862 by Capt. Hord, February 28, 1863 by Capt. Hord, October 30, 1863 by Maj. Bomar, December 31, 1863 by Maj. Ragan, February 29, 1864 by Maj. Ragan, & April 30, 1864 by Maj. Ragan. Left Cumberland Gap sick March 29, 1863 under orders from Surgeon W. T. Abrahams. Sent to hospital in Knoxville, TN. July 11, 1863. Sent to hospital in Macon, GA. by   Surgeon Murphy on October 9, 1864 remained in hospital until November 18, 1864 for recurring fever. Surrendered May 5, 1865 at Milledgeville, GA.

Private Jesse B. Edwards

Tennessee Confederate Pension Application 7218   Filed: July 19, 1905
Accepted   Disability: left arm paralyzed from shock received at the
Battle of Missionary Ridge & rheumatism.   Physician signing
application: Dr. James P. Hanner.   Witnesses: Eli Sherman & John
Gault   Notary Public: R. N. Richardson.   Residence at time of
application: Craigfield (Williamson Co.)   Assets listed in application:
I have nothing but one mare and a few hogs and cows & some household
& kitchen furniture worth $88. Wife has about 75 acres valued on the
tax books at $1 per acre.   Witnesses statement: " Said Edwards was a
faithful soldier in Baxter's Battery and surrendered with the company at
Milledgeville, GA. about May 1865. We both belonged to the same
Battery and know he made a good soldier and believe he deserves to be
pensioner. " Application was reviewed by Attorney R.N. Richardson of
Franklin, TN.

Married Nancy J. Bradford   (Born: June 17, 1850   Died: April 19,
1923) October 19, 1870 in Williamson Co., TN.

Corporal William M. Ellison   Born: 1842   Davidson Co., TN.   Died:
October 17, 1864 in Ocmulgee Hospital Macon, GA. Buried: Rose Hill
Cemetery   Macon, GA. Soldier's Square Section Row 16. Enlisted in
Baxter's Battery: October 30, 1862 in Dickson Co., TN. by Capt. E. D.
Baxter. Residence at time of enlistment: Dickson Co., TN.   Height:
5'6"   Complexion: Dark   Hair: Dark   Eyes: Dark   Occupation:
Farmer. Paid: December 31, 1862 by Maj. Hord, February 28, 1863 by

Capt. Hord, October 30, 1863 by Lt. Neal, December 31, 1863 by Maj. Ragan, February 29, 1864 by Maj. Ragan & April 30, 1864 by Maj. Ragan. Promoted to Corporal June 15, 1863 after the death of James McCrory.

Private A. L. Emlen   Born: 1844   Died: ?   Residence: Fayette Co., GA. Enlisted in Baxter's Battery: April 21, 1864 in Fulton Co., GA. by Capt. E. D. Baxter. Hospitalized at Ocmulgee Hospital in Macon, GA. October 4-27, 1864 for intermittent fever and December 7-29, 1864 for fever with debility and prostration by order of Surgeon Beauchamp. Never paid.

Private Joseph F. Foard   Born: 1833   Died: ?   Enlisted in Baxter's Battery: June 1, 1863 in Claiborne Co., TN. by Capt. E. D. Baxter. Furloughed for 30 days on June 26, 1863 by Gen. Gracie. Enlisted in 39th Tennessee Mounted Infantry March 16, 1862 at Rogersville Junction, TN. Elected Captain. Relieved at reorganization May 3, 1863. Served in Quartermaster department April 11, 1863 until July 30, 1863. Joined Company G 63rd Tennessee Infantry as a Private July 7, 1863. Appointed Hospital steward by Secretary of War. Joined 8th Tennessee Cavalry February 1, 1864. Captured in Jefferson Co., TN. December 28, 1864. Taken to Louisville, KY. to Ft. Delaware, DE., to Camp Hamilton, VA. Received by Confederate agent at Bermuda Hundred, VA. January 27, 1865 for exchange. 30 day furlough granted January 25, 1865. Paid in Richmond, VA. January 30, 1865

Corporal John Lambert Forehand   Born: 1837 Davidson Co., TN. Died: May 22, 1921   Buried: Eli Tidwell Cemetery   Hickman Co., TN. VA Marker. Enlisted in Baxter's Battery: December 3, 1862 in Hickman Co., TN. by Capt. E. D. Baxter.   Height: 5' 11" Complexion: Fair   Hair: Sandy   Eyes: Blue   Occupation: Farmer. Paid: December 31, 1862 by Capt. Hord, February 28, 1863 by Capt. Hord, April 30, 1863 by Maj. Hord, June 30, 1863 by Capt. Fowler, October 30, 1863 by Lt. Neal, December 31, 1863 by Maj. Ragan, February 29, 1864 by Maj. Ragan & April 30, 1864 by Maj. Ragan. Hospitalized at Ocmulgee Hospital in Macon, GA.   October 9 – November 12, 1864 for intermittent fever.

Cpl. John L. Forehand

Appointed Corporal December 12, 1864 upon demotion of Corp. McCaslin. Paroled April 28, 1865 at Macon, GA. Oath of allegiance taken May 4, 1865 at Chattanooga, TN. Ordered to report to Franklin. Married Mary Minerva Tidwell.

Tennessee Confederate Pension Application 4047.   Accepted   Filed: March 12, 1902   Disability: right arm and hand almost entirely disabled due to diseased blood contracted during the war.   Physician signing application: Dr. J. T. Cox   Witnesses: F. M. Tidwell, J. P. White, D. H. Lankford, H. A. Spencer & Wesley Welch.   Notary Public: Samuel Hammon (Co. K 11th Tenn. Infantry)   Residence at time of application: Tidwell (Hickman Co.)   Assets listed in application: I have 100 acres of land valued at $100 personal property of $60.   Witness Statements: " That he was a good and faithful soldier during the war."   D.H. Lankford & J.P. White.   Wesley Welch states that he has known J.L. Forehand since 1861 and was with him in the Confederate Army from 1862 to about the 18th of April 1865 the time that said Forehand and myself was surrendered and paroled. I further state that J.L. Forehand was a sound able bodied man when he entered the army in 1862. I was in army with him through the entire balance of the war. I further state that J.L. Forehand and myself were sent to the Hospital while at Macon, GA. with fever and while in the Hospital his right arm became diseased and continued to grow worse after he got home until he can't use it. It was thought for a long time that his arm would have to be amputated. This January 28, 1905

H. A. Spencer under oath stated that he was a comrade in the Confederate army with J. L. Forehand and well acquainted with his circumstances at home and that he has nothing to amount to anything except a small poor place, that he could not make a support, even if he was able to do manual labor, which he is not able to perform And that he was surrendered at Macon, Georgia and paroled about the 18th of April 1865 and he made a good soldier doing his duty and was of good character. F. M. Tidwell testified: That he has been acquainted with J. L. Forehand for fifty years and that he remembered seeing on his right arm shortly after he returned from the army a schurfy rough place the he complained of very much and it seemed to turn into irriceplus and I thought and so did every on that saw him thought that it would eventually cause his death and Mr. Forehand is a very poor man hasn't anything of any consequence outside of a very poor place that is worth but very little and he is totally unable to make a living by manual labor Franklin Attorney, Tom Henderson, assisted family in acquiring a government tombstone in 1938.

Private John L. Foster   Born: 1845 Died: ? Residence: Campbell Co., GA.   Enlisted: March 4, 1862 Co. G (Alleghany Rangers)) 52nd Regiment Georgia Volunteer Infantry, Army of Tennessee in Union Co., GA. Enlisted in Baxter's Battery: May 8, 1864 in Fulton Co., GA. by Capt. E. D. Baxter. Never Paid.

Private (Artificer) William P. A. Frashier   Born: June 28, 1831 in Dickson Co., TN. Died: August 14, 1919 Dickson Co., TN. Buried: Fraizer Cemetery Bear Creek Dickson Co., TN.   Enlisted in Baxter's Battery: December 16, 1862 in Dickson Co., TN. by Capt. E. D. Baxter. Residence at time of enlistment: Dickson Co., TN. Height: 5' 11" Complexion: Light   Hair: Dark Eyes: Gray. Paid: December 31, 1862 by Capt. Hord, February 28, 1863 by Capt. Hord, April 30, 1863 by Maj. Hord, June 30, 1863 by Capt. Fowler, October 30, 1863 by Lt. Neal, December 31, 1863 by Maj. Ragan, February 29, 1864 by Maj. Ragan, April 30, 1864 by Maj. Ragan & October 31, 1864 by Maj. Higgins. Appointed Artificer July 7, 1863. Hospitalized in Ocmulgee Hospital Macon, GA. October 12-29, 1864 for intermittent fever. Roll call for clothing at Lumpkin Hospital Cuthbert, GA. 12-28-64. Paroled April 28, 1865 at Macon, GA. Oath of allegiance taken May 4, 1865 at Chattanooga, TN.

Tennessee Confederate Pension Application 6171   Filed: April 22, 1904   Accepted.   Disability: rheumatism & inflammation of kidney. Physician signing application: Dr. E. W. Ridings   Witnesses: Daniel White & John Dillard   Notary Publics: Samuel Hammon (Co. K 11th Tenn. Infantry) & L. D. Wright.   Residence at time of application: Maple Ridge (Dickson Co.)   Assets listed on application $200--------- $100-------Witnesses statement: "That said Frasher was a dutiful soldier and that he is now in his 73rd year and that he is indigent and deserving. " He states in application that he was relieved as black smith for the company of artillery on account of rheumatism. He stated in application that " they was forced to take the oath of allegiance or the yanks would send him north to prison." Married Rebecca H. Parker (Born February 22, 1835 Died May 1, 1918) June 20, 1862 in Dickson Co., TN. He was a member of Bill Green Camp 933 of Tennessee Confederate Veterans in Dickson, TN.

Private James F. Garland   Born: 1843 Davidson Co., TN.   Died: January 1, 1930   Buried: Mt. Olivet Cemetery   Nashville, TN. Enlisted in Baxter's Battery: December 1, 1862 in Dickson Co., TN. by Capt. E. D. Baxter. Height: 5'7 ½"   Complexion: Fair   Hair: Dark Eyes: Blue   Occupation: Farmer   Paid: December 31, 1862 by Capt. Hord & February 25, 1863 by Capt. Hord. Left Cumberland Gap by order of Surgeon W. T. Abrahams on March 29, 1863. Sent to Hospital in Knoxville, TN.

Confederate report of June 1, 1863 shows deserted at Cumberland Gap. Federal Reports show captured May 6, 1863 at Richmond, KY. Taken to Lexington, KY., then to Camp Chase, OH. Prison.   Received at Johnson's Island Prison at Sandusky, OH. on November 4, 1863. Exchanged at Point Lookout, MD. Prison on October 30, 1864. Hospitalized at Chiambrazo Hospital in Richmond, VA. from November 28 to December 1, 1864. Brought furlough from Savannah, GA. for disease debility. Hospitalized in Jackson Hospital in Richmond, VA. April 3, 1865. On roll of POW'S captured in Richmond on April 3, 1865. Ordered transferred from Jackson Hospital on April 13, 1865.

Private John Gatlin Born: May 12, 1834 Williamson Co., TN. Died: May 1, 1920. Buried: Mt. Hope Cemetery Franklin, TN. Section F. Enlisted in Baxter's Battery: November 24, 1862 in Williamson Co., TN. by Captain E. D. Baxter.   Residence at time of enlistment:

Williamson Co., TN. Height: 5' 10"   Complexion: Fair   Hair: Dark
Eyes: Gray Occupation:Farmer. Paid:December 30, 1862 by Capt. Hord,
February 28, 1863 by Capt. Hord, April 3, 1863 by Capt. Hord & June
30, 1863 by Capt. Fowler. Deserted near Knoxville August 6, 1863.
Wife: Annie May Gatlin Born: May 12, 1894. Died: August 1, 1914.

2nd Lieutenant John M. Gault   Born: October 30, 1839 Franklin, TN.
Died: November 27, 1905 in St. Thomas Hospital   Nashville, TN.
Buried: Mt. Hope Cemetery Franklin, TN.   Section D-22. Residence
at time of enlistment: Davidson Co., TN.   Occupation: Merchant.
Enlisted: Company C 1st Tennessee Infantry Regiment on May 10,
1861 in Nashville by Colonel B. R. Johnson for 1 year. Unit enrolled
May 25, 1861 at Camp Cheatham. Re-enlisted on May 1, 1862 for 2
years in Corinth, MS. by Capt. J.R. Wholess. Discharged May 22, 1862.
Elected 2nd Lt. of Baxter's Battery December 11, 1862. Paid 40 cents
per day for use of horse. Hospitalized in Ocmulgee Hospital Macon,
GA. October 15-31, 1864 for recurring fever. Last record on file: present
December 31, 1864. Paid $90 per month as 2nd Lieutenant. Paroled May
1865 near Milledgeville, GA. He was a member of McEwen Bivouac #4
Association of Confederate Soldiers, Tennessee Division, Franklin, TN.
He attended the dedication of the Confederate statue on the Courthouse
Square in Franklin November 30, 1899.

Lt. John Gault

Tennessee Confederate Widow's Indigent Pension 6317   Filed: April 8,
1916 Accepted.   Mary Walton Polk Gault   Born: September 22,
1863 in Bastrop, LA.   Died: September 22, 1940 in Jackson, TN.

Buried: Mt. Hope Cemetery Franklin, TN. Married: April 12, 1887 in Franklin, TN. by Rev. Charles M. Gray, Rector of St. Paul's Episcopal Church. Witnesses: Eli Sherman & James P. Hanner Notary Public S. O. Maury

---

Sergeant William M. Gault Born: 1832 Williamson Co., TN. Died: >1880 Georgia ? Residence at time of enlistment: Williamson Co., TN. Enlisted in Baxter's Battery: November 8, 1862 in Williamson Co., TN. by Capt. E. D. Baxter Height: 5' 7" Complexion: Fair Hair: Dark Eyes: Dark Occupation: Brick Mason. Paid: December 31, 1862 by Capt. Hord, February 28, 1863 by Capt. Massengale, April 30, 1863 by Maj. Hord, June 30, 1863 by Capt. Fowler, October 30, 1863 by Lt. Neal, December 31, 1863 by Maj. Ragan, February 29, 1864 by Maj. Ragan, & April 30, 1864 by Maj. Ragan. Detached from Knoxville, TN. on February 15, 1863 by Gen. Gracie to forage for horses Hospitalized at Ocmulgee Hospital Macon, GA. October 16-27, 1864 for fever. Paid 40 cents per day for use of horse.

Paroled April 28, 1865 at Macon, GA. Oath of allegiance taken at Chattanooga, TN. May 4, 1865. Ordered to report to Franklin. Reported having family. Married Mary Medlin July 17, 1856.

Private (Artificer) Benjamin F. Gilliam Born: 1822 Williamson Co., TN. Died: 1899 Buried: Mt. Olivet Cemetery Nashville, TN. Enlisted in Baxter's Battery: November 8, 1862 at Williamson Co., TN. by Captain E. D. Baxter. Residence at time of enlistment: Cheatham Co., TN. Height: 5' 11" Complexion : Fair Hair: Light Eyes: Blue Occupation: Harness Maker. Paid: April 30, 1863 by Maj. Hord, June 30, 1863 by Capt. Deadrick, October 31, 1863 by Lt. Neal, December 31, 1863 by Maj. Ragan, February 29, 1864 by Maj. Ragan, & April 30, 1864 by Maj. Ragan. January & February absent on detached service in Cheatham Co., TN. to dispose of private horses by order of Gen. Gracie. Left Cumberland Gap March 29, 1893 sick by order of Surgeon W. J. Abrahams. Sent to hospital in Knoxville, TN. June 4, 1863 detailed for hospital duty by Maj. Gen. Buckner, June 30, 1863 due extra wages 88 days at 25 cents per day. Sent to hospital in Atlanta, Ga. December 14, 1863.

Paid $21.60 for use of horse.   Entitled to compensation for undrawn clothing up to October 8, 1863 balance due $ 83.24. Married Eliza Jane Isriel April 2, 1866.

Private Francis M. Godwin   Enlisted in Baxter's Battery: April 21, 1864 in Fulton Co., GA. by Capt. E. D. Baxter. Paid: October 31, 1864 by Major Higgins. Previous service in Co. H   17th GA. Volunteer Infantry Regiment.

Private William F. Goodgene   Born: 1839 Maury Co., TN.   Died: >1880   Enlisted in Baxter's Battery: November 22, 1862 in Williamson Co., TN. by Capt. E. D. Baxter.   Residence at time of enlistment: Williamson Co., TN.   Height: 5' 10"   Complexion: Fair   Hair: Light   Eyes: Blue   Occupation: Farmer.   January 1, 1863 AWOL, believed deserted in Williamson Co., TN. Never Paid. Married Maggie J. Hargrove September 19, 1859 in Williamson Co., TN.

Private James K. Gray   Born: 1841   Residence: Clayton Co., GA. Enlisted: May 1, 1861 Co. G. (Lewis Volunteers) 18th Regiment Georgia Volunteer Infantry, Army of Northern Virginia in Bartow County, GA. Deserted November 4, 1863. Enlisted in Baxter's Battery April 28, 1864 in Fulton Co., GA. by Capt. E. D. Baxter   Died in Ocmulgee Hospital Macon, GA. October 4, 1864 with spinal meningitis.   Never Paid. Buried in Soldiers Square Section Row 1 in Rose Hill Cemetery in Macon, GA.

Corporal (Artificer) Albert Green   Born: August 21, 1834 Williamson Co., TN.   Died: March 10, 1922.   Buried: Green Cemetery West Green Cemetery Road Bon Aqua, TN. VA Marker. Enlisted in Baxter's Battery: November 3, 1862 in Maury Co., TN. by Capt. E.D. Baxter. Residence at time of enlistment: Williamson Co., TN.   Height: 5' 8" Complexion: Dark   Hair: Dark   Eyes: Dark   Occupation: Blacksmith.   Left Cumberland Gap sick by order of Surgeon W. T. Abrahams. Sent to hospital in Knoxville, TN. May 1, 1863, reduced in rank from Corporal for incompetence.   Hospitalized at Ocmulgee Hospital Macon, GA. October 13-27, 1864. Paroled April 28, 1865 at Macon, GA. Oath of allegiance taken at Chattanooga, TN. May 4, 1865. Ordered to report to Franklin. Paid: December 31, 1862 by Capt. Hord, February 28, 1863 by Capt. Hord, June 30, 1863 by Capt. Fowler, October 31, 1863 by Lt. Neal, December 31, 1863 by Maj. Ragan, February 29, 1864 by Maj. Ragan, & April 30, 1864 by Maj. Ragan. Green also served as company dentist.

Cpl. Albert Green

Tennessee Confederate Pension application 6166   Accepted   Filed: March 28, 1904   Disability: rheumatism   Physician signing application: Dr. J. C. Daniel   Witnesses: B. F. Brown & H. A. Spencer   Notary Public: W. B. Williams.   Residence at time of application: Bon Aqua (Hickman Co.)   Assets listed in application: A small poor farm and about $250 personal property in all about $450. (Hickman County Trustee, Ed Russell listed 176 acre farm valued at $575.)

Tennessee Confederate Widow's Pension Application 7732   Filed: April 4, 1922   Accepted.   Mary Eliza Donnigan Green. Residence: Bon Aqua (Hickman Co.), TN. Born: February 27, 1851 3rd District of Dickson Co., TN. Died: July 1, 1923. Married: June 19, 1883 by A. P. Beard in Hickman Co., TN. Had 4 children. Witness: J. K. Myatt Notary Public: J. J.Tippit.

Private. Louis B. Griggs   Born: May 1, 1846 Adairsville, GA.   Died: >1896   Occupation: Painter.
Enlisted in Baxter's Battery: March 24, 1864 in Fulton Co., GA. by Capt. E. D. Baxter. Entitled to $50 bounty. Hospitalized at Ocmulgee Hospital Macon, GA. October 7-11, 1864 for recurring fever.
Paid: April 30, 1864 by Maj. Ragan & October 30, 1864 by Major Higgins.

Georgia Confederate Pension Application   Filed July 1, 1896 in Fulton County. Disability: rheumatism and catarrh of stomach.   Have suffered with rheumatism about 6 years during which time it has prevented me from working regularly, often having to lay in bed for weeks at a time. Assets: none. Physicians signing application: Dr. C. C. Greens & Dr. Evan Gaidsonover. Fulton County Ordinary: M. L. Calhoun. Witness to application W. S. Parrish. Witness statement: " I was in same company. Enlisted May 1863 at Atlanta in Baxter's Company River's Battalion. Served together 2 years. He was a good soldier, captured and paroled."

Private Minor Y. Griggs   Born: August 18, 1847   Died: >1930. Occuptaion: Painter. In 1930 was an inmate at Georgia Confederate Soldier's Home Atlanta. Enlisted in Baxter's Battery February 25, 1864 in Fulton Co., GA. by Capt. E. D. Baxter. Bounty due. Hospitalized at Ocmulgee Hospital Macon, GA. October 9-12, 1864 for recurring fever. Paid: February 29 & April 30, 1864 by Maj. Ragan. Paid $47.90 on December 8, 1864 by S. R. Proctor. Furloughed from Augusta, GA. hospital on October 17, 1864 for 60 days by Surgeon W. H. Doughty.

Georgia Confederate Pension Application Filed April 15, 1902 in Fulton County. Disability: Bright's Disease.   Witnesses to application: William Parrish, J. T. Speight, and Matthew Johnson.   Applicant's statement: "While stationed near what is now West End near City of Atlanta, Ga., there came a large carbuncle right under where the cartridge box pressed on my back, it was caused by wearing the cartridge box continually as I was required to do. The carbuncle had to be lanced, and I was at that time disabled for three months on account thereof & not able to do duty.   This carbuncle has several times since it first appearance, reappeared at the same point, just over my kidneys, and had to be lanced from the time said carbuncle first appeared until the date I have had a kidney trouble, my back and kidneys giving constant pains. The pressure of the cartridge box with constant wearing, I being forced to be on duty a great deal, so effected my back and kidneys that the results- above described caused & ruined my physical condition & recked my health-All these occurred while I was in the Confederate army & in active service and having been worked very hard & exposed to the worst of weather, took disease."   Witnesses Statements: " In the spring of 1864, said Griggs was in the Confederate Army, and while located at Atlanta, Ga. there appeared on his back a large carbuncle just over his kidney which had to be lanced and which disabled him from duty for about three months. The carbuncle was attributed to wearing a cartridge box and belt, said box rested upon the point where the carbuncle appeared. He was kept constantly on guard duty. We know that he has been crippled in his back ever since he had the carbuncle during the war. We have heard of the carbuncle reappearing at times since the war, but, of course, did not see it. Since Mr. Griggs is disabled on account of his physical condition described from earning a living". Pension Office 10-1-1901 It is not shown how and in what way carbuncle had during the war in producing Bright's Disease in 1901 or at anytime before. It must be clearly shown that the present condition is the sole and direct result of an injury received in the service and that from its affect alone he has been rendered incompetent to perform ordinary manual labor.   J. W. Lindsey Comm. of Pensions.   Pension Office 3-13-1908 Applicant's new testimony does not comply with commissioners note 10-1-1901. It is unreasonable to conclude that Applicant had Bright's disease for 38 years as the sole and direct result of the carbuncle of 1864. J. W. Lindsey Com. of Pensioners.   Assets: None. Physicians signing application: Dr. Evan Gaidsonover, Dr. W. C. Robinson, & Dr. A. S. Birdwell. Fulton County Ordinary John R. Wilkerson.

Private John D. Groves   Born: 1837   Dickson Co., TN.   Died: December 10, 1862 in camp at Bethesda, Williamson Co., TN. of hypertrophy of the heart. Enlisted in Baxter's Battery: October 30, 1862 in Dickson Co., TN. by Capt. E. D. Baxter   Residence at time of enlistment: Dickson Co., TN.   Height: 6' Complexion: Fair   Hair: Light   Eyes: Blue   Never Paid.
FIRST MAN IN BAXTER'S COMPANY TO DIE IN SERVICE

Private John T. Groves   Born: July 18, 1838   Died: March 15, 1914 Buried: Parker-Fowlkes Cemetery Dickson Co., TN.   VA Marker. Enlisted in Baxter's Battery: December 22, 1862 in Maury Co., TN. by Maj. J. L. House. Residence at time of enlistment: Dickson Co., TN. Left sick in Dickson Co., TN. May 24, 1863 by Lt. Herrin. Not heard from since. Never paid. Married Elizabeth D. Edwards
(Born: September 8, 1841   Died: September 17, 1930) April 7, 1862 in Dickson Co., TN.

Pvt. John T. Groves

Private Napoleon B. Groves "Poney" Born: 1840 Montgomery Co., TN. Died: >1880 Dickson Co., TN. Enlisted in Baxter's Battery: December 11, 1862 in Dickson Co., TN. by Capt. E. D. Baxter Height: 5' 9" Complexion: Dark Hair: Dark Eyes: Dark Occupation: Farmer. Paid: December 31, 1862 by Capt. Hord, February 28, 1863 by Capt. Hord, April 30, 1863 by Maj. Hord, & June 30, 1863 by Capt. Fowler. Deserted near Knoxville August 6, 1863.

Private Robert G. Hadaway Born: 1838 Died: ? Residence: Clayton Co., GA. Enlisted in Baxter's Battery: April 27, 1864 in Fulton Co., GA. by Capt. E. D. Baxter. Hospitalized at Ocmulgee Hospital in Macon, GA. October 20-November 3, 1864 by Surgeon Stuart for intermittent fever & chronic diarrhea.

Private James Henderson Hall Born: February 27, 1842 Dickson Co., TN. Died: February 23, 1911 at Jingo, Williamson Co., TN. Buried: Hall Family Cemetery Dice Lampley Rd. Fairview, TN. (located in Bowie Nature Park). VA Marker. Enlisted in Baxter's Battery: December 1, 1862 in Dickson Co., TN. by Capt. E. D. Baxter. Height: 5' 9" Complexion: Fair Hair: Light Eyes: Blue Occupation: Farmer. Paid: December 31, 1862 by Capt. Hord, February 28, 1863 by Capt. Hord, April 30, 1864 by Maj. Hord, June 30, 1863 by Capt. Fowler, October 30, 1863 by Lt. Neal, December 31, 1863 by Maj. Ragan, February 29, 1864 by Maj. Ragan, & April 30, 1864 by Maj. Ragan. February 15, 1863 detached at Knoxville, TN. to forage for horses by order of Brig. Gen. Gracie. Taken prisoner in hospital at the fall of Atlanta September 3, 1864. Oath of allegiance taken at Chattanooga, TN. on October 26, 1864.

Tennessee Confederate Pension Application 2711   Filed: April 27, 1900 Rejected.   Disability: rheumatism   Physician signing application: Dr. W. T. Clark   Witnesses: Eli Sherman, John M. Gault, James F. Buttrey & W. H. Bethshears.   Notary Public: J. A. Griffin.   Residence at time of application: Jingo (Williamson Co.)   Assets listed in application: " I have fifty acres is worth one hundred dollars. My personal property is worth one hundred dollars. "   Application states he was taken prisoner in hospital in Atlanta, GA. September 3, 1864 and was paroled and sent home. Witness statement of W. H. Bethshears: " I was in the same company with Mr. Hall under Capt. Baxter and know he was taken sick and sent to the hospital and I went there to see him the night before we left Atlanta".

Tennessee Confederate Widow's Pension Application 3833   Filed: March 14, 1911 Rejected.   Emaline Lampley Hall Born: March 13, 1844 Dickson Co., TN.   Died: July 13, 1915   Residence: Jingo, PO R.R. 2 Williamson Co., TN.   Married: December 19, 1864 by Rev. Frank McCaslin.   Had 8 children.   Witnesses: William H. Bethshears & T. E. Hall   Notary Public: C. G. Allen.   Williamson Co. Trustee H. T. Robinson.   Application states Private Hall was left behind sick in hospital in Atlanta, GA. by order of Captain Baxter when the company withdrew from Atlanta.

Corporal Robert G. Hall   Born: 1841 Dickson Co., TN.   Died: ? Buried: Hall Family Cemetery Fairview, TN. (unmarked grave ?) Enlisted in Baxter's Battery: November 5, 1862 in Williamson Co., TN. by Captain E. D. Baxter. Residence at time of enlistment: Wiliamson Co., TN.   Height: 5' 9"   Complexion: Fair   Hair: Light   Eyes: Blue   Occupation: Farmer. Paid: December 31, 1862 by Capt. Hord, February 28, 1863 by Capt. Hord, April 30, 1863 by Maj. Hord, June 30, 1863 by Capt. Fowler, October 30, 1863 by Lt. Neal, December 31, 1863 by Maj. Ragan, February 29, 1864 by Maj. Ragan, & April 30, 1864 by Maj. Ragan. Promoted to Corporal July 1, 1863 upon promotion of A. A. McCaslin. Hospitalized at Ocmulgee Hospital Macon, GA. October 19-November19, 1864 and January 3-25, 1865. Married Martha Jones July 30, 1860 in Davidson Co., TN.

2nd Lieutenant William Herrin   Born: 1825   Died: 1883 Davidson Co., TN. Buried: Herrin Cemetery South Harpeth Rd. Cheatham Co., TN. VA Marker. Appointed to Dickson County Home Guard of Minute Men June 10, 1861. Residence at time of enlistment: Dickson County, TN. Complexion: Light   Hair: Sandy   Eyes: Gray   Height: 5' 9" Elected 2nd Lieutenant December 11, 1862. Paroled Macon, GA. April 28, 1865. Oath of allegiance taken at Chattanooga, TN. May 4, 1865. Ordered to report to Nashville. Paid 40 cents per day for use of horse. Married Doreas Kinzer in 1849.

Sergeant William B. Hill   Born: December 12, 1832   Died: June 3, 1896   Buried: John Hill Cemetery Temple Rd. Williamson Co., TN. ? Residence at time of enlistment: Williamson Co., TN.   Enlisted in Baxter's Battery: November 20, 1863 in Williamson Co., TN. by Capt. E. D. Baxter Height: 6'   Complexion: Dark   Hair: Black   Eyes: Dark   Occupation: Farmer. Paid: December 31, 1862 by Capt. Hord, February 28, 1863 by Capt. Hord, April 30, 1863 by Maj. Hord, June 30, 1863 by Capt. Fowler, October 31, 1863 by Lt. Neal, December 31, 1863 by Maj. Ragan, February 29, 1864 by Maj. Ragan, April 30, 1864 by Maj. Ragan, & October 31, 1864 by Maj. Higgins. Promoted to Corporal May 1, 1863 upon demotion of Albert Green. Hospitalized at Ocmulgee Hospital Macon, GA.   October 16-29, 1864 for intermittent fever. Promoted to Sergeant December 12, 1864 upon demotion of A. A. McCaslin. Furloughed for 45 days on December 22, 1864 by Brig. Gen. Wachall. Paroled April 28, 1865 at Macon, GA. Oath of allegiance taken at Chattanooga, TN. May 4, 1865. Reported as having family. Married Nancy E. Ormes October 7, 1858 in Williamson Co., TN.

Sgt. William B. Hill

Sergeant George W. Hogan, Jr.   Born: 1842   Davidson Co., TN.   Died: October 1, 1921   Buried: Confederate Circle   Mt. Olivet Cemetery Nashville, TN.   Enlisted in Co. I 55th TN. Infantry Reg. (The Nashville Confederates) December 30, 1861.   Received medical discharge July 3, 1862.   Enlisted in Baxter's Battery: October 30, 1864 in Dickson Co., TN.   by Capt. E. D. Baxter.   Residence at time of enlistment: Williamson Co., TN.   Height: 5' 9" Complexion: Dark   Hair: Dark Eyes: Blue   Occupation: Farmer (he was a printer in Nashville after the war)   Paid: December 31, 1862 by Capt. Hord, February 28, 1863 by Capt. Hord, April 30, 1863 by Maj. Hord, June 30, 1863 by Capt. Fowler, October 31, 1863 by Lt. Neal, December 31, 1863 by Maj. Ragan, February 29, 1864 by Maj. Ragan & April 30, 1864 by Maj. Ragan.   Resigned at Sergeant July 1, 1863.   Hospitalized at General Hospital Macon, GA. October 9, 1864 by Surgeon Murphy for recurring fever & meningitis. Paid $24.80 for use of horse. Paroled May 12, 1865 at Macon, GA.   He was a member of Cheatham Bivouac #1 Association of Confederate Soldiers, Tennessee Division in Nashville.

Private (Chaplain) Henry Daniel P. Hogan   Born: 1839 Davidson Co., TN. Died: >1925   Rosedale, KS.   Height: 6' 0"   Eyes: Blue Complexion: Light Occupation: Farmer & Preacher. Enlisted in Co. B 24th TN. Infantry Regiment June 29, 1861.

Pvt. Henry Hogan

Captured at Battle of Murfreesboro.   After release from Union Prison at Camp Morton, IN., rejoined 24th Infantry and became Regimental

Chaplain. Requested to transfer to Baxter's Battery in January 1865 to be with his brother, George. Request was initially denied, but records show he was with Baxter's Battery for a short time in Macon. He was the only original member of Company B remaining in the 24th Infantry after the Battle of Nashville. Hospitalized at Ocmulgee Hospital Macon, GA. from February 18 to March 22, 1865. Paroled as a Private in Company K of 3rd Consolidated Tennessee Infantry Regiment May 1, 1865 at Greensboro, NC. He completed the Tennessee Civil War Veterans Questionnaire.

Private John N. Hood   Born: 1830   Died: ?   Buried: Warf Cemetery   Hickman Co., TN. (unmarked grave ?) Enlisted in Baxter's Battery: December 12, 1862 in Dickson Co., TN. by Capt. E. D. Baxter Left sick in Strawberry Plains in charge of non-commissioned officers April 16, 1862 by order of Brig. Gen. Gracie. Paid: April 30, 1863 by Maj. Hord. Deserted near Knoxville July 10, 1863.
Married E. C. Jackson September 1, 1857 in Dickson Co., TN

Private William J. Hood   Born: January 2, 1832   Died: January 12, 1908   Buried: Missionary Ridge Baptist Church Cemetery Bon Aqua, TN. VA Marker. Enlisted in Baxter's Battery: December 12, 1862 in Dickson Co., TN. by Capt. E. D. Baxter. Reported to company January 26, 1863. Paid: April 30, 1863 by Maj. Hord Deserted near Knoxville July 10, 1863. Married Manervia A. Hall on January 31, 1856 in Dickson Co., TN.

Private Thomas J. Hooper Born: 1839 Dickson Co., TN. Died: 1910 Buried: Rock Church Cemetery Dickson Co., TN. Enlisted in Baxter's Battery: December 11, 1862 in Dickson Co., TN. by Capt. E.D. Baxter. Residence at time of enlistment: Dickson Co., TN.   Height: 5' Complexion: Fair   Hair: Sandy   Eyes: Blue   Occupation: Farmer Paid: December 31, 1862 by Capt. Hord, February 28, 1863 by Capt. Hord, April 30, 1863 by Maj. Hord, June 30, 1863 by Capt. Fowler, October 31, 1863 by Lt. Neal, December 31, 1863 by Maj. Ragan, February 29, 1864 by Maj. Ragan & April 30, 1864 by Maj. Ragan. Hospitalized at Ocmulggee Hospital Macon, GA. October 4-15, 1864 & January 3-22, 1865 for intermittent fever. Reported deserted April 9, 1865. Oath of allegiance taken April 28, 1865 in Nashville, TN.

Tennessee Confederate Pension Application 2422   Filed: January 10, 1900   Rejected.   Disability: age and general physical condition prevents performing manual labor. He reported his duty was firing of the guns and his hearing was temporarily impaired and was shocked by jar of guns. Physician Signing Application: Dr. J. A. Venable of White Bluff, TN. Witnesses to application: J. M. Talley & M. B. Donegan. Notary Public: C. D. Hall of Dickson County. The following wrote the Confederate Pension Board on behalf of Hooper: T. B. Larkins letter notarized by J. A. Larkins. J. T. Beck & J. J. Johnson letters notarized by A. M. Petway and T. H. Whitfield. The following wrote letters to Captain E. D. Baxter on behalf of Hooper: A. Q. Tidwell of Bon Aqua, TN. H. A. Spencer of Bon Aqua, TN. A. A. McCaslin of Slayton, TN. & B. F. Brown of Burns, TN. Application reports and witnesses verify that Hooper was granted a 30- day sick leave, came home to Dickson County and was unable to return to the unit due to the large number of Federal Troops in the county. Also confirmed that the company had been surrendered before he took the oath of allegiance. Married E.J. Wright October 6, 1860 in Dickson Co., TN.

Private William R. Hooper   Born: 1841   Dickson Co., TN. Died: May 29, 1863 of typhoid fever in camp in Grainger Co., TN. Buried: unmarked grave near Bean Station, TN. Enlisted in Baxter's Battery: December 11, 1862 in Dickson Co., TN. by Capt. E. D. Baxter. Height: 5' 4"   Complexion: Fair   Hair: Light   Eyes: Blue Occupation: Farmer. Paid: December 31, 1862 by Capt. Hord, February 28, 1863 by Capt. Hord, & April 30, 1863 by Maj. Hord. Upon his death, personal effects were taken by his brother, Thomas Hooper. Married Susan F. Casey October 23, 1861 in Cheatham Co., TN.

Private Dewitt C. Houston   Born: 1844   Died: >1880   Buried: Houston Family Cemetery Marshall Co., TN. ? Enlisted: February 16, 1863 in Giles Co., TN. by Lt. Gunts. Residence: Marshall Co., TN. Complexion: Light   Hair: Brown   Eyes: Blue. Paid: December 31, 1863 by Maj. Ragan, February 29, 1864 by Maj. Ragan & April 30, 1864 by Maj. Ragan. Transferred from Company I 4th Georgia Cavalry to Baxter's Battery on November 15, 1863 by order of Gen. Braxton Bragg. Entitled to pay for horse from February 16, 1862 to July 10, 1863 at 40 cents per day. Hospitalized at Ocmulgee Hospital Macon, GA. October 7-13, 1864 and October 20 to November 19, 1864 for intermittent fever. Paroled at Macon, GA. April 28, 1865. Oath of Allegiance taken at Chattanooga, TN. May 4, 1865. Ordered to report to

Columbia, TN. No family reported. Married Nancy Gray September 16, 1876 in Sequatchie Co., TN.

Private George H. Isler   Born: 1824   Died: >1870 Residence: Long Marsh (Clark Co.), VA.   Enlisted in Baxter's Battery: August 4, 1863 in Knox Co., TN. by Capt. E. D. Baxter.   Detailed in Quartermaster Department by Maj. Gen Simon Bolivar Buckner's Special Order 97 on August 7, 1863   January & February 1864 Quartermaster duty Greeneville, TN.   March & April 1864 Quartermaster duty at Bristol, TN. with extra duty at Greeneville, TN.   May 1864 Quartermaster duty at Wytheville, VA.   August 1864   Quartermaster duty Asheville, NC. Paroled at Clarksburg, WV. May 4, 1865 by R. B. Grainger.   Paid on descriptive list.

Private Richard Parson Jackson "Dick"   Born: January 3, 1834 Dickson Co., TN.   Died: June 10, 1863 of typhoid fever in camp in Grainger Co., TN.   Buried: unmarked grave near Bean Station, TN. Appointed to Dickson County Home Guard of Minute Men June 10, 1861.   Enlisted in Baxter's Battery: December 19, 1862 in Dickson Co., TN. by Capt. E. D. Baxter.   Paid: December 31, 1862 by Capt. Hord, February 28, 1863 by Capt. Hord, & April 30, 1863 by Maj. Hord. Letter of administration for personal effects received by Lt. Herrin from Knox County Court.   Married Nancy P. Stuart June 30, 1857 in Dickson Co., TN.

Private John Jefferson Johnson, Jr.   Born: October 27, 1826 Hickman Co., TN. Died: May 16, 1912 White Bluff, TN. Appointed to Dickson County Home Guard of Minute Men June 10, 1861. Enlisted in Baxter's Battery: November 5, 1862 in Dickson Co., TN. by Capt. E. D. Baxter. Residence at time of enlistment: Dickson Co., TN.   Height: 5' 10" Complexion: Dark   Hair: Black   Eyes: Dark   Occupation: Farmer. Paid: December 31, 1862 by Capt. Hord, February 28, 1863 by Capt. Hord, April 30, 1863 by Maj. Hord, June 30, 1863 by Capt. Fowler, October 31, 1863 by Lt. Neal, December 31, 1863 by Maj. Ragan, February 29, 1864 by Maj. Ragan, April 30, 1864 by Maj. Ragan, & October 31, 1864 by Maj. Higgins.   Hospitalized in Macon, GA. October 7-29, 1864 for intermittent fever.   Paroled at Milledgeville, GA. May 5, 1865. Johnson was also a Mexican War Veteran having served in Company K 3rd Tennessee Regiment of Volunteers. Married June Harris (Born 1828 Died 1908) in 1852.

Private John Matthew Johnson   Born: 1847   Died: >1901   Residence at time of enlistment: Campbell Co., GA.   Resided in Atlanta after the war.   Enlisted in Baxter's Battery: April 27, 1864 in Fulton Co., GA. by Capt. E. D. Baxter.   Due $50 bounty.   Paid: April 30, 1864 by Maj. Ragan.   Paroled April 28, 1865 at Macon, GA.

Georgia Confederate Pension Application   Filed September 30, 1910 in Fulton County.   Disability: not stated.   Assets: none.   Witnesses: M. Y. Griggs & John T. Walker.   Fulton County Ordinary Marcellus M. Anderson.   Witness statement of M. Y. Griggs: " J. M. Johnson enlisted Feb. 1864 in Fulton Co. Baxter's Battery Rivers Battalion. Surrendered and paroled May 7, 1865 in Macon, Ga. by authority of Fed. Officer Gen. Wilson."

Private Felix M. Jones   Born: December 16, 1840   Dickson Co., TN. Died: August 7, 1907 Calloway Co., KY.   Buried: Mt. Pleasant Church of Christ Cemetery   Pilot Oak, KY.   Enlisted in Baxter's Battery: December 19, 1862 in Dickson Co., TN. by Capt. E. D. Baxter Residence at time of enlistment: Calloway Co., KY.   Height: 5' 11"

Private Felix M. Jones

Complexion: Light   Hair: Light   Eyes: Blue   Paid: December 31, 1862 by Capt. Hord, February 28, 1864 by Capt. Hord, & April 30, 1863 by Maj. Hord.   May 18, 1863 left sick at Cumberland Gap.   Reported deserted at Rock Springs, GA. on September 9, 1863.   Captured at Chattanooga September 12, 1863.   Oath of allegiance taken at Nashville, TN. September 21, 1863.   Sent to Military prison in Louisville, KY.

Released on oath and paroled on October 30, 1863 by order of Brig. Gen. Boyles. Married Catharine (Kittie) Othelia Emmerson.

Private Wilson B. Jones   Born: 1832 Robertson Co., TN.   Died: August 22, 1909   Buried: Mt. Olivet Cemetery   Nashville, TN. Enlisted in Baxter's Battery: November 20, 1862 in Williamson Co., TN. by Capt. E. D. Baxter.   Height: 5' 9" Complexion: Fair   Hair: Dark   Eyes: Dark   Occupation: Cooper. Detached for other duty by Gen. Bragg.   Later deserted. Never paid. Married Hulda A. Binkley February 10, 1855 in Robertson Co., TN.

Private John M. Kane Born: 1839 South Carolina Died: ? Residence at time of enlistment: Chatham Co., GA. Captured near Jonesboro, GA. September 1, 1864. Listed on roll of Prisoners of War exchanged by order of Maj. Gen. W. T. Sherman, Commander Military District of Mississippi, at Rough & Ready, GA. September 19 & 22, 1864. Previous service with Co. C 5th GA. Volunteer Infantry Regiment.

Private Thomas Kent Born: 1846 Georgia Died: ? Enlisted in Co. F 34th Alabama Infantry Regiment November 16, 1862 at Greeneville, AL. by Capt. Harron.   Deserted from Baxter's Battery at field hospital at Missionary Ridge October 25, 1863 and went to another company. Paid August 31, 1863 by Capt. Raigle. In 1880 resided in Prattville, Autauga Co., AL.

Private Napoleon B. Kile   Born: 1845   Died: ?   Residence: Fulton Co., GA. Enlisted in Baxter's Battery: February 2, 1864 at Fulton Co., GA. by Capt. E. D. Baxter. Ascertained to belong to another unit, 1st Georgia Infantry Regiment and returned to it. Never Paid

---

Private Noah Washington Kimberly Born: 1847 Georgia   Died: June 21, 1899 Hopewell, AL. (Cleburne County)   Enlisted in Baxter's Battery: April 26, 1864 at Fulton Co., GA. by Capt. E. D. Baxter. Residence: Fayette Co., GA. Wounded in hip July 22, 1864 in Battle of Atlanta.   Hospitalized at Ocmulgee Hospital Macon, GA. April 12-27, 1865 for intermittent fever by Assistant Surgeon Stuart. Paroled from Hospital.   Married Delila Walden   December 26, 1869 in Clayton County, GA.

Alabama Confederate Pension application No. 27920 Filed in Cleburne County April 14, 1897 Accepted. Disability: hip wound received in Battle of Atlanta. Assets: 2 mules valued at $80.

Alabama Confederate Widows Pension Application No. 5155 Delila Kimberly   Filed August 16, 1901 in Cleburne Co., AL. Accepted. Witnesses: John F. Cain and N. J. Cain of Morgan Co., AL. Assets: 80 acres of land worth $100, 2 mules valued at $60, 2 cows valued at $15, 2 hogs valued at $4, 1 gun valued at $2, 1 clock worth $1, $25 worth of household and kitchen furniture, $10 worth of bicycles and vehicles and tools worth $1.

Private Anderson King "Andy"   Born: 1826   Buncombe Co., NC. Died: >1890   Buried: Ranson King Cemetery (destroyed cemetery) Fairview, TN. Enlisted in Baxter's Battery: November 27, 1862 in Williamson Co., TN. by Capt. E. D. Baxter. Residence at time of enlistment: Williamson Co., TN. Height: 5' 8"   Complexion: Fair Hair: Light   Eyes: Blue   Occupation: Farmer   Hospitalized at Ocmulgee Hospital Macon, GA. October 17 to November 16, 1864. Paroled at Macon, GA. April 28, 1865. Oath of allegiance taken at Chattanooga, TN. May 4, 1865. Ordered to report to Franklin. Has family.

Tennessee Confederate Pension Application 4751   Filed: March 7, 1903   Rejected.   Disability: Almost total blindness & dropsy. Residence at time of application: Aden (Williamson Co.) Assets listed in application: small tract of land valued at $80. 76 years old being supported by nephew. Physician signing application: Dr. J.M. Drake Witnesses: Aaron Beard & W.H. Bethshears   Application states he was forced to take oath of allegiance or go to Northern prison.   Married Nancy Ann Mangrum November 8, 1858 in Williamson Co., TN.

Private Andrew Kite   Born: December 26, 1838   Fayette Co., GA. Died: >1900   Residence: Campbell Co., GA. Enlisted in Baxter's Battery April 18, 1864 at Fulton Co., GA. by Capt. E. D. Baxter. Previous service in Co. E 27th Georgia Infantry Regiment.   Due $50 bounty. Never paid.

Georgia Confederate Pension Application filed January 3, 1900 in Campbell County. Disability: Rheumatism & paralysis of right side. Physicians signing application: Dr. C. T. Tucker & Dr, C. H. Dauenpost.

Campbell County Ordinary R. C. Brown. Assets: none Witness: J. J. Buffington. Witness statement: " I know he served in Confederate Army. I commanded company in which he served. He enlisted April 1863 at Virginia in Co. F 27 Georgia Volunteers. Served 16 or 17 months. Was a good soldier & did his duty as such to the best of his ability. I was home wounded at the time of his discharge."

Private John O. Ladd Born: 1834 Granville Co., NC. Died: ? Buried: Ladd Cemetery Burns, TN. ? Enlisted in Baxter's Battery: October 20, 1862 in Dickson Co., TN. by Capt. E. D. Baxter. Residence at time of enlistment: Dickson Co., TN. Height: 5' 8" Complexion: Dark Hair: Light Eyes: Dark Occupation: Farmer Paid: December 30, 1862 by Capt. Hord, February 28, 1863 by Capt. Hord, April 30, 1863 by Maj. Hord, June 30, 1863 by Capt. Fowler, October 31, 1863 by Lt. Neal, December 31, 1863 by Maj. Ragan, February 29, 1864 by Maj. Ragan, April 30, 1864 by Maj. Ragan & October 31, 1864 by Maj. Higgins. 40-day furlough granted December 14, 1864 at Macon, GA. by Brig. Gen. Mackall. Oath of allegiance taken at Nashville, TN. on January 11, 1865 by Lt. Williiam H. Bracken, Assistant Provost Marshall Department of the Cumberland. Married Agness McKeehnie February 13, 1861 in Dickson Co., TN.

Private William Henry Ladd, Sr. Born: May 15, 1835 Granville Co., NC. Died: February 22, 1898 Buried: Ladd Cemetery Burns, TN. (Cemetery is located in Montgomery Bell State Park) Enlisted in Baxter's Battery: October 30, 1862 in Dickson Co., TN. by Capt. E. D. Baxter. Residence at time of enlistment: Dickson Co., TN. Height: 5' 9" Complexion: Fair Hair: Light Eyes: Blue Occupation: Farmer. Paid: December 30, 1862 by Capt. Hord, February 28, 1863 by Capt. Hord, April 30, 1863 by Maj. Hord, June 30, 1863 by Capt. Fowler, October 31, 1863 by Lt. Neal, December 31, 1863 by Maj. Ragan, February 29, 1864 by Maj. Ragan, April 30, 1864 by Maj. Ragan & October 31, 1864 by Maj. Higgins. Paroled April 28, 1865 at Macon, GA. Oath of allegiance taken May 4, 1865 at Chattanooga, TN. Ordered to report to Franklin, TN. Married Mary A. Luther September 30, 1862.

He was a member of James E. Raines Bivouac #14 Association of Confederate Soldiers, Tennessee Division, Dickson, TN.

Private Andrew Jackson Lampley "Bud" Born: 1829 Dickson Co., TN. Died: May 15, 1920 Buried: Lampley Family Cemetery Sugar

Camp Rd. Fairview, TN. (unmarked grave ?) Enlisted in Baxter's Battery: December 13, 1862 in Williamson Co., TN. by Capt. E. D. Baxter. Residence at time of enlistment: Dickson Co., TN. Paid: December 31, 1862 by Capt. Hord, February 28, 1863 by Capt. Hord & April 30, 1863 by Capt. Fowler. Deserted near Knoxville August 6, 1863.
Married Mary Jane McDaniel April 29, 1852 in Williamson Co., TN.

Private Andrew Jackson Lampley "Jack" Born: July 19, 1844 Dickson Co., TN. Died: May 23, 1920. Buried: Jack Lampley Cemetery Martin Rd. Dickson Co., TN. VA Marker. (land for cemetery was donated by him). Enlisted in Baxter's Battery: December 11, 1862 in Dickson Co., TN. by Capt. E. D. Baxter. Occupation: blacksmith, woodworker & preacher. Paid: December 31, 1862 by Capt. Hord, February 28, 1863 by Capt. Hord & April 30, 1863 by Capt.Fowler. Deserted near Knoxville August 6, 1863.

Tennessee Confederate Pension Application 11745 Rejected. Filed: January 7, 1910. Disability: rheumatism in hip and back. Physician signing application: Dr. J. E. Mathis Witnesses: Wesley Welch & John Forehand. Notary Public: Levi Johnson Tidwell. Residence at time of application: 3rd civil District of Dickson Co. Assets listed in application: About $800. Witnesses statements: " I Wesley Welch states that he knows of his own knowledge that applicant was in the confederate army and that of his own knowledge was in service 10 months and made a good soldier" " I, J. L. Forehand state that I do know of my own knowledge that applicant was a soldier in Ed Baxter's Company was a volunteer." Application states he was captured by the Federal Army at Lebanon, TN. the last of August 1863 and was taken to prison in Nashville and was paroled the last of August or first of September. Application states he took the oath of allegiance at the close of the war at Clarksville, TN.
Married Mary E. Bishop (Born March 28, 1844 Died January 15, 1892) July 4, 1862 in Dickson Co., TN.

Private Radford Tucker Lampley "Duck" Born: September 20, 1832 Dickson Co., TN. Died: January 14, 1922 Buried: Tomlinson Cemetery Dickson Co., TN. VA Marker. Enlisted in Baxter's Battery : December 11, 1862 in Dickson Co., TN. by Capt. E. D. Baxter. Residence at time of enlistment: Dickson Co., TN. Paid: December 31, 1862 by Capt. Hord, February 28, 1863 by Capt. Hord, April 30, 1863 by Capt. Fowler. Deserted near Knoxville, August 6, 1863. Married

Parthena McDaniel (Born October 28, 1841   Died   February 19, 1902) May 5, 1856 in Dickson Co., TN.   Later married Mary Spencer Lankford, widow of Arter Lankford.   Said to have received the nickname "Duck" when the battery first came under enemy fire and other soldiers yelled "duck Lampley, duck ", trying to get him down.

Private Reuben Lane   Born: 1825   Williamson Co., TN   Died: ? Enlisted in Baxter's Battery: November 22, 1862 in McMinnville, TN. by Lt. L Butler. Height: 5' 8"   Complexion: Dark Hair: Dark Eyes: Dark   Occupation: Farmer.   Believed deserted January 1, 1863. Since reported dead.

Private John S. Langley   Born: 1847   Died: ?   In 1870 resided in Lawrenceville, Gwinnett, Co., GA..
Enlisted in Baxter's Battery: April 11, 1864 in Fulton Co., GA. by Captain E. D. Baxter.   Entitled to $50 bounty.   Deserted August 6, 1864 at Atlanta, GA.   Never paid.   Previous service in Co. K   18th GA. Volunteer Infantry Regiment.

Sergeant Arter Radford Lankford "Fiddler"   Born: November 1, 1837 Dickson Co., TN. Died: January 22, 1899 at Aden (Williamson Co.), TN.   Buried: Parker-Fowlkes Cemetery Dickson Co., TN. VA Marker. Appointed to Dickson County Home Guard of Minute Men June 10, 1861.   Enlisted in Baxter's Battery: December 4, 1862 in Dickson Co., TN. by Capt. E. D. Baxter.

Sgt. Arter R. Lankford

Residence at time of enlistment: Dickson Co., TN.   Height: 6'
Complexion: Fair Hair: Light   Eyes: Blue   Occupation: Farmer.
Paid: April 30, 1863 by Maj. Hord, June 30, 1863 by Capt. Fowler,
October 31, 1863 by Lt. Neal, December 31, 1863 by Maj. Ragan,
February 29, 1864 by Maj. Ragan & October 31, 1864 by Maj. Higgins.
January & February 1863 Company report: Absent on detached service
in Dickson Co., TN. to dispose of private horses since January 20, 1863
by order of Brig. Gen. Gracie and reported sick. Rejoined unit in
February. Paroled April 28, 1865 Macon, GA. Oath of allegiance taken
May 4, 1865 at Chattanooga, TN. Ordered to report to Nashville. Has
family.   Married Mary Ann Spencer (Born January 29, 1840 Died
August 7, 1908) June 13, 1855 in Dickson Co., TN.

Private Dillard H. Lankford "Dee" Born: August 29, 1843 in Dickson
Co., TN.   Died: September 30, 1906.   Buried: Parker-Fowlkes
Cemetery Dickson Co., TN. VA Marker. Enlisted in Baxter's Battery:
December 4, 1862 in Dickson Co., TN. by Capt. E. D. Baxter.
Residence at time of enlistment: Dickson Co., TN.   Height: 5' 8"
Complexion: Fair   Hair: Light   Eyes: Blue   Occupation: Farmer.
Paid: December 31, 1862 by Capt. Hord, February 28, 1863 by Capt.
Hord, April 30, 1863 by Maj. Hord, June 30, 1863 by Capt. Fowler,
October 31, 1863 by Lt. Neal, December 31, 1863 by Maj. Ragan,
February 29, 1864 by Maj. Ragan, April 30, 1864 by Maj. Ragan, &
October 31, 1864 by Maj. Higgins.
Paroled April 28, 1862 in Macon, GA. Oath of allegiance taken May 4,
1865 at Chattanooga, TN.

Tennessee Confederate Pension Application 7273   Rejected.   Filed:
July 28, 1905   Disability: rheumatism of the back.   Physician
signing application: Dr. A. H. Abernathy   Witnesses: Daniel White &
John Dillard   Notary Public: L. D. Wright.   Residence at time of
application: Spencer's Mill (Dickson Co.)   Assets listed in application:
127 acres of poor and badly worn land valued at Three hundred dollars
and personal about $150.   Do you use intoxicants to any extent ? No,
except as medicine.
Witnesses statement: " We was with D.H. Lankford from the time we
enlisted, until the close of the war. We was paroled at Macon, Georgia
28 day of April 1865 and 4 day May 1865 at Chattanooga, Tennessee the
Federals forced us to take oath of allegiance to us or go to U S prison at
the same time we had our paroles in our pockets. We belonged to Capt.
Ed Baxter Battery."

Tennessee Confederate Widow's Pension Application 2163   Filed: November 7, 1908   Accepted.   Kiziah Hays Lankford   Born: October 14, 1843   Dickson Co., TN.   Died: February 23, 1915. Residence Burns PO RR 1.   Married June 14, 1865 in Dickson Co., TN. by James H. Tidwell.   Had 12 children. Witnesses to application: B. F. Brown & J. B. Thompson. Notary Public: T.J. Carr   Dickson County Clerk: T.R. Dickson.

Private Tillman P. Lankford "Till"   Born: October 18, 1832 Dickson Co., TN.   Died: March 1912.   Buried: Jack Lampley Cemetery Dickson Co., TN. VA Marker.   Enlisted in Baxter's Battery: December 15, 1862 in Dickson Co., TN. by Capt. E. D. Baxter. Residence at time of enlistment: Dickson Co., TN.
Height: 5' 7"   Complexion: Fair   Hair: Dark   Eyes: Blue
Occupation: Farmer.
Paid: December 31, 1862 by Capt. Hord, February 28, 1863 by Capt. Hord, April 30, 1864 by Maj. Hord, June 30, 1863 by Capt. Fowler, October 31, 1863 by Lt. Neal, December 31, 1863 by Maj. Ragan, February 29, 1864 by Maj. Ragan & April 30, 1864 by Maj. Ragan. 4th quarter 1864 hospitalized at Lumpkin Hospital Cuthbert, GA. disease not stated in records. Paroled April 28, 1865 at Macon, GA. Oath of allegiance taken May 4, 1865 at Chattanooga, TN.

Tennessee Confederate Pension Application 5504 Accepted .   Filed: August 22, 1903   Disability: lung problems due to measles contracted while in army.   Residence at time of application: Spencer's Mill (Dickson Co.) Physician signing application: Dr. E. W. Ridings Witnesses: W.M. Hogan, John Dillard, J.P. White & B. F. Brown Notary Publics: L.D. Myatt & Samuel Hammon (Co. K 11th Tenn. Infantry) Assets listed in application: 155 acres of land very poor land $200.   Witnesses statement: State of Tennessee Dickson County Personally appeared before me, S. Hammon a Notary Public for said county J.P. White and B.F. Brown and have made oath, that they are personally acquanted with T.P. Lankford, the applicant above mentioned for Pension that said Lankford is a comrade of theirs that said Lankford was a private member of Capt. Ed Baxter's Artillery Company, that said Lankford was sworn into the Confederate Army Dec. 1862. That said Lankford served faithfully and honorably in said Baxter's Artillery until he was taken prisoner at Macon, GA. April 1865. That said Lankford was honorably paroled on the 28th of April 1865 at Macon, GA. That said Lankford had the measles while in line of duty and that they served to greatly affect his lungs. That said Lankford is indigent, aged and physically exhausted that he has no means of support only such physical labor as he is able to perform. That said Lankford was a good faithful and obedient soldier and is a good citizen and neighbor and a strict member of the church. This Feb 5th 1904. J.P. White & B. F. Brown. Married Manerva Lampley (Born 1831 Died 1909) July 3, 1851 in Dickson Co., TN.

Corporal William J. Lankford "Billy" Born: 1841 Dickson Co., TN. Died: June 10, 1910 in 1st District Williamson Co., TN. Buried: ? Memorial VA Stone in Jane Jones Cemetery Fairview, TN. Enlisted in Baxter's Battery: December 5, 1862 in Dickson Co., TN., by Capt. E. D. Baxter. Residence at time of enlistment: Dickson Co., TN.   Height: 5' 10" Complexion: Dark   Hair: Dark   Eyes: Dark   Occupation: Farmer   Promoted to Corporal July 1, 1863 upon promotion of James F. E. Buttrey to Sergeant. Paid: December 31, 1862 by Capt. Hord, February 28, 1863 by Capt. Hord, April 30, 1863 by Maj. Hord & June 30, 1863 by Capt. Fowler. Deserted near Knoxville on August 6, 1863. Married L. Hutchison August 13, 1859 in Dickson Co., TN.

Private Thomas B. Laughlin Born: 1837 Williamson Co., TN. Died: >1880   Buried: Pleasant Hill (Old Finley) Cemetery Dyer Co., TN. ? Enlisted in Baxter's Battery: October 29, 1862 in Williamson Co., TN. by Capt. E. D. Baxter. Residence at time of enlistment: Williamson Co. TN.   Height: 6'   Complexion: Fair   Hair: Light   Eyes: Blue Occupation: Farmer.   Paid: December 31, 1862 by Capt. Hord, February 28, 1863 by Capt. Hord, April 30, 1863 by Maj. Hord, June 30, 1863 by Capt. Fowler, October 31, 1863 by Lt. Neal, December 31, 1863 by Maj. Ragan, February 29, 1864 by Maj. Ragan, April 30, 1864 by Maj. Ragan, & October 31, 1864 by Maj. Higgins. Paroled April 28, 1865 at Macon, GA.   Oath of allegiance taken May 4, 1865 at Chattanooga, TN. Ordered to report to Franklin. No family. Married Virginia A. Halstead January 23, 1869 in Cheatham Co., TN.

Private James G. Lewis   Born: April 13, 1844   Davidson Co., TN. Died: July 30, 1913   Buried: Mt. Liberty Church Cemetery   Dickson Co., TN. VA Marker. Enlisted in Baxter's Battery: November 5, 1862 in Dickson Co., TN. by Capt. E. D. Baxter. Residence at time of enlistment: Cheatham Co., TN. Height: 5' 11"   Complexion: Dark Hair: Black   Eyes: Gray Occupation: Farmer. Paid: December 31, 1862 by Capt. Hord, February 28, 1863 by Capt. Hord, April 30, 1863 by

Maj. Hord, June 30, 1863 by Capt. Fowler, October 31, 1863 by Lt. Neal, December 31, 1863 by Maj. Ragan & February 29, 1864 by Maj. Ragan. February 15, 1863 on detached duty from Knoxville to forage for horses by order of Brig. Gen. Gracie. April 16, 1863 left at Lea's Springs, TN. in charge of non-commissioned officers by order of Brig. Gen. Gracie. May 9, 1863 sick in S. A. Smith Hospital in Mossy Creek, TN. June 21, 1863 captured near New Market, TN. April 16, 1864 in Empire Hospital Atlanta, GA. October 16-27, 1864 and February 6-20, 1865 in Ocmulgee Hospital in Macon, GA. Paroled May 5, 1865 at Milledgeville, GA.

Tennessee Confederate Pension Application 18786   Filed: February 10, 1907   Accepted.   Residence at time of application: Perdue (Dickson Co.)   Disability: Old and disabled to work.   Physician signing application: Dr. M. Harper   Witnesses: John T. Beck & J. J. Johnson. Notary Public: T. H. Whitfield   Dickson County Court Clerk T.R. Dickson.   Assets listed in application: 56 & ½ acres of land valued at $500. Witnesses statement: " We were members of the same company with J.G. Lewis & know that he was parolled with us at Milegville, Georgy at the close of the war & that he was a good soldier & free from dishonor."

Tennessee Confederate Widow's Pension Application 5122   Filed: September 30, 1913   Accepted.   Lucy C. Whitfield Lewis   Born: 1854 Dickson Co. Died: 1922 Witnesses: W. L. Smith & R. A. Duke Notary Public: M. D. Story   Dickson Co. Trustee J. M. Thompson

---

Private Robert B. Loveall Born: 1844 Dickson Co., TN Died: April 13, 1863 of typhoid in Fairgrounds Hospital Knoxville, TN. Buried: Knoxville Confederate Cemetery ? Effects and two blankets valued at $15 turned over to Lt. William Herrin. Enlisted in Baxter's Battery: December 11, 1862 in Dickson Co., TN. by Capt. E. D. Baxter Height: 5' Complexion: Fair Hair: Dark Eyes: Dark Occupation: Farmer Paid: December 31, 1862 & February 28, 1863 by Capt. Hord.

Private John B. Maddox   Born: 1838   Coosa Co., AL.   Died: ? Enlisted: April 7, 1861 in Co. B 3rd Battalion Hillard's Alabama Legion at Clay Hill, AL. by Capt. Boatwright   Height: 5' 6"   Hair: Dark Eyes: Hazel   Complexion: Dark   Occupation: Farmer   Date of Enlistment in Baxter's Battery not stated in records. Granted a 15- day furlough February 15, 1864. Paid: October 31, 1863 by Lt. Neal & December 31, 1863 by Maj. Ragan.

Private John Calvin Mangrum   Born: August 3, 1833   Jefferson Co., TN.   Died: November 27, 1913   Buried: Ranson King Cemetery (destroyed cemetery)   Fairview, TN.   Enlisted in Baxter's Battery: November 9, 1862 in Dickson Co., TN. by Capt. E. D. Baxter. Height: 5' 8"   Complexion: Dark   Hair: Light   Eyes: Blue   Occupation: Farmer   Confederate Reports of June 1, 1863 show deserted at Cumberland Gap.   Federal reports show captured at Richmond, KY. on May 6, 1863. Taken to Lexington, KY. Received at Camp Chase, OH. Prison June 6, 1863. Departed Camp Chase June 20, 1863 for Johnson's Island Prison at Sandusky, Ohio. Sent to Point Lookout, MD. prison on October 30, 1863. Released on oath from Pt. Lookout on April 7, 1864, enlisted in Union Army in 1st United States Volunteer Infantry. Deserted Union Army in September 1864. Married Mary Jane King September 6, 1854 in Williamson Co., TN.

Pvt. John C. Mangrum

Tennessee Confederate Pension Application 12198   Rejected   Filed: October 14, 1910   Disability: double hernia   Physician signing application: Dr. J. P. Hanner   Witnesses: E. G. Sherman & C. W. Boyd   Notary Public: Thomas E. Haynes.   Residence at time of application; Jingo (Williamson Co.)   Assets listed in application: I have no estate of any kind.   Witnesses statement: He made a faithful soldier and no discredit could attach to him.

1st Lieutenant John Marshall, Jr.   Born: 1838   Died: June 5, 1874 (killed in railroad accident at Harpeth River on Northwestern Railroad line).   Buried: Mt. Olivet Cemetery Nashville, TN. Residence at time of enlistment: Franklin, TN. Enlisted in 20th Tennessee Infantry Regiment May 28, 1861 in Franklin for 1 year by Captain Skudder. Elected Orderly Sergeant. Unit accepted into Confederate service June 12, 1861 at Camp Trousdale in Sumner Co., TN. Appointed Captain as Assistant Quartermaster June 12, 1861. Resigned August 15, 1861. Elected 1st Lieutenant of Baxter's Company December 11, 1862 Paid 40 cents per day for use of horse.   Hospitalized at Ocmulgee Hospital Macon, GA. October 7-16, 1864 for recurring fever and October 31 to November 17, 1864 for intermittent fever.

Married Ellen C. McClung of Knox County, TN. Born January 30, 1843 Knox County, TN. Died: ?

(sister of Captain Hugh Lawson McClung of McClung's Battery Tennessee Light Artillery, CSA)

Sergeant James W. Martin   Born: July 5, 1825   Hickman Co., TN. Died: April 3, 1903. Buried: Mt. Hope Cemetery   Franklin, TN. Section A-88   Enlisted in Baxter's Battery: October 30, 1862 in Dickson Co., TN. by Capt. E. D. Baxter.   Residence at time of enlistment: Dickson Co., TN.   Height: 5' 8" Complexion: Dark Hair: Dark   Eyes: Dark   Occupation: Carpenter Reduced in rank from Sergeant on May 1, 1863 for incompetence. Paid $24.80 for use of horse. Hospitalized at Griffin, GA. December 5, 1863. Hospitalized in Ocmulgee Hospital in Macon, GA. October 4-November 19, 1864 for recurring fever and January 31 to February 6, 1865 for intermittent & recurring fever. Surrendered at Leesport, MS. Married Zilphy Brown January 14, 1851 in Dickson Co., TN.

Tennessee Confederate Pension Application 2615   Filed: March 21, 1900   Rejected.   Residence at time of application: Franklin, TN. Assets listed in application: I have none.   Disability: loss of hearing & diarrhea. Application states: "I was not wounded in battle. The disease contacted as a result of which I am deaf, caused by shooting of cannon and diarrhea was contracted while in line around Chattanooga." Physician signing application: Dr J. O. Shannon   Witnesses: E. G. Sherman & John M. Gault.   Notary Public: T. J. Wallace. Witnesses statement: He was a good soldier and never neglected his duty.

Ed Baxter wrote the pension board on his behalf.

1ˢᵗ Sergeant Matthew F. Maury   Born: January 17, 1829   Williamson Co., TN   Died: December 5, 1919.
Buried: Mt. Hope Cemetery   Franklin, TN. Section D-56.   Enlisted in Baxter's Battery: November 10, 1862 in Williamson Co., TN. by Capt. E. D. Baxter.   Height: 5' 9"   Complexion: Fair   Hair: Dark   Eyes: Gray   Occupation: Farmer   Paid $20.80 for use of horse. Detailed to Engineers May 6, 1863 by order of Maj. Gen. Dabney H Maury (his cousin).   Served as 2ⁿᵈ Lieutenant Company F 3ʳᵈ Confederate Engineer Troops. Paroled at Comstock, Georgia May 10, 1865.

Tennessee Confederate Pension Application 13469   Filed: March 19, 1912   Accepted.   Disability: rheumatism.   Physician signing application: Dr. James P. Hanner.   Witnesses: J. L. Sweeney & E. G. Sherman   Notary Publics: E.O. Green & A. O. Maury.   Witnesses statement: They say they both know M. F. Maury. He first was orderly Sergeant in Baxters battery and was afterward transferred to the engineering department. He remained in that service until the surrender of the army. We both know this to be true. We were members of Baxters battery. Nephew of Matthew Fontaine Maury (Pathfinder of the Seas), was his namesake, reared in his home & his education was financed & supervised by his uncle. Married Sarah Eliza Buford (Born: November 4, 1842   Died: September 15, 1918) February 26, 1858 in Williamson Co., TN.

Private Andrew J. May   Born: 1841   Died: ?   Enlisted in Baxter's Battery: September 27, 1862 in Claiborne, Co., TN. by Capt. Dillard. Hospitalized December 1, 1863.   40-day furlough granted February 3, 1864   Sent to hospital in rear at Atlanta on August 7, 1864. Last Paid April 20, 1864 by Maj. Ragan.
Married Sarah Peeps February 19, 1867 in Carter Co., TN.

Private Joshua May   Born: 1846   Died: >1900 Etowah Co., AL. Enlisted in Baxter's Battery: March 5, 1864 in Rockford, AL. by Capt. Hancock.   Residence: Coosa Co., AL.   Entitled to $50 bounty Hospitalized at Ocmulgee Hospital Macon, GA. October 4-27, 1864 for intermittent fever. Last paid April 30, 1864 by Maj. Ragan.

Private William F. May   Born: 1840. Died:?   Enlisted in Baxter's Battery: June 20, 1864 in Rockford, AL. by Capt. Hancock. Residence: Coosa Co., AL.   Height: 5'5"   Complexion: Fair   Hair: Dark

Eyes: Gray   Served in B Company 38th Tennessee Infantry. Wounded at Shiloh April 1862. Captured April 21, 1865 at Macon, GA. Paroled May 24, 1865 at Montgomery, AL. at 16th Army Corps Headquarters.

Private James R. McCallister   Born: 1820   South Carolina   Died: ? Enlisted: September 16, 1862 in (New) Co. A (Anthony Grays) 60th Regiment of Georgia Volunteer Infantry, Army of Northern Virginia, in Meriwether Co., GA. as a substitute for Adrian O. Trammell. Deserted at camp near Drewry's Bluff, VA. October 20, 1862. Enlisted in Baxter's Battery May 18, 1864 in Fulton Co. GA. by Capt. E. D. Baxter. Due $25 bounty. Hospitalized at Ocmulgee Hospital Macon, GA. October 19-November 19, 1864 for intermittent fever. Never Paid. In 1880 resided in Decatur, GA. (DeKalb Co.)

Sergeant Alfred A. McCaslin "Mac" Born: 1844   Dickson Co., TN. Died: February 16, 1928 at Stone Bluff, Oklahoma   Enlisted in Baxter's Battery: November 9, 1862 in Dickson Co., TN. by Capt. E. D. Baxter. Residence at time of enlistment: Dickson Co., TN. Height: 5' 6"   Complexion: Dark   Hair: Dark   Eyes: Dark   Occupation: Farmer. Paid: December 31, 1862 by Capt. Hord, February 28, 1863 by Capt. Hord, April 30, 1863 by Maj. Hord, June 30, 1863 by Capt. Fowler, October 31, 1863 by Lt. Neal, December 31, 1863 by Maj. Ragan, February 29, 1864 by Maj. Ragan, & April 30, 1864 by Maj. Ragan. Appointed Sergeant July 1, 1863 upon reassignment of A. P. Beard. Reduced from Sergeant December 12, 1864 for incompentcy, inefficiency and neglect of duty. Hospitalized in Ocmulgee Hospital Macon, GA. October 13-27, 1864 & January 3-March 28, 1865 for intermittent fever. Paroled April 28, 1865 at Macon, GA. Oath of Allegiance taken May 4, 1865 at Chattanooga, TN. Ordered to report to Nashville. No family.

Oklahoma Confederate Pension 4729. Application # 5834. Approved July 7, 1924 Disability: Old age Witnesses: Claud Woods & W. S. Gibson. Notary D. Edmonds Muskogee Co., OK. Wesley Welch & John Dillard Notary Public J. W. Herrin Dickson Co., TN. Witness statement of Wesley Welch: "That I walked home from Macon, Ga. with Alfred A. McCaslin after the surrender & stayed with him through the entire war. That there are only a few of our battery left to witness."

Private James A. McCowan   Born: 1846   Died: ?   Enlisted in Baxter's Battery: April 27, 1864 in Fulton Co., GA. by Capt. E. D.

Baxter. Residence at time of enlistment: Clayton Co., GA. In 1870 resided in Forsythe, GA. (Monroe Co.) Sent to General Hospital in Macon, GA. October 10-November 9, 1864 by Surgeon Murphy for recurring fever. Never paid.

Corporal James McCrory Born: 1830 Dickson Co., TN. Died: June 7, 1863 of typhoid in camp in Grainger Co., TN. Buried: unmarked grave near Bean Station, TN. Enlisted in Baxter's Battery: December 3, 1862 at McMinnville, TN. by Capt. Butler (widow's pension application states enlisted in Franklin, TN. in 1862 by Capt. E. D. Baxter) Height: 5' 5" Complexion: Fair Hair: Dark Eyes: Blue Occupation: Saddle tree maker.. Paid: December 31, 1862 by Capt. Hord, February 28, 1863 by Capt. Hord & April 30, 1864 by Maj. Hord. Letter of administration received by Lt. Herrin from Knox County Court to attend to personal effects, after his death.

Tennessee Confederate Widow's Indigent Pension 2778 Filed: July 22, 1909 Accepted Evaline Cummins McCrory Residence: Bellevue Davidson Co., TN. Born: 1831 in Davidson Co., TN Married: October 13, 1855 in Davidson Co., TN. by W. G. Smith, J.P. Had two sons born March 1860 and February 17, 1862. Witnesses: J.B. Thompson & T.J. Carr. Notary Public: T.L. Herrin Davidson County Trustee: P.M. Tamble

---

Corporal William McCrory Born: December 19, 1841 Williamson Co., TN. Died: February 11, 1882 Bellevue, Davidson Co., TN. Buried: Old McCrory Cemetery Pasquo, TN. (Davidson Co.) Enlisted in Baxter's Battery: November 18, 1862 in Williamson Co., TN. by Capt. E. D. Baxter. Residence at time of enlistment: Davidson Co., TN. Height: 5' 10" Complexion: Fair Hair: Dark Eyes: Blue Occupation: Farmer. Paid: December 31, 1862 by Capt. Hord, February 28, 1863 by Capt. Hord, April 30, 1863 by Maj. Hord, June 30, 1863 by Capt. Fowler, October 31, 1863 by Lt. Neal, December 31, 1863 by Maj. Ragan, February 29, 1864 by Maj. Ragan, April 30, 1864 by Maj. Ragan, & October 31, 1864 by Maj. Higgins. Appointed Corporal March 8, 1863 upon discharge of Edwin Paschall. Resigned as Corporal August 1, 1863. No pay due as Sergeant at $17 per month. One month pay due as private at $13 per month. Hospitalized at Ocmulgee Hospital Macon, GA. October 7-12, 1864 for intermittent fever . Paroled April 28, 1865 at Macon, GA. Oath of Allegiance taken May 4, 1865 at Chattanooga, TN.

Tennessee Confederate Widow's Pension Application 2308 Filed: February 17, 1909 Accepted Nannie Jane Taylor McCrory Born: July 29, 1851 Williamson Co., TN. Died: 1929 Buried: Mt. Hope Cemetery (Sec. G) Franklin, TN. Residence: PO Franklin, TN. RFD #1. Married: July 19, 1870 in Davidson Co., TN. by Rev. John Cox. Had one child. Witnesses: W. T. Parker, J. W. Deck, MD., J. L. Sweeney & C. A. Bond. Notary Public: R. L. Kennedy Williamson Co. Trustee W. T. Robinson.

Private Freeling H. McKay Born: February 29, 1844 Williamson Co., TN. Died: December 12, 1895. Buried: McKay Cemetery off Berry's Chapel Road 8th District of Williamson Co., TN. Enlisted in Baxter's Battery: November 7, 1862 in Williamson Co., TN. by Capt. E. D. Baxter. Residence at time of enlistment: Williamson Co., TN. Height: 5' 11" Complexion: Fair Hair: Black Eyes: Dark Occupation: Farmer Captured at Franklin, TN. while on duty December 27, 1862. Prisoner at Louisville, KY. on May 2, 1863. Discharged July 7, 1863 to Baltimore, MD. to City Point, VA. Hospitalized at Ocmulgee Hospital Macon, GA. from October 7-26, 1864 for recurring fever and November 4-7, 1864 diagnosis; nothing. Married Tennie Ballow (Born: November 8, 1846 Died: April 21, 1902) December 2, 1869 in Williamson Co., TN.

Private John W. McLaughlin Born: 1835 Williamson Co., TN. Died: April 18, 1867 Buried: Big Springs Cemetery Dickson Co., TN. Enlisted in Baxter's Battery: December 10, 1862 in Dickson Co., TN. by Capt. E. D. Baxter. Residence at time of enlistment Dickson Co., TN. Height: 5' 8" Complexion: Fair Hair: Dark Eyes: Blue Occupation: Farmer. Paid: December 31, 1862 by Capt. Hord, February 28, 1863 by Capt. Hord, April 30, 1863 by Maj. Hord, June 30, 1863 by Capt. Fowler, October 31, 1863 by Lt. Neal, December 31, 1863 by Maj. Ragan, February 29, 1864 by Maj. Ragan, April 30, 1864 by Maj. Ragan, & October 31, 1864 by Maj. Higgins. Hospitalized at Ocmulgee Hospital Macon, GA. October 19-26,1864 for intermittent fever. Paroled April 28, 1865 at Macon, GA. Oath of allegiance taken May 4, 1865 at Chattanooga, TN. Ordered to report to Nashville. Married Serena H. Clark February 4, 1855 in Dickson Co., TN.

Private William McPherson Born: 1829 Williamson Co., TN. Died:? Buried: McPherson Family Cemetery Old Franklin Road Fairview, TN. (near Turnbull Creek) VA Marker. Enlisted in Baxter's Battery:

November 5, 1862 in Williamson Co., TN. by Capt. E. D. Baxter. Height: 5' 8" Complexion: Fair Hair: Dark Eyes: Dark Occupation: Farmer. Paid: April 30, 1863 by Capt. Cate. Absent on 15-day sick furlough on December 31, 1862. Left Cumberland Gap sick March 29, 1863 on order of Surgeon W. T. Abrahams. Sent to Hospital in Knoxville. June 18, 1863 granted a 30-day furlough by Surgeon W. C. Hillard of Fairgrounds Hospital in Knoxville. Not heard from since, presumed deserted. Married Sarah Hullett February 21, 1851 in Williamson Co., TN. Married Susan McPherson February 25, 1875.

Private John B. Moore "Bailey" Born: 1835 Dickson Co., TN. Died: April 27, 1863 in hospital at Tullahoma, TN. Buried: Tullahoma Confederate Cemetery Tullahoma, TN. Enlisted: December 19, 1861 in Company C 44th Tennessee Infantry Regiment at Camp Trousdale (Sumner Co., TN.) . Dropped from rolls of 44th on March 8, 1863 by order of General Braxton Bragg. Transferred to Baxter's Battery. Does not appear on muster roll of Baxter's Battery, died before joining up with the Company.
Married Lucy Redden.

Private William A. Moore Born: June 1, 1842 Died: March 4, 1912 Buried: Rest Haven Cemetery Franklin, TN. Enlisted: April 1, 1863 at Tullahoma, TN. by Lt. Cross for 3 years. Residence: Williamson Co., TN. Height: 6' Complexion: Light Hair: Brown Eyes: Gray. Paid: December 31, 1863 by Maj. Ragan, February 29, 1864 by Maj. Ragan & April 30, 1864 by Maj. Ragan. Transferred from Company I 44th Consolidated Tennessee Infantry Regiment to Baxter's Battery on November 1, 1863 by order of Gen. Braxton Bragg. Hospitalized in Ocmulgee Hospital Macon, GA. October 7-27, 1864 for intermittent fever. Paroled April 28, 1865 at Macon, GA. Oath of allegiance taken May 4, 1865 at Chattanooga, TN. Ordered to report to Nashville. No family. Married Elizah Ann Ezell February 15, 1866 in Williamson Co., TN.

Private James Rad Morrow Born: September 12, 1845 Henry Co., GA. Died: August 2, 1929 in Atlanta, GA. Hair: Auburn Eyes: Yellow Complexion: Fair Height: 5' 5" Occupation: Farmer. Enlisted in Co. D (Clayton County Guards aka Estes Guards) 44th Regiment Georgia Volunteer Infantry, Army of Northern Virginia. Discharged due to disability at camp near Richmond, VA. on July 16, 1862. Enlisted in Baxter's Battery April 18, 1864. Residence:

Campbell Co., GA. Hospitalized at Ocmulgee Hospital Macon, GA. October 4-November 16, 1864 for recurring fever. Never paid. Furloughed home from Macon, GA. to be married March 25, 1865. Furlough to expire April 14, 1865.

Georgia Confederate Pension Application filed August 6, 1901 in Douglas County. Disability: Rheumatism, effects of typhoid and lung disorder. Assets: $20 to $30. Witness: John T. Walker Witness statement: "Enlisted in 1864 in Baxter's Battery Martin's Battalion Co. A. Served until the close of the war and was paroled during which time he made a first class soldier. Was paroled at Macon, Ga." Physicians signing application: Dr. O. H. Harris & Dr. T. R. Whitley. H. T. Cooper Douglas County Ordinary. Pension later transferred to Paulding County, GA.

Private Joseph C. Nall   Born: February 15, 1842   Died: March 19, 1888   Buried: New Hope Cemetery   Fairview, TN. VA Marker. Residence at time of enlistment: Williamson Co., TN. Height: 5' 8" Hair: Dark Eyes: Hazel Complexion: Fair   Paid: June 30, 1863 by Capt. Fowler, October 31, 1863 by Lt. Neal, December 31, 1863 by Maj. Ragan & February 29, 1864 by Maj. Ragan. Oath of Allegiance taken March 19, 1864 in Nashville by Capt. R. M. Goodwin, Assistant Provost Marshall, Department of the Cumberland.   Name appears on Roll of 10 rebel deserters released on oath of amnesty at Nashville, TN. March 19, 1864. Married Callie C. Bateman January 24, 1864 in Williamson Co., TN.

Private Linden A. Nall   Born: 1834   Died: >1880 Graves Co., KY. ? Buried: ?   Enlisted in Baxter's Battery: March 13, 1863(some records show enlistment date as March 15 & March 23, 1863) in Columbia, TN. by Maj. Nicholson.   Residence at time of enlistment: Dickson Co., TN. Entitled to bounty. Paid: June 30, 1863 by Capt. Fowler, October 31, 1863 by Lt. Neal, December 31, 1863 by Maj. Ragan, February 29, 1864 by Maj. Ragan, April 30, 1864 by Maj. Ragan, & October 31, 1864 by Maj. Higgins. Hospitalized at Ocmulgee Hospital Macon, GA. October 20-27, 1864. Paroled April 28, 1865 at Macon, GA. Oath of allegiance taken May 4, 1865 at Chattanooga, TN. Has family.   Married Martha Sellars January 3, 1859 in Dickson Co., TN.

Private George W. Neely   Born: 1836 Davidson Co., TN.   Died: ? Enlisted in Baxter's Battery: November 7, 1862 in Williamson Co., TN. by Capt. E. D. Baxter.   Height: 5' 9"   Complexion: Fair   Hair:

Red   Eyes: Blue   Occupation: Carpenter.   Left Cumberland Gap
sick March 27, 1863 by order of Surgeon W. T. Abrahams.   Sent to
hospital in Knoxville.   Last paid April 30, 1863 by Capt. Fowler .
Deserted near Knoxville August 6, 1863.

Private John Norris   Born: 1838   Died: February 4, 1865 of chronic
diarrhea at Union Prison at Camp Douglas, IL.   Buried: Block 3
Chicago City Cemetery.   Moved to mass Confederate grave in Oak
Woods Cemetery Chicago in 1867.   Enlisted in Baxter's Battery: April
18, 1864 at Fulton Co., GA.   Residence: Campbell Co., GA.   Entitled
to $50 bounty.   Deserted.   Captured at Decatur, GA. on September 8,
1864 by 23rd A. C. Department of Ohio.   Received at military prison and
turned over to Army of the Cumberland September 10, 1864.   Last paid
April 30, 1864 by Maj. Ragan.   Camp Douglas listing shows him
belonging to Company A of Georgia Reserve Artillery.

Private   Lindrey M. Norris   Born: 1844   Died: ?   Enlisted in
Baxter's Battery: July 11, 1864 in Fulton Co., GA. By Lt. William
Herrin Residence: Campbell Co., GA   Height: 5' 7"   Complexion:
Fair   Hair: Light   Eyes: Hazel   Deserted & captured at Decatur,
GA. on September 8, 1864.   Turned over to Army of the Cumberland
September 10, 1864.   Oath of allegiance taken November 18, 1864 at
Chattanooga, TN.   Last record in Military Prison Hospital in
Chattanooga on December 5, 1864.

Private Reuben J. Norris   Born: 1845   Died: >1924   Enlisted in
Baxter's Battery: April 18, 1864 Fulton Co., GA.   Residence: Campbell
County, GA.   Wounded by shell fragment September 8, 1864 near
Jonesboro, GA.   Home on furlough at time of surrender.   (No service
records found on Reuben Norris)

Georgia Confederate Pension Application   Filed: October 27, 1923 in
Fulton County.   Disability: not stated   Assets: none   Witness: J. T.
Walker.   Witness statement: "He was home on sick furlough at time of
surrender."   30- day furlough granted by Captain in command.   Fulton
County Ordinary Arthur R. Marbert.

Private Andrew J. Parker "Andy"   Born: 1844 Dickson Co., TN.
Died: >1880   Hickman Co., TN. ? Enlisted in Baxter's Battery:
December 4, 1862 in Dickson Co., TN. by Capt. E. D. Baxter
Residence at time of enlistment: Dickson Co., TN.   Height: 5' 7"

Complexion: Fair   Hair: Dark   Eyes: Dark   Occupation: Farmer.
Paid: December 31, 1862 by Capt. Hord, February 28, 1863 by Capt.
Hord, April 30, 1864 by Maj. Hord, June 30, 1863 by Capt. Fowler,
October 31, 1863 by Lt. Neal, December 31, 1863 by Maj. Ragan,
February 29, 1864 by Maj. Ragan & April 30, 1864 by Maj. Ragan. Sent
to hospital in Macon, GA. October 4, 1864 to March 8, 1865 for
intermittent fever by Assistant Surgeon Stuart. Paroled April 28, 1864 at
Macon, GA. Oath of allegiance taken May 4, 1865 at Chattanooga, TN.

Private Thomas Jefferson Parker "Jeff"   Born: January 27, 1842
Dickson Co., TN.   Died: April 15, 1914.   Buried: Parker-Fowlkes
Cemetery Dickson Co., TN. VA Marker.   Enlisted in Baxter's Battery:
December 30, 1862 in Dickson Co., TN. by Capt. E. D. Baxter.
Residence at time of enlistment: Dickson Co., TN.   Height: 5' 11"
Complexion: Fair   Hair: Sandy   Eyes: Hazel   Occupation:
Farmer. Paid: December 31, 1862 by Capt. Hord, February 28, 1863 by
Capt. Massengale, April 30, 1863 by Maj. Hord, June 30, 1863 by Capt.
Fowler, October 31, 1863 by Lt. Neal, December 31, 1863 by Maj.
Ragan, February 29, 1864 by Maj. Ragan & April 30, 1864 by Maj.
Ragan. February 15, 1863 detailed from Knoxville to forage for horses
by order of Brig. Gen. Gracie. Hospitalized in Ocmulgee Hospital
Macon, GA. October 16-November 7, 1864. Paroled April 28, 1865 at
Macon, GA. Oath of Allegiance taken May 4, 1865 at Chattanooga, TN.
No family.

Tennessee Confederate pension application 3457   Filed: June 18, 1901
re-filed under class "5" July 28, 1903 accepted.   1st application:
Disability: crippled, left knee stiff & hip badly shrunken. Physician
signing application: Dr. E. W. Ridings. Witnesses: F. F. Tidwell & W.
J. Mathis   Notary Public: W. B. Williams

2nd application: Disability: chronic bowel trouble & kidney trouble.
Physician signing application: Dr. E. W. Ridings.   Witnesses: John
Dillard, T. P. Lankford, J. F. Cunningham & T. J. Carr.   Notary Publics:
L. D. Wright & Samuel Hammon.   Residence at time of application:
Spencers Mill (Dickson Co.). Assets listed in application: None.
Witnesses statement: "That the applicant was a good soldier while in the
army & has bin a good and lawful citizen since the war." John Dillard &
T.P. Lankford
Personally appeared before me S. Hammon a notary public for said
county. J.F. Cunningham and T.J. Carr and made with in due form of

law that they are personally acquainted with T.J. Parker the applicant for pension being member of the same company with him in the Confederate army and that said Parker contracted diabetis and also diarrhea while in actual service in front of Chattanooga, Tenn.   In the fall and winter of 1863 from which diseases he seems to never have recovered and that he was honorably paroled at Macon, GA. April 28, 1865 and that he is in indigent circumstances is not the owner of any property either real personal or mixed except wearing apparel having no home or any children able to support & maintain him is now not physically able to care & support for himself. J.F. Cunningham & T.J. Carr sworn and subscribed Nov. 5, 1903.   Married Mary Harbison December 20, 1856 in Dickson Co., TN.

Private William S. Parrish   Born: 1834   Died: >1901   In 1900 resided in Atlanta.   Enlisted as 4th Sergeant of Co. H (Baldwin Co. Independent Volunteers) 57th Regiment Georgia Volunteer Infantry, Army of Tennessee on May 10, 1862. Reduced to ranks February 1863. Discharged   May 4, 1863 (or August 4, 1863).   Enlisted in Baxter's Battery July 15, 1864 in Fulton Co., GA. by Lt. William Herrin. Paroled April 28, 1865 at Macon, GA. Never paid.

Corporal Edwin Paschall   Born: April 15,1832   Granville Co., NC. Died: August 26, 1868   Cheatham Co., TN.   Buried: Rest Haven Cemetery Franklin, TN.   Enlisted in Co. C   1st Tennessee Cavalry Regiment May 28, 1861 at Franklin, TN.   Transferred to Humes' Belmont Battery October 16, 1861 and discharged January 1862. Enlisted in Baxter's Battery: November 24, 1862 in Williamson Co., TN. by Capt. E. D. Baxter.   Residence at time of enlistment: Williamson Co., TN.   Height: 5' 11" Complexion: Fair   Hair: Light   Eyes: Gray   Occupation: School teacher. Last paid December 31, 1862 by Capt. Hord. Medical discharge and final statement given March 7, 1863 at Cumberland Gap for secondary syphilis.   Later enlisted in Co. F 4th Tennessee Cavalry Regiment (The Williamson County Calvary).

Private George Peach Born: 1830   Williamson Co., TN. Died: >1880 Buried: Forehand Cemetery   Bellevue, TN. (Unmarked grave   ?) Enlisted in Baxter's Battery: November 24, 1862 in Williamson Co., TN. by Capt. E. D. Baxter.   Height: 5' 7"   Complexion: Fair   Hair: Light Eyes: Gray   Occupation: Farmer   AWOL January 1, 1863 In Williamson Co. believed deserted.   Married Emily Sears January 2,

1856 in Williamson Co., TN. Married Arbell Peach July 20, 1865 in Williamson Co., TN.

Private George A. Petty   Born: 1838   Davidson Co., TN.   Died: ? Enlisted in Baxter's Battery: November 7, 1862 in Williamson Co., TN. by Capt. E. D. Baxter.   Height: 5' 6"   Complexion: Dark   Hair: Dark   Eyes: Blue   Occupation: Boilermaker.   AWOL believed deserted January 4, 1863. Never paid.

Private Lewis H. Posey   Born: 1843   South Carolina   Died: June 1926 Jefferson Co., AL. Residence: Edgefield District, SC. Enlisted: March 11, 1862 at Marengo Co., AL. by Capt. Jones.   Absent since April 25, 1864 on 40-day furlough from Macon, GA. approved by Gen. Johnson. Hospitalized at Ocmulgee Hospital Macon, GA. October 7-11, 1864 for intermittent fever. Last paid October 31, 1864 by Maj. Higgins. On furlough at time of capture and parole.

Private James W. Powell   Born: 1845   Alabama   Died: >1880 Enlisted: August 5, 1861 in Co. B (Spring Place Volunteers) 3rd Battalion Georgia Volunteer Infantry, Army of Tennessee in Murray Co., GA.   Roll for December 31, 1862, last on file, shows him absent, drillmaster at Haynesville. Enlisted in Baxter's Battery June 8, 1864 in Fulton Co., GA. by Capt. E. D. Baxter.   July 22, 1864 wounded by minie ball in right leg, sent to Hood Hospital in Cuthbert, GA. in rear at Atlanta.   March 24, 1865 returned to duty. Never paid. In 1880 resided in DeKalb Co., AL.

Private George C. Randol   Born: 1846   Died: >1880   Enlisted in Baxter's Battery: November 14, 1864 in Corinth, MS. by Capt. E. D. Baxter.   Residence: Mississippi Co., MO.   Height: 5' 10" Complexion: Light   Hair: Light   Eyes: Blue   Paroled April 28, 1865 at Macon, GA.   Oath of Allegiance taken May 4, 1865 at Chattanooga, TN.   Name appears on roll of rebel prisoners of war received at Louisville from Nashville dated May 8, 1865. Took oath and was paroled to go North of the Ohio River May 9, 1865 at Louisville. $50 bounty due, never paid. In 1880 was a lawyer in Galena, Stone Co., MO.

Private John Ratteree   Born: February 4, 1834   Lancaster, South Carolina   Died: November 22, 1922   Buried: New High Shoal Church Cemetery   Dallas, GA. Enlisted in Baxter's Battery: June 2, 1864 in

Fulton Co., GA. by Capt. E. D. Baxter. Residence at time of enlistment: Paulding Co., GA. Never Paid. Also served as Sergeant in Company D 1st Georgia Regiment of State Troops. Discharged April 25, 1865 at Calhoun, GA. Married Ann Anderson October 30, 1859 in Paulding Co., GA.

Georgia Confederate Pension application   Filed September 20, 1920 in Paulding County. Disability: not stated. Assets: not stated. Witness: W. M. Turner. W. J. Baker Paulding County Ordinary.

Private William Reed   Born: 1831   Died: 1910 Knox Co., TN. Enlisted in Baxter's Battery: August 2, 1863 in Knox Co., TN. by Lt. William Herrin. Deserted August 19, 1863 near Knoxville. Never paid.

Private James Richardson   Born: 1829 Coffee Co., TN.   Died: ? Buried: Richardson Family Cemetery   Walker Road near Old Franklin Road in Fairview, TN. (unmarked grave ?) Enlisted in Baxter's Battery: November 5, 1862 in Williamson Co., TN. by Capt. E.D. Baxter. Residence at time of enlistment: Williamson Co., TN.   Height: 6' Complexion: Fair   Hair: Dark   Eyes: Blue   Occupation: Farmer (after war worked as a store clerk). Paid: December 31, 1862 by Capt. Hord, February 28, 1863 by Capt. Hord, April 30, 1863 by Capt. Cate, June 30, 1863 by Capt. Fowler, October 31, 1863 by Lt. Neal, December 31, 1863 by Maj. Ragan, February 29, 1864 by Maj. Ragan, April 30, 1864 by Maj. Ragan, & October 31, 1864 by Maj. Higgins.   Left Cumberland Gap sick by order of Surgeon Abrahams on March 29, 1863. Sent to hospital in Knoxville. Hospitalized in Ocmulgee Hospital Macon, GA. October 10-12, 1864 for intermittent fever . Paroled April 28, 1865 in Macon, GA.   Oath of allegiance taken May 4, 1865 at Chattanooga, TN. Ordered to report to Nashville.

Tennessee Confederate Pension Application 2710   Accepted   Filed: April 27, 1900.   Residence at time of application: Aden (Williamson Co.) Disability: paralysis of lower extremities and dropsy.   Physician signing application: Dr. W. F. Black   Witnesses: W. W. Walker, A. P. Beard, William Bethshears, J.F. Cunningham, J.F. Buttrey, John M. Gault & E. G. Sherman.   Notary public: T. J. Wallace.
State of Tennessee County of Williamson personally appeared before me, J.W. Hendricks, a Notary Public in and for said county and State duly elected, commissioned and sworn, J.F. Cunningham & J. F. Buttrey who being sworn according to law. Says that they was in the same

company with James A Richardson was well acquainted with him before the war and know he did not have rheumatism when he went into the army and that he taken rheumatism at Cumberland Gap and was sent to the Hospital and was there about three months. He went to the Hospital in Feby 1863 and came back to camps in May 1863 he was not well then. J.F. Cunningham, J.F. Buttrey. Sworn and Subscribed to before me this July 13, 1903 J.W. Hendricks Notary Public. Letter dated August 4-03 Camp Fraizer, Franklin, Tenn. from W.J. Whitehorne to Capt. John P. Hickman of the pension board states Jas. A. Richardson is a member of Leonidas Polk Bivouac, a guarantee of good record and a deserving man. (Note- this letter appears to be in reference to another James Richardson of Maury County who served in the 3rd TN. Infantry Regiment) Married Mary C. T. Orman June 28, 1853.

Private Isham Roberts   Born: 1839   Maury Co., TN.   Died: >1880 Enlisted in Baxter's Battery: November 22, 1862 in Williamson Co., TN. by Capt. E. D. Baxter   Height: 5' 7"   Complexion: Dark   Hair: Dark   Eyes: Blue   Occupation: Farmer.   Paid: December 31, 1862 by Capt. Hord & April 28, 1863 by Capt. Hord.   Confederate report of June 1, 1863 show deserted at Cumberland Gap.   Federal reports show captured May 6, 1863 at Richmond, KY.   Sent to Lexington, KY., to Camp Chase, Ohio.   June 20, 1863 sent to Johnson's Island Prison in Sandusky, Ohio.   October 30, 1863 sent to prison at Point Lookout, MD. Released on oath April 12, 1864.   Married Eliza J. Pace October 5, 1858 in Williamson Co., TN.

Private Samuel H. Saunders   Born: February 28, 1838   Maury Co., TN.   Died: April 4, 1913   Buried: Mt. Hope Cemetery   Franklin, TN. (unmarked grave)   Enlisted in Baxter's Battery: November 20, 1862 in Williamson Co., TN. by Capt. E. D. Baxter.   Height: 5' 7" Complexion: Fair   Hair: Dark   Eyes: Gray   Occupation: Cooper . Detailed as a government cooper by special order number 19 exact by Gen. Braxton Bragg dated Murfreesboro December 9, 1862. Deserted time & place unknown. Married Eliza J. Potts February 13, 1862

Private John Sayers   Born: 1826   Wythe Co., VA.   Died: ?   Buried: Mt. Hope Cemetery   Franklin, TN. (unmarked grave ?)   Enlisted in Baxter's Battery: November 29, 1862 in Williamson Co., TN. by Capt. E. D. Baxter.   Height: 6'   Complexion: Fair   Hair: Light   Eyes: Blue   Occupation: Farmer   Paid: December 31, 1862 by Capt. Hord,

February 28, 1863 by Capt. Hord, April 30, 1863 by Maj. Hord, June 30, 1863 by Capt. Fowler, October 31, 1863 by Lt. Neal, February 29, 1864 by Maj. Ragan, April 30, 1864 by Maj. Ragan & October 31, 1864 by Maj. Higgins.   Married Emeline Crowder December 26, 1878 in Williamson Co., TN

Private (Company Physician) Dr. Robert Baldwin Sayers "Bob"   Born: December 24, 1836 Talladega, AL. Died: July 28, 1901. Buried: Mt. Hope Cemetery Franklin, TN. Section A.   Enlisted in Baxter's Battery: November 5, 1862 in Williamson Co., TN.   Complexion: Fair   Hair: Dark   Eyes: Dark   Occupation: Physician Permanently detailed as company physician, paid 25 cents per day extra.   April 29, 1863 ordered to Lea's Springs, TN. by Capt. Baxter to bring medicine.   March 13, 1863 paid $96 by Maj. E. L. Hord for service from November 5, 1862 to February 28, 1863, $50 bounty included.   Left sick in Bean Station May 19, 1863 by order of Chief Surgeon W. T. Abrhams.   Detailed to hospital service by order of Gen. Simon Bolivar Buckner. Copy of order not furnished.   Later captured and took oath. Paid on descriptive list. Wife Josephine Sayers   Born: November 19, 1846   Died: May 13, 1871

Private Robert S. Scales   Born: August 12, 1843   Williamson Co., TN. Died: October 14, 1863. Buried: Absalom Scales Cemetery Rutherford Co., TN. (site was originally in Williamson Co.) Enlisted in Co. D 20th Tennessee Infantry   May 27, 1861 in Williamson Co., TN. by Capt. Scudder. Discharged August 1, 1861.   Enlisted in Baxter's Battery: November 8, 1862 in Williamson Co., TN. by Capt. E. D. Baxter. Height: 6' 1"   Complexion: Fair   Hair: Light   Eyes: Blue Occupation: Farmer. Paid December 31, 1862 by Capt. Hord. Medical discharge and final statement given at Cumberland Gap March 7, 1863 for hypertrophy of the heart.

Sergeant Hiram Sears   Born: 1825 Dickson Co., TN. Died: January 20, 1864 of chronic diarrhea in Catoosa Hospital Griffin, GA.   Buried: Confederate Cemetery   Griffin, GA.   Enlisted in Baxter's Battery: October 20, 1862 in Dickson Co., TN. by Capt. E. D. Baxter   Height: 5' 7"   Complexion: Dark   Hair: Dark   Eyes: Dark   Occupation Farmer.   Paid: December 31, 1862 by Capt. Hord, February 28, 1863 by Capt. Hord, April 30, 1863 by Maj. Hord, June 30, 1863 by Capt. Fowler, & October 31, 1863 by Capt. Bomar. $24.80 paid for use of horse. May 1, 1863 reduced in rank from Sergeant for incompetence. December 5, 1863 sent to Catoosa Hospital in Griffin, GA. Married Parthena Glass November 5, 1845 in Dickson Co., TN.

Private Joseph Marion Sears   Born: 1838   Dickson Co., TN.   Died: >1870 Fannin Co., TX. ? Enlisted in Baxter's Battery: November 27, 1862 in Williamson Co., TN. by Capt. E. D. Baxter. Residence at time of enlistment: Dickson Co., TN.   Height: 6'   Complexion: Light Hair: Light   Eyes: Dark   Occupation: Farmer   Hospitalized at Ocmulgee Hospital Macon, GA. October 16-26, 1864 for intermittent fever and January 3-16, 1865 with intermittent fever and February 4, 1865 for intermittent fever. Last paid October 31, 1864 by Maj. Higgins.

Sergeant Eli Gould Sherman   Born: April 3, 1836 in Augusta., GA. Died: September 12, 1916 Franklin, TN.   Buried: Mt. Hope Cemetery Franklin, TN. Section F-51.   Enlisted in Baxter's Battery: November 19, 1862 in Williamson Co., TN. by Capt. E. D. Baxter. Residence at time of enlistment: Williamson Co., TN.   Height: 5'10 ½ " Complexion: Fair   Hair: Dark   Eyes: Hazel   Occupation: Harness maker and saddle maker. Paid: December 31, 1862 by Capt. Hord, February 28, 1863 by Capt. Hord, April 30, 1863 by Maj. Hord, June 30, 1863 by Capt. Fowler, October 31, 1863 by Lt. Neal, December 31, 1863 by Maj. Ragan, February 29, 1864 by Maj. Ragan & April 30, 1864 by Maj. Ragan. Paid $17.20 for use of horse. Promoted to Sergeant upon demotion of Hiram Sears on May 1, 1863. Absent since December 27, 1863 furlough granted by Lt. Gen. Hardee. Entitled to compensation for undrawn clothing up to October 1863 balance due $24.17.   Sent to General Hospital in Macon, GA. on October 4, 1864 by Assistant Surgeon Stuart. Captured by 1st Brigade of 2nd Calvary Division April 21, 1865 at Macon, GA. Paroled at Macon, GA. April 28, 1865. Oath of allegiance taken May 4, 1865 at Chattanooga, TN. Ordered to report to Franklin. Has family. He was a member of McEwen Bivouac #4 Association of Confederate Soldiers, Tennessee Division Franklin, TN.

Tennessee Confederate Widow's Pension Application 6531   Filed: October 17, 1916 Accepted.   Sue Jones Sherman   Born: March 11, 1844 Williamson Co., TN. Died: 1926. Buried: Mt. Hope Cemetery Franklin, TN.   Section F-51   Residence: Franklin, TN.   Married: November 20, 1877 by Elder E. B. Cayce at Hillsboro, TN. Had 2 children.   Witnesses: W. W. Courtney & R. T. Cotton. Notary Public: R. G. Courtney. Williamson Co. Trustee B. B. Roberts

---

Private George Smallwood   Born: May 16, 1840 Baldwin Co., GA. Died: >1920 Harper's School House, AL. (Houston Co.)   Enlisted in Co. G 61st Georgia Regiment Volunteer Infantry, Army of Northern Virginia in Wilkes County, GA.   Enlisted in Baxter's Battery October 25, 1864 in Macon, GA by Lt. John Marshall. Paid: October 31, 1864 by Maj. Higgins.

Private William T. Smith   Born: 1835   Hickman Co., TN. Died: ? Enlisted in Baxter's Battery: November 7, 1862 in Williamson Co., TN. by Capt. E. D. Baxter.   Height: 5' 7"   Complexion: Fair   Hair: Red   Eyes: Blue   Occupation: Farmer Paid: December 31, 1862 by Capt. Hord, February 28, 1863 by Capt. Hord, & April 30, 1863 by Maj. Hord. Confederate report of June 1, 1863 shows deserted at Cumberland Gap. Federal reports show captured at Richmond, KY. May 6, 1863. Sent to Lexington, KY. to Camp Chase, OH. Prison. Sent to Johnson's Island Prison in Sandusky, OH. June 20, 1863. Sent to prison at Point Lookout, MD. on October 30, 1863. Released on oath April 11, 1864.

Private James Speights   Born: 1828   Died: >1900   Residence: Fayette Co., GA.   In 1900 resided in Atlanta.   Enlisted in Baxter's Battery: May 16, 1864 in Fulton Co., GA. by Capt. E. D. Baxter. Last paid October 31, 1864 by Major Higgins. Paroled April 28, 1865 at Macon, GA.
Married Lavina L. Mitchell December 28, 1842 in Fayette Co., GA.

Private Abraham S. Spencer "Abe"   Born: November 12, 1842 Dickson Co., TN.   Died: July 5, 1908   Buried: Hudgins Cemetery Fairview, TN. has CSA grave marker (not VA issue) Enlisted in Baxter's Battery: December 4, 1862 in Dickson Co., TN. by Capt. E. D. Baxter.   Residence at time of enlistment; Dickson Co., TN. Height: 5' 11"   Complexion: Dark   Hair: Dark   Eyes: Dark Occupation: Farmer   Paid: December 31, 1862 by Capt. Hord, February 28, 1863 by Capt. Hord, April 30, 1863 by Maj. Hord, June 30, 1863 by Capt. Fowler, October 31, 1863 by Lt. Neal, December 31, 1863 by Maj. Ragan, February 29, 1864 by Maj. Ragan & October 31, 1864 by Maj. Higgins.   Paroled April 28, 1865 at Macon, GA.   Oath of Allegiance taken May 4, 1865 at Chattanooga, TN. Ordered to report to Nashville.

368 CAPTAIN ED BAXTER & HIS TENNESSEE ARTILLERYMEN, C.S.A.

Tennessee Confederate Pension Application 7614   Filed November 2, 1905   Accepted.   Residence at time of application: Liepers Fork (Williamson County)   Disability: Rheumatism in left shoulder and deafness in right ear caused by firing of cannon at Chattanooga. Physician signing application: Dr. L. G. Hensley   Witnesses: J. B. Edwards & V. I. Barnhill.   Witnesses statement: " was with applicant in the army, he was a good soldier and stayed till surrender and is of good character." Assets: 150 acres of land valued at $150.00.

Tennessee Confederate   Widow's Pension Application 2580   Filed: April 22, 1909   Accepted. Judian Pewitt Spencer   Born: September 12, 1847   Williamson Co., TN.   Died: March 23, 1923. Residence: RT. 9 Franklin.   Married: August 24, 1871 by Isaac Ivy.   Had 5 children. Witnesses: A. P. Beard & J. B. Edwards   Notary Public: J. W. Hendricks.   W. T. Robinson Williamson Co. Trustee.

Corporal Hiram A. Spencer "High"   Born: August 24, 1835   Dickson Co., TN.   Died: January 19, 1912   Buried: Parker-Fowlkes Cemetery Dickson Co., TN.   VA Marker.   Appointed to Dickson County Home Guard of Minute Men June 10, 1861.   Enlisted in Baxter's Battery: December 10, 1862 in Dickson Co., TN. by Capt. E. D. Baxter.   Paid: December 31, 1862 by Capt. Hord, February 28, 1863 by Capt. Hord, April 30, 1863 by Maj. Hord, June 30, 1863 by Capt. Fowler, October 31, 1863 by Lt. Neal, December 31, 1863 by Maj. Ragan, February 29, 1864 by Maj. Ragan & October 31, 1864 by Maj. Higgins.   May 1, 1863 promoted to Corporal upon Eli Sherman being promoted to Sergeant. Paroled April 28, 1865 at Macon, GA.   Oath of allegiance taken May 4, 1865 at Chattanooga, TN.   Ordered to report to Nashville.   Has family. Married Celia Sowells February 5, 1857 in Dickson Co., TN.

Private Amos Spicer   Born: November 18, 1839   Dickson Co., TN. Died: 1918   Dickson Co., TN.   found dead near Turnbull Creek after being missing for several months.   Buried: Spicer Family Cemetery Dickson Co., TN. (lost cemetery).   Enlisted in Baxter's Battery: December 22, 1862 in Maury Co., TN.   by Maj. John L. House. Residence at time of enlistment: Dickson Co., TN.   Reported to company January 26, 1863.   Paid: February 28, 1863 & April 30, 1863 by Capt. Hord.   Deserted near Knoxville August 6, 1863. Married Mary Shelton Beck (widow of Private David Beck) in Dickson Co., TN.

Private Lewis T. Sudduth   Born: September 3, 1845   Fayette Co., GA. Died: >1898. In 1870 resided in Conyers Newton Co., GA. Enlisted in Baxter's Battery: February 16, 1864 in Fulton Co., GA. by Capt. E. D. Baxter.   Bounty due.   Last paid by Maj. Ragan on April 30, 1864. Enlisted in Co. F 4th Regiment Georgia State Militia Calvary September 1863. Unit disbanded five months later. Furloughed for thirty days from Macon, GA. on March 15, 1865. Never returned to service.

Georgia Confederate Pension initial application 602   Filed: July 1, 1896 in Fayette County. Accepted.   Disability: diabetes   Physicians signing application: Dr. J. E. Tucker and Dr. W. R. Russell.   Fayette Co., GA. Ordinary notarizing applications: D. M. Franklin. Witness to Confederate service: Noah W. Kimberly of Cleburne Co., AL. Witness statement: "We were with Baxter's artillery.   Me & him enlisted at Atlanta, Ga. We served about 12 months together. Saw him every day for that service. We were in same mess."

Private William Macie Sulliivan "Uncle Billy"   Born: August 23, 1826 Dickson Co., TN. Died: February 10, 1920 Buried: Hudgins Cemetery Fairview, TN. VA Marker. Enlisted in Baxter's Battery: December 10, 1862 in Dickson Co., TN.   Residence at time of enlistment: Williamson Co., TN.   Complexion: Dark   Hair: Brown   Eyes: Gray Occupation: Farmer   April 23, 1863 detailed to Strawberry Plains, TN. to care for sick and baggage by order of Captain Baxter. May 1, 1863 permanently detailed as a teamster. Paid 25 cents per day extra for 31 days of extra duty as a teamster.   Paid: December 31, 1862 by Captain Hord, February 28, 1863 by Capt. Hord, April 30, 1863 by Maj. Hord, June 30, 1863 by Capt. Fowler, October 31, 1863 by Lt. Neal, December 31, 1863 by Maj. Ragan, February 29, 1864 by Maj. Ragan, & October 31, 1864 by Maj. Higgins. Admitted to General Hospital at Macon, Ga. October 19 to November 19, 1864 with intermittent fever. Paroled April 28, 1865 at Macon, Ga.   Oath of allegiance taken May 4, 1865 at Chattanooga, TN. Ordered to report to Nashville. Has family.

Tennessee Confederate pension application 2189. Accepted. Residence at time of application: Craigfield (Williamson Co.)   Filed: September 25, 1899. Disability: rheumatism and deafness (application states lost hearing by concussion of artillery) Physician signing application: Dr. John T. Cox. Witnesses: John F. Cunningham, A.P. Beard, Albert Green & H.A. Spencer. Notary Public: J.W. Hendricks. Witnesses statements: Albert Green & H.A. Spencer: "He served with us in

Baxter's Artillery. He made a good soldier. His habits are good. Is in needy sercumstancees." Sept. 15, 1899. A.P. Beard & J.F. Cunningham who being sworn say that they were with William Sullivan when he was captured and paroled and that he was paroled the 28 day of April 1865 at Macon, Georgia. August 6, 1903. Franklin Attorney, Tom Henderson, assisted the grand children in getting a government headstone in 1938. Married Artimesa Green (Born: January 14, 1826 Died: September 23, 1914) May 4, 1848 in Williamson Co., TN.

Corporal Joseph Latimer Sweeney   Born: February 21, 1842 Williamson Co., TN.   Died: November 14, 1920   Leipers Fork, Williamson Co., TN.   Buried: Leipers Fork Cemetery Williamson Co., TN.   Enlisted in Baxter's Battery: November 8, 1862 in Williamson Co., TN. by Capt. E. D. Baxter.   Residence at time of enlistment: Williamson Co., TN. Height: 5' 11"   Complexion: Dark   Hair: Light   Eyes: Hazel   Occupation: Wheelwright   Paid: December 31, 1862 by Capt. Hord, February 28, 1863 by Capt. Hord, April 30, 1863 by Maj. Hord, June 30, 1863 by Capt. Fowler, October 31, 1863 by Lt. Neal, December 31, 1863 by Maj. Ragan, February 29, 1864 by Maj. Ragan, April 30, 1864 by Maj. Ragan, & October 31, 1864 by Maj. Higgins.   Reduced in rank from Corporal on December 12, 1864 for incompetence, inefficiency and neglect of duty.   Hospitalized in Ocmulgee Hospital Macon, GA. February 4-15, 1865. Paroled April 28, 1865 at Macon, GA.   Oath of allegiance taken May 4, 1865 at Chattanooga, TN.

Tennessee Confederate Pension Application 13562   Filed: May 20, 1912   Residence at time of application: Rt. 3 Franklin, TN. Accepted.   Disability: rheumatism of the shoulder.   Physician signing application: Dr. M. Drake.   Notary Publics: W. L. Pinkerton & C. A. Allen.   Witnesses: Matt Maury, W. H. Bethshears, & Aaron Beard. Witnesses statements: Matt. F. Maury, one of Affiants, say they were in the same company, were together at Cumberland Gap, Knoxville and other places. and affiant knows of his own knowledge that applicant, Sweeny was in the army, and made a good and faithful soldier, and that his condition is such that he needs the pension & that he is worthy & deserving in every respect & Affiant now is an old ex-confederate. Was in the army but not in the same company with applicant but knows of his own personal knowledge that applicant was in the war as stated, 7th day of May 1912. W.H. Bethshears & Aaron P. Beard who state upon their oaths that they know J.L. Sweeny of Franklin, TN, R. 3, personally, and that they served with him as members of Baxter's Battery in the late war, and that they know that he, the said J. L. Sweeny was paroled with them at Macon, GA., on or about the 25 day of April 1865, the same time that we and others of the company were paroled. We know too that he made an excellent soldier, and we feel that he is entitled to and is deserving of a pension under the law. W.H. Bethshears (O.R. Cunningham witness to his mark) & Aaron P. Beard.

Tennessee Confederate Widow's pension application 7498   Filed: December 24, 1920 Accepted.   Minerva Jane Gatlin Sweeney   Born: February 21, 1842 Boston, TN.   Died: 1934   Residence: Franklin, TN. RT 3.   Died: February 15, 1934.   Married: April 12, 1866 in Nashville, TN. by E. C. Trimble   Had 7 children.   Witnesses: M. A. Meacham & J. P. Redford   Notary Public: J. F. Mays. Williamson Co. Court Clerk T. E. Daniel.

Private David Basil Talley   Born: February 10, 1839 Williamson Co., TN.   Died: November 27, 1906 near Trimble (Dyer Co.) TN. Enlisted in Baxter's Battery: February 3, 1863 Dickson Co., TN. by Recruiting Officer B. T. Gilliam.   Residence at time of enlistment: Cheatham Co., TN. Height: 5' 7"   Complexion: Flourid   Hair: Brown Eyes: Gray Paid: April 30, 1863 by Maj. Hord, June 30, 1863 by Capt. Fowler, October 31, 1863 by Lt. Neal, December 31, 1863 by Maj. Ragan, February 29, 1864 by Maj. Ragan, April 30, 1864 by Maj. Ragan, & October 31, 1864 by Maj. Higgins.   Hospitalized at Ocmulgee Hospital Macon, GA. October 16-27, 1864 for intermittent fever. Paroled April 28, 1865 at Macon, GA. Oath of allegiance taken May 4, 1865 at Chattanooga, TN.

Tennessee Confederate Pension Application   Filed May 10, 1906 Accepted.   Residence at time of application: Trimble (Dyer Co.), TN. Disability: not stated. Physician signing application: Dr. J. H. Green. Witnesses: Frank Neely & George Thomason   Dyer County Trustee J. S. Todd.

Tennessee Confederate Widow's Indigent Pension Application 5517 Filed: July 14, 1914   Accepted.   Nancy Elizabeth Stovall Talley Born: November 29, 1836 Davidson Co., TN.   Died: November 8, 1925   Married: December 29, 1859 in Cheatham Co., TN. by Esq. Perkins.   Had 5 children, 3 boys & 2 girls.   Residence at time of application Union City (Obion Co.)TN.   Witnesses: H. D. Daera & W.

W. Moody   Notary Public: C.S. Tulley, Obion County Clerk.   Dyer County Trustee: George Johnson.

Private Benjamin H. Terrell   Born: 1832 Halifax Co., VA. Died: February 2, 1865 of chronic diarrhea at Union Prison at Camp Douglas, IL.   Buried: Block 2 Chicago City Cemetery.   Moved to mass Confederate grave in Oak Woods Cemetery Chicago in 1867. Memorial stone in Jane Jones Cemetery Fairview, TN.   Enlisted in Baxter's Battery: November 7, 1862 in Williamson Co., TN. by Capt. E. D. Baxter.   Height: 5' 11" Complexion: Fair Hair: Dark   Eyes: Blue Occupation: Farmer.   Paid: December 31, 1862 by Capt. Hord, February 28, 1863 by Capt. Hord, April 30, 1863 by Maj. Hord, February 29, 1864 by Maj. Ragan & April 30, 1864 by Maj. Ragan. Hospitalized in Knoxville, TN.   July 11, 1863.   Captured September 1, 1864 in Atlanta, GA.   Transported to Lousiville, KY. to Camp Douglas, IL. on November 23, 1864.   Married Louisa Hamilton January 7, 1858 in Dickson Co., TN.

Private (Artificer) Joseph R. Terrell   Born: 1823 in Halifax Co., VA. Died: May 28, 1863 of typhoid in camp in Grainger Co., TN. Buried: unmarked grave near Bean Station, TN. Memorial stone in Jane Jones Cemetery Fairview, TN.   Enlisted in Baxter's Battery: November 7, 1862 in Williamson Co., TN. by Capt. E. D. Baxter.   Height: 6' Complexion: Fair   Hair: Dark   Eyes: Blue   Occupation: Blacksmith.   Paid: December 31, 1862 by Capt. Hord, February 28, 1863 by Capt. Hord, & April 30, 1863 by Maj. Hord.   Was attended by private physician while ill at Bean Station. Personal effects reported taken by his brother, Benjamin Terrell.   Married Harriet M. Buttrey February 1, 1848 in Williamson Co., TN.

Private James Bouldin Thompson "J.B."   Born: January 1, 1844 Davidson Co., TN   Died: September 25, 1935.   Buried: Thompson Cemetery Burns, TN.   VA Marker.   Enlisted in Baxter's Battery: November 22, 1862 in Dickson Co., TN. by Capt. E.D. Baxter. Residence at time of enlistment: Cheatham Co., TN.   Height: 5' 10" Complexion: Dark   Hair: Dark   Eyes: Gray   Occupation: Farmer. Paid: December 31, 1862 by Capt. Hord, February 28, 1863 by Capt. Hord, April 30, 1863 by Maj. Hord, June 30, 1863 by Capt. Fowler, October 31, 1863 by Lt. Neal, December 31, 1863 by Maj. Ragan, February 29, 1864 by Maj. Ragan, April 30, 1864 by Maj. Ragan, & October 31, 1864 by Maj. Higgins. Paroled April 28, 1865 at Macon,

GA.   Oath of allegiance taken May 4, 1865 at Chattanooga, TN.   No family.

Tennessee Confederate Pension Application 8334   Filed: May 25, 1905   Accepted   Residence at time of Application: Burns (Dickson Co.)   Disability: rheumatism & piles   Physician signing application: Dr. J. J. Sledge.   Witnesses: T. J. Carr & T. L. Forehand   Notary Public: Lester Garton.   Witnesses statement: I was previously acquainted with J.B. Thompson and was with him two years and five months in the confederate army and we was paroled about the 28 of April 1865. J.L. Forehand & T.J. Carr.

Completed Tennessee Civil War Veterans Questionnaire at 77 years of age in which he stated: "Were in ditches at Atlanta about 9 months, lived mostly on tough beef and biscuit, wore regular old gray uniforms, slept on a blanket on the ground, not exposed to cold, (too far south), Got hungry many times and suffered from typhoid fever.   Was given transportation to Nashville and walked home to Kingston Springs at close of war. "   "During service at Missionary Ridge, I met Generals Hardee, Cayce, Williams and nearly all the head men of the Army of Tennessee.   I remember at one time they were all standing together laughing and shouting and watching the Federals retreat down the mountain, when a shell hit in fifteen or twenty feet of them and then the tune changed, they all left and in double quick time too."

Tennessee Confederate Widow's Pension Application 10893   Filed: October 16, 1935   Accepted.   Alice Richardson Thompson   Born: June 20, 1858 in Houston Co., TN.   Died: April 5, 1941. Residence: Burns, TN.   Married: October 8, 1879 by J. M. Stuart, J. P. in Dickson Co., TN.   Witnesses: B. M. Oliphant & Mary E. Oliphant   Notary Public: J. C. Berry Dickson Co. Trustee B. C. Nicks.

Private Lewis E. Thompson   Born: 1828   Davidson Co., TN.   Died: May 27, 1863 of typhoid in camp in Grainger Co., TN.   Buried: unmarked grave near Bean Station, TN.   Enlisted in Baxter's Battery: November 11, 1862 in Williamson Co., TN. by Capt. E. D. Baxter   Residence at time of enlistment: Cheatham Co., TN.   Height: 6' Complexion: Fair   Hair: Light   Eyes: Blue   Occupation: Farmer.   Paid: April 30, 1863 by Maj. Hord.   December 31, 1862 15-day sick furlough granted. January 15, 1863 unable to rejoin company.   Personal effects taken by nephew, James B. Thompson. Married Cornelia Nesbitt January 1, 1851 in Dickson Co., TN.

Private Aquilla Tidwell "Uncle Quilly" Born: July 14, 1838 Dickson Co., TN Died: December 19, 1908 Buried: Aquilla Tidwell Cemetery Bon Aqua, TN. VA Marker. Enlisted in Baxter's Battery: December 23, 1862 in Maury Co., TN. by Maj. John L. House. Residence at time of enlistment: Dickson Co., TN. Complexion: Florid Hair: Sandy Eyes: Gray Paid: February 28, 1863 by Capt. Hord, April 30, 1863 by Maj. Hord, June 30, 1863 by Capt. Fowler, October 31, 1863 by Lt. Neal, December 31, 1863 by Maj. Ragan, February 29, 1864 by Maj. Ragan, April 30, 1864 by Maj. Ragan, & October 31, 1864 by Maj. Higgins. Reported to company January 26, 1863. Paroled April 28, 1865 at Macon, GA. Oath of allegiance taken May 4, 1865 at Chattanooga, TN.

Pvt. Aquilla Tidwell

Tennessee Confederate Pension Application 6235 Accepted Filed: September 6, 1905 Residence at time of application: Bon Aqua (Hickman Co.) Disability: rheumatism Physician signing application: Dr. J. C. Daniel. Witnesses: Albert Green & W. A. Fraisher Notary public: T. J. Walker. Witnesses statement: "That they was with applicant in the army and that he complained of Rheumatizm there and he made a good soldier while able for duty and was an honorable man both in the army and at home and that applicant is a very poor man and not able to do but little labor and that he was paroled at Macon, GA. Apr 28, 1865 his character is good." 28th August 1905. Married Mary Ann Rebecca Russell December 14, 1859 in Dickson Co., TN. 2nd Wife Jane J. McMinn, 3rd Wife A. J. Redden , 4th wife Anna Allen.

Private John H. Tidwell   Born: 1834   Dickson Co., TN.   Died: 1915 Dickson Co., TN.   Buried: Maple Grove Cemetery, Dickson Co., TN. (unmarked grave ?)   Appointed to Dickson County Home Guard of Minute Men June 10, 1861. Enlisted in Baxter's Battery: December 15, 1862 in Dickson Co., TN. by Capt. E. D. Baxter. Residence at time of enlistment: Dickson Co., TN.   Paid: December 31, 1862 by Capt. Hord, February 28, 1863 by Capt. Hord, April 30, 1863 by Maj. Hord, & June 30, 1863 by Capt. Fowler. Deserted August 6, 1863 near Knoxville. Married Elizabeth Underhill October 17, 1859 in Dickson Co., TN.

Pvt. John H. Tidwell

Private Soloman Marsh Tidwell "Sol"   Born: January 20, 1844. Dickson Co., TN.   Died: February 8, 1929   Buried: Tidwell Family Cemetery on Sugar Creek near Bucksnort (Hickman Co., TN.) VA Marker.   Enlisted in Baxter's Battery: November 7, 1862 in Dickson Co., TN. by Capt. E. D. Baxter   Residence at time of enlistment: Dickson Co., TN.   Height: 5' 2" Complexion: Fair   Hair: Light Eyes: Dark   Occupation: Farmer. Paid: December 31, 1862 by Capt. Hord, February 28, 1863 by Capt. Hord, April 30, 1863 by Maj. Hord, June 30, 1863 by Capt. Fowler, October 31, 1863 by Lt. Neal, December 31, 1863 by Maj. Ragan, February 29, 1864 by Maj. Ragan, April 30, 1864 by Maj. Ragan, & October 31, 1864 by Maj. Higgins.

February 15, 1863 detached from Knoxville to forage for horses by order of Brig. Gen. Gracie.   Paid $74 bounty March 23, 1863 by H. T. Mapergod. Hospitalized at Ocmulgee Hospital Macon, GA. October 10-12, 1864 for intermittent fever. Paroled April 28, 1865 at Macon, GA. Oath of allegiance taken May 4, 1865 at Chattanooga, TN. Ordered to report to Nashville.

Pvt. Soloman M. Tidwell

Tennessee Confederate Pension Application 9735   Accepted   Filed: December 12, 1907.   Residence at time of application: Bold Springs (Hickman Co.)   Disability: rheumatism   Physician signing application: Dr. A. Norris   Witnesses: John Dillard & B. F. Brown Notary public: T. J. Carr. Witnesses statement: That S.M. Tidwell was their comrade and faithfully discharged his duty as a soldier until honorably paroled at Macon, GA. Apr 28, 1865 and has since been a good law abiding citizen. Dec. 11, 1907.   Married Lucinda Garton February 5, 1867 in Dickson Co., TN. Married Hannah Jane Wilkins

---

Private Felix Grundy Truett   Born: February 20, 1836 Williamson Co., TN. Died: November 25, 1893 Nashville, TN. Buried: Mt. Hope Cemetery Franklin, TN. Section A-65   Enlisted in Baxter's Battery: November 10, 1862 in Williamson Co., TN. by Capt. E. D. Baxter. Residence at time of enlistment: Williamson Co., TN.   Height: 5' 11" Complexion: Fair   Hair: Light   Eyes: Gray   Occupation: Farmer. Paid: December 31, 1862 by Capt. Hord, February 28, 1863 by Capt. Hord, April 30, 1863 by Maj. Hord, June 30, 1863 by Capt. Fowler,

October 31, 1863 by Lt. Neal, December 31, 1863 by Maj. Ragan, February 29, 1864 by Maj. Ragan, April 30, 1864 by Maj. Ragan, & October 31, 1864 by Maj. Higgins. Detailed for extra duty as a teamster by Capt. Baxter February 28, 1863. Permanently detailed as teamster March 1, 1863. Paid 25 cents per day extra for extra duty as teamster from October 1-31, 1863. Detached April 23, 1863 by Captain Baxter to Lea's Springs to care for sick and baggage. Paroled April 28, 1865 at Macon, GA. Oath of allegiance taken May 4, 1865 at Chattanooga, TN. Ordered to report to Franklin. Has family. Married Elizabeth Cook (Born: 1839 Died: 1911) July 2, 1859 in Williamson Co., TN.

Private Elisha Varden   Born: 1844   Davidson Co., TN.   Died: February 1910 at St. Elizabeth's Hospital (Government Hospital for the Insane) Bethesda, Maryland.   Buried: St. Elizabeth Hospital Grounds. Enlisted in Baxter's Battery: November 22, 1862 in Dickson Co., TN. by Capt. E. D. Baxter. Residence at time of enlistment: Cheatham Co., TN.   Height: 5' 10" Complexion: Dark   Hair: Dark   Eyes: Dark Occupation: Farmer.   Paid: December 31, 1862 by Capt. Hord, February 28, 1863 by Capt. Hord, April 30, 1863 by Maj. Hord, June 30, 1863 by Capt. Fowler, October 31, 1863 by Lt. Neal, December 31, 1863 by Maj. Ragan, February 28, 1864 by Maj. Ragan, & April 30, 1864 by Maj. Ragan. Reported deserted and captured at Jonesboro, GA. September 7, 1864. Transported to Louisville, KY. to Camp Douglas, IL. Enlisted in Union Army, 5th US Volunteers on April 6, 1865. Married Nancy E. Crawford January 21, 1869 in Cheatham Co., TN.

Private Middleton Vickory   Born: 1790 North Carolina   Died: ? Residence: DeKalb Co., GA. Enlisted in Co. K (Bartow Avengers) 38th Regiment Georgia Volunteer Infantry, Army of Northern Virginia on September 26, 1861. Discharged on account of old age and disability December 31, 1861.   Enlisted in Baxter's Battery   March 10, 1864 in Fulton Co., GA. by Capt. E. D. Baxter   Due $50 bounty. Never paid. Married Catharine Kinnard June 24, 1843 in DeKalb Co., GA.

Private John T. Walker   Born: 1844   Died: >1923   Residence: Fayette Co., GA. Enlisted in Baxter's Battery: July 19, 1864 in Fulton Co., GA. by Lt. William Herrin. Previous service in Co. F 28th Battalion Georgia Siege Artillery. Residence: Clayton Co., GA. Sent to General Hospital in Macon, GA. by Assistant Surgeon Beauchamp from October 4-27, 1864.   Hospitalized at Ocmulgee Hospital Macon, GA. December 11, 1864 to January 22, 1865. February 4, 1865 to April 18, 1865 & April

23-28, 1865 for intermittent fever. Never Paid. Paroled April 28, 1865 in Macon, GA.

Private Wesley Bowden Welch   Born: October 1844 Dickson Co., TN. Died: April 25, 1935   Buried: Jordan Cemetery Dickson Co., TN. VA Marker. Enlisted in Baxter's Battery: October 30, 1862 in Dickson Co., TN. by Capt. E. D. Baxter. Residence at time of enlistment: Dickson Co., TN.   Height: 5' Complexion: Fair Hair: Light   Eyes: Blue Occupation: Farmer & Butcher. Paid: December 31, 1862 by Capt. Hord, February 28, 1863 by Capt. Hord, April 30, 1863 by Maj. Hord, June 30, 1863 by Capt. Fowler, October 31, 1863 by lt. Neal, December 31, 1863 by Maj. Ragan, April 30, 1864 by Maj. Ragan, & October 31, 1864 by Maj. Higgins.   Sent to hospital at rear of Missionary Ridge September 27, 1863.   January & February 1864 in Blackie Hospital Madison, GA.   Sent to General Hospital Macon, GA. by Surgeon Murphy on October 9, 1864 for intermittent fever and severe anemic condition.   October 26, 1864 Floyd House and Ocmulgee Hospitals in Macon, GA. Transferred to hospital in Augusta, GA. December 1864. Returned to command at Macon February 15, 1865. Paroled April 28, 1865 at Macon, GA.   Oath of allegiance taken May 4, 1865 in Chattanooga, TN.

Pvt. Wesley B. Welch

Tennessee Confederate Pension Application 8483   Filed: October 13, 1906   Accepted.   Residence at time of application: Bon Aqua (3rd Civil District Dickson Co.)   Disability: diabetes & lung disease as a result of measles settling in lungs during the war.   Physician signing application: Dr. W. H. James.   Witnesses: Alfred McCaslin, H. A. Spencer, T. J. Parker & John Dillard   Notary Public: Levi Johnson Tidwell.   Witnesses statements: "That they know that he joined or enlisted in December 1862 in Baxter's Battery and served during the remainder of the war. Except what time he was in the hospital for fever & measles and was captured on the 28th day of April 1865 at Macon, GA. and was paroled and took oath at Chattanooga." John Dillard & T.J. Parker Nov 20, 1905.   State that they were with said Wesley Welch at Macon, Georgia when they surrendered and also were with him at the time they were paroled and they returned home together. H.A. Spencer & Alfred A. McCaslin September 30, 1907.

Completed Tennessee Civil War Veterans Questionnaire at age 77 in which he stated: "I lived in camp 3 years, 6 months and 5 days. I had not very much clothing. I slept on ground. Mostly I had beef, horse, beans, sugar, crackers & cornbread. That is what I had to eat. I were exposed to cold by not having sufficient clothing and eatables, I were in hospital 31 days. Nashville is the place I were discharged 1865 in May. I walked from Nashville home. I were bare footed, bare headed and my clothes half torn off me and worn pretty bad."

Corporal Daniel White "Dan"   Born: 1840 Dickson Co., TN. Died: 1925 Dickson Co., TN. Buried Parker-Fowlkes Cemetery Dickson Co., TN. VA Marker.   Enlisted in Baxter's Battery: December 8, 1862 in Dickson Co., TN. by Capt. E. D. Baxter.   Residence at time of enlistment: Dickson Co., TN.

Cpl. Daniel White

Height: 5' 6" Complexion: Dark   Hair: Dark   Eyes: Dark
Occupation: Farmer   Paid: December 31, 1862 by Capt. Hord,
February 28, 1863 by Capt. Hord, April 30, 1863 by Maj. Hord, June 30,
1863 by Capt. Fowler, October 31, 1863 by Lt. Neal, December 31, 1863
by Maj. Ragan, February 29, 1864 by Maj. Ragan, April 30, 1864 by
Maj. Ragan, & October 31, 1864 by Maj. Higgins.   Promoted to
Corporal May 8, 1863 upon promotion of John Cunningham.
Hospitalized at Ocmulgee Hospital October 10-29, 1864. Paroled April
28, 1865 at Macon, GA.   Oath of allegiance May 4, 1865 at Chattanooga.

Tennessee Confederate Pension Application 5462   Filed: August 11,
1903   Accepted.   Residence at time of application: Spencer's Mill
(Dickson Co.)   Disability: rheumatism in both arms and shoulders.
Physician signing application: Dr. E.W. Ridings.   Notary Publics:
Samuel Hammon & L. D. Wright.   Witnesses: B.F. Brown & D.H.
Lankford.   Witnesses statement: D.H. Lankford & B.F. Brown made
oath that they are personally acquainted with Daniel White, the above
applicant for pension.   That said White was sworn into the Confederate
Army as a member of Capt. Ed Baxter's Artillery Company Dec. 1862.
That said White contracted rheumatism while in the service and in line of
duty from which disease he has never recovered.   That said White was
honorably paroled at Macon, GA. April 28, 1865.   Said White was a
good faithful and obedient soldier and is a good citizen and neighbor and
a strict member of the church.   That said White is indigent, aged and
physically exhausted has no children able to support him.   This Feb. 5,
1904   Married Caroline Parker November 4, 1862.

He was a member of James E. Raines Bivouac # 14, Association of
Confederate Soldiers, Tennessee Division, Dickson, TN.   Tennessee
Confederate Widow's Pension Application 8279   Filed : June 2, 1925
Accepted.   Parthena Lankford White   Born: June 12, 1864 Dickson
Co., TN.   Residence: Burns P.O.   Died: November 11, 1935.
Married: June 9, 1907? In Dickson Co., TN. by Samuel Hammon, J. P.
Had 11 children.   Witnesses: Justin G. Tidwell & A. D. Underhill.
Notary Public: J. W. Herrin.   Parthena Lankford was daughter of
Tillman   Lankford   also   of   Baxter's   Battery.

Corporal James Polk White "J.P."   Born: February 23, 1844   Dickson
Co., TN   Died: October 6, 1927 Dickson Co., TN.   Buried: White
Cemetery   Dickson Co., TN.   VA Marker.   Enlisted in Baxter's Battery:
December 5, 1862 in Dickson Co., TN. by Capt. E. D. Baxter.
Residence at time of enlistment: Dickson Co., TN.   Height: 5' 7"

Complexion: Dark   Hair: Dark   Eyes: Dark   Occupation: farmer. Paid: December 31, 1862 by Capt. Hord, February 28, 1863 by Capt. Hord, April 30, 1863 by Maj. Hord, June 30, 1863 by Capt. Fowler, October 31, 1863 by Lt. Neal, December 31, 1863 by Maj. Ragan, February 29, 1864 by Maj. Ragan, April 30, 1864 by Maj. Ragan & October 31, 1864 by Maj. Higgins. Paroled April 28, 1865 at Macon, GA. Oath of allegiance taken May 4, 1865 at Chattanooga, TN. Ordered to report to Nashville. No family.

Tennessee Confederate pension application 6772   Filed: March 9, 1905 Rejected . Residence at time of application: Spencer's Mill (Dickson Co.) Disability: Chronic liver affliction, chronic bronchitis & nervous disorders. Physician signing application: Dr. J.M. Bagwell. Notary Publics: T.H. Whitfield & Samuel Hammon. Witnesses: T.J. Carr & John Dillard. Witnesses statement: " Said J.P. White was promoted to the rank of Corporal for soldierly bearing and was regarded as a soldier of the highest order by his Officers and comrades." February 25, 1905.

Second pension application 16227   Filed: July 11, 1927   Accepted. Residence at time of application: Burns Route 1(Dickson Co.) Disability: infirmities of old age. Physician signing application: Dr. J .J. Sledge. Notary Public: J.W. Herrin Witnesses: B.F. Brown & John Dillard. Witnesses statements: Served with him 28 months and know him as a good soldier and a good citizen and strictly a gentleman. 23 June 1927 B.F. Brown & John Dillard. Personally appeared before me, J.W. Herrin Notary Public in and for said County & State, the following named persons with whom I am personally acquainted: W.T. Jones, W.H. Lankford, W.S. Brown, W.J. Martin and W.M. Frazer who being duly sworn, made oath before me in due form of law, that they are personally acquainted with J. P. White, who is a citizen of Dickson County, Tennessee: that they have known said J.P White for many years, and that for many years they have lived in the same county and community in which he lives: that his character is good, and that his general reputation for truth and veracity is good, 12 day of July 1927.
W.R. White, son of J.P. White and administrator of his estate, wrote John Hickman of the pension board October 17, 1927, informing him of his father's death on October 6: "so that you could adjust his pension accordingly. Best wishes to you and the rest of the old boy's of the south."

Married Sarah Elizabeth Ford April 17, 1867 in Dickson Co., TN. He was a member of James E. Raines Bivouac #14 Association of Confederate Soldiers, Tennessee Division, Dickson, TN.

Private Jesse White   Born: September 3, 1833   Dickson Co., TN. Died: 1918   Buried: Stuart Cemetery   Burns, TN. VA Marker. Enlisted in Baxter's Battery: December 11, 1862 in Dickson Co., TN. by Capt. E. D. Baxter. Residence at time of enlistment: Dickson Co., TN. Height: 5' 4" Complexion: Dark   Eyes: Dark   Hair: Dark Occupation: Farmer.   Paid: December 31, 1862 by Capt. Hord, February 28, 1863 by Capt. Hord, April 30, 1863 by Maj. Hord, June 30, 1863 by Capt. Fowler, October 31, 1863 by Lt. Neal, December 31, 1863 by Maj. Ragan, February 29, 1864 by Maj. Ragan & April 30, 1864 by Maj. Ragan.   February 15, 1863 detached from Knoxville to forage for horses by order of Brig. Gen. Gracie.   Sent to hospital in Atlanta, GA. December 24, 1863. No disease.   Entitled to clothing allowance of $45.23 up to October 5, 1863. Captured September 7, 1864 at Decatur, GA. Sent to Camp Douglas, IL   December 1864 claimed to have been loyal and stated that he was "conscripted into the rebel army. Deserted to avail himself to the amnesty proclamation." Discharged from Camp Douglas May 12, 1865.

Pvt. Jesse White

Tennessee Confederate Pension Application 3218   Rejected.   Filed: March 15, 1901 Residence at time of application: Pinewood (Hickman Co.)   Disability: old age   Physician signing application: Dr. J. M.

Bagwell   Witnesses: Daniel White & Amos Spicer   Notary Public: T. H. Whitfield. Attorney reviewing application: Billy King of Pinewood. Witnesses statement: "We were both with the applicant, Jesse White, in the army belonged to his company & know he was in prison at the general surrender & that he is old & has no means of support & is unable to work." 14 day March 1901.
Married Adeline Mitchell December 20, 1855 in Dickson Co., TN.

Private Leonidas C. Whitmore Born: 1829.   Died: December 20, 1920 Habersham Co., GA. Occupation: Farmer. Enlisted: June 13, 1861 in Co. H (Rowland Highlanders) 18th Regiment Georgia Volunteer Infantry, Army of Northern Virginia.   In 1870 resided in Adairsville Bartow Co., GA.   Enlisted in Baxter's Battery March 29, 1864 in Fulton Co., GA. by Capt. E. D. Baxter. Entitled to $50 bounty. Never paid.

Georgia Confederate Pension Application   filed January 1, 1907 in Habersham County. Disability: Rheumatism and wound suffered at Battle of Seven Pines, VA. Assets: none   Habersham County Ordinary M. Franklin.

Georgia Confederate Widow's Pension Application   Filed: February 19, 1940 in Habersham County. Mrs. Sallie Vinson Whitmore. Born: January 15, 1878   Married August 6, 1905 in Habersham Co., GA. by Justice of the Peace W. T. Irwin.

Private John W. Williams   Born: 1829   Died: ?   Residence at time of enlistment: Williamson Co., TN. Complexion: Light Eyes: Blue Hair: Light Height: 5' 8".   Oath of allegiance taken March 19, 1864 in Nashville by Lt. R. M. Goodwin, Assistant Provost Marshall, Department of the Cumberland.   Name appears on: Roll of 10 rebel deserters released on oath of amnesty at Nashville, TN. March 19, 1864

Pvt. James T. Wright   Born: 1843   Jasper Co., GA.   Died: ? Enlisted: January 18, 1862 in Co. B 10th GA. Regiment of State Troops at Camp Walker, GA. Discharged due to disability February 6, 1862. Height: 5' 3" Complexion: Dark   Eyes: Dark   Hair: Auburn Occupation: Farmer. Enlisted: February 5, 1864 in Baxter's Battery in Fulton Co., GA. by Capt. E. D. Baxter. Deserted February 18, 1864 near Atlanta. Never paid.

BIBLIOGRAPHY

1. *War of the Rebellion: A Compilation of the Official Records of the Union and Confederate Armies.*
   129 volumes. Washington, D.C., 1880-1901
2. Alabama Department of Archives & History   Montgomery Compiled service records and pension applications of Alabama Confederate Soldiers.
3. Baxter, Edmund D. *Address to Tennessee Association of Confederate Soldiers at Nashville, TN.*
   October 3, 1889
4. Baxter, Edmund D. *Address to Tennessee Association of Confederate Soldiers at Franklin, TN.   1892*
5. Corlew, Robert Ewing   *A History of Dickson County*
   Nashville 1956
6. Cunningham, Sumner A., Editor   *Confederate Veteran*   490 Volumes
   Nashville 1893-1932
7. Demonbruen, John Foresythe   Civil War Letter 1864 contributed by his great-grand son,   Mr. Jerry W. Cook of Wartrace, TN.
8. Dickson County, Tennessee Quarterly Court Records
   June & August 1861
9. Dillard, John Bryant   Civil War Letters 1863-64. Transcribed by and contributed by his great grandson, Mr. Thomas A. Forehand, Jr. of Clarksville, TN.
10. Dyer, Gustavus & Moore, John Trotwood   *The Tennessee Civil War Veterans Questionnaires*   Volumes 1-5. Easley S.C. 1985
11. Fitzgerald, Nancy Tune; Warwick, Richard and Wilson Sadye Tune
    Letters to Laura- A Confederate Surgeon's Impressions of Four Years of War. Nashville 1996
12. Georgia State Library and Archives. Atlanta. Compiled service records and pension applications of Georgia Confederate Soldiers.
13. Hale, Will T. & Merritt, Dixon L.   *A History of Tennessee and Tennesseans*
    Chicago. 1913
14. Henderson, Lillian   *Roster of the Confederate Soldiers of Georgia*
    Vol. 1-6 Hopeville, GA. 1955
15. Holt, Prudence White   letters of 1955 & 1959   unpublished. Furnished by Mr. John G. White of La Mesa, CA.

16. Kentucky State Library & Archives   Frankfort
   Kentucky Confederate Pension Applications.
17. Lampley, Dennis J.   Collected family oral histories of men who served in Baxter's Battery & other local Confederate Soldiers. unpublished
18. Lampley, Dennis J.   *Confederate Soldiers of Williamson County, TN.-Final Resting Places*
   Dickson, TN. 2004
19. McMurray, W. J.   *History of the Twentieth Tennessee Regiment Volunteer Infantry, C.S.A.*
   Nashville. 1904
20. Oklahoma Department of Libraries & Archives   Oklahoma City
   Oklahoma Confederate Pension Applications.
21. Spence, W. Jerome D. & Spence, David L.   *A History of Hickman County, Tennessee*
   Nashville 1900
22. Tennessee Civil War Centennial Commission   *TENNESSEANS IN THE CIVIL WAR*   Volumes 1 & 2
   Nashville. 1964.
23. Tennessee State Library & Archives   Nashville   Compiled Service Records   Tennessee Confederate Soldiers, Tennessee Confederate soldiers & widow's pension applications
24. Thompson, James Boulin   Civil War Memoirs given to his granddaughter, Margurette Brown in 1937
   Unpublished
25. Watkins, Samuel R.   *"Co. Aytch," Maury Grays, First Tennessee Regiment*
   Wilimington, N.C. 1990.
26.Williamson County, Tennessee Quarterly Court Records
   May 1861

DENNIS LAMPLEY

Dennis Joe Lampley was born October 10, 1951 in Nashville, TN. At age 4 his family moved back to the family farm in the Liberty Hill Community of the 1st District of Williamson County. The land had been pioneered by his great-great-great grandfather in 1811. He and wife Irene, a member of the Tidwell family who were also pioneers of the area, continue to reside on the home place as the sixth generation on the same land.

Lampley graduated from Fairview High School and received his B.S. Degree in Agriculture from the University of Tennessee at Knoxville. After working in the dairy industry for several years, he now works for the Tennessee Department of Environment and Conservation.

Over the years, Lampley has been active in several agricultural, environmental and historical organizations.

Printed in the United States
200002BV00003B/234/A

9 781933 912837